CW01661113

THE UNOFFICIAL EVERTON TIMELINE

2014-2023: THE MOSHIRI YEARS

STEVE DICKINSON & LYNDON LLOYD

BRIGHTER FUTURES
PUBLISHING

Copyright © 2024 by Steve Dickinson and Lyndon Lloyd

Paperback ISBN: 978-1-7398994-9-3

E-Book ISBN: 978-1-7384977-0-6

All rights reserved.

No portion of this book may be reproduced in any form without written permission from the publisher or authors, except as permitted by the UK Copyright, Designs and Patents Act 1988.

Condition of Sale

This book is sold subject to the condition that it shall not, by way of trade or otherwise, be lent, re-sold, hired out or otherwise circulated in any form of binding or cover other than that in which it is published, and without similar conditions including this condition being imposed on the subsequent purchaser.

Limit of Liability/Disclaimer

While the publisher and the authors have used their best efforts in preparing this book, they make no representations or warranties with respect to the accuracy or completeness of the contents of this book and specifically disclaim any implied warranties of merchantability or fitness for a particular purpose. It is sold on the understanding that the publisher is not engaged in rendering professional services and neither the publisher nor authors shall be liable for damages arising here from. If professional advice or other expert assistance is required, the services of a competent professional should be sought.

Published by Brighter Futures Publishing Ltd., Queensgate House, 23 North Park Road, Harrogate, United Kingdom, HG1 5PD

Brighter Futures Publishing

Dear Reader,

When I became an author, I made the decision to set up my own independent publishing company.

It's called *Brighter Futures Publishing Ltd* - and it's the Indie publisher with a big heart.

The mission of *Brighter Futures Publishing* is: "To positively impact millions of people, through our published works, and to raise funds for cancer research charities."

Why is this important to me?

Well, my dad died of cancer. So did my grandad, my uncle and many others I have known and loved.

In fact, according to the World Cancer Research Fund, 1 in 2 people in the UK will be diagnosed with cancer in their lifetime.

It's a terrible disease. Research into cancer and its possible treatments is so important for all of us.

As an author, I choose to make zero profit from the sale of my books. My share of the proceeds remain in the publishing company.

And with my publisher's hat on, I am pleased to confirm that 75% of *Brighter Futures Publishing* profits are donated annually to Cancer

Research UK. Anything left is reinvested, for the future growth of the company.

We hope you enjoy this book, knowing your purchase is also contributing to cancer research.

Thank you for your generous support.

Steve Dickinson
Founder and CEO
Brighter Futures Publishing Ltd

CONTENTS

Dedication

You know how it goes. You pick up a book, flip to the dedication, and find that, once again, the authors have dedicated it to someone else and not to you.

Not this time.

Because you are an Evertonian/a friend or family member of an Evertonian/know an Evertonian somewhere in your life, you will understand the pain, passion and occasional jubilation that being an Evertonian involves.

Therefore, this one's for you.

Without pain, passion and occasional jubilation, this book would never have been written.

Up the Toffees!

Steve and Lyndon

Foreword - Window Closed

During the past four decades, I have crossed paths with all but one of the club's chairmen, directors and senior executives. The exception is Farhad Moshiri. That said, the *Liverpool Echo* did publish a photograph of him holding a copy of my autobiography which was released shortly after he purchased his initial shareholding in 2016. If by chance he scanned the contents, Mr Moshiri will be aware of my prediction of a narrow four-year window of opportunity for our beloved club to catch its traditional rivals.

In the wake of the fire sale of young Wayne Rooney, the failure of the subsidized Kings Dock initiative and the despondency of too many trophy-less decades sprinkled with false dawns, his arrival provided beams of dazzling light through the aforementioned window. Surely it was our turn to benefit from a billionaire's investment, ambition, and business savvy to develop the framework for a successful, sustainable and stable future by introducing aggressive plans, modern management systems and efficient decision making processes and employing proven trailblazers to exploit the commercial opportunities available to the then twentieth most valuable brand in global football.

In anticipation of this giant leap forward, I was convinced that Everton and its success-starved followers were poised at the threshold of a new era packed with unswerving commitments, fresh ideas, clear visions and bountiful resources plus a dash or two of patience required to rejoin the English elite and lead us towards royal blue heaven. Indeed in 2016, it was an exciting time to be an Evertonian.

Agonizingly, even though Mr Moshiri kept his promise and provided funds approaching £750 million, the club behaved like an inebriated lottery winner and squandered the windfall. While there have been mitigating factors such as the coronavirus pandemic, the suspension of sponsorships with USM, Megafon and Yota due to Russia's war in Ukraine and serious injuries to Bolasie, Tosun, Mina, Gomes and Gbamin, other pains have been self-inflicted. They include a haphazard approach to recruitment of new additions - few of which lived up to expectations, and the failure to dispose swiftly and efficiently of subsequent under-performers. To compound our plight, despite Mr Moshiri's desire for stability, he and the directors have overseen the engagement of eight managers and coaching staffs as well as three directors of football – most of who struggled to make the most of the expensive resources available at Finch Farm.

Looking back, the Moshiri era was an exhausting nightmare riddled with back-to-back flirtations with relegation, enormous operating losses, the trauma of a 10-points deduction for breaching financial regulations and the inflated expectations and subsequent anger of the Goodison faithful. After failing to realize his domestic or European goals, the majority shareholder decamped leaving our beloved club in the most precarious state in its long history. Sadly, even his legacy of a state-of-the-art stadium at Bramley-Moore Dock is undermined by the future burden of massive loan payments. As a result, it remains to be seen how the new owners will navigate through the chaos in order to prosper on the banks of the River Mersey.

The Unofficial Everton Timeline has been forensically researched and expertly produced by Steve Dickinson and Lyndon Lloyd, two royal blue wordsmiths. It provides a comprehensive and balanced account of events both on and off the field between 2014-2023, and is a must-read for anyone interested in the challenges facing Everton Football Club and its future well-being.

That said, I have encouraged the publisher to include a Warning Notice for Evertonians raised in the era of Sir John Moores, The Golden Vision and The Holy Trinity, that exposure to the book's contents may cause nausea, insomnia, uncontrollable crying and alcohol dependency.

Dr David France OBE
Life President, Everton FC Shareholders' Association
January 2024

Singing The Blues

Well, I never felt more like singin' the blues
'Cause I never thought that I'd ever lose
Your love dear, why'd you do me this way?
Well, I never felt more like cryin' all night
'cause everythin's wrong, and nothin' ain't right
Without you, you got me singin' the blues

The moon and stars no longer shine
The dream is gone, I thought was mine
There's nothin' left for me to do
But cry-why-why-why over you (cry over you)
Well, I never felt more like runnin' away
But why should I go 'cause I couldn't stay?
Without you, you got me singin' the blues

Well, I never felt more like singin' the blues
'Cause I never thought that I'd ever lose
Your love dear, why'd you do me this way?
Well, I never felt more like cryin' all night
'Cause everythin's wrong, and nothin' ain't right
Without you, you got me singin' the blues

Oh, the moon and stars no longer shine
The dream is gone, I thought was mine
There's nothin' left for me to do
But cry-why-why-why over you (cry over you)
Well, I never felt more like runnin' away
But why should I go 'cause, I couldn't stay?
Without you, you got me singin' the blues

Composed by Melvin Endsley. Published in 1956.

Introduction

In August 2010, the club unveiled the Everton Timeline at Goodison Park. Extracted from The Everton Collection and stretching around three sides of the stadium, the 123 photographic images in the timeline chart major events in the club's illustrious past.

Though updated periodically, the final image on Goodison Road celebrates the signing of Romelu Lukaku in 2014.

Did time stand still for Everton Football Club, or has it simply failed to acknowledge the struggles which occurred during one of the most eventful periods in its 145-year history? This is the book that fills in *all* the gaps, on and off the field, during the tumultuous years of Farhad Moshiri's ownership.

Welcome to *The Unofficial Everton Timeline.*

More than a book about modern-day football, *The Unofficial Everton Timeline* documents unbridled ambition crashing into chaotic reality between 2014-2023. It is a comprehensive and detailed chronicle of important matches, big dreams, colossal financial investments, unproductive transfers, property deals and engineering marvels. But most of all, it is a book about people: moneymen, conflicting egos in the boardroom, highly rewarded players, and the real heroes of the story - a community of passionate Everton fans.

***

Formed in 1878, and one of the dozen founding members of the Football League in 1888, Everton have played more games in the top-flight than any other, scored more goals in the top-flight than any other and, through iconic centre forward, Dixie Dean, still boasts the player who scored the record number of goals in one season. The Timeline illustrates the club's heritage: nine times English football league champions, five times FA Cup winners, one time UEFA Cup Winners Cup winner. For well over a century, Everton were one of the great success stories of English football.

Yet, it's more than twenty-eight years since the club last won a trophy, and for each of the last two seasons, it survived relegation from the Premier League only by the skin of its teeth.

There is a saying that success has many fathers. The roll-call of Goodison greats falls quickly off the tongue. Players such as Dean, Lawton, Hickson, Young, Ball, Harvey, Kendall, Royle, Latchford, Southall, Ratcliffe, Reid, Sheedy, Sharp...the list goes on and on.

Managers like Catterick and Kendall. Directors like Will Cuff and Sir John Moores.

They also say failure is an orphan. How did a club with the pedigree of Everton – one of the five architects of the English Premier League back in 1992 – end up facing a threat to its very existence? Who and what have been responsible for this cataclysmic decline in the club's fortunes?

If an existential threat sounds too far-fetched for an institution with the longevity of Everton we remember that, faced with the club's perilous financial situation and the possibility of relegation from the Premier League, the Everton directors were required to issue this statement on 31 March 2023 as part of the club's Annual Report and Accounts:

> ***"Collectively, the above conditions indicate the existence of a material uncertainty that may cast significant doubt about the group's ability to continue as a going concern." – Everton Football Club Report and Accounts 2021/22, Published 31.3.23***

If such a statement had come in the days when the club was owned by well-meaning, cash-strapped local entrepreneurs, it would have made more sense. Yet this stark warning came seven years after Farhad Moshiri, a billionaire businessman, who lives on a yacht in Monaco, acquired the club.

Moshiri's purchase of a 49.9% stake in Everton FC was ratified by the Premier League in March 2016. After considering submissions from the club regarding the Iranian-born billionaire's proposed investment, the League noted how he had sold a 15% holding in rivals Arsenal to Alisher Usmanov, his long-time business partner, paving his way to become Everton's largest shareholder.

Soon after taking over, Moshiri articulated his vision of returning Everton to the elite of modern-day footballing giants. He later backed up his words by increasing his shareholding to over 94%, and injecting more than £750 million into the club. Yet, despite that vast cash injection, the club found itself on a financial precipice in 2023 and fighting for its Premier League existence for a second consecutive year. Where did all the money go?

As the dust settled on the near-disastrous season of 2022/23, Everton faced a third battle to avoid the drop and financial ruin. 3 games into the new season, they had a record of Played 3, Lost 3, no goals scored, 6 goals against. It was the worst start in the club's 145-year history and, as events would soon show, the revival of the Blues' fortunes in the ensuing weeks under Sean Dyche would prove to be vital in the club's chances of avoiding relegation yet again.

At the time of going to print and following an unprecedented points deduction handed down by the Premier League in November 2023, the team had hauled itself out of the relegation zone, but the macro picture remained a grave concern. It was a picture of crippling debts, a paper-thin squad and uncertainty over the viability – not to mention the suitability of the Blues' potential buyers, 777 Partners.

***

So, it's time to take stock and examine what really happened after the club's 'messiah' owner arrived on the scene.

Over the following pages, we'll try to answer some big questions:

- What assumptions did Farhad Moshiri make before and after becoming the club's major shareholder?
- Why did things not work out the way he meant them to – not for the club and its fans, nor too for Moshiri?
- Would Moshiri ultimately achieve his goals and make a tidy return on his investment, or would he suffer a massive write-off and retire from this chapter of his life with his reputation in football circles in ruins?
- Most importantly, in what condition would Everton FC be at the end of the Moshiri era?

In short, we'll update the Everton Timeline. It's the unofficial version of events – the version guaranteed never to be included on the club's website, or on the walls of the stadium. We hope you stay with us from start to finish. It's a fascinating story.

2014: Bill Kenwright and Farhad Moshiri begin talks

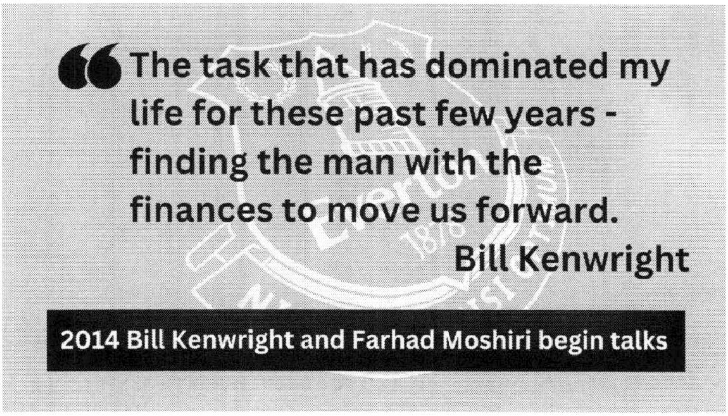

Bill Kenwright and Farhad Moshiri. Two men from very different backgrounds, whose paths would cross in 2014, and whose aims would centre around Everton Football Club.

According to Joe Strange, writing for The MailOnline in July 2016, [1]"Moshiri first met Bill Kenwright towards the end of 2014 and expressed an interest in buying a stake in the club."

Kenwright, a successful actor and theatre impresario, had been on the Board of Everton since 1989 and held the post of chairman since

2004. For years, he had made no secret of his wish to find a wealthy individual or investment group to take over at the club.

> "Once again, try as I might, I was unable to accomplish the task which has dominated my life for these past few years – finding the man, or the institution, with the finances to move us forward. Hopefully the day will come soon when I happily – even enthusiastically – hand over control of our beloved Club to a substantially wealthy individual or well funded investment group." – Bill Kenwright, Everton Annual Report & Accounts, 2011
> [2]

Moshiri, then 60, an Iranian-born financier, was the long-term business partner of one of the world's richest men, Alisher Usmanov. Moshiri had spent two decades advising and supporting Usmanov and, since 2007, they had each owned shares in Arsenal Football Club with ambitions to win seats on the Arsenal board before pushing through a complete takeover. For that plan to succeed, they would have to persuade majority shareholder, Stan Kroenke, to sell out to them. But Kroenke, the American magnate, had other ideas, and was determined not to sell to the Russian oligarch and his friend. It was this impasse in North London which prompted Moshiri to sell his shares to Usmanov and look for opportunities elsewhere.

Moshiri had entered the world of football as a financier with an accountancy background, rather than as a football fan, but his involvement at Arsenal had whetted his appetite for being around the

Premier League. It was a space he and Usmanov could see had good investment potential.

The investment in Arsenal by Usmanov and Moshiri, and Bill Kenwright's search for a mega-rich investor, came on the back of a major change in the preferred ownership model in the English Premier League, triggered in 2003 by the actions of another Russian oligarch, Roman Abramovich.

> "Looking back, it is hard not to regard the Abramovich takeover as the most significant single development in the Premier League era. Not in terms of what happened on the pitch, in a direct sense, but in terms of what it represented, both economically and culturally, for English football. 'We all knew,' [Sir John] Hall [formerly of Newcastle United] said. 'Doug Ellis at Aston Villa, Bill Kenwright at Everton, even the owners of Liverpool, Manchester United and Arsenal. We'd all put our money in, but the oligarch took everything to a new level. A billionaire came in at Chelsea and, overnight, there was no way we could compete financially.' – Oliver Kay, The Athletic, July 2023
> 3

In 2014/15, so-called "Chelski", backed by their Russian billionaire owner had romped away with the league.

Behind them, were Abu-Dhabi owned Manchester City, followed by Arsenal, Manchester United, Tottenham Hotspur and Liverpool. The "Top-6" seemed like a cartel.

Why not a Top-7, including Everton, the team which had played more games in the top-flight than all the others?

Kenwright argued to all potential investors that his club was a sound proposition. All it needed was more investment in players and facilities, to cement its place back among the elite of Premier League clubs.

If Chelsea and Manchester City could do it, why couldn't Everton?

The potential investment upside in Everton FC was enticing, and Moshiri knew it. He had taken counsel from David Dein, a close friend of Kenwright's and former vice-chairman of Arsenal between 1983 and 2007. When Moshiri began his due diligence process in 2014, on a potential investment in Arsenal's oldest rivals, it was only natural he would turn to Dein for advice.

David Dein had joined the Arsenal board when he bought a 16.6% stake in the club for £292,000 from Peter Hill-Wood, Arsenal's chairman. Hill-Wood described Dein as "crazy" to invest his money in the club, stating that, "to all intents and purposes, it's dead money."

Dein had built up his shares until, by 1991, he owned 42% of the club. Over the next decade, debts incurred forced him to sell just short of a 30% stake to co-director Danny Fiszman for approximately £11 million. By 2007, his remaining shares were worth around £60 million.

Alongside Philip Carter of Everton, Dein had been one of the architects of the Premier League in 1992, who reshaped the structure and finances of English football.

"I felt football was really a sleeping giant and had a long way to go," Dein said. "After seeing how the Americans operated their sport, particularly American football and baseball and basketball, I felt we were light years behind. We had so much more to give as an attraction."

Greg Dyke, later the chairman of the FA, stressed the central role of Dein in the Premier League's creation, saying "David Dein was the most revolutionary bloke I've met in football. David Dein created the Premier League. It was his idea."

During his time at Arsenal, Dein had an active role in transferring players and contract negotiations, including Ian Wright from Crystal Palace for £2.5 million and Dutch international Dennis Bergkamp for £7.5 million from Internazionale. He had been behind the appointment of the little-known Arsène Wenger for the manager's job in 1996. Under Wenger, Arsenal won the Premier League three times and the FA Cup seven times, and Dein strongly backed him and his transfer plans.

Dein had also been influential in the transformation of Highbury into an all-seater stadium. Following the Hillsborough disaster, the Taylor Report required Premier League clubs to introduce all-seater stadiums. Dein was behind introducing a bond scheme, which proved unpopular with the fans, to finance the redevelopment of Highbury's North Bank and Clock End terraces into all-seater stands.

He also helped Arsenal's entry into the group of major European football clubs in 2002 and became President of the G-14 in October 2006. He was also President of Arsenal Ladies Football Club, while Arsenal vice-chairman.

The Gunners had invested heavily in the development of their new stadium, which meant the club needed new revenue to service the heavy debts they had incurred as a result. The other board members allegedly signed a contractual agreement that they would not sell their shares for a year, and they jointly expressed their intention to keep their shares in the longer term. Dein, however, was in favour of a takeover of Arsenal by an external investor, and on 18 April 2007, he left the club due to "irreconcilable differences" between himself and the rest of the board.

In August 2007, and this is where it gets really interesting, David Dein sold his 9,072 shares (14.58%) in the club for £75million to Red & White Holdings, an investment vehicle owned by Russian metal billionaire Alisher Usmanov and his business partner, Farhad Moshiri. [4]

Usmanov and Moshiri appointed Dein as chairman of Red & White, which was at the time the largest shareholder in the club outside of members of the board of directors. In September 2008, he resigned as chairman of Red & White, with *The Times* suggesting it was to improve relations between Arsenal and Red & White.

But six years later, in 2014, relations between Red & White Holdings and the Arsenal board had gone from bad to worse.

With Arsenal still in a state of impasse, it was time for David Dein's close friend, Bill Kenwright, to enter the scene. Kenwright had been looking "24/7" for a 'messiah owner' to whom to sell Everton, and with it, some or all of his 26% shareholding in the club.

The relationships between Dein and Red & White, and between Dein and Kenwright, provided the green light for Kenwright and the Everton board to open discussions with Moshiri. It also opened the door to a potentially tantalising future deal with one of the world's richest men, should Alisher Usmanov ever sell his shares in Arsenal.

At the time talks began between Bill Kenwright and Farhad Moshiri, few people outside of Moshiri's circle of acquaintances knew much about him. An article published under the headline: *Iranian Moshiri Becomes Billionaire Helping Russia's Richest Man,* [5]provided some of the backstory:

"In 1989, Farhad Moshiri was an emigre in London pulling a pay check at Deloitte & Touche when he met Alisher Usmanov. Now, after a two-decade alliance with Russia's current richest man, the Iranian-born accountant is a billionaire himself.

"Moshiri who owns 5 percent of Usmanov's Metalloinvest Holding, Russia's largest miner of iron ore, and 15 percent of Arsenal Football Club, is worth at least $1.1 billion, according to data compiled by Bloomberg.

"Usmanov, 58, rewarded Moshiri, [then] 56, for years of service as an adviser and confidant in 2008, granting him a 10 percent stake in Gallagher Holdings, through which Usmanov controls Metalloinvest. 'He was consulting me for decades on different deals and exercised his option, fairly getting the stake,' Usmanov said in a telephone interview from Moscow. Usmanov and Moshiri both declined to elaborate on the terms of the option.

"Metalloinvest accounts for the bulk of Usmanov's fortune, which has swelled to more than $20 billion through timely bets on tech companies, including Facebook. Metalloinvest is worth at least $16 billion, valuing Moshiri's share at a minimum of $800 million. The company values itself at as much as $20 billion, chief executive Eduard Potapov said in February.

"For Moshiri, the road to riches started with a revolution. 'My parents fled Iran in February 1979, just before the Iranian Revolution,'

Moshiri, now a British citizen, said by e-mail. 'My father was an army doctor who trained as a pathologist and later became a senior military judge. My mother came from Iran's leading publishing house, Kayhan, which is now based in London.'

"The billionaire studied accounting at the University of London and worked at Ernst & Young and Pannell Kerr Forster before joining Deloitte & Touche. He said he met Usmanov through a mutual friend, Masoud Alikhani, when Usmanov was in London as part of a 'high-level delegation' seeking ways of setting up a political-risk insurance company to encourage foreign investment in the Soviet Union.

"'I was very taken at the time by his intelligence and the speed at which he absorbed complex ideas,' Moshiri said.

"The feeling was mutual, said Usmanov, who was born in the former Soviet republic of Uzbekistan, which, like Iran, borders Afghanistan.

"'We became friends almost at once,' Usmanov said.

"'With time, Moshiri actually became my financial mentor,' Usmanov said in the telephone interview. 'I appreciate his honesty and his encyclopaedic knowledge of finance and investments, although some of my most successful investments I did contrary to his opinion.'

"Moshiri has been chairman of Metalloinvest since 2006 and represents Usmanov on the boards of some of the other companies Usmanov owns shares in, including Norilsk Nickel, Russia's largest mining company, and MegaFon, the second-largest mobile-phone operator in the country.

"Not all of Moshiri's investments involve Usmanov. He bought 9.9 percent in 2007 of Panmure Gordon, one of Britain's oldest stockbrokers, without Usmanov's help. Now he holds 4.99 percent in the company.

"Still, the partners share a love of soccer, particularly Arsenal. Their Red and White [Holdings] venture bought 15 percent of the London club in 2007 and have since increased that stake to 30 percent, worth about $238 million, based on the April 3 closing price on the London Stock Exchange.

"Moshiri is an equal partner in the investment, according *to Arsenal's* website. A 15 percent stake in the club has a market value 'I love Arsenal, that's why I'm a shareholder,' Usmanov said in an interview last year.

"Moshiri said he was attracted to Arsenal's 'position as a top London club' that had just moved into a 'purpose-built' stadium that can seat 65,000 fans.

"It's one asset they may never sell. 'We're keen to invest further to secure the future success of the club on the playing field,' Moshiri said."

Ultimately, Farhad Moshiri's time at Arsenal was frustrating. Yet, he had gained knowledge and contacts which could be put to good use. The possibility of taking control of another Premier League club was opening up before him. Was this the time to strike out on his own?

---

1. Joe Strange, The MailOnline, July 2016

2. Everton FC Annual Report & Accounts, 2011

3. Oliver Kay, The Athletic, July 2023

4. "Dein sells Arsenal stake to Russian oligarch for £75m" – The Times Online

5. Iranian Moshiri Becomes Billionaire Helping Russia's Richest Man, Moscow Times, 12 April 2012

2015: Negotiations continue between Kenwright and Moshiri

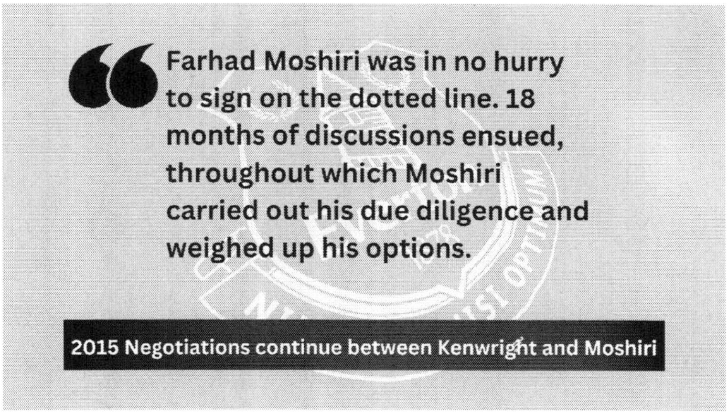

Why would anyone buy into Everton Football Club in 2015/16? And if they did, how much would it cost and what should they expect in return?

On the selling side of the negotiations was Bill Kenwright, representing himself and the other major shareholders. Kenwright, who joined the Everton board in 1989, became involved in a consortium to buy the club from the Littlewoods family in 1994 after the club avoided relegation. However, he lost out to Birkenhead-based Park Foods entrepreneur, Peter Johnson, who had owned a controlling stake in his local club, Tranmere Rovers since 1987. Johnson had agreed to inject £10 million into Everton via a rights issue, as advised by N M Rothschild from a Jersey-based family trust. When the deal was done, lifelong Liverpool fan Johnson appointed Kenwright as vice-chairman.

When the Football Association instructed Johnson to sell his interests in either Tranmere Rovers or Everton, it provided the perfect opportunity for Kenwright to realise his lifelong dream of owning Everton. He formed a new consortium that included Paul Gregg, Jimmy Mulville, Jon Woods and Willy Russell under a holding company called True Blue (Holdings) Ltd to buy Johnson's 68% controlling stake in Everton for £20 million on Christmas Eve 1999.

In an article headlined as '*Dream Script for Kenwright – Theatre impresario takes control of Everton for £20 million, as Johnson's gamble backfires,'* published in The Guardian on 26 January, 2000, Ian Ross [1]wrote:

"The theatre impresario Bill Kenwright yesterday finally assumed control of Everton. After more than 14 months of fundraising and at times acrimonious negotiation, Kenwright finally struck an irrevocable deal for the majority shareholding of the former chairman Peter Johnson.

"Kenwright met yesterday's non-negotiable deadline for completion with five hours to spare and will pay just over £20 million for Johnson's 68% stake - a deal which values one of football's oldest and most respected clubs at only £30 million.

"As Kenwright pondered how best to approach the task of transforming the fortunes of a sporting giant fallen on hard times, Johnson was left to rue a calculated gamble which backfired so spectacularly.

"The deal means that the Jersey-based businessman has not only received substantially less than he had been anticipating, but that he has also taken a loss of between £4 million-5 million on his investment when he seized control.

"Indeed, during the course of his pre-Christmas talks with Kenwright and other interested parties, Johnson was adamant that he would not do business at less than £1,200 a share, which would have valued his stake at around £29 million.

"Despite coming under pressure from the football authorities to offload his controlling interest in either Everton or the First Division club Tranmere Rovers, Johnson was content to extend his game of brinkmanship until a prospective buyer agreed to meet his price.

"However, the plan was to be undone just before Christmas when his bankers, anxious to recoup a loan he had taken out to buy Everton, insisted he accept any reasonable firm offer. Kenwright offered £857 per share, a bid which Johnson believed to be inadequate yet one which he had no option but to accept.

"With his bankers unhappy and the future of his primary business concern, the Park Food hamper group, very much on the line, Johnson gambled all believing that Kenwright would be unable to raise the funds to meet yesterday's deadline.

"As it approached, rumours began to suggest that Kenwright was struggling to pull together the strands of his consortium, meaning Johnson's gamble would have paid off. It did not. With the sort of flourish Kenwright normally reserves for his West End productions, he came up with the money to buy, at a rock-bottom price, the club he has always called his "life's passion".

"Obviously, I am very happy," he said. "It has been a long road, but I am thrilled and relieved that it is now done."

"Acquiring Peter Johnson's shares is only the first step to restoring a great club to where it belongs – to where it should be. If you are going to run a successful football club you need two qualities: you need to be realistic and you need a plan. I'm realistic and I have a plan," he added. Kenwright's consortium is made up of Paul Gregg, the head of the US entertainment company SFX, the Everton director Arthur Abercromby and John Woods, a member of the Everton Shareholders' Association.

"I do have tremendous confidence in my partners," said Kenwright, who will continue as Everton's vice-chairman. Sir Philip Carter [will be] chairman.

"To reduce a debt of about £14 million Everton will seek to sell a 9.9% stake to a media company such as NTL, Sky or Granada. There is also likely to be a new rights issue followed by discussions about the possibility of resurrecting Johnson's shelved plan to demolish Goodison Park and build a new stadium on the outskirts of the city.

"We have much hard work ahead of us but we are now on the way," said Kenwright.

The Everton manager Walter Smith can expect little benefit from the deal; he is likely to be informed that he must continue to run the team on a shoestring budget."

By the time Farhad Moshiri met Bill Kenwright in 2014, the market for Premier League teams was hotting up, and several clubs had recently changed hands. Valuations, ownership models and financing sources had been wide and varied.

Roman Abramovich had bought Chelsea for just £140 million in 2003. It had taken just 10 days for a deal to be agreed, and the meeting to iron out the heads of terms between then-chief executive Trevor Birch and Abramovich and his people had apparently lasted just 20 minutes.

The Glazer family had bought their first shares in Manchester United in 2003, escalating their shareholding until they finally had control of the club in 2005. They paid £790 million for Manchester United, but had come under heavy criticism for loading the club with over £700 million of debt.

Sheikh Mansour paid £210 million to purchase 90% of Manchester City from Thaksin Shinawatra in 2008. The Sheikh later paid extra for the remaining 10%, but it was the money he subsequently pumped into City which caused the most controversy over the years. Since their arrival in 2008, City's owners had spent more than £1.5 billion on player transfers alone.

In August 1991, the late David Moores, a member of the Littlewoods family, became chairman of Liverpool FC. Moores owned 51 percent of the club, and in 2004 expressed his willingness to consider a bid for his shares in Liverpool, Everton's rivals from across Stanley Park.

In August 2011, Andy Hunter penned an article in *The Guardian* under the headline: *Everton finances stretched to the limit, admits chairman Bill Kenwright – Kenwright tells fans' group why club is struggling. Chairman's 'desperate' search for new investors.*[2]

Hunter explained how: "Bill Kenwright has laid bare the scale of the financial problems at Everton, with a frank admission that their bankers have forced the club to reduce the overdraft and blocked additions to David Moyes's squad. In a remarkable exchange with representatives of The Blue Union, a coalition of supporters' groups alarmed at the lack of investment in Everton, the club chairman admitted that proceeds from recent player sales and Bellefield, the former training ground sold for £9 million, were taken by Barclays to reduce debts to £45 million."

The meeting turned out to be an embarrassment for Kenwright and the club, who as Hunter reported, "were now considering legal actions, amid claims The Blue Union broke an agreement not to make the conversation public. Kenwright reveals the mounting financial problems that have left Moyes without a net spend on players for three years, contradicts the evidence that Everton's chief executive, Robert Elstone, gave to a public enquiry and outlines his desperation to sell the club." They released the transcript of the three and a half hour meeting six days after the meeting which had taken place in Bill Kenwright's London offices on 12 August.

At one point, Kenwright allegedly said, "Look, we're desperate, I'm desperate."

Hunter also referred to Kenwright saying: "He is the only Premier League chairman not to take a salary or expenses from his club and reveals he has faced 'three periods of death threats' during his [then] 12 year reign as majority shareholder. He also confirmed that Keith Harris, Amanda Staveley – who was involved in the tortuous takeover process at Liverpool FC – the retail magnate Sir Philip Green, several banks and football agents, including Leon Angel, have all engaged in a fruitless search for new investment at Everton."

Andy Hunter's article ended with Kenwright's reported claim that he "was not worried about the future of Everton and that the club was looking at six sites for a possible new stadium." He denied that the billionaire Green had any involvement in the Goodison club. "He's not interested. He would say to me [adopts a mockney accent]: 'Bill, Bill, Bill, if I put facking money into Everton Football Club, you think Liverpool fans would buy from Topshop?' He's not interested. He's a total genius when it comes to money. He's like Mozart is to music. He's an adviser."

It took Bill Kenwright three more years of searching until his potential billionaire investor came along in late 2014. Yet, Farhad Moshiri was in no hurry to sign on the dotted line. 18 months of discussions ensued, throughout which Moshiri carried out his due diligence and weighed up his options.

As Alisher Usmanov's right-hand man, sitting on the board of many of his companies, Moshiri already had his work cut out. His favoured position at Usmanov's side clearly depended on him being available 24/7, 365 days a year. The case for investing in Everton may have looked attractive on paper, and both Usmanov and David Dein were supportive of the idea, but would it make sense for him personally to take on this additional project? And if he did, who would run Everton on his behalf? Who could he trust to do that?

It was time for Farhad Moshiri to prepare his business plan.

---

1. Ian Ross: 'Dream Script for Kenwright – Theatre impresario takes control of Everton for £20 million, as Johnson's gamble backfires,' The Guardian, 26 January, 2000

2. Andy Hunter ,The Guardian, 'Everton finances stretched to the limit, admits chairman Bill Kenwright – Kenwright tells fans' group why club is struggling. Chairman's 'desperate' search for new investors', August 2011,

2016: Moshiri's Project takes shape

> **"Was the Everton deal David Dein's, idea? Once lauded by Greg Dyke, later the chairman of the FA, who stressed the central role of Dein in the Premier League's creation. Dein undoubtedly had the brains, and the connections to mastermind Moshiri's acquisition of the Toffees. He was a close friend of Bill Kenwright and had been chairman of Red & White Holdings - jointly owned by Moshiri and Usmanov.**
>
> **2016 Moshiri's Project takes shape**

Every project begins with an idea, and either floats or sinks on a raft of assumptions. So whose big idea was it for Farhad Moshiri to 'buy and build' Everton Football Club?

Was it Alisher Usmanov's Plan B, after years of being rebuffed by Stan Kroenke and the Arsenal board? Billionaires, like Usmanov, spend their lives having big ideas, and taking massive risks. Their vast wealth is an indicator of the audacity of their ideas, the accuracy of their planning assumptions, and their ability to execute and deliver results.

As he entered his seventieth year in 2023, with an estimated net worth of $19.5 billion, Usmanov could look back on a lifetime of big ideas, many of which have delivered results in-line or ahead of his planned assumptions.

After spending six years of an eight-year sentence imprisoned in a remote Uzbek jail, on charges of which the Supreme Court of Uzbekistan later exonerated him, Usmanov steadily built up his empire through multiple mergers and acquisitions in sectors as widespread as steel, mining, publishing and mobile phones. He famously made huge returns by betting on high-tech companies. Facebook, Twitter, Groupon, Airbnb and Alibaba are among his successful investments. Even in his failed plans, such as the attempted acquisition of Arsenal FC, he walked away with a tidy profit.

Was the Everton deal David Dein's, idea? He undoubtedly had the brains, and the connections to mastermind Moshiri's acquisition of the Toffees. He was a close friend of Bill Kenwright and had been chairman of Red & White Holdings - jointly owned by Moshiri and Usmanov.

Could the idea have been the brainchild of Bill Kenwright? He had been looking for a billionaire to invest in Everton, ever since Roman Abramovich had arrived on the scene in 2003. It was an ambition he repeated in his Chairman's Statement in Everton's 2011 Annual Report and Accounts, where he wrote of his obsession with "finding the man, or the institution, with the finances to move us forward" [1]

The impasse between the Arsenal board and Red & White Holdings was clear, and through Dein, Kenwright would have known more than most. Did 'Chairman Bill' see Alisher Usmanov as his ideal 'substantially wealthy individual', and did he approach Usmanov and Moshiri with a tantalising proposition?

Or did the concept of buying Everton originate from Farhad Moshiri himself? Frustrated by years of achieving little at The Emirates, did he simply decide to sell up his shares at Arsenal, and buy out the Merseyside club to enable him to step out of Usmanov's shadow?

Through his association with Usmanov, Farhad Moshiri undoubtedly had experience in working on large, risky deals.

One of Moshiri's client accounts at Deloitte & Touche was Middlesex Holdings, a London-registered investment company in which Usmanov held shares. In 1993, Middlesex hired Moshiri, then aged 38, from Deloitte & Touche and within a few years made him an executive director. Over time, Moshiri began earning Usmanov's trust by analysing and challenging his investment ideas.

Whoever owned the original idea of 'the Everton deal': be it Usmanov, Dein, Kenwright or Moshiri; these four men came together to create an outline business plan, underpinned by a set of assumptions.

When later observing the financial mismanagement of Everton under Moshiri's ownership, it would be easy to assume there was no plan at all.

Business plans, profit-and-loss statements, balance sheets. These are the lifeblood of a person with a degree in accounting; someone with a professional career of working for major accountancy and consultancy companies for almost two decades. Moshiri had worked for Usmanov, the billionaire with a voracious appetite for acquiring businesses, for twenty-one years, employed as his principal tyre-kicker. Was there a business plan to acquire Everton FC? Of course, there was, and it was based on the club achieving success. Usmanov and Moshiri would not have touched the deal unless they believed they could bring their knowhow and capital to bear in a profitable way, and in an acceptable timeframe.

What's more, Moshiri was not walking into this deal cold. His experience as an Arsenal shareholder since 2007 had educated him in the running of an elite club within the English Premier League. From his seat next to Usmanov in the Red & White Holdings executive box at The Emirates, he had watched Arsenal play against their rivals season after season, with Everton never too far behind the Gunners:

- In 2007/08: Manchester United won the league, Arsenal finished 3rd, and Everton finished in 5th place.
- In 2008/09: Manchester United again finished top, with Arsenal 4th and Everton 5th.
- In 2009/10: Chelsea were champions, while Arsenal finished 3rd and Everton slipped down to 8th.
- In 2010/11: Manchester United were back on top, with Arsenal 4th and Everton 7th.
- In 2011/12: Manchester City were champions, Arsenal 3rd and Everton again 7th.
- In 2012/13: Manchester United were once again 1st, while Arsenal were 4th and Everton 6th.
- In 2013/14: Manchester City were champions once more, with Arsenal back in 4th place and Everton up to 5th spot.

Applying his 'encyclopaedic knowledge of finance and investments' to football, it's likely Moshiri knew more about the ownership structure and financial performance of every Premier League team than he knew about their tactics on the field, and some things must have seemed clear to him:

1. Winning the Premier League was increasingly the preserve of rich clubs. Whether that was because of the wealth of the Glazer family, Roman Abramovich, or Sheikh Mansour, the ability to fund large transfer fees and players' wages was a prerequisite to winning the ultimate domestic prize.

2. The Champions League generated a large part of Arsenal's turnover, in terms of gate receipts, commercial revenue and broadcasting income. A top 4 finish every season was therefore essential. Better still was to finish 1, 2 or 3 in the league, which led to improved seeding in the Champions League.

3. A top manager was worth his weight in gold. Alex Ferguson had proved this.

4. In Arsène Wenger, Arsenal also had a top manager. However, with the increased financial firepower of the Manchester clubs and Chelsea, the Gunners now lacked the monetary ammunition, and would likely remain as also-rans in the Premier League. Their last league title had been in 2003/04.

5. As things stood, Everton were never again going to win the league, but with comparatively meagre financial resources, they were deserving of their 'best of the rest' title.

6. Although the two clubs had once been close rivals in the Premier League, there was now a world of difference between their financial performance. For the season 2014/15 – during which Moshiri was conducting his due diligence on Everton FC, the financial comparison between the two clubs was stark.

By comparing the Arsenal Report & Accounts 2014/15[2] to Everton Report & Accounts 2014/15[3], it could be seen that the financial gulf between the two rivals was enormous.

- Arsenal's turnover of £344.5 million compared to Everton's £125.6 million.
- Arsenal's match day revenue (£100.4 million) was almost 6 times the level achieved by Everton's £17.9 million.
- Arsenal's commercial revenue of £100.3 million was 4 times that of Everton's £26.0 million.
- Arsenal's broadcasting income of £143.8 million was 76% higher than Everton's £81.7 million.
- The higher turnover enabled Arsenal to run a wage bill of £192.2 million, 2.5 times that of Everton's £77.5 million, allowing them to recruit more elite players into the squad and pay them better.
- Despite those enormous costs, Arsenal still spent a lower percentage of its turnover on wages (58.4%) than did Everton, at 61.7%.

- Arsenal made a pre-tax profit of £24.7 million, compared to Everton's loss of £4 million

- Arguably, Arsenal's greater financial muscle resulted in Arsène Wenger's side improving from a 4th place in season 2013/14 to 3rd place finish the following year, whereas Everton under Roberto Martinez dropped from 5th to 11th place.

Once discussions between Moshiri and Kenwright had opened in late 2014, and after signing a non-disclosure agreement from Everton's lawyers, Moshiri would have been privy to Everton's management accounts and other internal documents.

On the basis of their due diligence, Moshiri and his advisors drew conclusions which formed the basis of their business plan. Whilst the plan remains confidential, we can deduce some of **Moshiri's key business planning assumptions:**

- Usmanov's ongoing involvement in Arsenal prevented his direct investment in Everton, however, nothing prevented the Uzbek billionaire's companies acting as sponsors to the Merseyside club. Money, therefore, was seen as no barrier to success.

- Results in the Premier League had shown Everton progressing since Bill Kenwright and his True Blue Holdings consortium had taken over in 2000.

- Kenwright was a very experienced chairman of the football club. He had come highly recommended by David Dein, a man well trusted by Usmanov and Moshiri.

- Kenwright, Everton's self-proclaimed *Greatest Fan,* seemed to be well-liked by most of the Everton fan base, which would be a bonus for a publicity-shy character like Moshiri.

- Fan protests against Kenwright concerning the unsuccessful Kings Dock and Destination Kirkby stadium moves had showed the strength of feeling the fan base had over the stadium issue.

- Long-standing former-chairman, Sir Philip Carter, had passed away in April, 2015. Kenwright had been close to Carter, and his death had left a void within the Everton board.

- Moshiri had no wishes to involve himself in the day-to-day running of the club, nor did he have the time. As the club's majority shareholder, there would be no need for him to join the club's Board of Directors.

- In his place, he would appoint his young associate, Sasha Ryazantsev, to the Board. Ryazantsev was already advising Moshiri about the acquisition and future strategy of the football club.

- The relationship forged with Bill Kenwright during the 18-month long negotiations had been cordial. Kenwright was the consummate salesman, with a strong network of contacts within the club, within the wider football world, and on Merseyside. Kenwright had expressed a strong desire to remain active at the club.

- Appointing Kenwright as chairman made sense to Moshiri, as long as Ryazantsev was in charge of the purse strings, and could ensure Moshiri's strategy was being implemented.

- There would be evolution rather than revolution on the Board. CEO Robert Elstone would be retained and his performance evaluated.

- No further changes to the Board, including independent non-executives, were deemed necessary by Moshiri at that stage.

- Goodison Park was clearly on its last legs. Kenwright had said, either hyperbolically or disingenuously, that the stadium may fail its safety certificates.

- Kenwright and his team had identified several alternative stadium sites. The question was which one to choose, and how much would it cost to build the stadium and facilitate the move?

- A decision on selecting the new site could apparently be made in months.

- Planning approval would be swift, given the support of Liverpool City mayor Joe Anderson.

- Interest rates were low, and expected to stay low. A 40 year 'mortgage' could be easily arranged to fund the new stadium, as others – like Tottenham Hotspur- had proven.

- If Arsenal had been able to secure a £150 million naming rights deal on their new stadium, what could Everton expect for naming rights?

- Even with a limited budget, Everton had been able to recruit quality players such as: Lukaku, Stones, Arteta and Cahill. With more investment, the squad could only get better.

- Investment in the squad and team management would lead to progression, from average 7th place to Top 6 and eventually Top 4.

- Hiring a Director of Football (DoF) was essential. Everton had never previously employed one. This was a key change to improve the club's recruitment.

- The ideal DoF for Moshiri would act in an advisory capacity, with all key hiring and firing decisions requiring sign off by Moshiri and the Chairman.

- Roberto Martinez may need to be replaced. His performance would be monitored.

- There would presumably be no shortage of top managers willing to jump on board the 'hottest project in the Premier League.'

- Communicating with the fans via popular channels, such as

Jim White on TalkSport, would make Moshiri seem like a man of the people.

- A new stadium was paramount to the success of the club. It was essential to bridge the gap between Everton and the Top 6, and could help deliver regular European football.
- The rules of Financial Fair Play, introduced by UEFA in 2009, seemed to be largely ignored by the big clubs, and would probably not be an impediment to Moshiri's project at Everton.

Later on, we'll explore how these assumptions stood the test of time, but in the countdown to the deal, they provided Farhad Moshiri with a framework. He thought he knew how to take Everton into the Top 6, he assumed he had people to run the club on his behalf, and he was confident he had the financial resources needed to achieve his goal.

All he needed now, was to bring the deal over the line.

---

1. Everton Annual Report & Accounts, 2011
2. Arsenal Report and Accounts 2014/15
3. Everton Report & Accounts 2014/15

2016: Moshiri buys the club and sells the dream

Farhad Moshiri's signature on the contract to buy 49.9% of Everton FC in February 2016 meant Bill Kenwright's widely publicised search for a billionaire investor was finally over.

Moshiri's first communiqué – the dream he sold to the fans and other stakeholders - appeared on 12 March, 2016 in the match-day programme for Everton's FA Cup quarter-final match against Chelsea:

"I am delighted to join you here today at Goodison Park for my first match as a shareholder in Everton Football Club. I also felt it was fitting that my first message was in the matchday programme, with Everton being the first ever club to regularly produce one for home games. Indeed, it is this strong sense of tradition which appealed to me as I discussed this opportunity with Bill Kenwright to become part of the the future of the club. It is a testament to the enduring quality and consistency of the Club that Everton has remained in the top flight of English football since 1954. In more recent times this has been achieved under the stewardship of Bill, Robert Elstone and all the team behind the scenes at the Club. I am here to support them as required to ensure that the Club recaptures the glory days of the past and builds sustained success in the future. I know a lot of you want to know what my plans are. There is much to be done and things for me to learn, but I can confirm that I have committed to providing additional funds for transfers and retaining our key players to ensure that we have a strong core to build on for the future. We will also be looking at the best options in relation to our stadium. Goodison Park has served the Club extremely well but we need to make sure the Club has a suitable stage to perform on for the future. We will review the best options and how to finance, especially as it is likely to

> cost a little more than the £3,000 it apparently did in 1892. **Finally, and most importantly, Everton is about great football and winning matches.** Good luck to Roberto and the boys against Chelsea today."
> – Farhad Moshiri, 12 March 2016

Here, evidently, was a man with gravitas. A man who could spell out his understanding of the club and its history in less than 300 words. Here was a man of means, who could boldly state his vision, and his manifesto had four key elements:

- Provide additional funds for transfers,
- Retain key players,
- Look at the best options for the stadium, and how to finance it,
- Focus on great football and winning matches.

For all Evertonians, what was not to like?

***

Probably the first to break the news of Farhad Moshiri's investment in Everton, had been journalist Matt Lawton, writing in the MailOnline on 26 February, 2016[1]. He had claimed "exclusively" that a £200 million buy-out of Everton by a mystery Middle Eastern buyer could be announced in the coming days.

A report in Russia that Arsenal stakeholder Alisher Usmanov would become Everton's new owner was denied, but rumours immediately sprung up that his long-time business partner, billionaire Moshiri, was looking at purchasing the club.

For many Blues reading this news on social media, the rumours were received with scepticism. They had heard it all before.

But just three days later, the club's official website announced the news that: "Iranian-born businessman, Farhad Moshiri, has become Everton's largest shareholder."

Everton later confirmed that, pending Premier League approval, Moshiri had bought a 49.9% position that made him the club's largest stakeholder, and while it did not give him control overall, it effectively amounted to a takeover given the superior position it would afford him in the boardroom. American-based leisure tycoon Robert Earl had reportedly sold his 23% stake in Everton, while Jon Woods and Bill Kenwright reduced their own holdings from 26% and 19% respectively to usher in Moshiri as the club's biggest shareholder.

The Telegraph, along with several other media outlets including the BBC had reported that the funds had come from the sale of Moshiri's 15% interest in Arsenal to his long-time business partner, Usmanov, which was completed just one day earlier. The deal left Kenwright as chairman at Goodison, something that insiders suggested was an important factor for him personally, and which may have been one reason why an alternative investment proposal from the U.S. consortium led by John Jay Moores and Charles Noell had failed to come to fruition.

In a statement on the club website, Kenwright said of the news:

> "After an exhaustive search I believe we have found the perfect partner to take the Club forward. I have got to know Farhad well over the last 18 months and his football knowledge, financial wherewithal and True Blue spirit have convinced me that he is the right man to support Everton."

And Moshiri added:

> "I am delighted to take this opportunity to become a shareholder in Everton, with its rich heritage as one of Europe's leading football clubs. There has never been a more level playing field in the Premier League than now. Bill Kenwright has taught me what it means to be an Evertonian and I look forward with excitement to working with him to help deliver success for Everton in the future."

As Joe Strange reported in *TheMailOnline*, "After 18 months of discussions and due-diligence, a deal was struck, which included the option for Moshiri to increase his stake [at Everton] in the not too distant future."

For Everton fans, the news of the takeover and the unveiling of the mystery investor came as a welcome surprise. Suddenly everyone wanted to know about Moshiri and his connections with Usmanov, one of the world's richest men.

But it was not only the Everton fans who had taken an interest in Moshiri's background. The following year, the question of Usmanov's involvement in Moshiri's investment in Everton FC would be highlighted in a special report by the BBC programme, *Panorama*. [2]

The two-part investigation, broadcast on 5 and 6 November, 2017 focused on offshore tax havens and global finance as it pertained to some of the world's richest individuals.

By then, USM Holdings had already been announced as sponsors of Everton's Finch Farm training complex. Moshiri's directorship and part ownership of many of Usmanov's companies meant that the Uzbek-Russian's name was never too far from discussions about the Toffees' finances, but the club and the Premier League claimed there had been no conflict of interest.

Moshiri shrugged off the media's interest in his relationship with Usmanov. He said he needed to get on with the job of transforming Everton. He was a man in a hurry and would prove to be a hands-on owner, taking an active interest in the management of the first team, and the stage they played on.

---

1. Matt Lawton: MailOnline, 26 February, 2016

2. BBC Panorama: Paradise Papers: Who is in control of Everton? 6 November 2017

2016: New stadium high on Moshiri's to do list

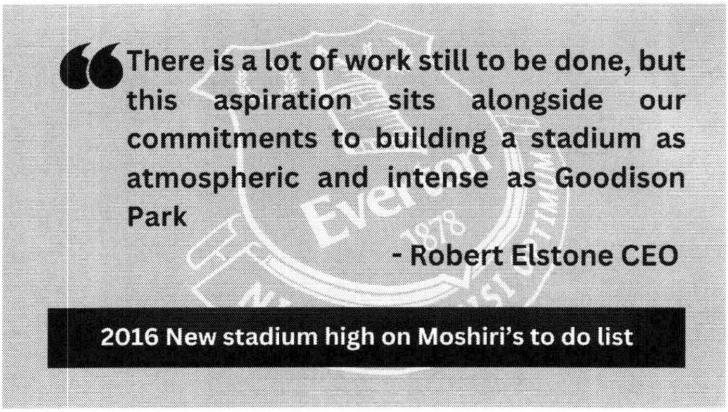

In the *Annual Report and Statement of Accounts 2000 of The Everton Football Club Limited* [1]- the first report and accounts since Bill Kenwright's True Blue Holdings consortium had taken charge - the late Sir Philip Carter wrote in his chairman's statement: "The stadium debate continued throughout the year and it is likely that whilst remaining at Goodison Park is still an option, we have indicated publicly that if we are to achieve a quality stadium with a capacity of 55,000, then an alternative site must be sought. Your Board will leave no stone unturned until this matter is finally resolved and again

Everton are at the forefront of stadium design; we must ensure that our rich traditions are reflected in any new design. I reiterate that before any final decision is made, the views of our supporters will again be canvassed. Supporters can be assured that only the best will be considered, and until the appropriate time we will remain in our ancestral home, which I am sure you will agree had a much needed facelift in the summer. The 'old lady' still has pride and we love her dearly."

Plans to move the club to a new stadium had actually been afoot since 1996, ever since the 1994 conversion of Goodison Park to an all-seater stadium had reduced its capacity to just under 40,000.

Every team in the league was facing similar challenges. Some had already moved forward, leaving Everton behind.

***

First out of the blocks were Manchester United. The club carried out major redevelopment works at Old Trafford starting in the mid-1990s, including the addition of extra tiers to the North, West and East Stands, which almost returned the stadium to its former capacity of 80,000. The expansion enabled a significant rise in gate receipts; which went from £43.9 million in 1994 to £87.9 million in 1997.

***

Because of restrictions on expanding the capacity at Anfield, Liverpool announced plans to move to a proposed Stanley Park Stadium in

May 2002. They received planning permission in July 2004, and in September 2006, the City Council agreed to grant Liverpool FC a 999-year lease on the proposed site. Following the takeover of the club by George Gillett and Tom Hicks in February 2007 and a redesign of the proposed stadium, the new plans were approved by the Council in November 2007. The club said the stadium would open in August 2011 and would hold 60,000 spectators. However, Gillett and Hicks had difficulty in financing the £300 million needed for the development and construction was halted in August 2008.

In October 2012, BBC Sport reported that, rather than build a new stadium in Stanley Park, Fenway Sports Group, the new owners of Liverpool FC, planned to redevelop their current home at Anfield. As part of the redevelopment, the capacity of Anfield was to increase from 45,276 to approximately 60,000, at a cost of £150 million. It was supposedly all part of a £260 million project to improve the Anfield area.

***

Arsenal had been denied planning permission by Islington Council to expand Highbury. Feeling the same pressures to comply with new safety standards, and needing to compete with their rivals by increasing match-day revenues, the club first explored the possibility of relocating to a new stadium in 1997.

After considering various options (including purchasing Wembley Stadium), the Gunners bought an industrial and waste disposal estate in Ashburton Grove in 2000. A year later, they received the council's approval to build a stadium on the site. Manager Arsène Wenger described the project as the "biggest decision in Arsenal's history." Relocation began in 2002, but financial difficulties delayed the work until 2004. In the interim, Emirates Airlines was later announced as the main sponsor for the stadium and Arsenal completed the project in 2006 at a cost of £390 million, with the club's former stadium turned into *Highbury Square*, an apartment complex.

***

Another significant stadium move took place 36 miles from Everton's Goodison Park, where The City of Manchester Stadium became the home of Manchester City. After the 2002 Commonwealth Games, the stadium was converted from a 38,000-capacity arena to a football stadium at a cost to the city council of £22 million and to Manchester City of £20 million. The club agreed to lease the stadium from the city council and moved there from Maine Road in the summer of 2003. The stadium instantly made the football club more attractive to potential investors. That culminated on 1 September 2008, when Abu Dhabi United Group Investment and Development Limited completed a takeover of Manchester City. The initial deal, worth a reported £200 million, was later dwarfed by the £1.5 billion or more the Abu Dhabi owners subsequently spent in the transfer market. In August 2015, a 7,000 seat third tier on the stadium's South Stand brought the capacity up to 55,000 in time for the start of the 2015/16 season.

***

The opening of Arsenal's new Emirates Stadium in 2006 was perhaps the catalyst for their North London rivals, Tottenham Hotspur, to make a move with their own stadium development. Announced in 2008, but beset by revisions, disputes and delays, construction finally began in 2015. The *Tottenham Hotspur Stadium* eventually opened on 3 April 2019. With a seating capacity of 62,850, it is a multi-purpose stadium and features the world's first dividing, retractable football pitch, which reveals a synthetic turf field underneath for NFL London games, concerts and other events. The project covered the site of the now demolished White Hart Lane ground, and areas next to it, with the intention being to sell the naming rights to a sponsor. A sponsorship deal has yet to be agreed, however, and fans occasionally refer to the stadium as New White Hart Lane.

***

Spurs' delays allowed another London rival, West Ham United, to overtake them in the race to play in a new, and larger home. With an all-seated capacity of 80,000 for the 2012 Summer Olympics and Paralympics, the London Stadium served as the athletics venue and as the site of their opening and closing ceremonies. Land preparation for the stadium began in mid-2007, with the construction officially starting on 22 May 2008. Following the Olympics, they renovated the stadium for multi-purpose use. When it re-opened in July 2016, it had 66,000 seats, but its capacity for football was limited to 60,000 under the terms of the lease. The decision to make West Ham United the main tenants was controversial, with the initial tenancy process having to be rerun.

***

Farhad Moshiri's announcement when he bought Everton, of 'a new stage for the team to perform on' had come 20 years after Peter Johnson first mooted the need for a new stadium, and after several unsuccessful attempts by the club to relocate. Yet this time there was a feeling in the city that Moshiri had not only the willpower, but also the finances to make things happen.

Speaking to BBC Merseyside, then Liverpool mayor, Joe Anderson expressed his belief that the Blues would kick off in a new ground by the start of the 2019/20 season. "I'm confident the new stadium will be up and running in three years' time," the mayor said. "I think there is a real acceptance by them, and I'm pretty confident that within three years there will be a new stadium for Everton Football Club in Liverpool."

While the club released no details of the potential sites under consideration, the Liverpool Echo reported one could be in the north docks area at Trafalgar Dock, and the other at the Stonebridge Cross site off the East Lancs Road in Croxteth.

The collapse of the Kings Dock project over a decade earlier had been a source of pain for Evertonians, who had dreamt of an iconic waterfront stadium that would have put the club on the map in more than one sense.

However, much of the property on the waterfront was now in the hands of Peel Holdings, the developers of the Liverpool Waters regeneration scheme. Peel had historically been reluctant to involve a football stadium in their plans, but, were reportedly warming to the idea once Everton made their interest known in the Bramley-Moore Dock site in Liverpool's north docks area, north of the Wallasey Tunnel.

Mayor Anderson had said in August 2016 that an announcement on the club's new home could happen "in a couple of months," but the docks site depended on the Blues meeting Peel's £30 million asking price for the land.

Anderson did not comment on the specifics, but said: "Things are really positive. No option is ruled out, but everyone knows my preferred option. Everyone knows the club's preferred option. There are discussions taking place and we're at the heart of that, trying to move things on. Really, given where we were 12 months ago, we are in a much different and healthier position. The obstacle with all these things is an agreement must be reached. We did that with Anfield. We had challenges, had to buy properties and move people on. It's about negotiation and making significant concessions."

In March 2017, interviewed by Adam Leventhal from Sky Sports News, Everton's then Chief Executive, Robert Elstone, spoke of the club's ambition and hopes of finally resolving the vexing stadium issue. The broadcaster's cameras were at USM Finch Farm, covering the Blues from all angles, and speaking to many key figures. They kicked the day off with Leventhal sitting down with the CEO and club ambassador Graeme Sharp.

Elstone talked of the renewed ability of Everton to take big steps towards rejoining England's elite group of clubs now that investor Farhad Moshiri was on board.

"One thing Evertonians are is fiercely ambitious," he began. "We are content where we are. Is it where we want to be? Is it where want to end up? Absolutely not.

"Everton fans and Everton Football Club wants to push on and that burning ambition is inherent in everything we do. In our manager, in our chairman, and indeed in our new majority shareholder, Farhad Moshiri, ambition really transcends the whole football club.

Leventhal asked Elstone how the club intended to balance the 'vision' of a new stadium and the wrench of moving away from Goodison Park.

He replied, "It's the most important decision we'll make in recent times. It's a decision that will live for us for generations, so we have to get it right. It's absolutely something we need to move forward. There are lots of features and qualities about Goodison that we wish to retain and take with us around atmosphere, about proximity to pitch, around intensity, around a place where opposition clubs really don't want to come and play. If we can bottle that and take that with us, then we'll have done well.

"Financially, it's a massive decision. This is a multi-million pound investment. For Everton in a stadium that we're currently filling at 40,000 seats, it's not as if we've got a huge waiting list of any army of fans ready to move in. We have to make sure that it works for us.

"For us, it's also about future-proofing because ultimately Goodison will need us to keep investing, and it's also about a statement of intent. Both of those things are harder to put down on a business plan.

"Having said all that, we're confident now that we're moving towards a solution for the problem that has remained with us throughout this of how we're going to afford it.

"It's a big investment — where's the money going to come from to build it? There's a lot of work gone into that and we're getting close, we hope, to resolving that problem."

Regarding the projected cost of the new stadium, Mike Keegan in The MailOnline [2]quoted a figure of £350 million, that estimate also being broadly in line with the construction cost of Arsenal's Emirates Stadium, which had opened in 2006.

***

Planning for the new ground at Bramley-Moore Dock continued, following the announcement that an agreement was in place with the landowner Peel Group to purchase the dock site. In May, with the 2016/17 season drawing to a close, Robert Elstone was back in the media, when he reaffirmed the club's proposed new stadium on Liverpool's waterfront, would be "as atmospheric and intense as Goodison Park."

The outline funding proposal called for a 50,000-seat venue, but there had been speculation among supporters and the local press that the final capacity could be larger. Elstone suggested that the Everton hierarchy were confident that they could fill a significantly larger ground than Goodison Park with it's 39,414 seats.

"Whilst the Council is lending valuable support, it is important to stress that the club is paying for the stadium in full," the Chief Executive confirmed. "We will pay for our new home with a long-term lease, likely to be 40 years.

"At the end of this time, the club will take sole ownership of the stadium. These two big steps forward were critical for the project to progress.

"They give us the confidence to proceed with the next phase of our work – the work required to define, in much greater detail, what the stadium will look like and the exciting role it will play in the future aspirations of the club.

"This phase of work will require substantial investment from the club, highlighting just how committed we all are to the success of the project.

"We have reason to be confident on capacity. As evidenced this season, Everton remains as ambitious as ever and will continue to challenge for a place in the Champions League.

"And, also, right now we have 10,000 prospective Season Ticket holders waiting for the release of around 3,000 seats, so we're confident that we can fill a considerably bigger stadium.

"There is a lot of work still to be done, but this aspiration sits alongside our commitments to building a stadium as atmospheric and intense as Goodison Park."

With anticipation and momentum growing around an expensive new stadium project, the manager and his team were under ever-growing pressure to deliver more success on the field.

---

1. Annual Report and Statement of Accounts 2000 of The Everton Football Club Limited

2. Mike Keegan: Daily Mail, 2 March 2017

2016: ROBERTO MARTINEZ PRAISES NEW OWNER MOSHIRI

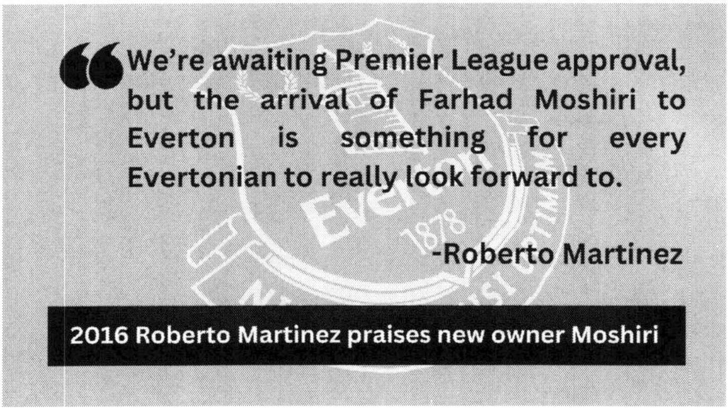

In 2013/14, Roberto Martinez had used his first season at the club to build on the sound defensive qualities of the squad he inherited from David Moyes. His masterstroke had been bringing in Romelu Lukaku on loan from Chelsea in September 2013. James McCarthy had also been a shrewd buy from Wigan, bringing energy and bite to the midfield; and Gareth Barry, an even more astute addition, initially also on loan. The team eventually finished a phenomenal fifth in the table.

Martinez' team had failed to kick on in 2014/15; this despite the conversion of Lukaku's loan to a permanent transfer, for a club record fee of £28 million in July 2014 – an event that proved worthy of inclusion in Everton's *Official* Timeline on Goodison Road.

A 1-0 home defeat at the hands of Spurs had confirmed a disappointing eleventh place in the table on the final day of the season. All eyes had been on Martinez at the start of the 2015/16 season, as he tried to reverse his side's downward momentum and push once again for one of the European spots.

Despite rumours that Lukaku was agitating for a move to a Champions League side, he had been regularly chipping in with crucial goals. By the turn of the year, he had already netted 18 times in all competitions. Stephen Naismith, Ross Barkley and Gerard Deulofeu were also hitting the target.

In search of additional firepower, and as cover for the prolific Lukaku, the club signed Oumar Niasse from Lokomotiv Moscow for a fee of £13.5 million at the end of the January transfer window.

January 2016 had been a winless month for Everton in the league, with away draws against Man City and Chelsea, and a demoralising home defeat to Swansea. With his team dropping out of the top half of the table, the pressure was ratcheting up on Martinez. When news of Farhad Moshiri's takeover emerged, the manager was quick off the blocks to welcome the new shareholder.

"It's really, really good news," Martinez said. "I met Mr Moshiri and the impression I got was that he is a gentleman with incredible values and someone who knows the Premier League inside out because he has been involved with another Premier League football club. He knows how difficult it is to have a vision in football and to put it into practice.

"Sometimes you get business people who don't understand it. Obviously, that is not the case here. He is someone who has been working closely with a Premier League club and he knows what it takes.

"He's someone that has been introduced to Everton and has followed the club very closely. It is fair to say, he has fallen in love with what Everton means, with the heritage and the history, and that's really exciting. Our chairman is the perfect person to introduce someone to Everton and I can speak from my own experiences.

"[He's a] new figure, someone who is going to bring a new vision and completely different push to our club. So you can imagine the excitement that we have. We're awaiting Premier League approval, but the arrival of Farhad Moshiri to Everton is something for every Evertonian to really look forward to."

Martinez expressed his belief that the change at boardroom level and the potential levels of investment that Moshiri could bring signalled a hugely positive development for the club. "What we've got is the perfect person to fit in at Everton, and you can't say that lightly. What I'm really excited about is that we're not going to lose any of the good things about the football club; it's the opposite. This is the start of a new era at Everton, without a doubt.

"We are going to show, as a football club, that we are ready to go to the next level. You can feel the excitement around the place and that's something we need to use out on the pitch. When I started, I said we have to look for the Champions League positions and we have to become a winning team. That is a very broad statement, and it's a difficult aim to achieve. Obviously, the investment and the involvement of Farhad Moshiri takes us into a different level in terms of accelerating the process.

"Clearly, it's an exciting time and every single Evertonian should know he is someone who knows our football club, someone who is a very strong addition and won't bring anything other than getting Everton to where we belong."

Behind the scenes, Martinez must have known the bar had been raised, and, if his team's performances did not improve quickly, his job would be on-the-line.

***

12 March 2016: Everton v Chelsea

Amid a raucous atmosphere at Goodison Park, and with Moshiri watching from the Directors' Box, the Toffees went toe-to-toe with the reigning Premier League champions in a tightly contested FA Cup Quarter-Final tie that featured plenty of effort and desire but precious few clear-cut openings.

Chelsea, hoping to keep their own season alive after exiting the Champions League at the hands of Paris Saint- Germain in midweek, had shaded the first half, enjoying most of the possession without really penetrating an Everton back line that was in uncompromising mood.

The first period was book-ended by a couple of Tom Cleverley shots that were comfortably gathered by Thibault Courtois, while the midfielder also dragged a shot across goal in the 25th minute, but it was a half notable more for the antics of Diego Costa.

No stranger to controversy or a bout of 'handbags' at Goodison, the Spain international was booked for catching Gareth Barry around the face in a clear act of retribution for an earlier coming together. And his teammate Kenedy was fortunate not to join him for a succession of fouls, benefitting from referee Michael Oliver's leniency.

The game picked up in terms of goalmouth incident after half-time, though. Ramiro Funes Mori rose highest to meet a Cleverley corner but could only steer his header over the bar. Costa then rounded the sprawling Joel Robles at the other but could only roll a shot across the face of the goal.

Everton had been stepping up the pressure on Chelsea's goal but had little more than set-pieces to show for it until Lukaku caught fire with 12 minutes to go, starting with a quite brilliant solo goal. The Belgian picked up a ball by Ross Barkley near the left touchline, shrugged off a foul by Cesar Azpilicueta, turned Gary Cahill inside and out before drilling a low shot inside the far post.

Three minutes later, Lukaku doubled his tally and the home side's lead with another unerring finish. Played onside by Azpilicueta, Everton's top scorer collected another pass by Barkley and drove the ball through Courtois' legs to send the bouncing Gwladys Street End into ecstasy.

Chelsea brought on Loic Remy to drag the Londoners back into the tie, but they undermined their efforts when Costa received a second yellow card for seemingly head-butting Gareth Barry with five minutes left.

Barry would follow him down the tunnel three minutes later when he too picked up a second yellow for a cynical trip on Cesc Fabregas, but Everton held on to progress to next month's semi-final at Wembley.

Could there have been a better start to the Moshiri era? It would be hard to imagine one.

Final score: Everton 2-0 Chelsea.

***

Interviewed after the Chelsea match, Farhad Moshiri said:

> "I bought into a great club. I felt it today. Let's enjoy the day and let's hope we can energise the club. I think you can never take over a club. You become part of a club and I hope to become part of the club. I bought into a new family. That's what special for me and I give them whatever I have."

The typically effusive Bill Kenwright, back at Goodison after an extended, illness-related absence, sat beaming next to Moshiri. He lauded Romelu Lukaku for two excellent goals that won the tie for Everton. He then paid tribute to his manager Roberto Martinez, who had come in for mounting criticism in recent weeks as inconsistent results in the Premier League had kept the Blues in the bottom half of the table.

> "I think we have got to acknowledge Rom's goal because it was an unbelievable goal, wasn't it?" the chairman said. "I thought his second goal was great,

> too. I thought they were all great today. I thought they were fantastic. You know what I thought today, though? What a manager. You can't hide the fact that there's been all kinds of criticism this week, [but] he's stood firm and just beaten Chelsea with some to spare."

Yet, after the euphoria of the Chelsea game had died down, the Blues recorded defeats against Arsenal and Manchester United, followed by draws against Watford, Crystal Palace and Southampton. Next up was one of the toughest matches of the season, and for Roberto Martinez, it was becoming a 'must win' game.

***

20 April 2016: Liverpool v Everton

Having suffered a 4-0 reverse in the Anfield derby during his first season in charge, Roberto Martinez' team had gained a creditable 1-1 draw in September 2014, when Phil Jagielka delivered that ninety-first minute Exocet into the Kop goal from 25 yards out, which went down in folklore as one of the greatest ever Merseyside derby goals.

In the days leading up to the 2016 all-Mersey clash on Liverpool's turf – and with an FA Cup semi-final against Manchester United due to take place just three days later at Wembley – the mantra from the under-pressure Martinez was, "We want to make our fans proud."

What ensued, however, was another 4-0 drubbing by the Reds. Instead of a proud performance, the team served-up Blues fans with utter humiliation in the worst arena possible.

Two of the goals had "Martinez regime" written all over them — acres of space afforded to the man crossing the ball, flat-footed defending and two simple headers — the first from Divock Origi and the second by Mamadou Sakho, given the freedom of Anfield in the six-yard box to nod home.

It was 'game over' by first-half stoppage time. The fight long gone out of his Everton team, Martinez stood, cross-armed and helpless on the touchline; his verbal battles now fought by his assistant, Graeme Jones.

Gareth Barry, back in the side to tie the Premier League record for games started, had to come off at half time with a groin injury that piled on the problems for the upcoming trip to Wembley. After Funes Mori received a straight red for a late stamp on Origi's ankle, Ross Barkley was also hooked; the white flag raised by the manager with dreaded thoughts turning already to the cup semi-final that could yet be his death knell, if he wasn't already out of a job before then.

If Simon Mignolet touched the ball at all in the second period, it would have come as news to Everton supporters. That the Reds weren't 4-0 up by the interval and that they didn't treble the 2-0 lead they took into the break was down to Joel Robles, who made some fine saves to deny Adam Lallana and Roberto Firmino in particular, and some poor finishing by Klopp's front line. Liverpool got it together up front on the hour mark, though, to carve the Blues wide open and present an easy chance to Daniel Sturridge to slot home. And Coutinho's accurate low drive from the edge of the box a few minutes later was well-placed beyond the Everton goalkeeper's reach to complete the rout.

Recent performances, and some damning goals for and against statistics in the last 30 minutes of matches, suggested the team weren't fit enough, didn't fight enough, weren't clinical enough, and that the mentality of the side was simply all wrong. The players seemed no longer to be playing for the manager – and when that happens, it's over.

Final score: Liverpool 4-0 Everton

***

After the match, the media found a chastened Martinez ruing a lapse in concentration at the end of the first half and a "chain of events" involving injury, illness and a red card in the horror show at Anfield.

"It was a horrible experience for everyone involved," a shell-shocked Martinez said to Darren Griffiths after the game. "You don't expect a game to change so radically. Three minutes before half time we got two actions that we don't defend properly, where we switch off and we allow a two-goal lead to be so soft in the manner that it happened."

***

23 April 2016: Everton v Manchester United (At Wembley Stadium)

In Roberto Martinez's own words, the period of the Anfield derby and the FA Cup Semi-Final against United, had promised to be a "defining week" for him and his players.

After the galling collapse at Anfield, Martinez needed a big performance, and the backs-against-the-wall, underdog spirit which had lifted Everton teams of the past against Man United, including at Wembley in 1995 and 2012. He eventually got something akin to it, whether by his own powers of motivation or, perhaps more likely, through a response from the players to the desperation pouring out of stands from 30-odd thousand Evertonians, and from the realisation their entire season was circling the drain.

The first 45 minutes produced tentative, defensive football that was lacking cohesion and organisation, and during which Everton fell behind to Marouane Fellaini's 34th-minute goal. But in the second half, the Blues suddenly discovered the intensity and drive that had been wholly lacking through a run of seven games without a win in all competitions, and they had Louis van Gaal's Red Devils on the ropes.

It yielded a penalty for the Blues, won by the otherwise disappointing Ross Barkley, who was felled in the box by Tim Fosu-Mensah. That was taken well enough by Romelu Lukaku but saved by David de Gea, a goalkeeper who had made a habit of bringing his best form into meetings with Everton over the previous couple of seasons. Then, after Phil Jagielka had denied Fellaini a second goal with an unseen handball almost on the goal-line, Everton levelled and threatened to turn the tie on its head with more pressure yet, sadly, fell short.

Instead, there was the latest in a succession of stings in the "tale" that Blues fans have had to deal with, as Martinez's defence succumbed one final time and Anthony Martial swept through the breach to plant a cruel winner beyond Joel Robles.

Little of what Martinez said in the aftermath of another crushing loss would have resonated with fed up Evertonians, but he was right that, on balance, Everton probably at least deserved to get to extra time. Their first-half display had been massively disappointing, an echo of the lifeless and unimaginative fare that had characterised a sequence of three draws and four defeats since that potentially catalytic victory over Chelsea last month.

It would have been easier to blame the loss of Seamus Coleman, the need to use Muhammed Besic as an emergency fullback, and Jagielka having to play through a hamstring injury but the second half from Martinez' side had been so much better.

The fightback, when it came, wasn't led by Martinez's self-proclaimed "style" of possession-based football; it was a last-ditch effort to raise the tempo by a group of players who were willed on by the masses of Evertonians banked in their thousands around one half of Wembley, with elimination from the cup rapidly closing in on them.

Had Lukaku prevailed from the penalty spot, things might have been so much different but, ultimately, the team had been undone by their failure to turn up for 50 minutes, their consistent failings at the back, and the leaking of yet another injury-time goal.

Final score: Everton 1-2 Man United

***

After the match, Roberto Martinez – who was insistent that his team was developing, and that he shared the Blues' ambitions – was asked if he was still the man for the job at Goodison Park. This despite another hugely disappointing season which had seen defeat over two legs to Manchester City in the League Cup earlier on, and now included a second cup exit at the semi-final stage.

"I am, yes," he replied. "I'm so attached to Everton and my ambition is exactly the same as their ambition. Over the last three years, we haven't invested any money. We've been handling assets really well. I think the squad is at a great valuation. We've got very good young players, we develop young players really well. I just share the drive that the football club has which is to getting into the Champions League, getting into positions where we can bring silverware to the football club and I'll give everything I've got to fulfil those expectations. I feel every season we are developing and showing certain things that can please our fans and bring the silverware they deserve. But clearly, at moments like this of true disappointment, it is very difficult to see through that the real good things we have developed over the last three seasons."

***

11 May 2016: Sunderland v Everton

Roberto Martinez' words after the FA Cup semi-final defeat would ring hollow in the aftermath of what proved to be his final match in charge as Everton manager. His team offered another shameful away performance, going down meekly to Sunderland who easily picked up the three points they needed to safeguard their membership of the Premier League and send Newcastle and Norwich down to the Championship.

The Blues fell behind 2-0 by the half-time interval to goals by Patrick van Aanholt and Lamine Kone. They then conceded another when Joel Robles could only parry to the feet of the Ivorian defender and he converted from close range.

Coming in the wake of the previous Saturday's abject capitulation at the King Power Stadium to newly crowned champions, Leicester, and the even more embarrassing surrender at Anfield in the Merseyside derby in the previous month, the outcome of this game came as little surprise to those Evertonians who had made the journey to the northeast.

Seven goals conceded in those two prior away fixtures soon became ten, as the Black Cats capitalised on Everton's inability to convert superior possession into chances and preyed on the Toffees' notorious weakness at set pieces.

All three goals came as the result of dead-ball situations. The first and third were incidents that Robles would want to forget, but none of the defenders covered themselves in glory and were it not for a couple of other important stops by the Spanish goalkeeper, the score might have been higher.

It had been another miserable evening for Everton. The club may have wished to delay a decision about the manager's future until after the final game against Norwich, but had he still been in charge by then, disgruntled Everton fans would have been sure to make their feelings known at what was supposed to be an upbeat occasion to see out the season.

Final score: Sunderland 3-0 Everton

2016: Roberto Martinez sacked

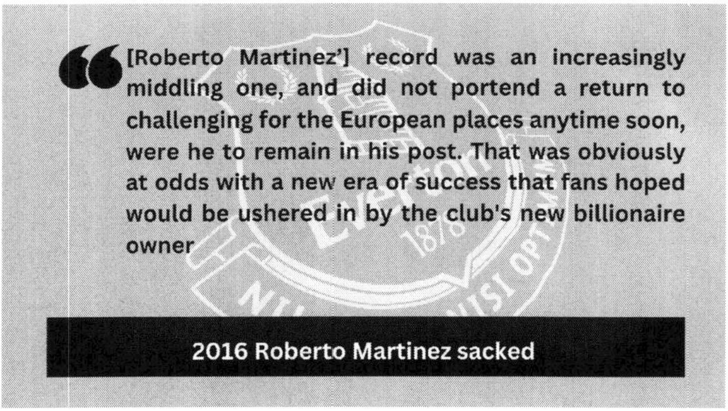

The day after the Sunderland defeat, the club made an official announcement on Twitter and evertonfc.com that Roberto Martinez had been relieved of his duties as manager of Everton.

Bill Kenwright and the Board of Directors expressed their thanks to Martinez for his "dedication and commitment" and for conducting himself "with the utmost integrity and dignity."

The decision had come towards the end of a second-successive season in which the Toffees would finish in the bottom half of the Premier League. The defeat at the Stadium of Light had been the latest chapter in an alarming run of results stretching back to early

March 2016, in which Everton had won just twice in 12 matches in all competitions.

Humiliation at Anfield in the Merseyside derby and failure in the FA Cup semi-final had finally made up the mind of Farhad Moshiri that Martinez's time was up. While there had been rumours that the board was split on dismissing the Catalan, privately there had been a desire to see out the season and make an announcement regarding his future in the coming weeks.

The dreadful showings at Leicester City and at Sunderland, coupled with a growing clamour from supporters for his removal, forced the club to announce his departure, and head off planned protests at the final home game of the season.

While there was little doubt in the end that Martinez had to go, his departure was nonetheless tinged with regret. He had joined the Toffees in June 2013 on the heels of his FA Cup Final triumph with Wigan Athletic, but also after the Latics' relegation from the top flight. Such contrasting achievements would be reflected during his time at Goodison Park.

In his first season, he guided Everton to a fifth-place finish and their best points tally since the formation of the Premier League in 1992. It was success that not only prompted an extension to his contract, but also fostered genuine excitement among supporters that his exciting brand of football might finally deliver on the promise of the Moyes years.

The Catalan battled, however, to match the achievements of his first season at Goodison Park, with the club struggling through consecutive seasons of under-performance that ended in disappointing mid-table finishes.

In 2014-15, Martinez had become the first Everton manager to oversee exits from the domestic cups at the first hurdle, although he fared much better in the Europa League, until his side lost to Dynamo Kiev in the Round of 16 in March 2015. Many cited his decision to deploy defender Antolin Alcaraz in central defence on that miserable evening, rather than John Stones, as being indicative of the manager's defensive weaknesses that were becoming more and more damaging the further the club moved away from the solid foundations put in by his predecessor.

Martinez had steered the Blues to the last four of both the Carling Cup and FA Cup in his final season, eventually losing to the two Manchester clubs respectively, but registered another unwanted record with Everton's worst home league record in the club's history to that point, when adjusted to three points for a win.

In short, his was an increasingly middling record and one that did not portend a return to challenging for the European places anytime soon, were he to remain in his post. That was obviously at odds with a new era of success that fans hoped would be ushered in by the club's new billionaire owner.

***

Speculation soon shifted to whom the club might target to replace Martinez, with a slew of names, ranging from Frank de Boer, Manuel Pellegrini and Southampton Head Coach, Ronald Koeman.

De Boer, whose agent suggested he would love to manage a club like Everton, had just parted company with Ajax after narrowly failing to land his fifth Dutch title, while there had been tabloid claims that

Pellegrini would be interested in a job that would keep him in the Premier League and in the northwest of England following his departure from Manchester City.

The media asked Koeman on 13 May about his contract situation and his future at his pre-match press conference ahead of the weekend's final games in the Premier League.

He replied, "I am manager of Southampton. Everyone knows I have one more year of my contract," Koeman said. "What I said last week when I got [asked] the same question, is that we will sit together and analyse this season and talk about the future. That's what the news is today."

Asked outright if he would stay as Saints boss, Koeman simply stated: "Yes."

However, Moshiri would soon come calling to pitch a very attractive proposition from Everton, one the Dutchman would find very hard to turn down.

***

15 May 2016: Everton v Norwich

Three days prior to the end of of a disappointing 2015/16 season, Everton announced that Under 21s coach, David Unsworth, and former Blues manager, Joe Royle, would take temporary charge of Everton for the final match of the campaign against Norwich City, following the dismissal of Roberto Martinez as manager.

Everton also announced the postponement of their awards gala to mark the end of the season. The club followed their confirmation that the Catalan would leave his post by advising supporters that the End of Season Awards night at St George's Hall would no longer be taking place.

It was a phrase barely used in the last few weeks of his tenure at Goodison Park, but Martinez had spoken frequently of his desire to see his players "enjoying their football." It reflected his almost relentless optimism, but for all the sunniness of his disposition, it had become quite clear by the Anfield derby and beyond that Everton's players were no longer enjoying anything.

Fast forward to three days after what most Evertonians now felt was his overdue and necessary dismissal and there was much joy to be found at the Grand Old Lady — from the stands to the pitch, there were smiles and a noticeably elevated mood as the club began looking to a potentially brighter future than the stagnant one that has faced them in recent months.

As Unsworth's well-received team selection and the impressive displays by its youngest members showed, that optimism for what lay ahead was not just confined to the search for a new manager to take the helm at Everton. Four fresh graduates from the club's academy featured prominently in a handsome 3-0 victory over relegated Norwich City, lending credence to the stand-in boss's confident assertion that the next permanent manager would inherit some real gems mined from the youth system.

Matthew Pennington, starting again at right back in the absence of Seamus Coleman, would have been more familiar to Toffees fans, having featured in recent games. He would manage just 28 minutes before succumbing to the same injury as his more senior teammate and being replaced by Jonjoe Kenny — the captain of Unsworth's Under-21s side when he wasn't on loan helping Oxford United gain promotion from England's fourth tier — who made his senior bow in impressive fashion.

In midfield, the much-anticipated Kieran Dowell didn't disappoint with his hour-plus on the field and was involved in two of the Blues' goals, but it was Tom Davies who emerged as the star of the show and finishing the game as many people's man of the match. Still just 17, Davies exhibited a wonderful blend of touch, skill, steel, awareness and maturity in the middle of the park that defied his tender years, more than justifying his selection. No wonder Unsworth had made repeated mention of the need for the next manager to cherish and nurture Everton's stable of young players.

The blooding of those precocious young Blues wasn't the only refreshing thing about the Everton side that took to the field for this finale to another disappointing season. The attitude, tempo, and intensity that a team blending youth with seasoned experience brought to the contest from the first whistle was in stark contrast to the insipid, pedestrian fare that plagued them for so much of 2016.

There was also a confidence coursing through players' veins where in recent games, with perhaps the exception perhaps of 45 minutes at Wembley, there appeared to be none. That was beautifully illustrated in the 19th minute, when a lightning-quick move started by Tim Howard, making his last ever appearance, went straight down the centre of the field through James McCarthy and then Dowell, with the Irish midfielder continuing his run to meet a loose ball 25 yards from goal and bending a wonderfully crisp shot inside John Ruddy's post. Criticised by fans for his staid, one-dimensional and crab-like performances, this was evidence of the player McCarthy could be when the shackles of a flawed system were discarded.

Norwich, with their own weight lifted off their shoulders, did their best to feed off the home side's energy, and they had a couple of good moments in the first half.

Their best chance fell to Matt Jarvis a few minutes before the break, but thankfully, while he'd capitalised on space in front of him as he cut in from the left, he hammered his shot over the bar when he should have done better.

It left him to rue that miss a couple of minutes later when, at the other end, Lukaku collapsed in the Norwich box under the attentions of Robbie Brady and the referee pointed to the spot. It looked harsh on the Canaries but Baines took responsibility for the penalty as Howard declined an invitation to mark his send-off with a goal and, restored to spot-kick duties, the fullback made no mistake, slotting past Ruddy to send Everton into half-time 2-0 up.

The third goal was the one that put the game beyond Norwich's reach, but it was the one that would have Evertonians most excited by the future, given that it involved all three of the impressive-looking teenagers. Davies snapped into a tackle midway inside the Canaries' half and the ball broke to Dowell. He nudged it on to McCarthy, who fed Kenny on the overlap and his low centre benefitted from a deflection before arriving at the feet of Mirallas, who swept it into the empty net.

It was an afternoon that could only have gone better for Everton if they had piled on a couple more goals. Compared to what the day threatened to be if Martinez had still been in the dugout, it was an occasion pregnant with relief, hope for the future, and expectation at the rebuilding job ahead over the summer.

2015/16 was a season that supporters would be glad to see the back of, as the emotional toll has been a heavy one. For the second year running, Everton finished 11th in the league.

Final score: Everton 3-0 Norwich

***

Everton continued to fill the back pages as speculation over the new managerial appointment increased, and as the Blues got their search underway for Roberto Martinez's replacement, David Moyes, the man whom the Catalan had replaced at Goodison in 2013, said he would be open to returning to the club as manager. With Moyes out of work following his sacking first from Manchester United and then Real Sociedad, his name had inevitably come up in connection with the Everton post, and the former Preston boss said he would be interested seeing as there appeared to be the need for some rebuilding of the team.

"Would I consider going back? I've said if I get an exciting challenge and something that makes me feel I could get my teeth into it, then I would be really interested," he said in *The Times.*

"When we took over, we had 11 great and successful years, but we also had to rebuild the club a little bit. I just think now the change has been made, and Everton need to now go and do it again.

"If you give David Moyes an opportunity, he tends to rebuild a club, and he tends to get it going in the right direction and making sure that things are correct and I'm looking forward to getting the chance to do that again."

Rumours abounded that Bill Kenwright was supporting the return of 'The Moyesiah', but there were real hopes the club could go out and make a top-drawer managerial appointment instead. Moyes was, therefore, never going to be a popular choice. There was a tangible sense by the 2012/13 season that he had taken the club as far as he could; so there was unlikely to be broad enthusiasm for his return to Everton after a three-year absence.

In any case, this was the first opportunity for Moshiri to make his mark on the club. The fan base and the media waited to see whether he would go with Kenwright's man, or strike out in a different direction.

2016: Everton Board secure #1 Target Ronald Koeman

By mid-June 2016, the managerial speculation was at an end. Everton finally confirmed the appointment of Ronald Koeman as the club's next manager, days after reaching a £5 million compensation agreement with Southampton and completing all the remaining details over personal terms.

The Dutchman left St Mary's Stadium with a year remaining on his term there, signing a three-year contract with the Blues that would tie him to Goodison Park until 2019.

Koeman's arrival marked the completion of a process that had begun almost as soon as Martinez departed, as the 53-year-old had been touted as Farhad Moshiri's first choice to lead his new era at Goodison.

Initially, Saints CEO Ralph Kruger and director of development, Les Reed had been confident they could persuade Koeman to stay at St Mary's Stadium, at least to see out the final year of his contract. But the lure of a significantly increased salary (believed to be £6 million per year), a reported £100 million transfer war chest, and the promise of Moshiri's ambitious plans proved decisive.

"I am very excited to be Everton manager," Koeman said on his appointment. "I believe in the Club, in the team, in the fans and in our ability to achieve things in the future. Everton is a club with a great history and real ambition, and it is a proud feeling for me to be part of what we want to go and do, together with the chairman and Farhad Moshiri. I am looking forward to meeting everyone at the Club and to preparing for a big season in the Premier League."

A world-class defender in his playing days, Koeman had starred for all three of the Netherlands' big clubs: Ajax, PSV and Feyenoord. At Barcelona, he was a member of Johan Cruyff's "Dream Team" of the early 1990s, and on the international stage for his country he won the European Championships in 1988.

As manager, he had managed six teams in the Eredivisie and also had stints in Portugal and Spain before he came to England to continue the renaissance of Southampton begun by Mauricio Pochettino — despite seeing some of that club's best players sold over the past two summer windows. He led the Saints to 7th place in his first season and then 6th place in his second term, finishing just three points off the top four but securing Europa League qualification for the second year running.

Expectations of Koeman's continued success were running high at Goodison Park, and the fanbase was eager to see how Farhad Moshiri would deliver on his promises.

2016: New DoF and New Board Members Appointed

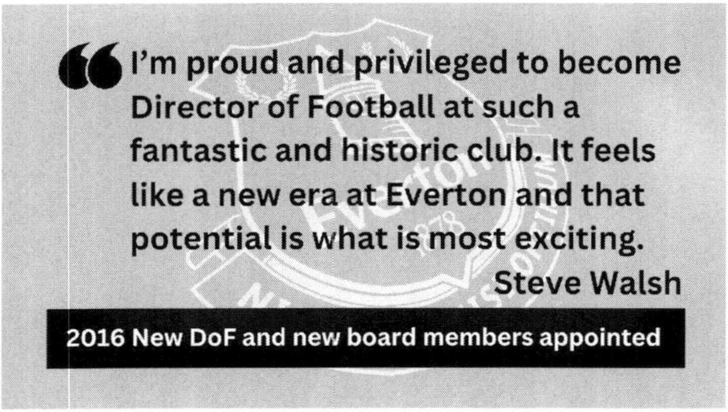

A week after Koeman's appointment, Everton announced they had also secured the services of Leicester City's highly rated head of recruitment, Steve Walsh, as the club's new Director of Football.

The 63-year-old, once described by Sir Alex Ferguson, as the most influential figure in the 2015/16 title race, filled a new position at Goodison Park and Finch Farm, one that new major shareholder Farhad Moshiri had identified as a vital part of his plans for the club.

Walsh, who once served as a European scout under Jose Mourinho and Andre Villas-Boas at Chelsea (where he helped sign Didier Drogba, Gianfranco Zola and Michael Essien) and was assistant boss to both Nigel Pearson and Claudio Ranieri at Leicester, achieved credit for uncovering the likes of Riyad Mahrez, Jamie Vardy and N'Golo Kanté, three of the main driving forces behind the Foxes' stunning 2015/16 Premier League title triumph.

Besides his 16 years at Chelsea, for whom he initially worked part time while holding down a PE-teacher role in Chorley, he had spells at Newcastle United, and Hull City. His brother Mickey, a football agent, was a Republic of Ireland international who played 29 times for Everton in the 1978/79 season, as well as also representing Blackpool, QPR and Porto.

Despite having signed a new contract with Leicester City, Walsh followed Kanté out of the King Power Stadium, as the French midfielder made a £30 million switch to Stamford Bridge.

It was reported that Koeman had recommended Walsh to Moshiri.

"I'm proud and privileged to become Director of Football at such a fantastic and historic club," Walsh said on his arrival. "It feels like a new era at Everton and that potential is what is most exciting.

"I know the club well. My roots are in the north-west and my brother, Mickey, was an Everton player in the Bob Latchford era and always proud of that fact. I also did my initial teacher training at Liverpool Hope University many years ago. I'm genuinely excited to be here at the club and very much looking forward to getting down to work."

Koeman, meanwhile, welcomed the Lancastrian to Everton by saying: "It's really good for the club to have Steve, who has shown his quality in his job at a number of clubs over many years. That's the experience and quality he will bring to us at a good time in the season. He has a great deal of knowledge about building for the long-term and the magnificent work he did at Leicester on top of the job he did at Chelsea makes us excited to have him here at Everton."

***

Alexander (Sasha) Ryazantsev had joined the Board of Directors of Everton Football Club in March 2016 following a successful career in finance and investment banking spanning over 20 years.

He graduated from the Russian Plekhanov University of Economics in 1995 with a BSc in Economics and Commercial Management, later working as an investment analyst at Global Natural Energy PLC, where future Everton major shareholder Farhad Moshiri was CEO.

After completing his Masters in Finance from the London Business School in 2002, Ryazantsev joined ABN AMRO Bank, where he led a team advising European consumer brands on their capital structures and corporate financing. He joined the corporate financing and risk solutions team at RBS in 2007, and handled bond issues and mergers and acquisitions across Europe, the Middle East and Africa.

In early 2016, Ryazantsev advised Farhad Moshiri on the acquisition of Everton, and on the future strategy of the football club.

Born into a footballing family - his father was a goalkeeper at several clubs across the former USSR in the 1960s and 1970s - and Sasha played at right-back for Dynamo Moscow boys until the age of 16 but then turned his focus towards his studies.

Darren Griffiths interviewed Ryazantsev at Finch Farm for evertontv, and he confirmed the board were delighted to have secured their top pick to succeed Roberto Martinez as Everton manager.

"[Ronald] was absolutely our number one choice from day one of the search process," he said. "It took us a while to get to him, but in the end we have absolutely no doubt we made the right decision.

"We are now one of the four north-western clubs that have brilliant managers and [there's] such a concentration [of big clubs] in the northwest that we couldn't have fallen behind. Therefore, it was very important to get someone of that stature into the club.

"Bill Kenwright ... has been the driving force for the last many years. Obviously, he is an Evertonian, and it is very important for us to keep that culture.

"We very much hope that the new manager will be the guardian of that culture as well, and that we all move forward as a big Everton family."

Moshiri had embarked on what seemed to be an ambitious process of reshaping Everton and restoring its image as one of the big players in the Premier League, with plans for squad strengthening that summer and a long-awaited resolution of the stadium issue.

Many had described his new investment in the Toffees as a 'project' but Ryazantsev felt it was bigger and more long-term than that description suggested.

"I don't know if 'project' is the right word to use," he continued. "It's probably more than that. Of course, we have the team, the performance on the pitch and, of course, we have the appointment of Ronald is the very first step we had to make in that regard.

"But we have other projects like the stadium going forward as well, and we very much want to win and be successful in whatever we do."

***

The club also announced that Deputy CEO, Denise Barrett-Baxendale MBE had become the latest member of the Board of Directors. Long considered a potential successor to Robert Elstone as the club's Chief Executive, Barrett-Baxendale had been nationally recognised for her work in heading up the award-winning charity, *Everton in the Community.*

***

In October of that year, Keith Harris, the former London banker whom Everton had enlisted to help seek investors in the club was also appointed to the Board of Directors.

Harris was previously chairman of the Football League and spent six years as Director of Wembley National Stadium until 2007 but had become noted as a broker in the sale and purchase of a number of football clubs, among them Chelsea, Crystal Palace, Swansea City, West Ham United, Aston Villa, Fulham, Manchester City, and was believed to be involved with bringing Farhad Moshiri to the table at Goodison Park, leading to his purchase of a 49.9% stake in the Toffees in February.

"I am truly delighted to be joining the club at such an exciting time," Harris said upon the announcement of his appointment. "I've known the chairman and Mr Moshiri for a long time, so I have a good understanding of their ambition. I have visited Goodison Park numerous times over the years and really enjoy the authenticity of the club and passion of the fans. The atmosphere I experienced at Goodison for the FA Cup tie against Chelsea last season reminded me just how special Everton is and I am looking forward to sharing many more experiences like that in the future."

Harris, 63, joined long-standing Chairman Bill Kenwright and deputy chairman Jon Woods on a newly expanded Everton Board of Directors which included CEO Robert Elstone, Moshiri's representative Sasha Ryazantsev and deputy CEO Denise Barrett-Baxendale.

"We've strengthened our board significantly over the last six months and I'm really pleased that we've been able to add even more experience by bringing Keith in," Kenwright said. "He has a unique set of credentials and experience, combining roles at the highest level of international business with some of the most senior positions within football in this country, and will be a great asset."

Moshiri's back-office team had taken shape. Now Evertonians were watching closely to see how the transfer funds he had promised on the footballing side would be spent.

2016: Squad changes: Money can buy you Stones

> "There is much to be done and things for me to learn, but I can confirm that I have committed to providing additional funds for transfers and retaining our key players to ensure that we have a strong core to build on for the future.
>
> \- Farhad Moshiri

2016 Squad changes: Money can buy you Stones

It was clear the Everton first team squad needed strengthening in the summer of 2016 after two consecutive seasons of disappointment.

Roberto Martinez' January signing, Oumar Niasse, had looked well off the pace of the Premier League. So holding onto Romelu Lukaku was, therefore, the main priority. The Belgian's agent at the time, Mino Raiola, had hinted at some back-tracking over Lukaku's desire to leave Goodison Park, after weeks of suggestions that he would move on before the start of the upcoming 2016/17 season. The player's desire for Champions League football, coupled with his impressive goals return for the Blues, had made him an obvious target for many clubs. In remarks made to the Belgian press in the build-up to Euro 2016, Lukaku had indicated a desire to join a team that summer that represented a "project" and could offer him the chance to play in Europe's elite club competition.

However, following Koeman's appointment and a reported meeting between Blues' director Sasha Ryazantsev and Raiola, where the former outlined Moshiri's ambitions and the possibility of a much-improved deal for the player, there appeared to have been climbdown in the agent's rhetoric for his client's Everton future.

"Everton don't need the money anymore but Romelu wants to play for a club that can win trophies," Raiola told *Sportwereld* in Belgium. "Something's changed at Everton. There's a new project. If he leaves, it has to be a good deal for all parties. Romelu certainly has the qualities to play in Italy," he said. "But as the Italian landscape currently looks, there's no team that can afford him. He is too expensive for Serie A. Only a global power can pay for him – the top clubs in England, Barcelona, Real Madrid and Paris Saint-Germain."

Lukaku had talked of potential moves to Juventus or Paris Saint-Germain, two clubs that could have afforded him and offered him Champions League football. Meanwhile, a dubious report from Italy claimed Arsenal could launch a paltry £31 million bid for him, as Jamie Vardy's proposed move from Leicester to the Emirates looked to be off.

With the club now backed by Moshiri's money and with Koeman at the helm, even more players than usual were linked with Everton during the closed season. A reported fee of £30 million had been agreed with Zenit St Petersburg for Lukaku's Belgian team mate, Axel Witsel, with the expectation being that a deal could be completed after Euro2016.

Meanwhile, Everton continued to be linked with Juan Mata, more by rumour than media coverage, who may have been surplus to requirements at Manchester United.

By early August, however, with only one new signing in place, Everton's Assistant Manager, the manager's brother, Erwin Koeman, was fielding questions. He cited a combination of the delay caused by Euro2016 on the summer transfer market, the relatively late introduction of a Director of Football following Steve Walsh's switch from Leicester, the need for Koeman to fully assess the players he inherited from Roberto Martinez, and the obstacle to attracting top-class talent because of Everton's lack of European football next season as being contributory factors to the protracted wait for new faces. With the new season just around the corner and the transfer deadline four weeks away, Erwin Koeman, said his brother and the chairman were very busy, stepping up their efforts to bring in new players. Interestingly, there was no mention of Steve Walsh in terms of recruitment efforts.

The following day, the club confirmed Idrissa Gana Gueye as an Everton player, after putting pen to paper on a four-year deal.

After goalkeeper Maarten Stekelenburg's arrival the previous month, the 26-year-old midfielder became Ronald Koeman's second acquisition of the summer in a £7.1 million deal, after the club activated his release clause at Aston Villa.

Gueye had been odds-on to join the Toffees from Villa Park, when reports of their interest first emerged, and the Midlands club's new boss Roberto di Matteo admitted they had been resigned to losing him to Everton.

Meanwhile, eyebrows were raised around Goodison Park, when Roberto Martinez was named as the boss of the Belgian national team, replacing Marc Wilmots, who left the role after the European Championships. The Catalan had provided studio analysis for ESPN at the tournament and was interviewed by Anderlecht before also being linked with the vacancy at Hull City.

Back at Goodison, Everton signalled their faith in up-and-coming midfielder Tom Davies by handing the teenager a five-year contract with the club. The 18-year-old, who had only made his first-team debut in April, put pen to paper on the extended deal, which no doubt came with improved terms.

"It's great motivation knowing I'll be here for five years and that I can really push on and hopefully develop to become a really good player for the team and go on to do really well," Davies told evertontv. "Coming back from the off season and going straight back with the first team has been a good insight for me into what's required of me for the season and to be around the players, play as much as I have and train with them, it's been vital for my progression as a player.

"I just want to become a regular first. That's something I am going to work towards and hopefully, with the help of the staff and learning from other players, I can get there."

The following week, Everton sealed the signing of highly experienced Wales captain, Ashley Williams, from Swansea City in a deal that was officially undisclosed but reportedly worth £9 million.

The news of Williams signing followed confirmation of John Stones' sale to Manchester City in a deal that would eventually be worth the reported £50 million transfer fee that Everton had been holding out for that summer. Fans on social media were asking whether Farhad Moshiri was being true to his word of retaining key players, if those of John Stones' calibre were being allowed to leave the club at the first opportunity.

Interviewed later in the month, however, Stones opened up to the media about how his relationship with ex-Everton manager Roberto Martinez had deteriorated the previous season and led to his departure for Manchester City that summer, despite Ronald Koeman's arrival.

The defender, who left for what was, at the time, a club record £47.5 million fee for an outgoing player, was often played out of position or dropped for poor performances, and he said the Catalan hadn't explained why he wasn't picking him. "It was a tough period because I was doing everything right," Stones said. "I was being professional. I was carrying myself well. I wanted to do everything right, try to get in the team, how everyone should, and fight for my place.

"I felt I was doing everything I could and deserved to play and still wasn't. That's when I found it hard. It's probably a question you should have asked him at the time because he wasn't telling me.

"Roberto had his style of play and kind of changed that towards the end of his career at Everton," Stones continued. "He changed the whole style of the team and things weren't working out at that time so you could say it wasn't the best decision.

"As you know, the gaffer got sacked. It wasn't enjoyable. We weren't winning games. When we don't do that a few games on the trot, it starts to eat away at you, no matter who you are. It was a good test for me. I learned a lot about my football, about myself."

That prompted him to think about leaving Everton, three years after he arrived as an unknown teenager from Barnsley. He had put in a transfer request the preceding year when Chelsea mounted a concerted effort to sign him but, with the Gwladys Street adapting the Beatles song 'Money Can't Buy You Love' with the words 'Money Can't Buy You Stones', Martinez and the Blues' hierarchy had rejected the offer and refused to sell him so close to the 2015 transfer deadline.

A year later, he was on his way to Manchester but, having signed the veteran Williams to plug the gap in the short term, Koeman believed he had another player who could step into Stones' shoes in the form of the young defender picked up from Barnsley by Martinez in the summer of 2015.

Simon Jones in The Daily Mail[1] wrote of Ronald Koeman's faith in Mason Holgate:

> "The ink was barely dry on John Stones' Manchester City contract when the question was posed: where do Everton find the next John Stones? Ashley Williams arrived from Swansea and Lamine Kone was courted at Sunderland, but their strengths are leadership and aggression. The simple fact is Ronald Koeman believes he may have the answer right in front of him. Mason Holgate is a tall, stylish ball-playing defender that Everton signed as a teenager from Barnsley for £2million after barely 20 first team games. Sound familiar? He can play right back or centre back and has such insouciant temperament that Koeman thought nothing of asking him to mark Zlatan Ibrahimovic

> during Wayne Rooney's testimonial at Old Trafford last week. You have to understand that he is 19 years old but maybe he showed more confidence than some other players on the pitch," purred Koeman afterwards. "He's a big talent." Everton players will testify, earning Koeman's praise does not come easy and Holgate is not taking his first team graduation for granted. The manager has been great to me and not just because he put me in the team!" Holgate says. "Before I went out at United, he just said it doesn't matter whether you are 19 or 36, I'm putting you in because you are ready and you are good enough. Don't have any fear, just show what you can do. I know I have to work to impress him, I wouldn't expect anything else but it's nice to know I could get a chance this season if I keep at it. The United game was a great experience."

Koeman's efforts to improve the squad he had inherited from Martinez continued. August 15th saw Everton announce their fourth signing of the summer when Crystal Palace winger Yannick Bolasie arrived on a 5 year deal worth a reported £22.5 million that had the potential to reach as high as the club record that Everton had paid Chelsea for Romelu Lukaku, if all appearance-related add-ons were triggered.

On the same day as Bolasie signed, Farhad Moshiri said on Sky Sports there were plans to further strengthen the team before the end of the transfer window.

> "We are very pleased about today's signing," Moshiri said in the statement, "but remain anxious to further strengthen the squad. The chairman, Bill Kenwright is relentlessly pushing things forward with total support for him, for Steve Walsh and Ronald Koeman."

Two more names were added to the squad on 31 August 2016, Transfer Deadline Day, when Everton announced they had agreed a fee of £1.5 million for young Sheffield United striker Dominic Calvert-Lewin. The 19-year-old had been a target for the Blues for most of the summer. Ecuador striker, Enner Valencia also came in on loan for the season from West Ham. Proposed moves for Moussa Sissoko and Yacine Brahimi collapsed.

Valencia's impact would prove to be limited, but in Calvert-Lewin Everton had signed someone who would go on to become a hugely important player for the club and score one of the most important goals in Goodison Park's history.

Described as being physically strong with good aerial presence, Calvert-Lewin was in England's U20 squad, having made it into the Blades' senior squad in 2015 following a loan spell at Northampton Town.

The coup of acquiring him was credited to Under 23s coach, David Unsworth, who had seen his rich potential as a raw 16-year-old while coaching him at Sheffield United.

"This is an opportunity of a lifetime for him," Unsworth said once Calvert-Lewin had put pen to paper on a 5 year contract. "To go from League One to the Premier League is a massive jump, but he certainly has all the attributes to make that jump, given time, hard work and the desire I know he has."

Since Moshiri had purchased his 49.9% stake in Everton in March 2016, the club had already felt his impact and decisiveness. Through his representative on the Board, Sasha Ryazantsev and chairman Bill Kenwright, he had dismissed former boss Roberto Martinez and brought in both Ronald Koeman from Southampton and Steve Walsh from Leicester, by negotiating compensation packages with both clubs.

Off the field, the Board were still moving ahead under Moshiri's direction with plans for a new stadium, and an interim facelift for Goodison Park was also underway.

It all felt so promising, but would the team deliver?

---

1. Simon Jones: Daily Mail, 10 August 2016

2016: New season off to a bright start

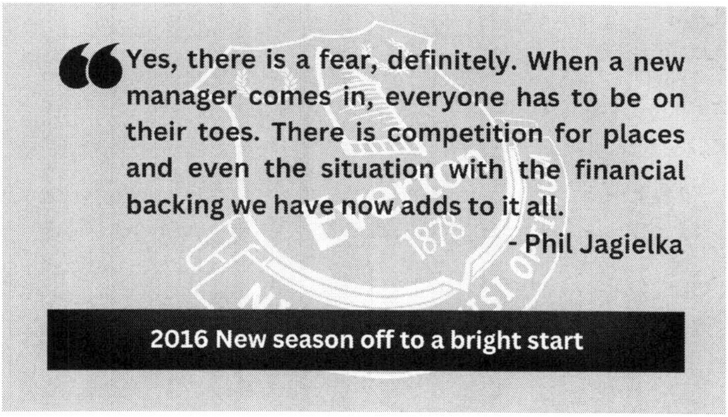

Though there had been disappointment that the club hadn't been able to hold onto defender John Stones, Evertonians were buoyant going into the 2016/17 season. Ronald Koeman had been lured away from Southampton to complete what Farhad Moshiri described as a quartet of "Hollywood managers" in the northwest, alongside Jose Mourinho, Pep Guardiola and Jurgen Klopp. Furthermore, Romelu Lukaku had opted to stay at Goodison to spearhead the Blues' attack under the new regime.

The new-found optimism following two disappointing seasons under Roberto Martinez appeared to be well-founded, as Everton began the new season with a six-match unbeaten run in all competitions.

A 1-1 home draw to Spurs was followed by four successive wins: 2-1 away at West Brom, 4-0 at home to Yeovil in the League Cup, 1-0 at home to Stoke and 3-0 away at David Moyes' new club, Sunderland. By the time Middlesbrough came to Goodison, Everton were sitting pretty, in third place in the Premier League table.

***

17 September 2016: Everton v Middlesbrough

Old habitual instincts may die hard but, with each passing game under Ronald Koeman's assured leadership, Evertonians were allowing confidence to creep back into their psyche.

1-0 down to a controversial 'Boro goal, the cavalier Blues side of early 2015/16 might well have fought back but ended up throwing the game away again; whereas the more brittle version under Roberto Martinez might have caved altogether in the face of injustice, the size of the task and the frustration pouring out of the stands.

Confidence is a powerful thing in football, though, and Koeman was restoring it in spades at Everton, to the point where they simply brushed off an awful decision by Lee Mason who overlooked Alvaro Negredo's foul on Maarten Stekelenburg and allowed Middlesbrough to take the lead after 20 minutes. Everton then turned the match on its head and had it effectively won by half-time.

Much of that was down to the combination of a vastly improved defensive setup, a visibly fitter collection of players, and their consequent work-rate that started with the front players and extended to the back, where the gladiatorial duo of Phil Jagielka and Ashley Williams refused to give 'Boro an inch.

In front of them, the imperious Idrissa Gueye, who turned in another man-of-the-match display of stunning effectiveness, again supported Gareth Barry. The Senegalese seemed to cover every blade of grass, tackled anything that moved, and again weighed in with an assist, all of which added to his burgeoning reputation as the best signing of the summer.

The game was won, however, with Everton's superior talents at the other end, once they had gathered the impetus to have a real go at Aitor Karanka's outfit. Middlesbrough had started confidently, and through their discipline and organisation, made things difficult for their hosts throughout.

It was a deep cross by George Friend that led to the opening goal. Negredo's head connected with Stekelenburg's arms rather than the ball. Everyone expected the referee to blow for the foul, but he didn't. There was disbelief and fury when he pointed to the centre circle but Everton channelled that emotion into an almost immediate response.

The second of two successive corners was swung in from the Everton left. Williams almost connected in front of the goalkeeper, and when the ball bounced through towards the back of the area, Barry had peeled away smartly to sweep it home with a nicely controlled finish.

'Boro's resistance then melted in the face of a neat move three minutes before the break, as Gueye picked out Coleman's run and the Irishman dribbled inside two defenders and drew the 'keeper, opening up both sides of the goal, to allow him to tuck the ball into the corner with aplomb.

And four minutes after that came the killer third. Bolasie engineered space for a teasing cross from the right that caught Valdés in two minds as Lukaku looked certain to get decisive contact on the ball but, whether with the aid of the merest of touches from the striker or not, it swerved into the far corner to make it 3-1 at half-time.

The second half was a bit of a non-event, save for an injury that forced Lukaku off to the benefit of debutant Enner Valencia and further evidence that the manager's decision to keep Barkley in the side was being vindicated by a purposeful display from the 22-year-old. It was he who came closest to padding the scoreline, but his powerful drive from the angle was denied by Valdés' save.

Final score: Everton 3-1 Middlesbrough

***

Asked after the game whether the combination of Koeman's more regimented management and Everton's greater financial resources had increased the pressure on the players to perform, club captain Phil Jagielka confirmed as much.

"Yes, there is a fear, definitely," Jagielka said. "When a new manager comes in, everyone has to be on their toes. There is competition for places and even the situation with the financial backing we have now adds to it all.

"Not one player is guaranteed a place in the squad, let alone the team. If the manager wants to go and buy a player in January, then the cheque book is open.

"It does put added pressure on the players, but it is a good pressure.

"That proves he has not done a bad job. At the moment, it is going well. I wouldn't say we are playing amazing, but we are getting fantastic results, and that breeds confidence."

Had Jagielka spoken prematurely? Maybe so, because Everton's encouraging start under Koeman quickly evaporated following the victory over Middlesbrough. The club's customary early exit from the EFL Cup occurred with a 2-0 home defeat at the hands of Norwich three days later. That was followed by a 1-0 away defeat at Bournemouth, two 1-1 draws against Crystal Palace and Man City, then a 2-1 away defeat at Sean Dyche's Burnley. The net result was Everton were out of a cup, and by early December they had slipped to ninth in the Premier League having won just once in 10 games.

One player who definitely wasn't enjoying life under Ronald Koeman was Oumar Niasse, whom many felt was treated harshly by Koeman.

Billed as a goal-scoring backup for Romelu Lukaku, the striker had arrived on a big-money transfer in February under Koeman's predecessor, but the new manager had decided over the summer the Senegalese should look for a new club. A move to Galatasaray had reportedly fallen through while a late loan opportunity back to Lokomotiv Moscow also failed to materialise, amid rumours Niasse's wife didn't want to return to Russia.

That left the 26-year-old in limbo, banished by Koeman to the Under-23s, without a squad number or a locker, and with just a couple of run-outs for the second-string to his name to start the season.

"It's sad, it's really sad," Niasse said in *The Guardian* at the time. "And, to be honest, I think I don't deserve this, but what I can do is just keep my head and fight to change things. I'm not going to make a drama over this. I just deal with it. I know it's just one period.

"I couldn't understand how [the manager's] decision could have been made after 45 minutes [of a pre-season friendly] but I just said: 'OK, thank you.' It's his decision. He's the manager. What can I do? I called my agent, and he said he would look into the opportunities for me. To be honest, I didn't ask Koeman to explain his reasons. I just thought, even if I asked why, I would never understand. After just 45 minutes, you cannot say to me: 'You are no good. He took my shirt number, and he told me I wasn't allowed to be in the dressing room for the first team; that I wasn't going to train with them. I had to go with the second team.

"I said: 'OK, no problem.' When you say you don't need a player, you don't have to see him. I've just kept working in training. Even if I'm training with the Under-23s, I give them the respect.

"Anything can change. Koeman just wants the best for himself and, in two months, if I can be the best for him, he will take me, because he doesn't have any problem with me and I don't have any problem with him. It's football and bigger players than me have had this problem with their coaches."

***

30 October 2016: Everton v West Ham

When West Ham arrived at the end of October, Everton were looking to arrest a run of five games without a victory in all competitions since making an unbeaten start to the new season. The Hammers were hoping to build on three successive wins in the League and EFL Cup, but they came up against a very different proposition in Koeman's outfit.

It was an Everton team featuring three changes from the one that had started against Burnley eight days previously — among them was captain Phil Jagielka who paid the price for two very poor performances with a place on the substitutes' bench — had begun the contest in less than encouraging fashion, with West Ham on the front foot for the first quarter of the match.

However, Everton headed into the break looking the more likely of the two sides to break deadlock and so it proved within five minutes of the restart. After Lukaku failed to gather a heavy infield ball from Oviedo, Reid despatched a weak defensive clearance straight to Barkley. His pass met Coleman's run on the outside where the Irishman drilled a near-post shot that Adrian could only parry and Bolasie showed remarkable speed and desire to burst past two claret shirts, swing the ball on the stretch back into the goalmouth where Lukaku had the simple task of heading into the vacant net.

West Ham began to re-assert themselves to find the equaliser but Payet's attempt to drive a free kick under the wall failed. Robles came to the rescue following an awful lapse by Ashley Williams. Substitute Andre Ayew was denied a clear goal-scoring opportunity by Oviedo's superb covering block, and when Noble attempted an impressive curling effort that looked destined to sneak inside the far post, Robles beat it away two-handed and at full stretch to keep West Ham at bay.

That paved the way for Barkley to kill the game at the end of another nicely-worked move between him and Lukaku, the former arriving in the box and meet the latter's chipped centre with a controlled left-foot finish inside the post.

It was an excellent result for the home side, earned on the back of an increasingly strong performance that was worthy of all three points in the final reckoning. Apart from Lukaku's consistent scoring record, most pleasing for Koeman was the offensive production of Barkley and Bolasie, who weighed in with assists while the former finally scored his second Premier League goal of the season.

Everton had successfully navigated an important game, keeping themselves up with the leading pack and maintaining morale as they headed into the most difficult month of the campaign so far. But would it be enough to satisfy the hierarchy?

Final score: Everton 2-0 West Ham

2017: Moshiri at AGM: 'Don't want to be a museum'

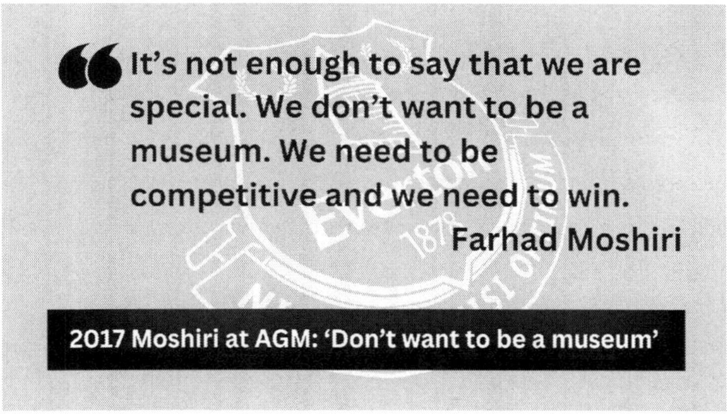

The first Annual General Meeting of Everton shareholders to take place since Farhad Moshiri had purchased his 49.9% stake in the club was held on the evening of 4 January, 2017 at Liverpool's Philharmonic Hall. Moshiri was in attendance along with his representative on the Board of Directors, Sasha Ryazantsev, and it was an occasion which offered plenty of good news, even if it did not provide a definitive update on the stadium situation.

Besides covering successful motions to reappoint Robert Elstone, Denise-Barrett-Baxendale, Ryazantsev and Keith Harris to the Board,

CEO Robert Elstone gave a review of the financial results for 2015/16, concluding the club would have made a profit but for the compensation paid out to Roberto Martinez and his staff when the Catalan departed in May.

He also announced that the club's commercial revenue would grow by £6 million that season and turnover was forecast to top £170 million for 2016/17 – a massive £50 million increase, thanks largely to the bumper new TV broadcast deals. Furthermore, the club had concluded £75 million in new commercial deals in the previous six weeks, including naming rights for Finch Farm. Elstone also expected the new shirt sponsorship revenue to increase by 300% under the current arrangements with Chang.

Elstone also said that: "Everton would save around £5 million a year on interest payments following the recent consolidation of debt under Moshiri, who had provided the club with an £80 million interest-free loan."

When it came time to take questions from the floor, the greatest interest from shareholders was in the search for a new stadium, on which Elstone was only able to report on "solid" progress with Liverpool City Council, and said the next couple of months would "be critical" to secure a location.

Everton had started an investigation into two brownfield sites within the city for suitability for a new ground, with plenty of speculation suggesting that a site at Bramley-Moore Dock on the waterfront was preferable to one at Stonebridge Cross on the outskirts of town in Croxteth.

There were enough hints from both Bill Kenwright and Liverpool Mayor Joe Anderson to confirm the waterside location was the one

Everton wanted, but the latter admitted it was a complex issue. One shareholder cautioned the Board over the prospect of moving to the outskirts of the city.

Elstone responded by saying: "Kirkby was clearly a very divisive location. In terms of Walton Hall Park, we really believed we had a viable scheme. Site location is critical. We do learn lessons. We have to find the right location. I think we can do it this time."

Kenwright backed that up by hinting that the dockside location was the one everyone wanted. "There's no real question as to where we want to be and we have alternatives, but we are working studiously towards that," he said.

The Mayor then said: "I think the elephant in the room is the waterfront site, which everyone, me included, wants but it is a complex issue. We've got plan Bs but everyone is working extremely hard to deliver on the site that you want - that we all want. On Friday, we announced £20 million for a road directly into the dock site. The reality is, there is a railway station being built there. This is the most exciting opportunity this club has had in decades."

Kenwright then discussed the arrival of Farhad Moshiri at the club, saying:

> "After meeting Farhad 18 months ago, instantly it was clear he had an astonishing love of football. I felt instantly this was a man who could get us out of the problem times we were having. This is a very special moment, I believe, in our football club."

Finally, Farhad Moshiri addressed the AGM, and in his speech said:

> "I had looked at a number of clubs. I was involved at Arsenal. Meeting Bill at his office, you couldn't be negative. His enthusiasm was infectious. The atmosphere at Goodison has far exceeded my expectations. They are really special fans. They keep buying beer for me! I don't even drink! It's not enough to say that we are special. We don't want to be a museum. We need to be competitive and we need to win. The gold standard is the Premier League (not the FA Cup). We need to do well in the league. That's where Everton's competitive edge will be measured. We don't have all the time in the world. We have a window to establish ourselves and we'll do everything we can. We need a sustainable base to be among the elite. It takes time but we're committed. That's why we're here."

2017: KOEMAN SIGNS SCHNEIDERLIN IN JANUARY WINDOW

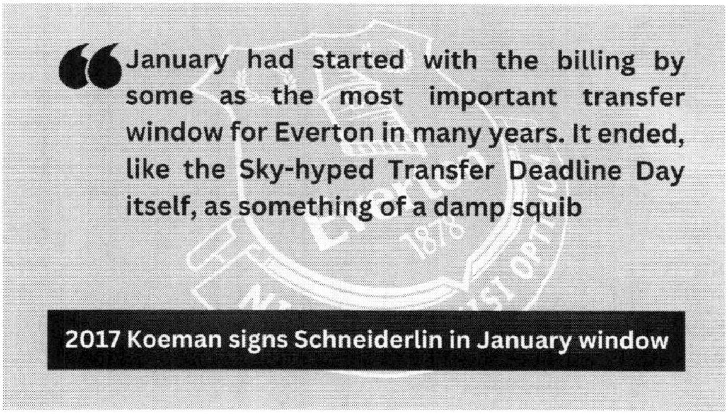

Everton had struggled through October and November by picking up just one win in a 10-match sequence, culminating in an ugly defeat at Watford in early December. The rest of the month offered hope, however, that Ronald Koeman could right the ship again in anticipation of a stronger second half to the 2016/17 Premier League campaign.

Arsenal and Leicester City were vanquished at Goodison Park either side of a crushing loss in the Merseyside derby to Sadio Mane's injury-time goal, and when Koeman's former club Southampton were comfortably beaten 3-0 in the New Year, the Toffees sat in seventh place.

January had started with the billing by some as the most important transfer window for Everton in many years. It ended, like the Sky-hyped Transfer Deadline Day itself, as something of a damp squib. However, by then there seemed to be acceptance among supporters that, despite only bringing in two players, the club had done fairly well out of January.

Certainly, the wailing for a complete squad overhaul following the defeat at Watford in December felt like it a distant memory, as did Ronald Koeman's frustrated reaction to the FA Cup defeat to Leicester at Goodison on 7 January, where he appealed to the hierarchy to speed up the recruitment process in short order.

The acquisition of Morgan Schneiderlin from Manchester United a few days later seemed to represent the beginning of a shopping spree that would transform the squad. In the final reckoning, the Frenchman was the second and last signing of the month after Everton got cold feet over the Ishak Belfodil deal and, presumably, Koeman and Walsh's other top targets proved to be out of reach for the time being.

Of course, the dissipation of the previous urgency was due almost entirely to Everton's run of form in the Premier League since the turn of the year. Three successive wins, three clean sheets, and the impression that Koeman seemed to have finally found a reliable combination of personnel and formation lessened the perceived need for reinforcements.

Undoubtedly, new talent was needed in certain positions. That view hadn't changed, even if there was no broad consensus over which positions needed attention first. Some Evertonians had pined for a new goalkeeper, or a top-class centre-half as a long-term replacement for Phil Jagielka. Others were focused on the more attacking areas of the team where, inconceivably, there was just one reliable goal-scoring centre-forward on the books.

The collapse of Arouna Kone's move to Crystal Palace ensured that he would stay with the club until the summer, but was unlikely to be called upon at all unless something went seriously awry on the injury front.

Koeman had named Enner Valencia as the nominated backup to Romelu Lukaku, even if no one was under any illusions that he could adequately replace the club's top scorer.

It meant that Everton would muddle through another half season hoping that Lukaku stayed fit, and the manager presumably felt comfortable enough with the fact that between Valencia, Kevin Mirallas, Ross Barkley, Dominic Calvert-Lewin (when fit, perhaps by the end of the month) and even young Ademola Lookman, there were enough forward options in the side to cover for the Belgian.

The previous few games (that cup debacle against Leicester aside) may have created a false sense of security in the squad and it wouldn't take too many poor results before the voices of dissent moaned about the missed opportunity in the winter window to strengthen the side for a tilt at the top 6 or higher.

There was a nagging feeling that Everton could do better than seventh this season and that an injection of quality in January could have made the difference. With the club's powder staying largely dry until next July, however, it prepared everyone for a summer or real progress on the transfer front, one where Koeman and Walsh could take the team to the next level in terms of quality and the ability to compete for the top 4. Koeman had said he always planned for a marathon, not a sprint, and his three-year plan still appeared to be on track.

2017: City Game One of Few Highlights

> "Lord knows it hasn't been easy being an Evertonian for much of the last three decades, but the intervening period since the Blues' glory days of mid-1980s had been punctuated by moments, special matches and turns of events that reminded you why this football club is so deeply embedded in your heart and your soul and why you keep coming back.

2017 City game one of few highlights

Between the turn of 2017 and mid-March, Ronald Koeman and Everton did a successful job of putting their autumn downturn behind them, stringing together a run of just two Premier League defeats in 15 matches that included nine wins.

The Blues were frustrated in that time by the form of those clubs above them and, despite the upturn in form, they were unable to lift themselves above seventh place over the remainder of the season.

Nevertheless, it was a promising spell, the best sequence of results under Koeman and it featured the high water mark of his tenure at Goodison Park – a comprehensive victory over Manchester City that inflicted the heaviest defeat in Pep Guardiola's managerial career to date.

***

15 January 2017: Everton v Man City

It hasn't been easy being an Evertonian for much of the last three decades, but the intervening period since the Blues' glory days of mid-1980s has been punctuated by moments, special matches and turns of events that reminded you why this football club is so deeply embedded in your heart and your soul and why you keep coming back.

This was one of those matches, and much more; an almost perfect afternoon, which layered on memorable moment after memorable moment, building to a crescendo as Everton inflicted on Pep Guardiola the heaviest defeat of his much-lauded managerial career. It was the Spaniard's first match at Goodison Park and, as images of him sitting slumped and shell-shocked in the dugout amid a rocking, triumphant atmosphere illustrated, it's one that would live long in his memory, too.

Had nothing of note happened for the 56 minutes after Romelu Lukaku put the Blues into the lead, the game would likely have been a special enough occasion in its own right. It had started with pre-match poignancy as the Belgian carried Bradley Lowery, the little Sunderland fan diagnosed with Neuroblastoma who was mascot for the day, onto the field, followed by a minute's applause for Graham Taylor and Jim Greenwood, both of whom had recently passed away.

Those heart-warming moments coupled with a 1-0 win, delivered by a well-worked, expertly finished goal and underscoring the incremental progress being made under Ronald Koeman, would have represented a lovely afternoon for the home fans on their own. What unfolded was as unexpected as it was thrilling.

The days leading up the game seemed focused on Morgan Schneiderlin and the hope that, following last weekend's chastening cup exit at the hands of Leicester and the manner of it, the Frenchman might make an instant impact to mark the next phase of Koeman's rebuilding process.

The expectation and, perhaps, fear was that the new signing would replace Tom Davies if they deemed him fit enough to start. In the end, while being named on the bench and coming on after 65 minutes to replace Kevin Mirallas, Schneiderlin's appearance was a footnote in the narrative of this game, as Davies took top billing on a day full of potential headlines.

The 18-year-old midfielder kept his place in the side, alongside Gareth Barry in a line-up featuring just one change from the previous weekend - that of Mirallas for Enner Valencia - but by the final whistle Davies had come of age with a personal performance to savour.

It was his anticipation of Gael Clichy's forward pass which illustrated his versatility as a central midfielder. Davies' beautifully-weighted pass to Mirallas split three opposition players down the right channel and created the first goal. The Belgian's cutback to his compatriot near the penalty spot was perfect and Lukaku side-footed confidently past the wrong-footed Claudio Bravo to make it 1-0 in the 34th minute.

If the visitors felt aggrieved going into the break a goal down, it was down to Robles, who kept his place despite Maarten Stekelenburg's return to fitness, and to Davies who ensured the Blues took a clean sheet into half time by clearing off his own goal line in first-half stoppage time.

Any attempt by City to get back into the game early in the second half was superbly halted by Everton, who doubled the lead within two minutes of the restart and then took a stranglehold on the contest as every player in royal blue seemed to grow in stature.

Mirallas, whose personal rejuvenation under Koeman's stewardship over the previous month had perhaps flown under the radar, checked his run masterfully to stay onside, receive a pass from Lukaku and made no mistake with the opportunity, rifling a low shot into the far corner to make it 2-0.

That almost nothing of note in terms of chances happened for the next half an hour was testament to how Everton stifled City's much-touted attack, but then they increased their lead with a sublime third goal 11 minutes from time, one which ended up being one of the most memorable Everton goals of the Moshiri era.

Holgate dispossessed Sterling just outside his own area. Davies picked up the loose ball and took off down the right flank. Leaving Clichy and Touré for dead with an audacious "Ronaldo chop" on the touchline, his role in the attack seemed to have ended by a collision with Stones. The teenager sensed opportunity, however, picked himself up in time to collect another precise Barkley pass and picked his moment to clip the ball over the advancing Bravo. Time seemed to slow down as it bounced goal-wards by the near post, Lukaku arriving to make sure the spin on the ball didn't carry it wide before Davies wheeled away in almost incredulous celebration in front of the Gwladys Street end.

A brilliant first ever goal for a player already rapidly blossoming into an Everton star felt like the icing on the cake, but just when you felt it couldn't get any better, the day had one last moment of magic to offer.

Koeman sent new signing Ademola Lookman on in the 89th minute to savour the atmosphere and get a few minutes under his belt as an Everton player, but within minutes he would etch his name onto that fabulous Blues performance with a moment of anticipation and a confident finish that rounded out the win in style.

In a similar fashion to Everton under Roberto Martinez, City had spent much of the first half trying to play their way out from the back, sometimes in the most risk-defying manner, so it was ironic that Stones's attempt to just knock the ball into the stands in the final minute of stoppage time ricocheted off Coleman and bounced into Lookman's path. The 19-year-old took one touch to put the ball in front of him and then buried a shot between the 'keeper's legs before he, too, made for the Street end in elation, knee-sliding towards the corner flag before being mobbed by his teammates. Robles ran the length of the field to join the party as Lukaku bear-hugged the stunned teenager, the celebrations were the last act before Clattenburg blew the final whistle as demoralised City kicked off for the final time.

More so than the win over Arsenal a month previously, where the Blues seemed to turn the game on its head through force of will, Evertonians hoped this was a transformative moment in Koeman's first season. More performances like that and Koeman's goal of a top-six finish didn't seem far-fetched.

Final score: Everton 4-0 Manchester City

***

After the free-scoring win against Manchester City, Everton ground out a 1-0 win away at Palace and a 1-1 draw with Stoke at the Britannia Stadium. It was then back to Goodison for what turned out to be a remarkable game of football.

***

4 February 2017: Everton v Bournemouth

With a mad game like this one, perhaps the best place to start is to simply acknowledge a brilliant performance from Romelu Lukaku, and a personal haul that left him as the top scorer in the Premier League at the time.

Surprisingly, after waiting almost three decades for a consistent striker capable of scoring 20-plus goals in a season, there had been calls for Everton to cash in on their greatest asset. Lukaku, one of the best in the modern game still graced Goodison Park. Yet some supporters preferred to get hung up on his attitude and work-rate, when his goals return spoke simply and loudly for itself.

On his day, Lukaku was unplayable and after having precious little bearing on the proceedings at Stoke in midweek, he was in that familiar "beast" mode against the Cherries — bullish, clinical, spectacular, unstoppable. From the quick-fire build-up play involving Morgan Schneiderlin and a one-two with James McCarthy, to the curling finish that bent majestically around Artur Boruc's despairing dive, his first goal of four very different strikes on the day was a thing of pure beauty.

Goals two and four showed his opportunism and lethality; his third and, arguably, most important was a deft volley following an equally impressive disguised pass to Seamus Coleman, whose pitching-wedge centre it was that he guided past the hapless Bournemouth goalkeeper to make it 4-2.

Just for good measure, he created the second goal for McCarthy almost out of nothing, with quick feet, strength and awareness along the by-line, underscoring his peerless tally of Premier League goals in which he has been directly involved.

On any other day, Ross Barkley would probably be the one hogging the headlines. He too had had a night to forget in the Potteries on Wednesday evening, but against Bournemouth, he delivered his most complete performance of the season. Diligent in his pressing, tenacious in his tackling, purposeful, creative and incisive on the ball, and both clinical and impudent with the coup de grâce that made it 6-3 in second-half stoppage time, the 23-year-old was excellent and a close runner-up behind Lukaku for man of the match.

Everton's attacking display was breath-taking, but there were nagging frustrations with the team's overall showing, particularly on the defensive side and the way the Blues dropped off for long periods and allowed the visitors to run the game. And by the 70-minute mark, memories of the 3-3 debacle at the Vitality Stadium in November 2015 were flooding back as the visitors rallied back to 3-2.

Haunting thoughts of the home defeats to Leicester, Stoke and West Ham last season weren't too far behind. But whereas many would bet that an Everton team under Roberto Martinez would have given up the lead this afternoon, under Koeman they were a different proposition... even if some of the defending by Ramiro Funes Mori and Ashley Williams looked like it belonged in the previous regime.

Credit to Koeman, however, for making some tactical adjustments in the final half hour to help steer the course of the game back in his team's direction. His response to the visitors drawing to within one goal was immediate. Kevin Mirallas came on in place of Lookman, whose precociously dazzling footwork and daring had been a delight at 3-0 but his comparative lack of experience on the defensive side made him surplus to requirements now that the game needed to be shut down.

But it wasn't until Mason Holgate replaced Barry with 10 minutes to go and the Blues transitioned into a back five, with the tactical shift that was missing in the last two seasons under Martinez, that the tide turned back in their favour.

Everton broke the contest open again with some wonderful attacking football. And once again, the end of the move was all down to Lukaku as he completed a brilliant hat-trick in the 83rd minute, steering home a left-foot volley before adding a fourth a minute later, while surging between two defenders and picking his spot past Boruc to bury the ball into the bottom left-hand corner.

Bournemouth's spirit was unshaken, though, and they would strike back again the final minute of the regulation 90 when Arter bundled the ball over the line to make it 5-3.

The Cherries were still going for more goals in the fourth minute of stoppage time, but in doing so, Everton picked them off one final time. Funes Mori sent Barkley away with a raking forward pass that drew Boruc well out of his box. The Blues' No.8 knocked it past him nonchalantly and, with the empty net gaping in front of him, he had time to spread his arms wide in celebration (perhaps with retribution for the winner that was taken away from him by Junior Stanislas at Dean Court 16 months ago on his mind) before slotting it home.

Koeman acknowledged after the game that he was concerned how much his team sat back at 3-0 up and invited Bournemouth back into the game. But he couldn't hide his admiration at the quality of the goals or his satisfaction at the effect his tactical tinkering had had the desired effect on the result.

That was further evidence of the progress being made under the Dutchman's stewardship. A year before, few would have bet against Bournemouth completing their comeback and sending Blues fans away muttering about defensive collapses and the team's frail mentality after throwing away a seemingly unassailable lead.

After the draw at Stoke, the three points were paramount, but the supporters gleaned plenty of confidence from the impressive way in which Everton put their foot back on the accelerator and powered their way back to a three-goal lead. Seven games unbeaten and a 100% start to 2017 at home in the Premier League showed that the Toffees under Koeman were gathering momentum at just the right time to capitalise on any slip-ups by the teams above them.

Final score: Everton 6-3 Bournemouth

***

Two days after the Blues' high-scoring win over Bournemouth, Gareth Barry lauded Romelu Lukaku's work ethic and commitment to self-improvement, but said the Belgian marksman shouldn't be in a hurry to leave Goodison Park in search of elite European football.

Lukaku had made no secret of his desire to play Champions League football, or his belief that he was now ready for it, but Barry said that Everton were once again on course to make that dream a reality with his goals capable of propelling them there.

"I don't think I have met a player who is so hungry to score goals," the veteran midfielder told evertonfc.com. "He is desperate to keep on improving. He is a great finisher already, but he won't stop there — he is working hard all the time.

"There is still room for improvement and he has got that personality and character to want to improve, so I'm sure he won't stop now. He will be desperate to keep on breaking records.

"There have been a few stories over the last couple of years about Rom wanting to play football at the highest level, and that is the Champions League.

"I'm sure he would have had conversations with the powers at the Club, and they are desperate to get there. With the signings we are making and the manager we have got at the minute, that is the road we want to go.

"Sometimes you have to be patient, but I'm confident that, if Rom sticks around, Everton can get there."

There were signs Barry's message was getting through. Just three days later, Lukaku's agent, Mino Raiola, restated his belief that his client would sign a new contract at Everton, saying talks were ongoing. Despite erroneous suggestions made in *The Express* that Lukaku had already signed a new £100,000-a-week deal with the Toffees in December, the striker had yet to reach a final agreement that would likely make him the highest-paid player in the club's history.

Raiola remained confident, however, that his client would agree new terms, although he didn't put a timescale on it.

"There are no problems right now between the player and the club, Raiola told TalkSport. "Talks are ongoing. He will sign."

***

1 April 2017: Liverpool v Everton

Prior to the 2016/17 edition of the Anfield derby, confident speeches were emanating from the Everton hierarchy.

On the playing side, Steve Walsh talked of his role at Everton and how he and Ronald Koeman were working together to assemble a team built to take the club back to the top

He was one of several club figures interviewed by Adam Leventhal during Sky Sports News' behind-the-scenes coverage from USM Finch Farm in the build-up to the game, and he explained his ethos and working relationship with Koeman.

"You're always planning and looking at good players, trying to make your team better. The fundamental question you have always got to ask is: does that player fit into what we are trying to do? If that's the case, then we try to take that forward.

"It's not just position specific - it's about trying to find out about as much as you can about that player such as his personality, has he got drive, does he want to do what we want as a football club?

"You can only do that with time. But we are certainly better than the team that started in the summer, and I think the fact we have bought people like Schneiderlin shows we have got better and will get better.

"The first thing I did [when I arrived] was I sat down with Ronald and looked at how he wanted to play. There's no point me bringing in players that don't fit with how he plays. We talked about systems and structures, and built on that.

"The most important thing is the recruitment of players for the first team, but I'm also conscious of the fact we have a good academy and good young players coming through.

"Doing that is the hallmark of a successful club. We will build on what we've got and take the club forward.

"We want to be successful. We want to get into the top four and you only do that over a period of time. Given time, we are going to get there. There's no doubt about that."

***

Would all these fine words and ambitions translate into a long-awaited win for the Blues at Anfield? Unfortunately, not that year. Another Anfield derby, passaging another season without a victory on Liverpool's patch and another painful post-mortem for Everton following a third successive defeat in the all-Mersey tussle. Blues fans had become numb to it, although the pain would never truly go.

On that occasion, the form book favoured Everton, but ultimately the league table was a better indicator of the likely destination of the points, and on an occasion that demands that star players rise above the fray, Liverpool were simply better. The Blues were badly wanting in almost all departments.

The injuries that disrupted Ronald Koeman's back line were significant, particularly that of Seamus Coleman, but it was hard to see Everton winning this game even had the Irishman been fit. Not for the first time away from home against a top-four side, the manager got his tactics wrong, and this time was let down by his main enforcer, Idrissa Gueye.

Once more the Dutchman opted for a five-man defence and, just as it was at Chelsea and Tottenham, this exposed the space in front of the defence. Pennington's inexperience, Gueye's dereliction of duty and Koeman's mystifying delay in addressing a demonstrably flawed formation were all important factors in the 3-1 defeat.

With Tom Davies, 18, in midfield and Dominic Calvert-Lewin, 20 up front, it was a very youthful Blues line-up, but it was the failure of Koeman's "big-game" players on the one hand, and the success of Jürgen Klopp's on the other, that ultimately proved to be the significant difference.

And it only took eight minutes. While Everton, and Ross Barkley in particular, succumbed unnecessarily to the increasingly out-dated imperative to indulge in the blood-and-thunder fare of the local grudge match — the Blues' No. 8 was fortunate to avoid a yellow card just six minutes in, and then a red card later in the first half — Liverpool (Emre Can aside) largely eschewed the frenetic and played the way they often do these days under Klopp: with speed and energy in attack.

Sadio Mané evaded a limp attempt at a tackle by Gueye in the centre of the park, accelerated past Davies's despairing lunge and then sucked three Everton defenders to one side of the box before screwing a shot across Joel Robles and into the far corner of the goal. The defending was atrocious really, and it threw a harsh spotlight on both Pennington and the decision to select him for such a difficult match.

Everton levelled in the 28th minute, however, with their first chance of the game. Leighton Baines's out-swinging corner was flicked on by Jagielka at the near post. Dejan Lovren couldn't react quickly enough to hack it clear and the ball fell invitingly to Pennington, who couldn't miss in front of goal.

The return to parity lasted just three minutes, though, and once again it was a failure to show Coutinho inside that would prove costly. The Reds' midfielder picked the ball up in space in central midfield and with no one closing him down until Gueye threw a lazy leg at him as he danced past, he advanced into the box, tied Pennington up in knots before curling an unstoppable shot inside Robles's left-hand post.

Liverpool's match-winners were showing up; Everton's were hugely disappointing and Barkley benefited from leniency from referee Anthony Taylor when he went over the ball and caught Lovren mid-shin, seeing his name go into the book rather than receiving his marching orders. Truth be told, apart from his failure to book James Milner for deliberate handball in the second half, the much-maligned official managed the game very well.

The expected changes from Koeman at half time never came. The manager had not been shy about replacing players or switching formations when clear they weren't working, but there was no activity from the bench until the 67th minute and by then it was too late.

There wasn't enough to suggest that keeping the five-man back line or persisting with the willing but limited Calvert-Lewin up front was going to be enough to turn the tide.

Klopp, meanwhile, made a change when Mané pulled up injured; but his replacement effectively sealed the game. Divock Origi came on in the 57th minute when Mané couldn't continue and within three minutes, he had scored.

Pennington played Holgate into trouble against the touchline. His attempted pass was picked off by Coutinho, who breezed past the lead-footed Gueye and slipped a pass to Origi behind the back-pedalling Williams. The Belgian took aim from 20 yards and smashed a shot almost down the centre of the goal.

The margin and manner of the Reds' victory were emphatic enough to render thoughts of a late push by the Blues for the top four as fanciful. Even allowing for the injuries that prompted Koeman into his ill-advised line-up, there was an unsettling gulf in ability between the two teams that sharpened the focus once more on the Dutchman's task when the summer transfer window opened.

It would also have reignited the debate over Lukaku who was, again, virtually anonymous against a top-four team and failed to register a shot in the entire 90 minutes for the third time this season, after blanks against Chelsea and Manchester United.

There was much to be said for the argument that a striker of his style can't do much without support, and without his teammates giving him the ball. Certainly, service to him was poor, just as it was in the Goodison derby in December. On the rare occasions he saw the ball, however, his touch was poor and his distribution was just as bad. Just when Everton needed him to be on razor sharp, inventive and unplayable. He was anything but.

At the end, it was a defeat that in many pundits eyes would cement Everton as only a top-seven side that season.

Final score: Liverpool 3-1 Everton

***

21 May 2017: Arsenal v Everton

The petering out of Everton's season concluded at the Emirates as 10-man Arsenal still ran out 3-1 victors against a Blues team seemingly with its mind on the summer.

The home side went ahead when Alexis Sanchez drove to the by-line, Danny Welbeck failed to connect in the centre and Hector Bellerin had the simple chance of converting from a central position to make it 1-0.

The visitors received a clear boost when Laurent Koscielny flew into Enner Valencia, scything the Ecuadorian down in full flight and referee Michael Oliver brandished a straight red card. Yet it failed to have the desired effect on Everton's performance, even after Ross Barkley replaced Tom Davies in the 26th minute, as Koeman tried to add some more guile in the final third.

Arsenal doubled their lead a minute later as Sanchez took advantage of a criminally static Blues defence, firing home Welbeck's pass across goal, after his initial shot had cannoned off Phil Jagielka.

Everton rallied briefly late in the first half and might have scored six minutes before the break, but Valencia and Barkley scuffed shots in front of goal, and Lukaku's effort was blocked near the line.

Idrissa Gueye then brought a flying save from Petr Cech with a powerful shot from distance and the Gunners' keeper had to push a header from Lukaku over his crossbar.

The second half failed to draw the requisite desire or pressure from Everton to test Arsenal, ever after Rob Holding handled in his own area and Lukaku planted a well-struck penalty to Cech's right, notching his 25th league goal of the season.

Valencia had what looked to have been the equaliser chalked off, when his impressive header from Mason Holgate's great cross was ruled-out for a push on Per Mertesaker. But it was Arsenal who got their third in stoppage time, when Ramsey took advantage of a yard of space ahead of him on the edge of the Everton box and curled an unstoppable shot around Robles to make it 3-1.

With seventh place long since guaranteed, the result had no bearing on Everton's season, but the disappointing manner in which the season meandered to a close had Evertonians eagerly awaiting the summer transfer window, when improvements to the squad were evidently needed.

Final score: Arsenal 3-1 Everton

2017: Everton lose Lukaku, sign 4 Number 10-s but no striker

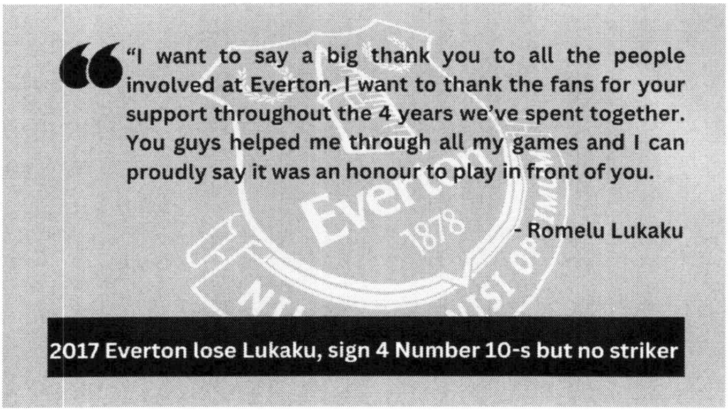

By the summer of 2017, Steve Walsh had been director of football for a year, and in that time was developing his relationship with Ronald Koeman.

The pair had been working to identify which areas of the squad needed improving after a 2016/17 season that showed progress on successive 11th-place finishes under previous boss Roberto Martinez, but which ultimately underscored a deficit in quality and depth in certain positions.

With the close season only a fortnight old and the transfer window itself not officially open for another four weeks, Walsh insisted he, his team, and Koeman had been working hard to identify the personnel they would try to sign.

"Planning never stops," Walsh said in the Liverpool Echo.

"From the day the window closes until the day it opens again, you are always looking at your possibilities. We are no different.

"We've done a lot of work behind the scenes to get the correct information about the players. I have sat down with Ronald and gone through those. Obviously, we discuss it all the time and we want to improve things, build on what we have got. That's the key message.

"My department is very well run, very organised and we make sure we get as much information about the player that we possibly can. If we like the player, I've got to try to convince Ronald that he's the player for us. It could well be that Ronald has seen the player as well, so it's a collective decision at the end of the day."

***

What followed was a series of deals that would shatter Everton's transfer record for both incoming and outgoing players. It was a clear statement of intent and ambition from Farhad Moshiri as he sought to take that next, potentially decisive step towards realising a three-year project to reach the Champions League, and it set a tone of continuing largesse in the market for the next three years.

The ramifications for the club's financial future and its ability to simply remain in the Premier League would be felt a lot further down the line, but the feeling at the time was that Everton were moving in the right direction, and that Moshiri's ambition and willingness to maintain loose purse strings would support a sustained push for qualification into Europe's elite club competition.

***

With Enner Valencia leaving at the end of his temporary loan spell, Everton were soon in the race to sign Sandro Ramirez - a striker from Malaga who had scored a remarkable 14 goals in La Liga in 2016/17 - but it would take a while to land the Spaniard in a £5.2 million deal.

It looked as though Sandro would stay with Malaga, hoping to join Atletico Madrid in January when the latter club had its transfer embargo lifted, but he eventually joined the Blues when the move was finally completed on 3 July.

***

Just four days later, Everton completed the capture of Jordan Pickford in a record deal for an English goalkeeper that would eventually be worth up to £30 million.

Having undergone a successful medical, Pickford signed a five-year contract that would make him not only Everton's most expensive player at the time, but also the most expensive British player in his position.

The Blues agreed a deal with Sunderland that saw them pay around £25 million up front for the 23-year-old, who would officially become an Everton player on 1st July when the club could register him with the Premier League.

"It's great to sign for the club," the Washington-born player said. "Last season was my first in the Premier League, so to get this opportunity with Everton now, to be able to go forward with my career and show everyone what I can do with Everton is unbelievable.

"It's a great club, a massive club and I think it's a great opportunity and the right time for me to come to Everton and show what I can do.

"This is an exciting time for the club and for me, too, with the ambition being shown. I just want to be the best I can be to help."

For manager Ronald Koeman, Pickford's signing came after a season's worth of assessment of both Joel Robles and Maarten Stekelenburg for the mantle of first-choice goalkeeper at Everton.

"I'm really pleased we've made what I'm sure will be a significant signing for Everton Football Club," Koeman said after announcing Pickford's signing. "Jordan is a very talented young professional who also has a real hunger for success, and that's important for us as we now look to make further progress in the seasons ahead.

"We've seen the quality he has through his performances in the Premier League last season and, given his young age, we're sure he will get even better."

***

Later that same day, Dutch midfielder Davy Klaassen became an Everton player after he too agreed personal terms with the club, and a £24 million move from Ajax. The 24-year-old captain of the Amsterdam side had had a stellar season with Ajax, and the Blues had led the chase for his signature before he was unveiled as Everton's second signing of the day.

"I spoke a few weeks ago with Ronald Koeman about Everton," Klaassen told evertontv. "I wanted to come here and check if this was the right club for me and since I came here, I feel so happy. It's a great club.

"The moment that I spoke with the manager directly, I got a good feeling. He's an honest guy. We talked about the club, about the way he wants to play and that gave me a positive feeling.

"It's difficult to leave Ajax, but I think this is a good step for me now and I'm really looking forward to my time here."

***

On the final day of June, Everton also completed the signing of exciting prospect Henry Onyekuru from KAS Eupen in Belgium for an officially undisclosed fee, reported to be around £6.8 million.

The Blues beat off competition from Arsenal, Paris St Germain and West Ham to land the 20-year-old who signed a five-year contract to become the club's third signing of the summer, and he was followed by another major acquisition in the form of defender Michael Keane from Burnley for £30 million.

The 24-year-old became the fifth player to be signed by the Blues during a busy transfer window, making Everton the highest spending club in the Premier League for 2017 to that point, with more than £92 million splashed out in the period since January.

Keane had been one of Ronald Koeman's and Steve Walsh's top targets, with the Everton manager breaking a self-imposed protocol by making his interest in the player public earlier in 2017 after it became common knowledge that he would leave Turf Moor over the summer.

Keane signed a five-year contract and added important competition to the back line for the upcoming season, as Everton prepared to mount a bid to make it into the Europa League group stages, as well as challenge for the Premier League's top four.

"I'm absolutely delighted to be at Everton," Keane said, "a fantastic football club with passionate fans and a great tradition, and I can't wait to come into training tomorrow to meet all the lads.

"First and foremost, the manager was a big factor in me coming to the club. He played in my position when he was a world-class player for a great Barcelona side and a great Dutch side and the style of football he likes to play will suit me, I believe.

"He's convinced me he can still improve me in certain areas of my game. I'm only 24, which, for a centre-half in the Premier League, is relatively young. I've still got a long way to go and I know this and hopefully under his guidance I'll keep improving."

***

Unfortunately, the widely expected departure of the club's star-striker finally came on 10 July, when Romelu Lukaku's club record-breaking £75 million move to Manchester United was announced, with the Belgian signing a five-year contract at Old Trafford.

Interviewed by ESPN about his switch from Goodison Park to Old Trafford and, after expressing his delight at joining the "world's biggest club" with "the best fans", Lukaku sent a farewell message to the club he had joined four years earlier, initially on loan and then permanently from Chelsea for £28 million:

"To the staff at the stadium and training ground, thank you for making me feel home from the first day I walked in. To my teammates, it was great to play with you guys. To the technical staff, thank you for helping me become a better player. Working with you guys has been a pleasure and I'll take your advice throughout the rest of my career. Thank you Everton Football Club."

***

Moving in the opposite direction was Wayne Rooney. The 31-year-old had grown up in Croxteth as a Toffee-mad kid on the Blues' books, but left the club as a teenager for Manchester United in 2004 after bursting onto the Premier League and international scene. He spent 13 years amassing a trophy cabinet full of honours and was hoping to help end Everton's trophy drought and make a concerted push for the top four under Ronald Koeman.

He put pen to paper on a two-year contract after months of speculation about his future and took the mantle of the No.10 jersey vacated by Romelu Lukaku.

"Throughout the summer I've been working out where I was going to go," Rooney said on evertonfc.com. "I spoke to my agent and said: 'Listen, you need to speak to Everton, see if it can happen.'

"He said it could, so I told him to speak to the club and get it done as quickly as possible. It's happened. I'm delighted and I'm ready to go.

"[Wearing the shirt] feels as special as it did 13 years ago and I'm just looking forward now to getting out on the pitch with it on. "[Goodison Park] has always been a special place, even when I've been on the opposing team," he continued. "You always get that feeling when you walk out of the tunnel, so to actually do it again in an Everton shirt will be a special moment for me. "I've kept it quiet for the last 13 years, but I've actually been wearing Everton pyjamas at home with my kids. I had to keep that a bit quiet!"

***

Meanwhile, his new manager was excited to have added genuine experience and savvy to the team to blend with the youthful additions he and Steve Walsh have been busy making this summer.

Rooney was the elder statesman, when compared with Jordan Pickford (23), Davy Klaassen (24), Sandro Ramirez (21), Henry Onyekuru (20) and Michael Keane (24), but he had played on the biggest stages for club and country and still kept a burning desire to push his former club back towards the top of the English game.

"Wayne has shown me that ambition that we need and that winning mentality," Koeman said. "He knows how to win titles and I'm really happy he's decided to come home.

"He loves Everton, and he was desperate to come back. He is still only 31 and I don't have any doubts about his qualities. It's fantastic he's here.

"It's all about his fitness and his desire, but he has shown me that ambition that we need. He knows how to win titles, as I said. He wants to play at the highest level that is possible for him. We have spoken several times about Everton and what we are striving to achieve."

***

Another player who could potentially play in the Number 10 role was Nikola Vlašić who completed a move from Hajduk Split to Everton at the end of August for an initial fee of around £8 million. An attacking midfielder who could operate across the forward line, Vlašić had made 87 league appearances and scored 11 goals for Hajduk since breaking into their team in 2014.

"Nikola is one of those players who can play a big part in Everton's future and in what we want to achieve as a club," Ronald Koeman said of the new acquisition.

Vlašić, meanwhile, expressed his delight at finalising the move. "When there is a manager like Ronald Koeman who wants you, there is no need to talk about it much," he said. "I wanted to come here because of the manager, because of the big players, because of the reputation of the club. It is the opportunity of a lifetime. I played a lot of games for Hajduk Split but the Premier League is something else. I am very excited about the opportunity to play for this big club. The Premier League is the best league in the world and this is one of the top clubs in England. It is such a big honour for me to be here."

***

Playing out against the backdrop of what was a busy summer of incomings and outgoings – that had seen injury-prone midfielder Darren Gibson, unfancied Tom Cleverley, Costa Rican fullback Bryan Oviedo, erratic winger Aiden McGeady, and the popular but mercurial Spaniard winger Gerard Deulofeu all leave the club along with Lukaku – was the saga of Everton's attempts to sign Gylfi Sigurdsson.

The Blues had pursued Sigurdsson for a year and seen successive offers starting at a reported £25 million rebuffed by Swansea City, including a £40 million bid in early August 2017. The Swans looked as though they were going to dig their heels in over their £50 million valuation of their star player, but they eventually negotiated a compromise package of around £40 million with a further £2.5 million dependent on appearances. It took until 15 August for the Gylfi Sigurdsson deal to finally conclude.

That deal smashed Everton's previous club record fee of £30 million paid for Jordan Pickford in June, but now, backed by Farhad Moshiri, Ronald Koeman and Steve Walsh had their top targets in place.

The open question was, after signing a goalkeeper, another centre-half, four No.10s and two untried young strikers, how would the team fill the 25-goals-a-year gap that Lukaku's departure had created?

2017: Poor Start After Massive Investment in Squad

Finishing seventh in the league in 2016/17 meant that Everton had only qualified for Qualifying Round 3 of the Europa League, and that entailed a shortened pre-season and an unusually early start to competitive action in late July.

Their opponents were MFK Ružomberok and it was hoped that the two-legged tie against the Slovakians would provide Ronald Koeman's side with the ideal ramp into the new season.

It was then that Everton's struggles under Koeman began, with the Dutch manager seemingly incapable of arresting a slide that would cost him his job in late October.

***

27 July 2017: Everton v MFK Ružomberok

Ronald Koeman fielded £60 million of new talent in his first starting line-up of the 2017/18 season, but it was the man snapped up for just £5.2 million from La Liga and a veteran fullback who made the difference in the first leg against Ružomberok.

Wayne Rooney started as expected, and there were debuts for Michael Keane, Cuco Martina and Davy Klaassen, while Jordan Pickford and Sandro Ramirez were on the bench.

Maarten Stekelenburg was in goal given Pickford's lack of pre-season preparation, while Leighton Baines captained the side.

With large sections of the Main Stand closed for renovations aimed at improving facilities for disabled supporters and Ružomberok bringing just a smattering of travelling fans, the atmosphere inside Goodison had a decidedly pre-season feel as the Blues' season got off to a pedestrian start.

Everton had their chances in the first half, but Idrissa Gueye – arguably the standout player of the first 45 minutes – as well as Rooney and Klaassen all failed to find the target, at least until the Senegalese midfielder stung the palms of Macik from distance and Dominic Calvert-Lewin saw the last effort of the half comfortably saved.

Emboldened by their hosts' torpor, the visitors controlled the early exchanges in the second half and Daniel had a half-chance, but hooked it wide before Stekelenburg had to intervene with an excellent save when he finger-tipped Maslo's header onto the crossbar.

In between, Klaassen missed with a header from Martina's cross, Mirallas's accurate drive was pushed behind by Masik, and Keane's header from a free kick deflected behind as Sandro stripped off in readiness to come on in place of Calvert-Lewin.

The Spaniard's introduction provided an immediate spark of urgency and when Everton won a corner in the 65th minute that was cleared to the feet of Baines, the captain rattled a shot goalwards that took a decisive deflection off Daniel and past Macik to hand the Toffees the lead.

With time winding down, Koeman introduced Ademola Lookman for Mirallas, but it was Ružomberok's own substitution that almost paid dividends when the ball fell to the feet of Lacny 10 yards from goal. Thankfully, he could only shoot tamely at Stekelenburg, and Goodison breathed a sigh of relief.

Final score: Everton 1-0 MFK Ružomberok

***

The return leg was played in Slovakia on 3 August in front of 4,752 fans, with Dominic Calvert-Lewin scoring the only goal, and ensuring a 2-0 aggregate win for the Toffeemen.

***

12 August 2017: Everton v Stoke

If the wisdom of Everton re-signing Wayne Rooney from Manchester United wasn't universally accepted, the 31-year-old's display over two legs in the Europa League tie with Ružomberok seemed to confirm the fears of the doubters that it wasn't so much the Prodigal Son who had returned, but the Prodigal Pensioner.

Rooney wasn't alone in performing beneath himself on the European stage — the whole team had been alarmingly disappointing against the Slovakian side — but if his contribution to the 2017/18 Premier League opener was any sign of the season to come, then Messers Koeman and Walsh (and Kenwright, too, no doubt) would be vindicated in the decision to bring the Boyhood Blue home.

Rooney grabbed the headlines by scoring the winner against Stoke, but it was the manner in which he dictated much of this contest, particularly in the second half, that was so pleasing to the Goodison faithful. Playing metronome to a side that had visibly settled once the manager had dispensed with a lopsided and, frankly, questionable formation, the Croxteth-born forward ran the show for Everton, spraying balls around at one end and chipping in with vital defensive interventions from set-pieces at the other.

His celebration following the only goal in first-half stoppage time was also a wondrous sight; the joy of scoring for Everton undiminished by 13 years away in Manchester with United.

That strike, a composed header back across Jack Butland from Dominic Calvert-Lewin's sumptuous cross at the end of the best move of the match, was also the highlight of an otherwise abysmal first period.

With Koeman determined to find a way of playing a three-man central defensive unit, Calvert-Lewin played in an advanced wingback role, one that saw Idrissa Gueye occasionally dropping off to the touchline to cover DCL's advances forward.

It was a role to which the young striker looked wholly unsuited; thankfully, he was relieved of it for the second half when Cuco Martina came on in place of Ashley Williams and Koeman reverted to a more conventional back four.

Overall, the Blues' tactics were puzzling, with a succession of floated balls to the flank aimed at Calvert-Lewin more often that not missing their target. Even the set-pieces were odd; Rooney and Sandro insisted on taking corners short, depriving the team of strikers of chances to pick up the pieces in the box.

Stoke, looking every inch a Potters side with plenty of height sprinkled with flashes of limited end product from the likes of Bojan Krkic and Xherdan Shaqiri, offered even less threat in the first half.

The visitors had a brief flurry immediately after the restart but Everton soon established control of proceedings and Calvert-Lewin, now playing up top in a three, had two chances to double the lead but saw one shot blocked and another saved at the near post by Jack Butland.

Morgan Schneiderlin may have had another off day to go with those iffy evenings in the Europa League, and Davy Klaassen struggled to make an impact (his role in the goal where he drew defenders away to leave Rooney unmarked might get overlooked) but Gueye was excellent. And Tom Davies, the unfortunate one to drop to the bench, showed how difficult Koeman's midfield team selection will be when he came on for Klaassen after an hour to put in another accomplished display.

Despite their hugely improved second-half showing, Everton endured a somewhat nervy last 10 minutes as Hughes threw on Peter Crouch and Stoke lumped more and more balls into the home area, hoping for something to fall their way.

It was from the more cultured foot of Shaqiri that they almost grabbed a point at the death. The Swiss picked the ball up in central midfield following a corner, advanced into space and unloaded from 25 yards with a shot that was searching out the far corner. Pickford, whose only real involvement up to that point had been to display some pleasing command of his area with decisive decision-making and action, was equal to it; diving to his left to turn the ball behind his post. It was a match-winning save from the young England U21 'keeper and the first return on the massive transfer fee that had brought him to Merseyside from Sunderland.

Overall, while there was plenty to ponder from that first half, the Blues grew stronger after the break and Rooney, spurred on by his goal, employed all his experience and savvy to help control the contest after half-time.

Koeman acknowledged afterwards that the wingback idea hadn't worked as he had expected, while also admitting that his team needed to improve significantly if it was to achieve its aims this season.

He and Steve Walsh would also have to keep busy until the deadline, in finding recruits to fill the obvious gaps in the team, such as another seasoned striker who could hold the ball up and provide a physical presence up front.

Final score: Everton 1-0 Stoke

***

9 September 2017: Everton v Tottenham Hotspur

It had only been a few weeks since that Everton's expensive transfer business had been heralded by a usually ambivalent national media, and the Blues were being talked about as genuine top-four contenders.

The return of Wayne Rooney, admittedly past the peak of his powers but a world-famous name, gave the show of ambition an added layer of legitimacy and Evertonians waited for the two or three additions to the squad that would top off an excellent transfer window.

Those signings never came, of course. Romelu Lukaku, the source of football's most important currency — goals — departed for huge money but wasn't replaced. There was also no cover for 32-year-old Leighton Baines and, if there was any desire by the management to add pace and/or genuine creativity to the side, there was precious little evidence of it.

The product of this one-dimensional approach to recruitment over the summer of 2017 had resulted in Everton's uninspiring start to the new season, one which had quickly lurched from concerning into the realm of deeply demoralising.

Worse still, the team looked like a collection of individuals bereft of a plan, an identity, or any consistent attacking threat. So when the wheels came off defensively, Evertonians witnessed the humbling of their team against Tottenham Hotspur.

Seldom, if ever in the Premier League era, had a Spurs side enjoyed such an easy ride at Goodison Park, a venue that had become a veritable fortress for Koeman's side since the turn of the year. By the same token, it was hard to recall the Blues looking so lacking in desire or spirit in a home game against highly-fancied opposition other than the 3-0 reverse against Chelsea, hitherto their only defeat at Goodison in 2017.

For the first time in the league that season Koeman had abandoned the five-man defensive line he had been using, perhaps to keep one of his experienced centre halves in reserve with an eye on the upcoming trip to Italy in the Europa League, or perhaps because he had identified something in Tottenham's makeup that was better tackled with a flat back four.

Cuco Martina made his first Premier League start in an Everton jersey — many hoped, in vain, that it would be his last — while Davy Klaassen and Morgan Schneiderlin returned to the side, and Sandro Ramirez played alongside Rooney in attack.

The opening exchanges didn't offer much hint of the debacle to follow but the warning signs for the Blues would come before the match was a quarter of an hour old and the opening goal for the visitors wasn't too far behind.

A corner eventually ended up on the Tottenham right where Harry Kane tried to swing in a cross, but he ended up drifting his centre over Jordan Pickford and under the crossbar to make it 1-0 with 27 minutes gone.

Sandro saw one snapshot at the other end cannon off Toby Alderweireld's head from close range after good work by Rooney, but it was a rare opening for Everton that was swiftly followed by a second goal for the visitors.

Sucked into his six-yard box, Martina waved a leg at a cross that was flighted over everybody in the middle, which left Davies in space to force Pickford into a save but he could only push it out to Chrsitian Eriksen who converted the rebound from close range.

Dele Alli should have buried Everton in stoppage time but, completely unmarked in the middle, he mis-kicked yet another delivery from wide on Tottenham's left before Martina gifted the ball to Kane and the striker dragged his shot wide.

Kane made no mistake less than a minute into the second half, though. Laying the ball out to Davies with Martina badly exposed again, he continued his run untracked by Schneiderlin and calmly side-footed a first-time finish past Pickford to make it 3-0.

That goal ripped up whatever plan Koeman had had for the second period. Having thrown on Tom Davies and Calvert-Lewin for Klaassen and Sandro, and for the next 20 minutes, Spurs created all the chances.

Everton sputtered into a bit of life too late in the proceedings as the game ticked through the last 10 minutes after Nikola Vlasic had come on for his debut following his deadline-day move from Hajduk Split. It was a cameo that featured some neat touches and confident running that ensured he would walk off at the end as one of a tiny number of Blues players to emerge with any credit from a pitiful performance.

In the final reckoning, though, Everton had just one shot on target and failed to trouble Lloris with a shot all game... as damning a statistic as you can imagine for a team supposedly challenging today's opponents for a place in the top four.

There were supposedly mitigating circumstances: this was a team featuring several new faces, some of whom were new to the Premier

League and Everton had had a tough start to the new league season but they generally looked poor, toothless and utterly directionless.

Koeman, a man steeped in the Total Football of Holland's finest era and a Barcelona legend in his own right, was presiding over some awful yard-dog football that was marrying the worst elements of his three predecessors' reigns: the striker-less days of Walter Smith, the defensive and cowing disposition of some of David Moyes's teams, and the spineless and defensively shambolic performances in the worst days under Roberto Martinez.

Tactically, he looked to be a novice despite his lengthy CV. His team had no width, no pace, no creativity and too many like-minded players stuffed into the same line-up, not least in midfield where Sigurdsson, Klaassen, Gueye and Schneiderlin struggled to gel. The team looked lost, and it was difficult to see progress, despite an outlay of £140 million on new players.

There was plenty of time, of course but the feeling was that the manager needed to step up and figure out a way to get his side playing basic football again – or else it promised to be a very long, frustrating season.

Final score: Everton 0-3 Spurs

***

After the match, Koeman cautioned against raised expectations following the Blues' big-spending summer.

"In the second half you could see we were far away from Tottenham, but in the first half an hour we were much closer," Koeman said, following his team's second successive defeat. "I've said before, I think, along with Manchester City, Spurs are the best footballing side (in the Premier League). The difference is they have had the same group of players for a long time now.

"If you think we are trying to join them in that [top six] pack, it will be really difficult."

"I know how it works in football. If you sign some players, people stop being realistic," he said.

"Everybody is talking about Everton and the top six. But if you know the qualities, and the individual qualities of the players in the top six, it is a challenge. It is our ambition, but we need to realise it is difficult.

"We will learn from the mistakes today and we have enough games coming up to have a good reaction."

***

Throughout October, speculation concerning Koeman's position was reaching fever pitch. At the start of the month, Farhad Moshiri had once again used *Sky Sports* and *TalkSport* presenter Jim White as the conduit for a message to supporters where he gave his backing to Koeman, as the manager struggled to turn around the team's poor start to the season.

The Blues had lost 1-0 to Burnley at Goodison Park on 1 October, and left the field to boos from the home fans for the second time in three days following the 2-2 draw with Apollon Limassol in the Europa League.

Just two Premier League wins had left Everton in 16th place in the table, increasing the pressure on the manager following a significant outlay on players over the summer.

Jim White, who claimed to have a close relationship with Moshiri and who regularly passed on updates from the billionaire investor, tweeted a quote purported to be from the Monaco-based billionaire.

In the message, Moshiri said that the Burnley match was the only match so far where a defeat was unexpected, arguing that Everton had faced four of the title contenders and were tired from having to play Europa League qualifying games.

Moshiri's statement, said:

> "We're in a bad moment. But we have played the four title contenders, three away. Today was the only unexpected loss. The four Pre qualifying UEFA games and two group games on Thursdays haven't helped. There is mental and physical fatigue and seven injuries. These are early days and Koeman has my total support. We have great fans and they deserve better. We know the honest and objective expectations of our supporters and will not let them down."

On Friday, 13 October, Moshiri reportedly dropped in at USM Finch Farm.

MailOnline reported that the Iranian-born businessman was joined by chairman Bill Kenwright at the club's training facility primarily to discuss plans for the new stadium at Bramley-Moore Dock. He also spoke with Koeman, a move that was seen by some as further backing for the Dutchman, who was under pressure following a sequence of poor results that meant Everton went into an important fixture against Arsenal sitting in 16th place in the Premier League.

***

22 October 2017: Everton v Arsenal

The Arsenal match turned out to be an unmitigated disaster and it signalled the end for Ronald Koeman less than 18 months into his much-vaunted tenure. It beggared belief, really, when thinking of the vast sums Everton had spent on new players over the summer and the optimism that had been coursing through Evertonian veins just three months previously. Yet the club was once again embroiled in crisis.

Sitting in the relegation zone for the first time in 12 years and with a poorer goal difference than eventually doomed Sunderland had at the same stage of 2016/17, underscored the trouble that the Koeman regime was in.

The season before, the Arsenal fixture had marked a turning point, at least in Everton's home form in the League. It paved the way for the 4-0 demolition of Manchester City, as a cock-sure Blues side romped through Pep Guardiola's team with abandon, and six more wins at Goodison Park after that before Champions-elect Chelsea broke the sequence.

The only turning point this visit of Arsenal to L4 was likely to spark, however, was an abrupt one in Koeman's employment status... although there was no guarantee the Everton Board would be so decisive. Farhad Moshiri was seen to mouth "oh, no" as the fifth goal went in while Bill Kenwright visibly shared the pain of every Evertonian watching. It was hard to see a way back for Koeman — he looked bereft of answers.

The game exposed Everton's technical limitations and defensive frailties, while underscoring that energy and tenacity alone is not enough against sides like Arsenal when they can slice through disorganised defences like a whipsaw. The Gunners weren't at their best, but when they reached their potential, the porous Toffees couldn't live with them.

In some respects, there was a measure of sympathy to be had for Koeman here, albeit not enough to mask the mess over which he presided. He had asked for "aggression" from his players and mostly got it in the opening half hour as the forward line harried the Arsenal defence, and the likes of Idrissa Gueye were making full-blooded challenges like the one that set Wayne Rooney up for the opening goal.

Getting a boot to the ball before Hector Bellerin, the Senegalese midfielder prodded it towards Rooney and drawing on the self-belief and execution with which he announced himself to the world as a raw teenager 15 years ago almost to the day, he swept it past Petr Cech from 20 yards.

But it was over-exuberance from Gueye — in the absence of Morgan Schneiderlin, his job being to protect the back four — that got him into hot water with referee Craig Pawson 11 minutes before halftime, and which ultimately cost him his place on the pitch half an hour later when he picked up a second yellow card for one late sliding tackle too many.

Despite grabbing the relatively early goal that might have provided the foundation from which they could prey on the low morale of an Arsenal side that came into the game without an away win all season, there wasn't much more in terms of offensive production from Everton.

Jordan Pickford made himself the leading candidate for the Blues' man of the match by tipping a shot from Alexis Sanchez wide, diverting Alexandre Lacazette's shot behind to safety and making an excellent close-range save to deny the French striker after Aaron Ramsey had picked him out with an accurate centre from the Gunners' right flank. He was busy again pushing away Sanchez's free kick and then denying Aaron Ramsey from the rebound, but Arsenal's increasing pressure told. Five minutes before the break, a wrong-footed Pickford could only parry the ball into the path of Nacho Monreal and he smashed the rebound home.

Goodison was deflated, and it left plenty wondering if the Blues had it in them to re-establish a lead against a Gunners team that looked very much up for it, and was slicing through them at will.

And eight minutes into the second half, when the ball came to Sanchez, he delayed until he spotted Mesut Özil's unchecked run. One chipped cross later, the German had guided a header past Pickford to make it 2-1.

Koeman would lament after the match that Gueye's dismissal had made an already difficult task for his team impossible, but much of the fight had already gone out of them by that point. Arsenal with their tails up were just too good.

While the massed Evertonians watched angled ball after angled ball float out of play on the right touchline - the result of the manager's directive to go more direct - Wenger's men passed with speed and precision, moving through the gears with an efficiency that Blues fans could only dream of.

With 16 minutes left, Arsenal extended their lead when they carved their hosts open once more after Nikola Vlasic had uncharacteristically given it away in their half. Only the hapless Michael Keane was in the middle of defence as Ozil surged down the right flank and crossed to Lacazette, who couldn't miss from the centre of the goal.

Substitute Jack Wilshere split the defence to pick out Ramsey for the Gunners' fourth as regulation time expired but there was farce still to come in added time as Cech tried to dribble away from Oumar Niasse and the striker robbed him to knock the ball into the empty net.

Sanchez would still exert his will on the game with a final act in the final minute of stoppage time, though. Driving his way past a rank of Blue shirts, he eventually engineered space for a shot that he whipped across Pickford and into the far corner to complete the misery among those Evertonians who had remained behind to the bitter end.

But for Pickford's heroics, the result could have been much, much worse. And, even accounting for the final quarter of the contest played with 10 men, it was bad enough.

The flawed transfer strategy that saw Everton exit the transfer window with an unbalanced squad, woefully deficient in some areas and over-weight in others, was clearly a significant factor behind the slump, but the lack of consistency and clarity in Koeman's methods, team selections and tactics – and the resultant collapse in confidence among the players – were compounding the problem to a degree that was unsustainable.

There was a shortage of imagination, and what came across as a lack of passion and desire from the manager. When the buck ultimately stops at that one role, there is usually only one course of action to take. And take it, Moshiri did.

Final score: Everton 2-5 Arsenal

2017: Ronald Koeman sacked

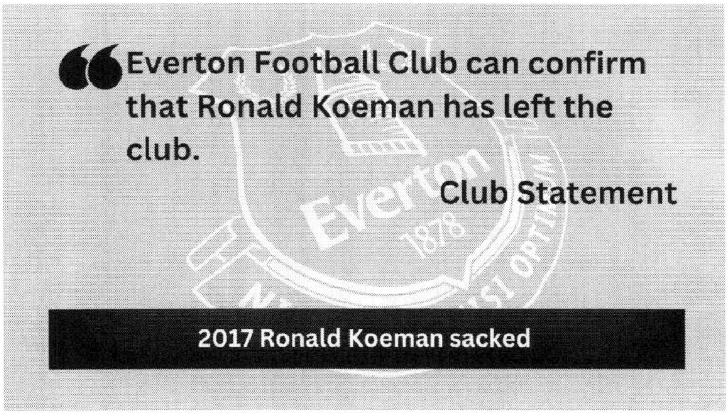

Everton sacked Ronald Koeman in the wake of that chastening 5-2 defeat by Arsenal, which had left the team sitting in the relegation zone for the first time since 2005.

A statement on the club's official website confirmed a decision from Farhad Moshiri and chairman Bill Kenwright that had become increasingly likely, despite the recent vote of confidence in the manager from the Blues' major shareholder.

Besides Everton's nose-diving form in the Premier League, the club was bottom of their Europa League group, having lost two and drawn one of their games, the worst such record for an English team in the competition to date.

Koeman had arrived at Goodison Park in June the previous year, billed as a "Hollywood" replacement for Roberto Martinez.

The Dutchman, an experienced coach who had won the title in the Netherlands three times before coming to England, had guided unfancied Southampton to seventh and then sixth place in the Premier League. Moshiri had seen him as the ideal candidate to take Everton forward.

Backed by unprecedented investment on the playing side and a club-record £6 million-a-year salary, Koeman's job was to steer the Blues into the Champions League, but what he regarded as an initial three-year project derailed in dramatic fashion with five defeats in nine league games.

The 54-year-old was insistent after the heavy loss to Arsenal that he was the right man to turn Everton's fortunes around, but a visible loss of confidence among the players and no sign of an upturn in results forced the hierarchy to act.

Koeman took training as normal at Finch Farm, but was informed shortly afterwards by CEO Robert Elstone and chairman Kenwright of the Board's decision to end his contract, including those of his backroom staff, comprising his brother and assistant Erwin, fitness coach Jan Kluitenberg, and goalkeeping coach Patrick Lodewijks. First team coach Duncan Ferguson would stay with the club.

The club statement read:

> "Everton Football Club can confirm that Ronald Koeman has left the Club. Chairman Bill Kenwright,

> the Board of Directors and Major Shareholder Farhad Moshiri would all like to express their gratitude to Ronald for the service he has given to the Club over the past 16 months and for guiding the Club to seventh place in last season's Premier League campaign."

Koeman had presided over 24 wins during his 58 games in charge, with 14 draws and 20 defeats. Though there were some misgivings among supporters about the standard of football his Everton team played, in the latter half of his first season at the club he appeared to have his team moving in the right direction.

There was, however, a feeling from club insiders that Koeman was a poor fit for the Toffees' culture, and that became a greater problem the worse results got in the weeks leading up to the dreadful display against Arsenal that triggered his dismissal.

It would also be revealed that Koeman and the club's sporting director Steve Walsh had increasingly divergent views on how to take the team forward.

Writing in *The Sportsman* on 9 November, Patrick Boyland [1]pinpointed the failed partnership between Ronald Koeman and Steve Walsh, saying that any new manager needed to learn lessons. He wrote:

> "It perfectly highlights the disconnect between Koeman and Walsh as far as the last few windows are concerned. In the case of the former, players seemingly able to deliver short-term gains were targeted in an attempt to meet a series of lofty goals over

the course of his three-year contract. As such, Morgan Schneiderlin, Davy Klaassen and Gylfi Sigurdsson were all bought on the recommendation of the Dutchman. Walsh, by contrast, largely chose to place faith in younger, hungrier players and hidden gems. In Ademola Lookman, Sandro Ramirez, Michael Keane and Jordan Pickford, the former Leicester City head of recruitment sought to buy players who would grow to form the backbone of Everton sides way into the future. The two contrasting visions have left Everton's squad lacking identity. Some players have youthful exuberance on their side and others the nous that comes with experience, but few in the ranks have both. With reliable heads thin on the ground, the Blues have been forced to place too much faith in a creaking elder statesmen and young bucks with rough edges to iron out. Whichever path is taken, Everton's director of football and new manager simply have to be on the same wavelength when it comes to recruiting players. As Koeman's demise has shown, contrasting visions cannot be reconciled. In that sense, those in power in L4 would be well advised to learn lessons from the failures of the past when appointing Koeman's successor."

***

David Unsworth, assisted by John Ebrell, was placed in charge of the first team as interim coach. With no immediate successor to Koeman lined up, the former Everton player was effectively handed an open-ended trial period to prove that he could take the job on, at least in an interim capacity, perhaps until the end of the season.

***

5 November 2017: Everton v Watford

In what was David Unsworth's fourth match in charge as caretaker boss, the Blues faced Watford at Goodison. His record in the role, up to that point, had been less than impressive. An unfortunate 2-1 defeat away at Chelsea in the League Cup was followed by 2-0 loss against Leicester in the Premier League, and a more alarming 3-0 thrashing by Olympique Lyonnais in Group E of the Europa League.

Unsworth named another changed line-up to face Watford, with Phil Jagielka, Leighton Baines and Wayne Rooney all returning to the starting XI, and with Michael Keane available again following his recovery from a leg infection, but genuine chances remained at a high premium in the first half.

The best chance of half had fallen the visitors' way when Richarlison drove forward for Watford and caught Pickford in no-man's land, but the Brazilian could only find the side-netting from the angle with the open goal gaping.

Richarlison made amends just 30 seconds into the second half, however. Everton were carved wide open again, and the forward took it wide to the left around Pickford once more and slammed it past Jonjoe Kenny on the line to make it 1-0.

By the 64th minute, Everton found themselves 2-0 down. Christian Kabasele rose highest from a corner, having lost his marker, and powered a header home.

Everton grabbed a lifeline three minutes after that, though, and sparked a dramatic and memorable comeback when Niasse toed the ball past the keeper, who had come flying out of his area. Despite being tripped as he charged through, he scored into the empty net.

Dominic Calvert-Lewin replaced Rooney, and when Leighton Baines swung in a corner, the substitute was there at the back post to head home and send Goodison into bedlam at 2-2.

As the match reached 90 minutes, it appeared the clincher had come. Holebas felled recent substitute Aaron Lennon and the Blues received the opportunity to take the lead. Baines stepped up to take the spot kick and, despite a short run-up, he placed it perfectly past the keeper to complete a stirring comeback. Yet still the game was not over.

Watford piled on increasing pressure and sunk Evertonian hearts when they too earned a penalty 10 minutes into stoppage time. Richarlison looked odds on to score his second as he neatly side-stepped Pickford in front of the goal, but the 'keeper tripped him trying to make a last-ditch tackle, and the spot kick was awarded.

Tom Cleverley stepped up with the chance to drive a stake into his former team's heart, but he screwed his penalty kick wide to spark more wild celebrations around the Old Lady; and the Blues held out for the final couple of minutes to claim a crucial victory.

This was only the second time since the relegation-defying win over Wimbledon that Everton had come back from a two-goal deficit, and it could not have come at a better time. With 10 minutes in the second half gone, the club had been staring a long battle against relegation firmly in the face. But a brilliant fightback had not only lifted Everton out of the relegation zone, it had offered hope that this collection of players had the stomach for any fight to survive in the top flight.

Final score: Everton 3-2 Watford

***

After the match, the 44-year-old Unsworth was full of praise for his players, many of them young and relatively inexperienced.

"Incredible!" Unsworth beamed in the tunnel after the game. "I'm just delighted for the club and the fans that they can go home tonight happy. I didn't expect the second half to pan out like the way it did, but to get the win, and the manner of being two goals down [makes it] very special, and it's a night that will live in the memory for a long time.

"The players have been magnificent. I've said all along that they've given me everything and they have. We've had a tough run of fixtures, but that's no excuse. When you play for this great club, you know that you've got to go away from home and give big performances and get results because our fans demand that.

"It's really important that we always go into every game and try to win. It was great to come back here tonight, to come home and get 40,000 Evertonians behind us, and that one's for them tonight."

Unsworth's prospects of succeeding Koeman permanently appeared remote before kick-off after three successive defeats, but he stressed he did not know if they would offer him the post considering the win, or if the board would look elsewhere for a new manager.

"Whatever will be, will be," Unsworth said. "I have been the proudest man in the world to take charge for the last two weeks, and no one can take that away from me.

"I know nothing about it. I'm sure I'll speak to the chairman and owner, and I'll keep giving my best for this wonderful club."

***

Unsworth's hopes of building on his first win were tested when, a day after the Watford match, Morgan Schneiderlin came out to reports he had been "sent away" from training on the preceding Saturday, as he reaffirmed his commitment to Everton.

The French international midfielder had been omitted from David Unsworth's squad for the Premier League fixture against Watford, three days after being sent off in Lyon for two bookable offences in the Blues' 3-0 defeat in the Europa League.

Speculation had been rife that both Schneiderlin and Kevin Mirallas, also left out of the team, either walked out of training on Saturday for failing to take it seriously or were told to leave by coach Duncan Ferguson if they couldn't knuckle down.

Schneiderlin, however, rejected the reports, posting a statement to social media that read: "I have seen press stories today about me 'being sent away from training'. The stories are not true. I am fully committed to Everton and will continue to work hard for the Club and the fans in training and on the pitch."

Mirallas also addressed the situation, albeit in rather more vague terms. The Belgian posted on Instagram thanking fans for all their messages to him.

"It's a difficult situation for me," his post read. "But in life there are things much more serious than my personal situation."

Mirallas, who had signed a new three-year contract earlier in the year but then angled for a move back to Olympiacos during the transfer window, had not featured for the team since being substituted at half-time at Leicester nine days previously.

---

1. Patrick Boyland: The Sportsman, November 2017

2017: Moshiri delighted to confirm Sam as manager

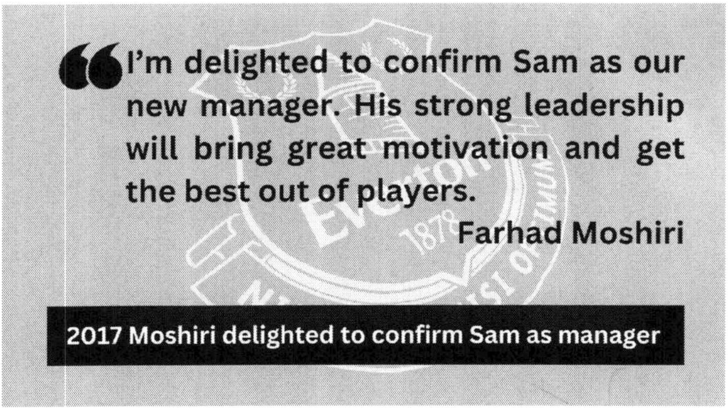

Three weeks on from the win over Watford, speculation was reaching fever pitch over who would replace Ronald Koeman. On the field, things had gone from bad to worse despite David Unsworth's best efforts. The dramatic victory over the Hornets had turned out to be a flash in the pan. A 2-2 draw away at Crystal Palace preceded a 5-1 Europa League thrashing by Atalanta at Goodison, which was followed by a heavy 4-1 away defeat at Southampton. With Everton humiliated in Europe and hovering just above the relegation zone, it looked increasingly unlikely that David Unsworth would be retained as caretaker manager for much longer.

***

29 November 2017: Everton v West Ham

The answer as to who would take the reins on a more permanent basis finally came on a bitterly cold day, when Everton were due to play a vital midweek Premier League fixture against West Ham at Goodison.

63-year-old Sam Allardyce had re-emerged as the front-runner, with a number of reliable media outlets all claiming the club had turned to the man who had built a reputation over the years for rescuing teams from relegation.

Once again, important club news was channelled through Jim White, while Everton took the unusual step of issuing a brief statement saying that Allardyce would travel to USM Finch Farm that afternoon to complete his deal.

White then passed on another message, purportedly from major shareholder Farhad Moshiri that read:

> "I really want to give [Allardyce] the support he needs. He can go as far as he wants. We need a strong leader, he gives us that."

Despite the 'official leak', stand-in manager David Unsworth took charge of the match against West Ham United, seemingly his last task in charge of first-team affairs before Allardyce would take over.

The reports claimed Allardyce had negotiated an 18-month deal on an annual salary of almost £6 million a year, and planned to bring in ex-Liverpool player Sammy Lee as his assistant. Craig Shakespeare, fired earlier this season as Leicester City's manager, would also join the backroom staff.

If Unsworth has sported the look of a harrowed man over the preceding few days, he left Goodison Park with a rueful smile, having left the post of caretaker manager with a thumping 4-0 win over the Hammers to savour.

Having lost 4-1 at Southampton just four days earlier, and seen his team fall apart in similar fashion against Atalanta the previous Thursday, the former defender knew it was only a matter of time before a permanent successor to Koeman appeared. He looked hurt in his pre-match press conference, and for stepping into the breach in hugely difficult circumstances, he fully deserved to leave his temporary post with a victory.

And how! One look at the Blues' recent form and a patched-up back four, featuring the much-maligned duo of Cuco Martina and Ashley Williams, as well as Mason Holgate, who only proved his fitness the previous night, suggested that confidence-sapped Everton might be in for a difficult evening. Instead, with controversial new hire Allardyce watching on from the Directors' Box, Wayne Rooney claimed a first hat-trick for his boyhood club in the most spectacular fashion and the home side kept its first clean sheet in the Premier League since the opening day of the season.

Despite the emphatic nature of the scoreline, it wasn't an entirely comfortable evening for a home crowd that was quiet and circumspect during an opening quarter of an hour. That the supporters could go home happy was also down to a vital penalty save from Jordan Pickford 13 minutes into the second half, and what was, apart from Jason Cresswell's shot that crashed off the face of the crossbar, a woeful attacking performance from West Ham on David Moyes's latest chastening return to Goodison. Rooney's world-class intervention eight minutes later, followed by atonement for Williams, merely confirmed that it was going to be the Toffees' night.

When viewed as a whole, this was not a great performance, but in the panic that had gripped the club after Sunday's defensive debacle at St Mary's Stadium, it was certainly good enough and there were some very encouraging individual performances.

With his years advancing, many observers had suggested that Rooney's best position could be in a deeper role than he occupied under Koeman and, finally, Unsworth took the much-called-for step of dispensing with two holding midfielders at home to accommodate the veteran in that more influential role.

Rooney responded by running the game from midfield, offering the industry and vision that has been sorely lacking from Morgan Schneiderlin while still chipping in with his customary striker's position for Everton's second goal after 28 minutes. His deployment as a roving "No.8" probably also left him perfectly positioned to score the third in spectacular fashion from inside his own half.

Rooney would get a deserved ovation when replaced by Beni Baningime with five minutes left on the clock, but in between Ashley

Williams scored Everton's fourth, a looping header from a corner after he had lost his marker.

And so to the impending transfer of managerial duties from the truest of Blues to the far less felicitous Allardyce, with the stabbing irony that this result confirmed what many had felt — that even hampered by injury to three more first-teamers, this Everton side was far better than performances and results had suggested this season. Indeed, several players had let Unsworth down badly since he assumed the helm six weeks earlier.

Unsworth may always regret that he wasn't able to draw better out of the team, and give the Board of Directors more time to avoid the panicked decision that had led them down the road to appointing the man sacked by England in disgrace.

It was just Sod's Law that the ink was probably still drying on Allardyce's contract as the Blues rattled in four goals, alleviated at a stroke the fear that had taken hold after their thrashing at the hands of Southampton, and removed much of the need for a relegation specialist at all. It left the Everton support having to back a manager that the vast majority didn't want, and the Board having to balance Allardyce's transfer needs in the upcoming January window with the longer-term needs of the Farhad Moshiri/Steve Walsh project, which had been on hold until the new man's hiring.

That would be an issue to wrestle with in the coming days. Rooney may have grabbed the headlines, but this had been "Rhino's" night.

Final score: Everton 4-0 West Ham

***

The day after the West Ham match, Everton 'officially' announced Sam Allardyce as their new manager, after he completed the formalities on a deal set to run until the end of 2018/19.

The arrangement represented a plain compromise between the two parties, with Allardyce agreeing to a shorter 18-month term than the three years he was reportedly after.

Everton, meanwhile, were paying him £6 million a year, a substantial increase on the £2.5 million annual salary he had been on at Crystal Palace.

Allardyce immediately called for unity and commitment from the squad following the Toffee's dreadful start to the season. "Let's try to get a healthy spirit around the club," he said. "I think that whatever's happened before we've just got to all rally around, because we are all in it together, and let's all pull in the same direction.

"We have to give the players every possibility to play to their best, really give them no excuses for not playing to their best, and get them right back up to the top level we believe they're capable of.

"Peter Reid is one of my best mates, so are Andy Gray and Paul Bracewell, whom I worked with at Sunderland. These people have always made me aware of just how special and unique a club Everton is, and I feel really enthused and energised to come in as manager."

Known as the man struggling clubs turned to steer them away from relegation, Allardyce was greeted by Everton fans with a mixture of displeasure and indifference. He was widely regarded as one-dimensional and unsophisticated. His arrival was seen by some as a sign of how far their grand old team had fallen.

Born and raised in Dudley in the West Midlands, Allardyce got his start in football as a player with Bolton Wanderers in the 1970s.

His first managerial assignment was also in the northwest with Blackpool before he moved to Notts County, the only club to that point where he had overseen relegation.

After joining Bolton, he led them to the Premier League and eventually into European competition via a sixth-place finish, but left in 2007. A stint at Newcastle followed, and he would go on to ensure the Premier League safety of Crystal Palace, West Ham, Sunderland and Blackburn Rovers before his arrival at Everton, cementing a reputation for always bringing stability and order to struggling teams headed for relegation from the top flight.

Though his achievements at Bolton remained the pinnacle of his managerial career, Allardyce's biggest appointment prior to the Everton job was that of England manager in 2017.

Hired to replace Roy Hodgson, it was an opportunity he hoped would allow him to dispel his image as a firefighter and manage at the top of the game. His spell lasted just one match, however, as the FA sacked him, following a sting by *The Telegraph* in which they recorded him apparently negotiating with an undercover reporter posing as a Far Eastern business executive looking to pay money for help in skirting FIFA's rules over third-party ownership of players.

Having rehabilitated his image somewhat at Crystal Palace, he elected to retire from the game when they parted company at the end of 2016/17. But he answered the call from Farhad Moshiri and the Everton Board in order to stabilise what had thus far been a chaotic 2017/18 season at Goodison.

***

2 December 2017: Everton v Huddersfield Town

Everton began Sam Allardyce's tenure with a second successive home win, as goals from Gylfi Sigurdsson and Dominic Calvert-Lewin were enough to see off Huddersfield Town.

Having adapted to the visitors' energetic pressing and found their own rhythm in the second half, the Blues pressed home their superiority with two goals in a match that was otherwise short on goalmouth action.

After watching Everton dismantle West Ham on Wednesday evening in David Unsworth's last game in charge, Allardyce elected to go with the same starting XI despite the availability of Oumar Niasse and Michael Keane.

That meant Calvert-Lewin played up front again, Wayne Rooney occupying the deeper-lying role in which he proved so effective against the Hammers, and Cuco Martina continuing to deputise for the injured Leighton Baines at left back.

And it was Martina who had the best chance of a physical first half, where opportunities were at a premium at both ends. The Curacao international benefited from strong hold-up play by Calvert-Lewin and hammered a right-foot shot that Jonas Lössl had to parry away with both hands.

At the other end, Laurent Depoitre came closest to breaking the Terriers' long goal drought away from home when the ball fell to him at a corner, but Jordan Pickford did enough to get a hand to it before the ball was hacked away to safety.

The second half was only a couple of minutes when Everton took the lead. Aaron Lennon's pass into the penalty area was flicked beautifully into the path of Sigurdsson by Calvert-Lewin and the Iceland international swept confidently home from a central position.

The Blues had increasingly got the measure of Huddersfield and when Idrissa Gueye won the ball in his own half and found Rooney, the veteran forward released Calvert-Lewin behind the visitors' defence with another pin-point pass. The striker bore down on Lössl's goal and profited from a slight deflection from the covering defender's lunging tackle that carried it over the 'keeper's arms into the net.

Tommy Smith had a deflected late effort saved by Pickford, but Huddersfield, who hadn't scored on their travels since the opening day, would not find a way past the Blues' back line, which kept its second clean sheet of the week.

The result lifted Everton into 10th place in the Premier League and moved them eight points clear of the bottom three.

Final score: Everton 2-0 Huddersfield

***

10 December 2017: Liverpool v Everton

Before the season started, many an Evertonian might have been eyeing this fixture as the one where the Blues would finally end their wait for a first derby victory at Anfield since 1999. Back in August, with £100 million on new players spent and the promise of more to come, 2017/18 felt like it could be the one where Everton could travel across Stanley Park as equals and with genuine prospects of winning.

15 League games and four months of the ruinous Ronald Koeman reign later and those expectations had been scaled down radically. Avoiding a Martinez-scale 4-0 humiliation was, perhaps, top of mind and if ever a performance needed to be viewed in its proper context, this was it.

In that context, the eventual reward of a point was important, because this was a horrible match to watch from the Blue perspective. The 79% of possession ceded to Liverpool was, apparently, a Premier League record at the time, which was not surprising.

Everton probably couldn't have given the ball away more if they had tried. Even Sam Allardyce, a manager given to direct, back-to-basics football, was critical afterwards of his side's inability to keep possession. And yet, the Blues escaped Anfield with a point, extended their unbeaten run to four games and took another step on the road to stability in a season that was spiralling into chaos just a fortnight ago.

That Allardyce fielded two strikers in Oumar Niasse and Dominic Calvert-Lewin, was a sign that his game plan was based on more than just defending. Unfortunately, the two spent so much time chasing wayward forward balls from Jordan Pickford that they could never get close enough to form any kind of partnership.

It meant that the ball kept coming back at Everton time after time, but two dogged banks of four bolstered by gritty performances from Mason Holgate and Jonjoe Kenny and the work rate of Idrissa Gueye meant it would take a special piece of individual play for Liverpool to get their noses in front by half time.

For all the crowing about Jurgen Klopp's attacking quartet — he had the hubris to leave two of the four, Philippe Coutinho and Roberto Firmino on the bench — they had really only threatened on one occasion prior to the 42nd minute when Mohamed Salah took matters into his own hands. He shoved Cuco Martina away from a challenge just inside the box, dribbled past Gueye and bent a shot around Pickford and inside the far post.

What should have been 2-0 and game over, came in first-half stoppage time. Sadio Mané easily side-stepped Ashley Williams as he committed himself to a sliding tackle he had no hope of winning, and raced into a four-on-one situation with just Martina and Pickford in front of him. But rather than squaring it for Salah, the Senegalese international went it alone and screwed his shot across goal and wide. Salah himself would also miss a gilt-edged chance on the other side of the break, when he headed narrowly wide with a free header from Milner's cross.

Allardyce withdrew Niasse at half time in favour or Aaron Lennon — the winger with his industry was a positive addition — and Calvert-Lewin remained on the field to provide the outlet that eventually won Everton only their second penalty at Anfield in 80 years.

In between, it was something akin to a training-ground exercise of attack-versus-defence; it was one-way traffic towards the Everton goal, but apart from an overhead kick from Mané, Pickford had nothing to do. That established the platform from which Everton could remain in the game, until it entered the final quarter of an hour, when they went in search of the equaliser.

Rooney raked a ball over the top for Calvert-Lewin, who knocked it on into the Liverpool box with his thigh with Dejan Lovren on the chase. The defender ended up shoving the striker in the back and, seeming to contact his right leg, sent him crashing to the turf and prompting referee Craig Pawson to point to the spot.

Rooney smashed the resulting penalty straight down the middle with Mignolet diving in vain to his left and it was 1-1.

While no one in Blue would have enjoyed the performance, it yielded a satisfying result, particularly given how worked up Klopp and Lovren were at the final whistle.

The point ensured a share of the spoils, avoided another painful derby defeat and kept Everton in 10th place with two games against teams below them up next. And all the while, Allardyce and his team were learning about the players they had inherited, and what they needed to do when the winter transfer window opened. It would be interesting to see how things looked by the end of January.

Final score: Liverpool 1-1 Everton

***

After the game, Sam Allardyce spoke of the positives, from what he saw as an impressive defensive display that saw Everton withstand Liverpool's dominance in possession, to grind out a point.

"It was a huge point," Allardyce said, "because we didn't create much in possession of the ball today, which was very frustrating [given] the quality of the players we have."

2018 Allardyce and Walsh sign Tosun to replace Lukaku

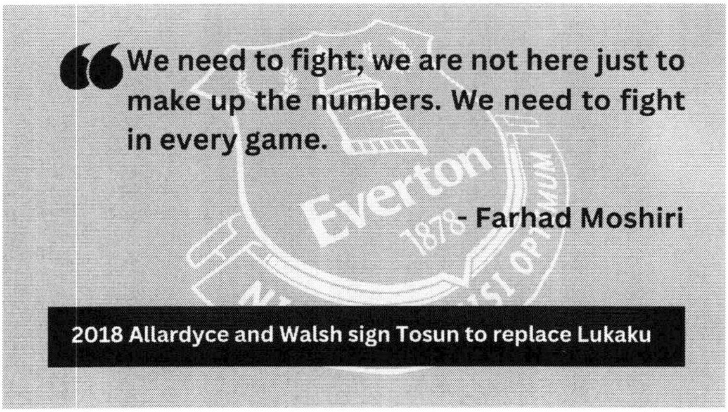

As Christmas 2017 approached, Everton announced record turnover and a post-tax profit of £30 million for the 2016/17 year. The club's turnover topped £171 million, almost £50 million more than the previous record set two seasons prior, thanks largely again to the Premier League broadcast revenue bonanza.

With such financial power seemingly at the club's disposal, the fans were optimistic about filling a Romelu Lukaku shaped gap in the first team. The Belgian had been sold to Manchester United over the summer but had not been adequately replaced.

The Turkish striker, Cenk Tosun, was rumoured to be on Everton's radar, but apparently his move to Everton hung in the balance as rival clubs looked to swoop. Everton sent Steve Walsh and a delegation to meet face-to-face with Besiktas officials to land the Turk ahead of competition from Europe.

"It's in the wind," Blues boss Sam Allardyce said of the Tosun transfer when asked if he could confirm the speculation. "There's obviously an interest because we're actively looking for a front man, but whether we are the ones to complete that deal or not, I don't know. The interest from other clubs around Europe is our biggest worry if we are to secure that transfer."

Ultimately, Everton were successful in signing Tosun in a £21 million deal. Tosun finally completed his move on 5 January.

Allardyce then turned his attention to trying to sign midfielder Steven N'Zonzi from Sevilla, a player with whom Allardyce had worked during his Blackburn Rovers days and was keen to link up with him again, but the attempt proved unsuccessful.

***

On 9 January 2018, Everton's major shareholder and de facto owner, Farhad Moshiri spoke of his confidence that the club were making significant progress on what he saw as a long road to getting the Blues back to their place among the elite of the English game.

Speaking in a rare video interview at Finch Farm, the Iranian-born billionaire shared his thoughts on the recent setbacks to his vision for Everton created by the team's unexpectedly poor start to the season and his determination to deliver a new stadium at Bramley-Moore Dock, the new cost projection for which was £500 million.

The interview on evertonfc.com was released against the backdrop of that evening's Annual General Meeting of Shareholders at the Liverpool Philharmonic Hall.

Moshiri talked about having a plan that would take several years to fully execute and one which began with investment in the playing staff and the infrastructure that supports it.

He cited the new sponsorship deal with USM at Finch Farm, the sleeve sponsorship agreement with Rovio for Angry Birds, and suggested that more arrangements along those lines were in the pipeline.

> "We have invested quite heavily in infrastructure. What you see is the visible part — buying — but there is an awful lot going on behind the scenes to make success sustainable. The commercial side is developing really well. There are a lot of other sponsorships which are coming in. On the stadium we have [also] made great progress. We have to have a [new] stadium and we will have a stadium. When the building work starts, that will be the proof of the pudding so we want to get to that stage. But until we get to that, we are in the preparation stage but we are progressing well. We have secured the land which is the most essential [part], we've picked the [site] that we think the fans would prefer. It's an iconic thing, something that Everton needs," Moshiri continued, perhaps hinting at a desire to unveil a ground superior to Anfield, "to

> have a better stadium — and that's what we have to do. I think the first part of the exercise is to make the team competitive so that the owner, the Board, the fans and the employees can be proud of the team," he said. "We need to fight; we are not here just to make up the numbers. We need to fight in every game – Farhad Moshiri, Everton AGM, 9 January 2017

***

A week after the AGM, striker Theo Walcott completed his move from Arsenal to Everton in a reported £20 million deal, becoming the Blues' second signing of that transfer window.

The 28-year-old had followed Turkish striker Cenk Tosun through the door as manager, Sam Allardyce, and director of football, Steve Walsh, looked to strengthen a forward line that had struggled to put shots on target let alone score goals in recent matches.

Everton had beaten off competition from Walcott's former club Southampton, by securing the England international's signature on a 3½-year contract and taking their spending for January past the £40 million mark. Walcott would wear the No.11 jersey vacated by Kevin Mirallas, who had joined Olympiakos on loan in the same month.

Walcott had made his name at Arsenal where he had 270 Premier League appearances, scoring 65 goals and providing 43 assists.

Despite scoring 19 goals in all competitions for the Gunners in 2016/17, Walcott had become a peripheral figure at the Emirates Stadium and hadn't started a Premier League game under Arsène Wenger for nine months.

Walcott no doubt viewed his move to Goodison Park as a fresh start where he could put himself back into the mind of England manager Gareth Southgate ahead of the upcoming World Cup in Russia, having missed the cut for Euro 2016.

"I've come to Everton because I'm very ambitious and I want the club to push to the next level," Walcott said upon signing. "I'm very excited to be starting a new chapter and felt this was the right place for me to be.

"The fact there's a new stadium going to be developing in the next few years, it's exciting times for Everton Football Club.

"I'm dead excited and I just want to do what I do best, which is playing football and expressing myself because I'm excited again. I really am.

"I do really believe that I'm going to give it my all, which is what I always have done, and this place is going to get even more out of me.

"There's something about this move which I've just felt good about."

Evertonians were keen to see whether the new strike force of Tosun and Walcott would revitalise the team's goal threat.

2018: EVERTON BOTTOM OF SHOTS ON GOAL TABLE

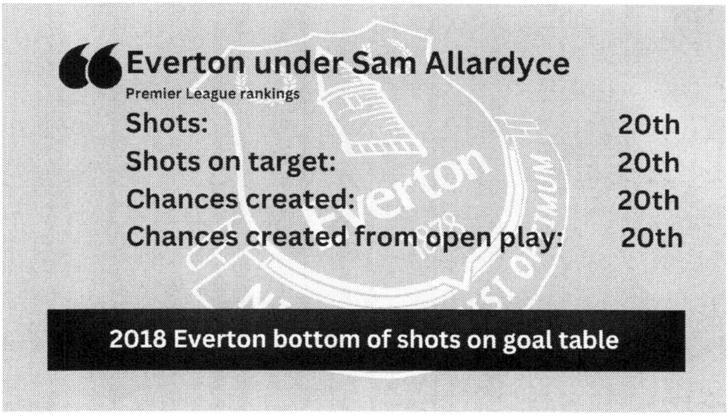

The final games of 2017 were a mixed bag for Sam Allardyce and Everton, with wins against Newcastle and Swansea, draws against Chelsea and West Brom, and an away defeat at Bournemouth.

With everything crossed for a happy New Year, the match at Goodison on New Year's day turned out to be a disappointment, with a 2-0 defeat against Man United.

Next up was an away tie at Anfield in the third round of the FA Cup, for which the expectations were low, given the Blues abysmal record at Anfield this century. That proved prescient because, for the second season running, the Toffees' FA Cup road would come to an end almost as soon as it had begun, as Everton succumbed to a 2-1 defeat.

***

13 January, 2018: Tottenham Hotspur v Everton

What happened at Wembley on this mid-January fixture was not, in theory, supposed to happen anymore after Sam Allardyce was appointed as Everton boss. The Premier League's famed "fire-fighter" had been employed to whip together a sorry bunch who had, thanks to the flawed leadership and inadequate recruitment of his predecessor, plunged into the bottom three and destroyed all the pre-season optimism generated by an unprecedented spending spree.

He was expected to shore up the defence, make the Blues hard to beat, and slowly instil in the players a confidence that they could take on anyone in the top flight and get a result. And yet, Evertonians were sat staring at another after a 4-0 drubbing – the fourth successive defeat – and with the team conceding at a rate of 2½ goals a game. Allardyce's unique selling point, defensive solidity and backs-to-the-wall defiance, has gone up in smoke since Boxing Day. It left Blues fans wondering: so what now?

Allardyce had made a decent start, going seven games unbeaten in all competitions and steering the Toffees to the comfort of ninth place in the Premier League table. However, successive defeats to Bournemouth, Manchester United and Liverpool in the FA Cup Third Round had seen Everton begin to revert to type with worsening attacking metrics that would eventually be the worst in the top flight.

This, against Spurs in their temporary home at the national stadium, was an utterly miserable performance, one only briefly lifted above the turgid and the hapless by a fleeting moment here and there early on by debutant Cenk Tosun and the brief, quickly extinguished, elation at a Wayne Rooney goal chalked off for offside.

Beyond that, there were almost no redeeming facets save the continued shot-stopping form of Jordan Pickford... that is when he wasn't left completely exposed by a flat-footed or simply non-existent back line.

Everton finished the contest having failed to register a shot on target for the third Premier League game in the previous five, and undergoing a collapse in the second half that echoed the nadirs of the Roberto Martinez and Ronald Koeman regimes.

To hear Allardyce speak afterwards of having to now make his side more boring and less adventurous afterwards beggared belief for Evertonians. The manager talked as if their maverick spirit had been punished as they poured forward in attack when, in fact, the Blues did precious little by way of getting forward beyond sending missiles forward from the boot of Jordan Pickford, aimed in the general direction of Tosun's head.

The Turk was as isolated as his predecessors in the role before he was withdrawn in the second half — proof, as if it were needed, that you can't just throw a striker into this team and expect all the problems going forward to melt away.

And for all Allardyce's renowned defensive bent, Tottenham picked their way through a system supposedly bolstered by twin defensive midfielders and around the fullbacks with ease.

The deluge began in the 26th minute as Serge Aurier took advantage of an ocean of space on Everton's left flank and drove a hard and low ball into the 6-yard box where Son Heung-min simply side-footed home from close range.

Tottenham's second was almost a mirror image of the first although this time the freedom of the flank afforded Son came from Jonjoe Kenny's inexperience as the South Korean expertly rolled him, leaving him for dead. Kane was offside when the ball was delivered to him but the defending in the middle was just as lax, with the striker easily able to steal between Jagielka and Martina.

Kane plundered a second as blue jerseys ambled about and Eric Dier then simply passed the ball into the 6-yard box again behind the static Mason Holgate and Jagielka to toe it over Pickford.

And Christian Eriksen, the like of which Everton so desperately need in attacking midfield, finished off the rout at the end of an impressive Spurs move when he swept home Dele Alli's flick.

It could have been worse. Pickford made a number of stops to deny Kane, Aurier, Kane and Son. Son also rattled the post in the second half prior to the third goal while the Blues offered nothing going the other way.

Final score: Tottenham 4-0 Everton

***

Later in January 2018, events that would have ramifications for both Everton and Sam Allardyce were playing out in Hertfordshire when Watford sacked Marco Silva as their manager on 21 January, citing

Everton's approach for the Portuguese manager the previous November, as the "catalyst for this decision".

Silva had been top choice of the Blues' hierarchy to succeed Ronald Koeman, following the Ronald Koeman's dismissal in October, but Watford had rebuffed Everton's attempts to prise him away, even after the Goodison side reportedly offered £10 million in compensation for Silva's services.

Watford fans were critical of Silva's rhetoric at the time, where he appeared reluctant to state his unreserved commitment to seeing out his contract at Vicarage Road in the midsts of reports he wanted to take the Everton job.

A statement from the Hornets said: "The Club is convinced the appointment of Silva was the right one, and had it not been for the unwarranted approach by a Premier League rival for his services, we would have continued to prosper under his leadership.

"This has been a difficult decision and one not taken lightly. The catalyst is that approach, something which the board believes has seen a significant deterioration in both focus and results to the point where the long-term future of Watford has been jeopardised."

Watford had hired Silva on the back of his impressive spell at Hull City, where he gave the doomed Yorkshire club a fighting chance of staying in the top flight with a string of home wins. He looked to be adding to his burgeoning reputation in 2017/18 and had overseen a flying start to the campaign, but after beating Newcastle 3-0 in late November, the Hornets won just once more in 11 Premier League games.

Neither Watford's faltering form nor the controversial circumstances behind Silva's form would deter Farhad Moshiri who remained determined to bring the promising young coach to Everton,

***

31 January 2018: Everton v Leicester City

The humiliation at the hands of Spurs was followed by a 1-1 home draw against West Bromwich Albion, with the Blues' saviour that day turning out to be none other than Oumar Niasse, who had survived Koeman's reign and had popped up with a 70th-minute equaliser after Jay Rodriguez had netted for the Baggies in the seventh minute.

In search of their first win of 2018, Everton faced Leicester City at Goodison at the end of January.

Allardyce made six alterations to the starting XI that started against West Brom but they appeared to have little effect on the performance in the early stages, with Everton lacking in both cohesion and direction, and overly reliant on high and direct balls aimed at Niasse up front. They managed a rare shot on target early on when new signing Theo Walcott forced Kasper Schmeichel to push a bouncing shot wide, but the tale of the first quarter of the contest was one of the home side's weakness defending set-pieces.

Everton settled, however, and when Cuco Martina pressured Ben Chilwell and the ball broke to Gylfi Sigurdsson wide on the right, the Icelandic international cut it back to meet the run of Walcott who tucked a first-time shot inside the post to make it 1-0 with 24 minutes gone.

Walcott led the way again six minutes before the interval. Michael Keane contested for Rooney's flighted ball into the box and his looping header fell invitingly for the former Arsenal forward, who volleyed it back across Schmeichel and into the far corner.

2-nil and the the Blues were flying, but their momentum did not carry through to the second half, which became a much more even affair, even if the Blues were still carrying the greater attacking threat.

Jamie Vardy scored from the spot for Leicester in the 71st minute, which led to an inevitably nervy conclusion as the home side threatened to fall to pieces under renewed pressure from the visitors. The woodwork saved them in the 77th minute, however, as substitute Kalechi Iheanacho watched a deflected effort bounce off the bar before he rapped the rebound off the post.

Everton's back line threatened to buckle again when Martina had to hack the ball out of the goalmouth to safety and Pickford flapped badly at successive crosses towards his six-yard box but escaped when Jamie Vardy curled well wide of his goal.

Everton eventually saw the game out to collect three vital points that moved them eight points clear of the relegation zone, and just three wins shy of the 40-point mark that usually guarantees safety.

Final score: Everton 2-1 Leicester

***

Just three days after that morale-boosting win over the Foxes, the Blues suffered a humiliating but all-too-familiar reverse at The Emirates

Stadium, losing 5-1 to Arsenal in what was Sam Allardyce's second defeat by four goals in North London in less than a month.

The manager was scathing of his team's inconsistency and what he described as a "pathetic" first-half display.

Aaron Ramsey scored a hat-trick and there was a goal, allowed despite a clear offside, for Gunners debutant Pierre-Emerick Aubameyang as Arsene Wenger's side racked up five goals against the Toffees for the second time that season.

Dominic Calvert-Lewin came off the bench to score a consolation goal to make it 4-1 as Everton improved after introducing Tom Davies for the hapless Michael Keane at the interval, but Arsenal's fifth underlined the paucity of the visitors' defending.

Allardyce, who vowed that the defensive capitulation he witnessed against Tottenham last month couldn't happen again, watched on from sidelines as his defence opened up again for Ramsey to complete his treble. He expressed his anger and "bitter disappointment" to evertontv after the match and suggested that the performance made it look as though he and his staff were not doing their job properly.

"The first half was a disaster," Allardyce told the cameras. "I have a lot of trouble with the players [not] taking onto the pitch what we actually asked them to do.

"That is a big worry for me. I have to say, the longer I go on, the players are showing so much inconsistency that I have to face the uphill battle of trying to get them to be more consistent and to perform at their best level, week in and week out.

"It's no good playing okay in the second half, getting the goal and trying to make the score look respectable. It's far too late. It's just a pathetic first-half performance.

"At the end of the day, I can pick as many systems as I want to pick, but if a player plays like they did today — and I'm talking about all 11 in the first half — then you've really got no chance. Tactics and systems mean absolutely nothing."

***

17 March 2018: Everton v Stoke

Performances throughout February and March resembled a yo-yo. There was a 3-1 home win against Crystal Palace, consecutive away defeats against Watford and Burnley, and a 2-0 home win against Brighton. The Blues were typically winning at home, but losing away. The away match at Stoke provided an opportunity to break that pattern.

With Gylfi Sigurdsson injured, it forced Sam Allardyce to change things in midfield where he brought Idrissa Gueye back into the side after he missed the win over Brighton through illness. The Senegalese international slotted in defensive midfield alongside Wayne Rooney, with Tom Davies given license to push forward between wingers Yannick Bolasie and Theo Walcott.

Everton struggled to get going in a dreadful first half that was not aided by periodic spells of heavy snow that settled over two-thirds of the pitch. Poor distribution from the back and a general lack of cohesion in attack meant that, not for the first time this season, they failed to register a shot on target before half time.

Stoke, who came into the match sitting in the bottom three, weren't much better, although they tested Jordan Pickford with a couple of efforts from distance, one from Peter Crouch that the 'keeper spilled before gathering at the second attempt.

Some in the Potters' ranks had declared this game as their "cup final" in their bid to beat the drop, but Charlie Adam critically undermined their cause with half an hour gone. The Scot lunged into a late tackle on Rooney midway inside the Everton half that caught the Blues' midfielder on the ankle and referee Martin Atkinson had little hesitation in brandishing a red card.

The visitors made little headway in making the numerical advantage tell, however, until there were a little over 20 minutes to go. Yannick Bolasie whipped in a cross from the right onto which Cenk Tosun got the merest of glances. Butland could only parry it to Dominic Calvert-Lewin, but Konstantinos Stafylidis stopped it on the line. Tosun was on hand to tap the loose ball home, however, scoring what should have been the decisive goal.

The Blues, however, came undone in familiar circumstances from a set-piece. Gueye pulled back his man, and when Joe Allen dropped the resulting dead-ball delivery into the space between Pickford and his back line, Maxim Choupo-Moting stole in to plunder the equaliser.

Everton wrestled the initiative back, though, with Tosun himself scoring the winner with his fourth goal in three games. This time, Theo Walcott was the provider with a cross from the right and Tosun stooped in ahead of Ryan Shawcross to power the ball into the corner.

The victory, Everton's first on their travels in three months, finally lifted Allardyce's side to the "magic" 40-point mark. Though the performance left much to be desired — even allowing for the conditions, which veered from bright sunshine to near blizzard, the manager's only concern was those three points, and the end of a run of six games without an away win in all competitions.

Final score: Stoke 1-2 Everton

***

Though Ronald Koeman had paid for his own failings as head coach of Everton's first team, the club's first Director of Football Steve Walsh had continued in his post following the Dutchman's dismissal and the appointment of Sam Allardyce.

Walsh had faced criticism, however, for the club's recruitment policy over the preceding 20 months and there was growing speculation by the spring of 2018 that he would be moved aside in favour of PSV Eindhoven's highly regarded technical director, Marcel Brands. Sky Sports were claiming from their sources that Brands, would become the Blues' latest appointment once the Dutch side were confirmed as Eredivisie champions.

Speculation concerning Allardyce's future at the club was also growing. The Dudleyite had faced routine questions about his standing at the club in the preceding weeks, amid the increasing clamour among Everton fans for him to be moved on in the summer now he had fulfilled his initial remit of keeping the Blues away from relegation danger.

He insisted he had received the clarity he sought over his future from the club's major shareholder, Farhad Moshiri, after a meeting in London but in the wake of further questions following a poor performance against Southampton in the penultimate match of the season, Allardyce admitted that he would have benefitted from public backing.

"It would have helped, yes," the 63-year-old said, "but I can't control the board, I can't control what they say.

"They are my bosses, so I can't be dictating and telling them what they should or should not do, obviously, but that has fuelled more speculation. I think results speak for themselves personally.

"You know, at the end of the day it is where it is."

Moshiri had spoken about Allardyce in glowing terms around the time of the Annual General Meeting in January, but the naturally media-shy Monaco-based businessman had said little publicly on any topic since.

The length of his initial contract suggested that Moshiri and the Everton board might have had a short-term time horizon when they hired the Premier League's renowned 'firefighter', and there had been plenty of media speculation that the Blues would move to replace Allardyce with a longer-term candidate capable of rebuilding and reshaping the team over the next few years.

Marco Silva, the man originally targeted to succeed Koeman in the autumn of 2017 before Watford refused to let him go, remained the subject of newspaper chatter, as did his compatriot Paulo Fonseca, whom Everton had also approached. Other more up-and-coming managers also cropped up in the various press stories, including the likes of Mikel Arteta and Patrick Vieira.

Former Everton players were weighing in with their opinions too.

Toffees favourite, Tim Cahill had expressed his dismay at the club's loss of identity in recent years. The Australian international became a linchpin of the team built by David Moyes, one that routinely punched above its weight in the Premier League and enjoyed forays into European competition thanks to a renowned team spirit.

Everton and Moyes battled for years on a shoestring budget while Bill Kenwright continued his stated search for a billionaire to transform the club's fortunes and to enable them to compete with the increasing riches in the old top four.

Farhad Moshiri's enormous spending had not yet propelled the club back among the top flight's elite, and the chaos that had unfolded at Goodison Park, with the sacking of Koeman and the controversial appointment of Allardyce had left Everton looking unrecognisable from Cahill's time with the Toffees.

"It's confusing. They are confused too," Cahill said on *Goals On Sunday*. "They have lost their identity as a club. There is nothing they are really building around.

"Before, there was a basis and a group of players that was built and we were adding to it and looking for the long-term plan of how to evolve as a football club.

"Now it seems like they are just making signings and the chemistry is not there, and on the pitch they are not linking well.

"It's difficult to watch because of the quality. You have to be careful what you wish for. If you want an owner with lots of money, they have that, but it doesn't always bring success overnight.

"The fans want some passion and identity. When you look back at Roberto Martinez, for example, maybe it was impatient and waiting for that style, and under David Moyes maybe they thought it was getting stale, but now you can appreciate what they have lost."

Interviewed on *Sky Sports,* former Blues forward, Kevin Campbell predicted Sam Allardyce would never gain the full support of Everton fans.

"I think Sam Allardyce has done the job he's meant to do by coming in and solidifying the club," Campbell said. "But taking it forward, I don't think the fans really take to him. I don't think they ever will and I think there's going to be a change in the summer because Everton are a year behind in their game plan.

"They really need to get somebody in there, get the plan in place and get that recruitment drive going. It might take some drastic measures to rip things up, but if that's what has to happen, that has to happen."

***

13 May 2018: West Ham v Everton

Sitting in a reasonably comfortable ninth position, after the win at Stoke, Everton lost their next home game to Manchester City, and then ground out a 0-0 against Liverpool, also at Goodison Park. Two more draws, this time at Swansea and Southampton bookended wins over Newcastle and Huddersfield which left the Blues sitting in eighth place heading into the final match of the 2017/18 at West Ham's London Stadium.

Before this match, David Moyes' reunions with the club where he spent 11 reputation-building years had been exercises in defeat. Beaten home and away as manager of Manchester United four seasons prior, the Scot had the same treatment meted out to him as manager of Sunderland in 2016/17 season and received his heaviest defeat against

Everton in November 2017 when the Blues romped to a 4-0 win under David Unsworth.

Add to that the fact that in the Premier League era, West Ham were Everton's favourite opponents; throw in a meaningless end-of-season game and you had the ingredients for an occasion where even Sam Allardyce could throw caution to the wind and go for it a bit.

The much-maligned manager did finally experiment with two strikers, although their lack of experience playing together, coupled with West Ham's first-half dominance and Everton's crippling lack of creativity meant that they weren't able to link up like a genuine strike partnership at any stage. Allardyce largely nullified any nod towards attacking adventure by deploying three centre-halves and two holding midfielders. And, if the intent was to release Leighton Baines and Seamus Coleman to conduct raids down the flanks, it didn't work.

The result was a performance that mostly made the Hammers, who began the day in 15th place, look a significantly better team than their record and recently-averted crisis suggested they were and, eventually, resulted in a defeat that may have seemed harsh when comparing chances created but which was wholly deserved on the balance of play.

Indeed, in the first period in particular, all the "joined up" football was coming from the home team, with the visitors reliant on direct balls forward and attempted penetrating passes from deep. West Ham were next to bottom when Allardyce came on board at Goodison and while he had spent the previous few months moaning that his team couldn't play with style because of the players at his disposal, Moyes simply got on with the job of getting his side playing some pretty decent football.

The Hammers were moving the ball around crisply in midfield, but after Oumar Niasse robbed Angelo Ogbonna and was denied by Adrian in the hosts' goal, Mario Lanzini capitalised on embarrassing defending by Everton to give West Ham the lead. An innocuous-looking pass from Cheikhou Kouyaté deceived Keane as it eluded the toe of Arnautovic, and Lanzini, who had started the move near the halfway line, continued his run between two blue shirts to pick up the loose ball and slot it home.

Allardyce responded at half time by withdrawing Ramiro Funes Mori, who had done nothing to suggest he has been hard done-by being excluded from the starting XI since he regained his fitness, and introducing Davy Klaassen into a midfield that now boasted four central midfielders and no width.

It resulted in more possession for Everton but precious little service to the strikers or threats to the Hammers' goal, apart from a tame effort from Klaassen from around 20 yards out, that Adrian claimed easily. Instead of taking one midfielder off and going for a more attacking formation, Allardyce stuck to type, and hooked Cenk Tosun when it came time to throw Theo Walcott on, much to the Turk's visible disgust.

Blues fans probably matched his fury; as a decision, it made no sense under the circumstances. Two minutes later, it was 2-0 from a goal largely out of nothing. Picking up a pass in a benign area outside the Everton box, Arnautovic simply rolled Keane, who was too tight and too slow to recover and smashed a shot practically through Pickford's gloves from 25 yards. The replays weren't kind to the young goalkeeper who appeared to crouch, expecting the ball to dip towards the ground before it lifted slightly at the end, and flew past him.

Niasse gave Everton hope 11 minutes later, showing some deft control and an emphatic finish to make it 2-1 from a corner, but Moyes' men restored their two-goal advantage and effectively sealed the game eight minutes later.

Lanzini was the marksman again, profiting from the yard or two's space afforded him by Seamus Coleman at the corner of the area and curling a shot towards the top right corner. Pickford went for it with his opposite hand and got fingers to it, but could only guide it onto the post and in.

It had been a disappointing end to a poor season.

Final score: West Ham 3-1 Everton

***

In fact, it had been an awful season, forgettable in almost every way except for the stain it would leave on the Blues' Premier League era.

The threat of the drop, if it existed with 24 matches left in the campaign, was largely extinguished fairly soon after Allardyce arrived. It was hard to believe there had been 12 teams worse than Everton, the paucity of quality in the top-flight rendering a finish as high as eighth flattering in the extreme.

The interim had seen a frustrating succession of dull performances, moribund football, lifeless defeats to the teams that finished above them, and a near constant yearning for 2017/18 to be over.

Now that the season was done, supporters hoped the club's hierarchy would make their key decisions – starting with the removal of the manager – that would ensure that the next season would be nothing like what had just transpired. As a fanbase, patience was being replaced by apathy, but it was not irretrievable. Another big summer was on the cards, but only if those in the corridors of power were ready to take the bull by the horns and steer it in the right direction.

2018: Sam Allardyce sacked

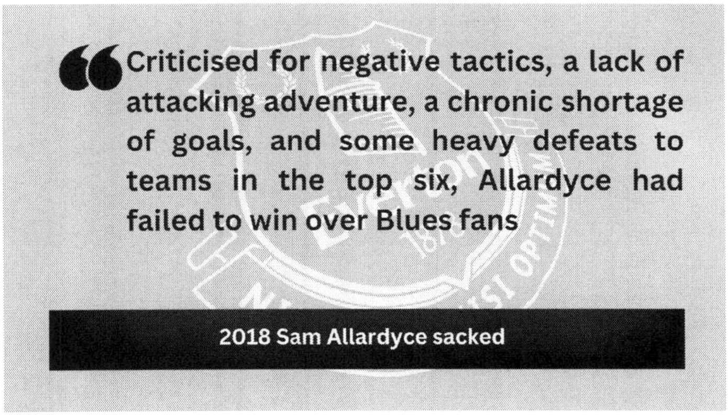

Just 24 hours after the final fixture of the 2017/18 season against West Ham, Sam Allardyce's tenure as Everton manager was over, amid reports the club would relieve him of his duties within the next 48 hours.

The Dudleyite met with major shareholder Farhad Moshiri, when he was, as expected, told they would not keep him beyond the end of the current season.

Allardyce had guided Everton into the top half of the table and to within six points of Champions League-chasing Tottenham by mid-December, but could not sustain a consistent run of form to mount a challenge for Europe. The Toffees eventually clung on to eighth place despite losing that season finale to the Hammers.

Criticised for negative tactics, a lack of attacking adventure, a chronic shortage of goals, and some heavy defeats to teams in the top six, Allardyce had failed to win over Blues fans, and was the subject of increasingly vocal chants from the stands calling for his dismissal over the final weeks of the season. That, combined with a desire on Moshiri's part to kick start his stalled project with a fresh appointment, had led to the decision to cut ties.

Marco Silva remained the favourite to take the Everton managerial reins, although media reports suggested that his appointment would not be entirely straightforward, with the Portuguese still in a legal dispute with Watford over £750,000, he felt they owed him because of his premature dismissal from the Hertfordshire club in January.

It was also thought the Hornets Board could still pursue legal action against Everton, if they hired Silva, for what they deemed an illegal approach for him last November; that despite reports that the Blues had offered Watford upwards of £10 million to part with him.

With three managerial sackings under his belt in two seasons, the focus was once again on Farhad Moshiri. What would he do next, and would his next managerial appointment get the Blues back on track? But before that decision would be made, other senior changes were afoot.

2018: Brands in. Walsh out

> “Marcel’s record of achievement has cemented his reputation across Europe and I am extremely pleased that we will be bringing his drive, energy and expertise to Everton.
>
> - Farhad Moshiri

2018 Brands in. Walsh out

One day after Sam Allardyce departed, Everton confirmed Marcel Brands as the club’s new director of football from PSV Eindhoven.

The 56-year-old Dutchman signed a three-year contract after turning down improved terms in Eindhoven in favour a fresh challenge on Merseyside.

Brands, who had formed a vital part of the team management setup at PSV that had overseen three Eredvisie titles in the previous four years, replaced Steve Walsh, who would leave the club after nearly two years rather than accept a chief scout role.

It represented a successful pursuit of the Dutchman by Farhad Moshiri, who first identified Brands as a target when he was looking to appoint Everton's first director of football two years earlier.

"At that moment I had already given my word to PSV, and I did not want to leave," Brands said of the Toffees' first approach in 2016. This time, having helped deliver another Dutch title for PSV, he felt the time was right.

"The Premier League is, of course, a great thing," Brands said on PSV's official website. "It is the biggest competition in the world in all respects. I now get the chance to do something in my own way. I am really looking forward to that."

Moshiri welcomed Brands to Everton on the club's official website, and expressed his pleasure at having landed a long-time target:

> "Marcel's record of achievement has cemented his reputation across Europe, and I am extremely pleased that we will be bringing his drive, energy and expertise to Everton. It was clear to me in our conversations that he shares in the vision we have for the club and he has much to contribute in making us better and more equipped to challenge the top teams in the Premier League."

Born in 's-Hertogenbosch in the Netherlands, Brands had an unremarkable career as a player, spending the bulk of it at RKC Waalwijk while also spending two seasons with Feyenoord.

It was as a sporting and technical director that he really made his name in Dutch football, however, first at Waalwijk and then at AZ

Alkmaar, where he worked under future Holland and Manchester United boss, Louis van Gaal.

In five years there, he helped transform the fortunes of the club as AZ won the Eredivisie in 2009, breaking the dominance of the traditional "big three" of Ajax, PSV and Feyenoord, and reaching the last eight of the Europa League.

He joined PSV as their technical director in 2010 and had developed what observers describe as an immense reputation for spotting playing talent and working the transfer market.

"It is a privilege to be joining Everton as Director of Football and I am incredibly excited to take on this challenge," Brands said on evertonfc.com. This is a great club — footballing royalty – with the best, most committed fans, and I can assure every single Evertonian that I am completely committed to driving our club forward and making the most of the opportunities that we have.

"I know what the priorities are and I'm determined that we make progress in these areas. It's also important to me that we make our progress in the right way – in the 'Everton way' – and this includes listening, consulting and collaborating on all important club matters.

"The fantastic passion of the fans for their club, the magnificent history of the club over the years and the ambition and purpose we have as people tasked with driving the blub forward all mean that we need to be competing for honours against the Premier League elite.

"It is no straightforward challenge, but this must be our motivation each and every day.

"It is only a challenge such as this which could have persuaded me to leave PSV where I am indebted to the many people whose collective effort led to some great achievements.

"Now we will look to build something really strong and lasting here at Everton."

It was also announced that Steve Walsh had stepped down as Director of Football after almost two years in the post

After first being approached by Everton two summers previously, when Walsh was eventually brought on board to become the Blues' first DoF, Brands replaced the former Leicester City scout to embark on what could become a career-defining project if he succeeds.

Incoming CEO, Professor Denise Barrett-Baxendale, said in a statement on the club's official website:

"I'm very much looking forward to working closely with Marcel, whose experience in the areas of player recruitment and development pathways for young players has forged an outstanding reputation in European football. I know that Marcel will bring an unsurpassed level of quality and prowess to his work at Everton.

"Chief among my priorities, is to structure and resource our club to enable us to fully achieve our ambitions. We will work alongside Marcel on the recruitment of a new manager, which is now our biggest focus."

"On behalf of the Board and Mr Moshiri, I'd like to express our thanks to Steve Walsh, our first ever Director of Football, who has now left the club. We all wish Steve well for his future."

***

Winding the clock forward to January 2019, Marcel Brands was appointed to Everton's Board of Directors and handed broader powers covering all aspects of the playing side at the club.

Everton's newest Board member spoke on stage at the club's Annual General Meeting at the Philharmonic Hall in Liverpool on 8 January with Master of Ceremonies Darren Griffiths, where he described how the club has exceeded his expectations so far.

"I hope to do the best things for our football club," Brands said. "To be honest, the club is more than I expected. I was working in a great club in Holland and was happy there, but I had a very good feeling about Everton from the start and that became even better when I started here. So many people have blue blood here."

Brands' promotion was one of several issues touched on during the meeting and, naturally, the executives discussed the proposed new stadium at Bramley-Moore Dock.

"Everton is transitioning through one of the most important periods in the club's history," CEO Professor Denise Barrett-Baxendale stated.

"I am aware of our long and complicated history in delivering a new stadium. We have several funding opportunities available [for the project]."

The club's recently-appointed deputy chairman, Keith Harris, talked further about what he described as a "real cracking opportunity" for Everton, saying that the goal was to build "a stadium everyone can be proud of" and "recreate the history and rich traditions" of Goodison Park.

"We are having very advanced discussions now with financial institutions which are encouraging. The money will be available. The money will be available for us to do this. Most of our raw materials will be imported.

"We cannot promise an end date because we haven't broken ground. We are hoping to put a spade in the ground next year and it would be wonderful to do it in two years, but we certainly should do it in three and it will be a wonderful stadium."

Meanwhile, Director of Finance, Sasha Ryzantsev, said that the majority shareholder, Farhad Moshiri, had committed to contribute "some equity" towards the projected £500 million cost of Bramley-Moore Dock.

Moshiri himself spoke of the stadium proposal:

> "The delivery of a new stadium, quite frankly, has nothing to do with my vision. It is a necessity. We have been given a great site which is extremely expensive. It has cost £100 million more for ground preparation, but we have to get on with it. It's a little like Mastermind — we've started, so we have to finish — and I have people I trust to execute it. I have spent £250 million to turn a museum into a competitive outfit. Throwing money at it is not the answer. You have to get it right. We always want to be top of the table. We want to be consistent, we want to do well, and we need to play a style of football which fills a 52,000 stadium."

It would not be long before details of that new stadium would begin to emerge.

2018: Dan Meis preaches to the faithful

> “During the Q&A at the first of the workshops, Dan Meis was also asked what he had been told by the club concerning funding for the new stadium. Richard Kenyon, then the club's Marketing Director interjected. He said, “I can assure you that funding will be no problem.”

2018 Dan Meis preaches to the faithful

In April 2018, the club, together with the new stadium’s appointed architect, Dan Meis, began the next phase of supporter engagement over the proposed ground at Bramley-Moore Dock with workshops at St Luke’s Church, next to Goodison Park.

With Everton having solicited feedback from fans through a survey based on 11 Key Principles that would guide the move away from Goodison, Meis was meeting with fans at the site of the Blues’ current home to gather further ideas and present initial concepts.

The first images of those concepts had been surfacing on social media and they featured components that had been prominent in the minds of many Evertonians when thinking about the new development, including proximity of the stands to the pitch, a large, imposing home end and the possibility of a safe-standing section.

The conversation around capacity has also been a prominent one over the preceding weeks, ever since CEO Robert Elstone's remarks at a Liverpool business meeting in which he had intimated that the capacity at Bramley-Moore Dock would not represent a massive jump from Goodison's ~40,000.

Meis himself has also hinted that the maximum attendance at the new ground would be guided by the need for intimacy and to create an intimidating venue, and he backed that up again at St. Luke's. Meis remarked that while 99% of Evertonians wanted a 50,000-plus capacity, he was cautious of going as high as 60,000, the number favoured by most Blues.

According to the *Liverpool Echo*'s Chris Beesley, Meis said that he believed in scarcity of seats and the importance of selling out a venue. He said that the last 10,000 seats in a stadium are the most expensive and bring in the least revenue."

During the Q&A at the first of the workshops, Dan Meis was also asked by a supporter, Steve Dickinson, what he had been told by the club concerning funding for the new stadium. Richard Kenyon, then the club's Marketing Director and emcee for the workshop interjected. He said, "I can assure you that funding will be no problem."

***

Elsewhere, Liverpool Mayor Joe Anderson had revealed an alternative funding scenario for Everton's proposed stadium at Bramley-Moore Dock, whereby Liverpool City Council could build the ground and lease it back to the club.

Both Everton and LCC were discussing ways in which the club could raise the estimated £500 million cost of the stadium on the banks of the Mersey, with the leading proposal being for the City take out a £280 million loan at ultra-low interest rates that is then repaid by the club over 25 years.

Under that scheme, the ground and the club would act as security with the Council netting £7 million a year in interest payments it otherwise wouldn't receive if the Blues went entirely their own way. Everton would still need to raise the remaining £220 million privately.

Under the Mayor's alternate proposal, he told Liverpool Business News that LCC could fund the new stadium entirely if the club could not raise their share of the cost via private investment.

"There is an open door to the possibility. It is not ruled out," said Mayor Anderson.

"Everton want to own their own stadium and they are still confident they can raise the money that would allow them to do that."

Anderson explained that, "there would have to be a completely different securitisation package to go along with that," under the terms of this different arrangement and it could mean less leverage for Everton where the design, capacity, use and revenue from the Bramley-Moore Dock stadium are concerned.

The original proposal had its share of critics, with some opponents fearful of risk to city taxpayers, even though the terms of the project would put all the risk on Everton. This Plan B option would involve significantly more capital and risk on LCC's side.

Anderson gave assurances of full transparency in the process and confirmed a vote of the full council would be taken before any agreement was signed.

***

On 25 July 2018, Everton Shareholders' Association chairman John Blain had a second informal chat with Everton's major shareholder and Bill Kenwright.

As well as reaffirming his commitment to the Director of Football model at Everton and a focus on youth to bring the average age of the Blues' squad down, a key takeaway was the proposed new stadium at Bramley-Moore Dock which Moshiri still said would open in 2022. The funding model for the project was still not completed, a delay which had already contributed to the targeted date slipping by a year, and it was Blain's assessment that Moshiri envisioned the capacity of the new ground being between 52,000 and 55,000, lower than the target capacity of 60,000 favoured by most supporters (not to mention John himself), if the polls on social media were correct.

2018: SILVA WILL BE A VERY GOOD MANAGER: BRANDS

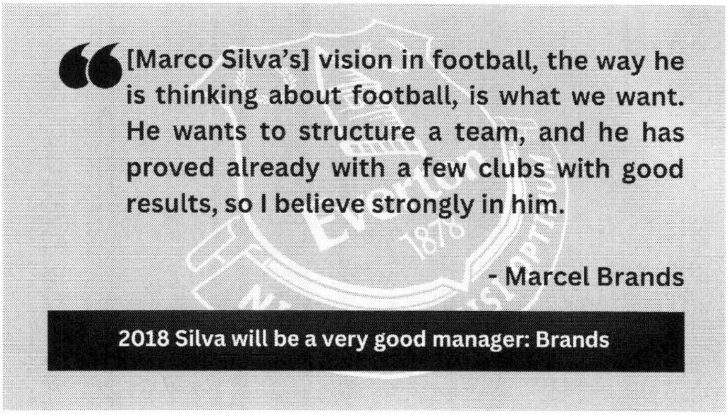

It would take until 31 May 2018 before the club announced Marco Silva as Everton's new manager, following weeks of speculation suggesting he would become the long-term successor to Ronald Koeman.

The 40-year-old signed a three-year contract with the Blues, seven months after they first tried to lure him away from Watford and four months after the Hornets had eventually fired him for a sequence of poor results.

Silva's arrival came two-and-half weeks after the club had sacked Sam Allardyce.

"I'm really proud to be the new Everton manager," Silva told evertontv. "I'm excited and I'm really happy to take this big challenge for us as a club and for me as a manager.

"I want to express my thanks to Farhad, to the chairman, to the Board of Directors and to Marcel as well, for the confidence in my work. I know the huge history of Everton as a club and what the fans expect. I'm sure with everybody working together, I will be ready for this challenge.

"We have a lot of work to do in this next month and it is important to prepare everything in the right way. But there will be even more important work to do from the start of pre-season into the first Premier League match of next season.

"I know what our fans expect - they expect results but not only results. I want our fans to be proud when they see our team on the pitch. I want them to feel that we are committed, that we are working hard and enjoying our football because that is important as well.

"We want to build a great connection between the squad and the fans, and I'm sure that with our attitude and demands of commitment, then our style of play will see that, I believe."

The acquisition of the Portuguese was the latest in a succession of changes at boardroom and team-management level following a hugely disappointing 2017/18 season.

Marcel Brands, who had arrived as the club's new Director of Football in place of Steve Walsh on 16 May, said: "His vision in football, the way he is thinking about football, is what we want. He wants to structure a team, and he has proved already with a few clubs with good results, so I believe strongly in him. He's an open guy who wants to work together with good staff and in an environment at Finch Farm, which is conducive to building something strong."

Silva brought with him a reputation for improving every team he had managed, his last few weeks at Vicarage Road notwithstanding. After attracting attention for his exploits as a young coach on the Continent, he had gained experience of managing in the Premier League from two short stints at Hull City and Watford

Between the time he hung up his playing boots in 2011 to take up the managerial reins at Estoril Praia and his departure from Olympiakos in 2016, Marco Silva had emerged as one of the fastest-rising young managers in the European game.

Originally hired in a director of football role by Estoril, he quickly shifted to the position of manager with the small Portuguese club 10th in that country's second tier. With a run of just three defeats in the remaining 24 matches of the campaign, Estoril won the division as champions under Silva and gained promotion to the Primera Liga.

The following season, Silva steered Estoril to fifth place and qualification for the Europa League for the first time in their history and eventually left the club in 2014, having gone one better with a fourth-place finish and attracted the attention of domestic giants Sporting.

Silva spent just one season at Estádio José Alvalade where he guided the Lions to third place before being dismissed just days after landing the Taca de Portugal, their first piece of silverware in seven years, apparently because he refused to wear an official club suit in an earlier round of the competition.

He joined Olympiakos that summer to replace his compatriot Vítor Pereira where, again, he would only spend a year, but not without notching some more impressive achievements. He led the Greek club to the title by a league record 30 point margin winning 28 of their 30 league games, which included a 17-match winning streak, another record.

Silva was the surprise choice to whom Hull turned in January 2017, when they needed a miracle to escape relegation from the Premier League. The Tigers were rock bottom with just 13 points from 20 games when he arrived, far away from safety. They ended the season with 34 points, eventually falling short of what would have been an incredible escape from relegation, while also reaching the League Cup semi-final. The young Portuguese had, however, done enough to convince Watford to make him their latest manager that May after he had stepped down at the KCOM Stadium.

With a quarter of the 2017/18 campaign complete in October, Watford were sixth in the table and looking capable of finishing in the top seven and, perhaps, claiming the final European berth that Burnley eventually did.

However, the Hornets' hierarchy blamed the collapse in Watford's form in the ensuing weeks on Everton's overt approach for Silva following Koeman's sacking. Just one win in 11 matches was enough for the Hertfordshire club to dismiss him after 24 league games and lodge a formal complaint with the Premier League accusing the Blues of "tapping" their former manager up.

Mentioned in connection with recent vacancies at Southampton, Stoke City and West Ham, Silva reportedly turned down overtures from China and Continental Europe in order to become the 10th full-time Everton manager since 1992.

His staff at Finch Farm would include Duncan Ferguson, who was first promoted to first-team coaching duties under David Moyes, and Ryland Morgans, who would continue as Performance Director.

Silva named João Pedro as his assistant manager, Hugo Olivera as his goalkeeping coach, Antonis Lemonakis as his technical scout and Pedro Conceição as the fitness coach.

With a new Technical Director and a new Manager in place, expectations were high that the team would receive some much needed reinforcements during the summer transfer window.

2018: Rooney out. Richarlison in

Only days after Marco Silva's appointment, Marcel Brands warned that Everton would need to trim its bloated squad of surplus players and wages before he and Marco Silva could make the targeted signings they believed would improve the team.

The Blues' new Director of Football and the new manager underwent an analysis of the playing personnel they had inherited from Ronald Koeman, Sam Allardyce and Steve Walsh, with Brands admitting that some difficult- but necessary – conversations would have to take place with certain players.

At issue was a senior squad boasting around 38 players, and some hugely inflated transfer fees and wages which were paid and offered to the preceding year's recruits in order to get them through the door.

When asked whether there would be a repeat of last summer's open chequebook, Brands was frank in his assessment, whilst also admitting that it was going to be hard to offload some players because few clubs could match their current salaries.

"No," he said in *The Guardian*. "First, we need to offload players to raise money [for transfers], and also salary-wise. But it's not only a money thing. Of course, money is important but also, for a coach, it is not workable to start with 38 players in your squad.

"We have to look for a squad Marco can work with and I think there always has to be space for young players to come to the first team.

"That has to be, let's say, 25-30 players. Now there are 38 and a lot are not young anymore. They are players who have arrived.

"We have to be honest when we take the decision with these players. Do they have prospects here at Everton? Some of the conversations will not be nice, but I think Marco must start with a squad that everyone is eager to play for and has prospects to play."

Wayne Rooney was predicted to be first out the door, as his slow-moving negotiations over a switch to DC United were nearing conclusion. According to other reports, Morgan Schneiderlin and Davy Klaassen were two more players signed by Ronald Koeman on wages north of £100,000 a week who could have followed him.

Schneiderlin seemed keen on finding a new club, with speculation linking him with a return to France. Sandro Ramirez, who had arrived for just over £5 million but was also on a big salary, had stressed he had no desire to play for Everton again after securing a loan move to Sevilla in January.

Klaassen, meanwhile, had publicly stated his desire to stay at Goodison Park to fight for his place but was reportedly being eyed by Besiktas, initially on loan. According to *The Mirror,* Yannick Bolasie was the subject of interest from at least one Premier League club.

"If you make a new signing," Brands continued, "with the salaries in England and the player is not successful, then what do you do? In most countries, players cannot make the wages they get in the Premier League, so a lot of players who don't play here cannot play anywhere, because the salaries are not comparable.

"Hopefully, I will succeed in offloading the right players. They are good players, so I hope there will be interest for a few of our players."

***

The first manifestation of the changes Brands had intimated was Wayne Rooney's move to DC United, with confirmation he would officially sign for the Major League Soccer club coming on 10th July 2018.

According to the Washington Post, the 32-year-old had agreed a 2½-year contract, with an option for a third year, and a $13 million (£10 million) compensation deal that would seal his departure from Everton for the second time in his career.

Rooney, who left Goodison Park as an 18-year-old star-in-the-making in 2004 before returning in the summer of 2017 on a 2-year deal, was keen to see out the final year of his current terms with the Blues, but was informed that he was not part of the club's plans.

Everton would ease their wage bill to the tune of £8m for the coming season with Rooney's transfer.

Rooney could not play for DC United until after the MLS transfer window opened, which meant that the first match for which he would be eligible was his new team's home game on 14th July, which also marked the opening of Audi Field.

When asked about his feelings on leaving Everton for a second time, Rooney said, "It's football. Everton is the team I grew up supporting and I was grateful for the chance to go back there last summer. But in football you never know what's round the corner. I've made the decision to come here and I'm sure there are a lot of questions on why I left Everton and the people who want to know can ask Everton Football Club and let them answer it. But I've made the decision to come here and, as I keep saying, I'm excited and I'm just looking forward now to the first game."

***

On American Independence Day, Everton's new management team reportedly travelled to London to discuss transfer strategy with Bill Kenwright.

According to the *Liverpool Echo*, Marcel Brands and Marco Silva made the trip to the Capital for a first summit with the club's chairman, showing the duo were preparing to make their first signings.

To that point, three first-team players had left what Brands had admitted was an overly large squad — Wayne Rooney and Ramiro

Funes Mori were both sold, while Joel Robles was released after his contract expired. They would be followed by Davy Klaassen whose hugely unsuccessful stint in England came to an end when he joined Werder Bremen for half the fee Everton had paid for him 12 months earlier. Yet, while there had been plenty of links to potential targets, Blues fans were still awaiting the first acquisition of the summer.

Silva and Brands had hoped to start the new season with a group of just 25 players, having trimmed the wage bill from the previous year, and they set about making targeted additions aimed at bringing down the average age of the squad and ensuring that the bulk of Everton's incoming signings would have a resale value should they need to be moved on before their contracts expired.

***

The marquee acquisition of that summer would be Richarlison who arrived in July on a five-year contract, in a deal worth a reported £40 million. It was a big price tag around his neck but he was a player with enormous potential.

The move represented a reunion with new Toffees' boss, Marco Silva, who had signed Richarlison from Fluminese for a little over £11 million the year before, persuading him to join the Hornets rather than Dutch giants Ajax.

The then 20-year-old had starred for his country at the U20 World Cup, and showed his star quality with five goals in his first 12 games for Watford as they ascended to the top six early in 2017/18.

He had begun his career in his native Brazil with América Mineiro from Belo Horizonte, where he scored nine times in 24 games in

2015/16. Fluminese bought him for the following season, and he struck another nine goals in 42 appearances before Watford came calling.

"I want to have a lot of success with Everton," he told evertonfc.com after they announced his arrival. "I think it is going to be important for me here to be with Marco Silva again. I will learn more because I am still learning as a player and I aim to develop and grow here.

"Everton have put their faith in me and I intend to honour this shirt and demonstrate on the pitch why I came here.

"I want my dreams to become a reality here at one of the biggest clubs in England."

***

The signing of Richarlison was followed by that of Lucas Digne, whose move from Barcelona to Everton was announced on 1 August, when he signed a five-year deal with the club. A fee, reported to be worth around £18 million, was negotiated with the Spanish club, and the 25-year-old used the time to mull over a decision between regular football at Everton and the prospect of playing second string at the Nou Camp.

Digne ultimately opted for the fresh challenge on offer in England where he would provide long overdue competition for Leighton Baines, before eventually replacing the Goodison favourite at left back.

***

The rest of Everton's transfer business, of what proved to be a busy summer, culminated on Transfer Deadline Day of 9th August 2018 when four more key additions were made to Silva's squad.

With all incoming deals needing to be done by 5pm that day, time was running out to plug the few holes in the team that still needed to be addressed.

The Blues started the proceedings by unveiling Bernard, their third major signing of the summer, who was acquired as a free agent from Shaktar Donetsk.

There was high confidence that Yerry Mina would complete a £28 million switch from Barcelona and despite late reported interest from Manchester United and Lyon, Everton won the race for his signature.

He was joined by Andre Gomes, another Barcelona player deemed surplus to requirements at the Nou Camp, who was signed on a season-long loan. That just left a late scramble to land Kurt Zouma from Chelsea, also on loan. A deal sheet for the central defender was submitted to the Premier League just before the deadline which gave Everton's staff two hours to complete the deal, which they did successfully to conclude the summer's business.

2018: RICHARLISON BRACE GETS THE NEW CAMPAIGN UNDERWAY

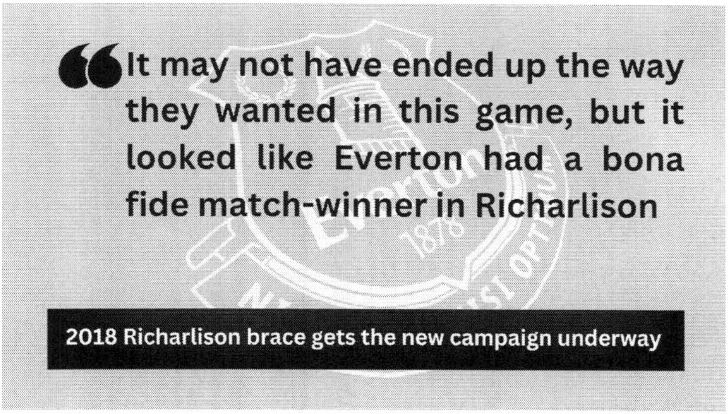

Several watchwords had characterised the following of Everton since the surprising 2013/14 season under Roberto Martinez and one of them was *frustration*. It was the overriding feeling again as the Toffees kicked off their first campaign under Marco Silva against Wolves at Molineux.

***

11 August 2018: Wolves v Everton

The Blues were 10 minutes from a first opening-day win away from home in 17 years and, had they been able to hold on to the lead handed back to them by a moment of brilliance by new signing Richarlison, it would have felt like a huge victory in several ways.

After all, it was only a few short months ago that largely the same XI was labouring under Sam Allardyce's limited stewardship, struggling to register shots on target, let alone win games with any regularity. It was only a week since a similar starting XI had looked worryingly ill-prepared for the resumption of the Premier League when they had lost a friendly curtain-raiser to Valencia at Goodison Park.

But having proven categorically that they were ready after all, Silva's men had the rug pulled out from underneath them by a moment of controversy at the end of the first half against Wolves, one that contributed significantly to the loss of two points.

Having largely quelled the enthusiasm and momentum that Wolves carried into their first game back in the top flight, amid pyrotechnics that illuminated and echoed around this famous old ground before kick-off, Everton were riding into the half-time interval on the back of a 1-0 lead at the time thanks to Richarlison's first goal for the club since his big-money move from Watford.

The 21-year-old debutant had been in the right place at the right time after 16 minutes when Michael Keane challenged for a corner from the Blues' left, the ball dropped to his feet and he had the simple task of firing home from close range to open the scoring and silence the buoyant home crowd.

Joao Moutinho's rising half-volley midway through the first period was as close as Nuno Espirito Santo's men had come to troubling Jordan Pickford, while Everton had looked composed and good value for their lead.

But then a momentary lapse of concentration... a square pass from Keane squirmed away from Phil Jagielka and towards Diogo Jota arriving on his blind side. Desperately trying to atone for his slip, Jagielka slid through the ball, diverting it forward before catching his opponent's foot and sending him sprawling. "Over the ball" it was not, but his stretch meant that he led with his studs and it was one of those incidents where the tackled player's reaction can have a huge bearing on the referee's course of action. No surprise, then, that as the Wolves player writhed in pain on the turf, referee Craig Pawson went straight to his pocket to pull out the red card.

Wolves added insult to the injury, with an equaliser; one which owed plenty to Ruben Neves surreptitiously moving the ball forward — unseen or unchecked by the officials — five yards into the ideal spot for a curling free kick over the wall. The Portuguese's shot was spot-on; Jordan Pickford's fateful step to his right to peer through his wall less so, meaning he got his fingertips to the ball but couldn't keep it out.

Credit to Everton after half-time, because they could have folded, and under any of Silva's immediate predecessors, they might have done. Kudos also to the manager himself, whose faith in Richarlison was demonstrated by the decision to keep him on the field, although he had picked up a yellow card in the 14th minute.

The Brazilian rewarded that faith midway through the second half. Collecting Tosun's lay-off near the touchline, Richarlison took a few steps into the Wolves box before whipping a bending low shot around the goalkeeper's despairing dive and inside the far corner. It was a strike where the element of surprise in its early despatch was as important as the crispness and accuracy of the finish and it felt like a massive goal for the 10 men in Blue.

They couldn't keep the lead, though. Holgate and the much improved Michael Keane repelled cross after cross at the back, but the numerical disadvantage meant that stopping those deliveries from the wide areas was much more difficult.

With ten minutes remaining, Neves capitalised on the space wide on the left to check back and curl a wicked cross over Keane's jump to Jimenez, who buried his header at the back post to make it 2-2.

It denied Silva a memorable victory in his first game in charge at Everton, but there was plenty to admire about his team and much that gave hope for a strong season ahead if the performance showed what was to come.

Importantly, there was a spirit and fight in the face of adversity that had been absent for so much of the previous season, which hinted at both a unity of purpose in the ranks and the effects that true competition for places can bring.

It may not have ended up that way in this game, but it looked like Everton had a bona fide match-winner in Richarlison. Even better, all four of Silva's deadline-day signings, among them Bernard and Andre Gomes, had yet to make their first appearances. It felt like exciting things were just getting started.

Final score: Wolves 2-2 Everton

***

After the game, Silva was fulsome in his praise of his players' work ethic and commitment.

"I saw a fantastic attitude, fantastic spirit in our squad and good organisation even with 10 players," he said afterwards. "I believe we were better with our organisation, even with the 10.

[After we scored] we didn't give them any chances and [it was] one really harsh decision from the referee. Of course, not only was there a red card but they score a goal as well, so it made a big impact on the match.

"Because we were having a good game, but one decision can impact the match. We felt it was not the right decision and where there are moments where something [like this] happens, we are to work together to help each other, which is what we did in the second half."

***

29 August 2018: Everton v Rotherham

A week after the promising performance at Wolves, the Blues opened their account at Goodison with a 2-1 win against Southampton. Seven days later, they led 2-0 at Bournemouth, before being pegged back to 2-2 by Eddie Howe's side. Twice in away fixtures Everton had led, twice they had had a player sent off in controversial circumstances — this time it was Richarlison given his marching orders for a barely perceptible motion towards Adam Smith's forehead — and twice they had come away with only a point.

Marco Silva's first cup match in charge was against Rotherham United. A crowd of 31,972, the highest attendance for a League Cup second round tie at Goodison Park for 50 years, turned up at Goodison and watched Everton ease into the draw for the Carabao Cup third round after what was a comfortable win over the Championship side.

Everton started in nervy fashion at the back but scored just shy of the half-hour mark to settle the nerves. Sandro Ramirez took on his man and fired the ball across the box. Gylfi Sigurdsson stuck out a leg and diverted it past the 'keeper to make it 1-0.

Rotherham came very close to equalising almost immediately, but the ball ricocheted off Kurt Zouma and bounced wide of Maarten Stekelenburg's goal. It wasn't until an hour had elapsed that the Blues doubled their advantage when Digne swung a cross to the back post where Calvert-Lewin nodded home.

Niasse should have made it three not long afterwards, but he headed Sandro's cross over from six yards out and though Rotherham rallied late in the game and went disturbingly close to making the game interesting, Calvert-Lewin cut back on his right foot and curled a beauty over Price and inside the far post to restore Everton's two-goal advantage.

Final score: Everton 3-1 Rotherham

***

21 October 2018: Everton v Crystal Palace

Progress in the cup at Rotherham's expense was followed by a 1-1 draw against newly-promoted Huddersfield Town draw at Goodison. Then came a home defeat to West Ham, and the customary away loss at Arsenal, resulting in a slide down the table to twelfth position.

The positive vibes felt in August suddenly seemed like a distant memory. A 3-0 home win against Fulham restored some confidence, but could the Blues find some consistency?

Next up was Southampton, in Round 4 of the League Cup at Goodison. The match finished 1-1, a tie decided on penalties. Everton went out after Richarlison skied his spot kick over the bar, and Theo Walcott's effort was saved.

Four days later, Everton were on the road again, recording their first away success under Silva with a 2-1 win at Leicester.

After the international break, it was back to Goodison for another Premier League match. This time, Everton and Silva engineered victory when it appeared a typically obstinate Crystal Palace side would shut them out.

Recent years had seen frustrating encounters against Palace, starting with a crushing 3-2 defeat in Roberto Martinez's first season, that effectively ended the Blues' Champions League hopes. It was the same scoreline the following campaign despite Romelu Lukaku getting the home side off to an early lead, and the following two seasons featured annoying 1-1 draws. A 3-1 win over the Eagles at Goodison Park in 2017/18 had bucked the recent trend.

Another point looked to be on the cards in this match as well until all three of Silva's substitutes weighed in to win it with a thrilling conclusion. Fortune favoured the brave because on an afternoon when little had worked for Bernard, when Theo Walcott had been ineffective, and when Richarlison had often been guilty of over-elaboration or a stubborn refusal to give up the ball, it needed something different to pick the lock to the visitors' defence.

Pleasingly, Ademola Lookman supplied a deft cross for Dominic Calvert-Lewin to steer a header past Wayne Hennessey and Cenk Tosun, forced back to the bench for the last two games, rapped home the killer second goal, all within the space of less than two of the dying minutes.

Blues fans were also toasting Jordan Pickford for that third successive Premier League win. The England international pulled off a brilliant stretching save in the first half to deny Cheikhou Kouyaté, as Everton almost buckled from another set-piece, and then made a superb stop with his trailing foot to prevent Luka Milivojevic from putting Palace ahead from the spot with an hour gone.

The penalty save proved to be the turning point of what was a scrappy and testy affair, punctured incessantly by referee Anthony Taylor's whistle. It was also the moment that ignited a Goodison crowd that was becoming anxiously Everton weren't going to find a way through.

After all, besides Palace's reputation as playing the spoiler at Goodison and the recent stumbles against Huddersfield and West Ham, Everton had a miserable record in Sunday televised matches, and there was the rather curious statistic that the last time they had won one without Tom Davies playing was December 2016... and the 20-year-old midfielder was not in the starting XI for this match.

That was because the manager had handed André Gomes his long-awaited home debut, ten long weeks after he signed on a season-long loan from Barcelona. Finally deemed fit after picking up a hamstring injury on the Spanish club's pre-season tour in America, the Portuguese international had lined up alongside Idrissa Gueye in a partnership that immediately looked like it would be the way forward for Silva that season, if both could stay fit and healthy.

Gomes's Premier League baptism was a hugely encouraging one, as were the performances of Michael Keane, Kurt Zouma and Lucas Digne at the back, as they restricted Palace to few real chances of note from open play.

Three league wins in succession and a move back into the top ten had Silva's side well placed as they prepared for their next game, a trip to Old Trafford. It would be difficult matches like those that would show just how far Everton could conceivably go that season so early in the new manager's tenure. The future looked bright and the future looked blue.

Final score: Everton 2-0 Crystal Palace

***

Afterwards, Silva credited his team for their patience as they eventually prevailed over a typically stubborn Palace.

"Tough game, tough game, like we expected," Silva said. "Like I told my players, always when Crystal Palace come here to play, it's always a tough game for us.

"[To make Goodison a difficult place for teams to play] is what we want. The Premier League is really hard. Opposition teams respect our team, they come here to wait, to keep good defensive organisation and we have to find the solution to play faster in some moments.

"But we are creating and today our team had the patience and moments to not lose our balance too easily. Our fans, they were fantastic because they didn't lose patience as well; they kept supporting our team the whole time and in the end everybody is happy because we played together, us and our fans."

2018: Ryazantsev: 'We learn from others'

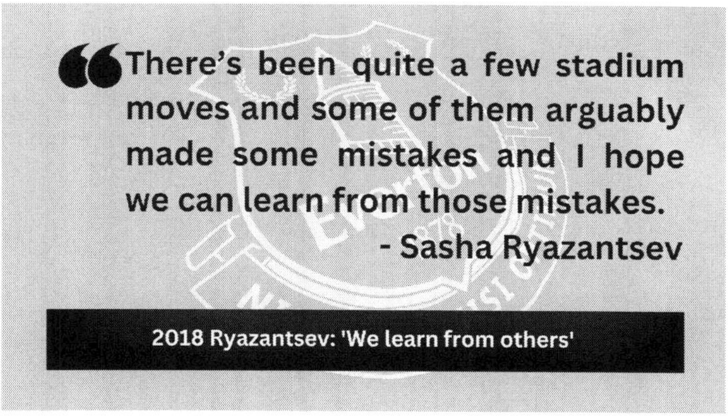

While Everton were beginning life under a new manager in the Autumn of 2018, off the pitch planning for the new stadium at Bramley-Moore Dock was continuing apace. In October, the Toffees' Director of Finance said the club would use the experiences of rival clubs as learning opportunities.

Speaking at the Leaders Sports Business Summit at Chelsea's Stamford Bridge, Sasha Ryazantsev said that while the decision to leave the Blues' current home at Goodison Park was a hard one, avoiding some mistakes made during the planning and construction of other stadiums would make their transition to the banks of the Mersey that much smoother.

Ryazantsev, who joined the club with Farhad Moshiri in 2016, as the owner's presence in the Boardroom, didn't mention any specific examples in the quotes attributed to him, but the delays and cost over-runs of Tottenham Hotspur's new stadium served as the most obvious instance.

West Ham's move to the London Stadium, meanwhile, had been fraught with complaints over policing and a lack of atmosphere in the wide expanses of a former athletics venue.

Ryazantsev said that if Everton could get their move right, it could be the catalyst for propelling the club back into the elite of the English game, while also providing enormous financial benefits to the city of Liverpool.

"There's been quite a few stadium moves and some of them arguably made some mistakes and I hope we can learn from those mistakes," Ryazantsev said.

"Sometimes it's good to be a trailblazer, but when you're not first, you can learn from others' mistakes. It is a very long-term project and it will take several years before we move.

"We see it as an opportunity to close the gap on the top six and the stadium itself will create a huge amount of new life.

"It will breathe new life into the team, create new jobs in the area and be worth one billion pounds of economic value to the city."

The proposed new ground at Bramley-Moore Dock still had a target completion date of 2022 but the financing of the project had yet to be finalised, leaving the planning application, final capacity and design up in the air.

It was a message Ryazantsev repeated in June 2019, two weeks after the opening of the Tottenham Hotspur stadium. He said that Everton's proposed move to Bramley-Moore Dock was vital to the club's future. He also commented that Spurs had shown how it was possible to remain competitive while still funding such a large-scale project.

Speaking to fcbusiness magazine, Ryzantsev explained that the new ground would give Everton a leg up in terms of commercial performance, with increased matchday revenue and wider sponsorship possibilities. He reiterated that the club's hierarchy envisaged that the build would take three years from the time the planning application was approved and the first spade plunged into the ground at the historic north docks site.

"We see the new stadium as an opportunity to further move the club towards the Premier League elite again," Ryazantsev said. "We will have more capacity and more concourse space, enabling us to offer a better fan experience.

"We also hope to attract better partnership deals and earn more broadcasting revenue with an iconic setting for our stadium on the Liverpool waterfront.

"And the one thing that we very much hope to bring from Goodison is the atmosphere of our amazing fans.

"I think every year in the Premier League is a challenge for all of us, whether it is a new stadium, competing for the title, European places or if you're in a relegation battle. It is a very challenging league.

"I would almost rephrase it: would it be challenging for us not to move to a new stadium over the next decade? I think that it would be a much bigger challenge.

"If you look at the obvious example of a similar project recently," Ryazentsev continued, referencing the Tottenham Hotspur Stadium, "that team has managed to build a new stadium and compete on the pitch.

"We hope we can learn from that in terms of managing the construction process while also performing on the pitch and increasing our commercial growth."

Ryzantsev was asked where Everton were regarding plans for the new stadium and when the club envisage breaking ground.

"We have made steady progress so far," he replied. "We are on track to submit a full planning application for a new stadium before the end of the year.

"In terms of funding, we are in a good place; we have options available to us in both the private and public sector and will carry out due diligence on the best deal for the club.

"I am as keen as every Evertonian to break ground, but we have been clear that this can only happen once we get planning permission and once we do, we estimate it could be a three-year build."

He concluded with the message that the club continued to plan for the team kicking off at Bramley-Moore Dock for the first time in 2023, but everything depended on the planning application and securing the required funding.

2018: Blue Crimbo at Moshiri's Liver Building

The prospect of a gleaming new stadium on the banks of the River Mersey allowed Evertonians to dream of reclaiming a significant share of the local limelight from neighbours Liverpool, and the club's *de facto owner,* Farhad Moshiri, took a step towards that in 2017 when he led a consortium to buy the iconic Liver Building on the city's waterfront.

Together with Luxembourg-based Corestate Capital and a group of international investors, Moshiri bought the grade 1 listed building for £48 million, with the British-Iranian businessman understood to own 49.9%.

With a view of the club's future home a mile and a half to the north at Bramley-Moore Dock, Moshiri moved Everton's operational headquarters to the Liver Building, and the world-famous Liver Birds atop the two towers were lit up in Everton blue for Christmas in 2018, triggering a spectacular firework display above the River Mersey.

They floodlit the iconic statues in blue to launch the Football Club's *Blue Crimbo* campaign and it would remain a fixture of the city's skyline throughout December.

Everton chairman Bill Kenwright and X Factor finalist Anthony Russell pulled the lever that covered the top of the Liver Building in the Club's colours, with hundreds of fireworks immediately shooting skywards to mark the occasion.

First-team stars Yerry Mina and Michael Keane, Director of Football Marcel Brands and former WBC cruiserweight boxing champion Tony Bellew were also on stage, along with Ambassadors Ian Snodin and Graham Stuart, joining 350 invited supporters and guests in attending the high-profile waterfront event.

"We've got a wonderful community programme and we've established Blue Crimbo over the last seven years, but tonight was something for everyone, a feeling of Liverpool, the best place in the world," said Kenwright.

"It's the start of Christmas and, of course, we all want Anthony to do well for us this weekend.

"He's a real Blue, a typical Scouser. He's up against two extraordinary vocal talents but it's called the X Factor and he's got it."

Everton Chief Executive, Denise Barrett-Baxendale said: "It's been fantastic. Despite the wind and rain, Evertonians have collected outside to come and see the start of our Blue Crimbo campaign."

It wasn't the last time that the two mythical Liver Birds would be lit up in Everton blue – the club would take the opportunity to do so ahead of Merseyside derby matches in future years – and it was a visible sign that the city's first club was beginning to take back some of its former prominence.

2019: Results show Silva's Blues can't defend set pieces

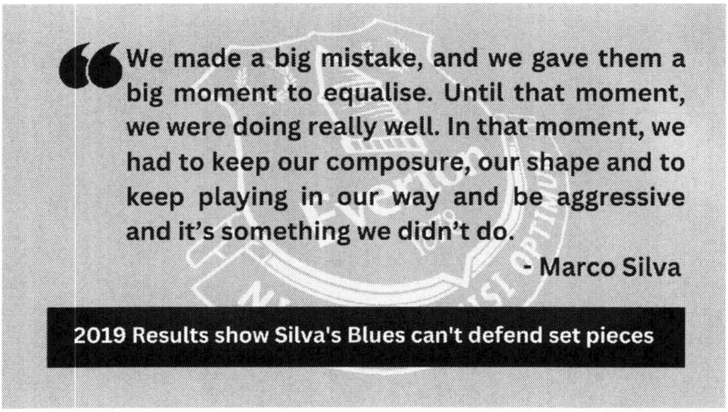

Back on the field, Marco Silva's largely positive start, which had seen his team lose just three of their opening 13 matches in the Premier League between the opening day and late November, had given way to a more difficult patch that would see them slip from sixth place to mid-table.

There had been defeats in away games at Manchester United, Liverpool and Manchester City. However, 'Fortress Goodison' had seen wins against Brighton and Cardiff City, followed by draws against

Newcastle United and Watford. Another stern test would be in store for the Blues when Spurs were the visitors two days before Christmas.

***

23 December 2018: Everton v Tottenham Hotspur

If Everton had shown what they were capable of in their five previous meetings with the top five that season, this latest meeting with Spurs was supposed to be the moment they finally fulfilled that promise, on home turf against a "big six" team.

The attacking adventure they had shown at the Emirates in September, ultimately let down only by poor finishing and the fine form of Petr Cech, defensively robust displays at Stamford Bridge and Anfield in November where chances to score went begging, not to mention some promising spells against Manchester United at Old Trafford in October... it all hinted at what the new Everton, the positive, attack-minded Marco Silva Everton, could produce.

With the backing of the Goodison Park faithful and fuelled by the determination to make up for recent disappointments, the Blues hoped they could finally put together a complete performance. Instead, a veritable nightmare before Christmas unfolded at a stunned Goodison as Spurs meted out a thrashing of unforeseen proportions.

It left in tatters for the time being, any notion that Silva's nascent Everton revolution could keep the top five within reach and capitalise on any continued upheaval at Manchester United. His Everton team was miles away from touching that elite clutch of clubs, and there could have been no doubt about the scale of the task required to bridge that gap.

This was an agonising result, on a weekend where supposedly inferior teams like Crystal Palace and Leicester achieved what Everton couldn't do in recent weeks — namely win away against a top-5 team. It was now 23 games since a Toffees side had recorded a win over England's six richest clubs, and if they played like they did that day against Spurs, it would be a good deal longer before they got another.

Once again, this was a game littered with poor performances up and down the Everton ranks, with only Lucas Digne, Gylfi Sigurdsson and, perhaps, Dominic Calvert-Lewin emerging with any credit. Sigurdsson helped create one goal with Calvert-Lewin, and he scored with a brilliant solo effort of his own. While the young striker, DCL, was hugely unfortunate to have a headed goal disallowed. That, coupled with the episode of Keystone Cops at the other end shortly afterwards, proved pivotal in the contest.

Where the rest were concerned, it was hard to know where to begin. Jordan Pickford added another howler to further tarnish the glowing reputation he took from the World Cup in Russia; Richarlison was anonymous save for two off-target headers; Theo Walcott converted the opening goal with aplomb, but did nothing else for 90 minutes; Tom Davies, André Gomes (before he went off injured) and Morgan Schneiderlin (after he had come on for the Portuguese) cut gallingly vulnerable figures without the injured Idrissa Gueye when they didn't have the ball; and, with a black hole of a midfield in front of them, the rest of the back four simply caved as Spurs romped through them, seemingly at will.

The players' collective display, as bad as anything the Goodison faithful had endured the previous season under three different managers, only told half the story, though. The other component of this collapse was naïve tactics by their manager and a stunning inability or refusal to make any alterations to address a midfield being badly overrun.

Trying to play Spurs at their own game with an attacking bent, a dangerously high defensive line, and an inconsistent high press, they invited one of the most dangerous teams in the country to pick them off with balls over the top or into the channels or simply parted the waters to allow the visitors to stream through.

Harry Kane helped himself to yet another brace. The hugely impressive Hueng-Min Son bagged two of his own and there were crisp first-time strikes from Dele Alli and Christian Eriksen to underline the talent assembled at Tottenham in recent years. They stood as the example that Everton had to follow, but it felt like an awfully long road on days like these.

Final score: Everton 2-6 Spurs

***

Silva admitted that his team had made critical mistakes against Spurs and the humiliating result left Evertonians in familiar doldrums going into Christmas, with the Blues sitting outside the top half of the table with no wins in five games.

"Of course we have to feel really bad," Silva told Sky Sports afterwards. "For sure, we wanted to do something different than the score we achieved.

"We started really well. Of course, we scored first and scored the second goal as well — it's a key moment in the game, in my opinion, when we scored the second goal but the referee saw something there and didn't give the goal to us.

"Afterwards we made a big mistake, and we gave them a big moment to equalise. Until that moment, we were doing really well. In that moment, we had to keep our composure, our shape and to keep playing in our way and be aggressive and it's something we didn't do.

"At this level, when you make mistakes against a team like Tottenham, they can create problems and we lost many, many things after that moment."

***

26 December 2018: Burnley v Everton

Everton responded to the mauling by Tottenham by putting five past Burnley and recording their biggest away win since 1985.

Yerry Mina scored his first Premier League goal to set Marco Silva's men on their way inside two minutes, Lucas Digne added two fine strikes in either half, while Gylfi Sigurdsson scored from the spot, and Richarlison came off the bench to put the icing on the cake in stoppage time.

The four-goal margin might not have shown the general pattern of play — Everton only shaded possession and there were long spells where they were content to sit back a little and see what Burnley could come up with — but you can't argue with a 5-1 victory.

The win moved Everton back into the top eight but, of course, one impressive score-line in isolation would mean very little if it wasn't followed up with a string of positive results over the upcoming seven games before the next meeting with a top-six side.

Win at Brighton in the following game, and follow it up with a victory over Leicester on New Year's Day and Silva could legitimately feel that his side had recovered somewhat from the Spurs debacle, to embark on a long road to Wembley in the FA Cup and remount a challenge for that sixth place that Manchester United currently occupy.

Final score: Burnley 1-5 Everton

***

Afterwards, Silva praised his players for the manner in which they bounced back from the humiliation by Tottenham and thanked the fans for their support.

"We learn every time, not just when we have a bad result," Silva explained. "We had a really tough result in the last game and even today we won the match clear, but we learned as well, for sure. It's part of our process as a team.

"My first words are for our fans and for our players. The fans welcomed our players before the match [which was] fantastic after a really tough result.

"And our players deserved this win and the three points. It was a good win for us. We got three important points for us and now is the time to rest and prepare for the [next match].

"Our last game wasn't a normal one from us, but we are here to fight, to compete, and to show the ambition we have as a club."

***

5 January 2019: Everton v Lincoln City

The Burnley result turned out to be the only win recorded by the Blues in December 2018, and there remained a lack of fluidity and confidence about Everton that suggested it would continue to be a difficult road. The manager searched for the answers to the poor run of form that began with the Merseyside derby in early December, with its last-minute punch in the gut. That had been followed by disappointing home draws against Newcastle and Watford, defeats against Manchester City, Tottenham and Brighton, and a 1-0 home reverse against Leicester City on New Year's Day.

For a team struggling through that run of poor form midway through the season, a home tie against a side in the fourth tier of the English football was precisely what you would want. Any game against a lower league side is a potential banana skin but a healthy home win to calm the nerves was surely on the cards.

That it didn't turn out that way underlined the shortage of confidence and composure that had suddenly afflicted Marco Silva's team. The Toffees won, but the manner in which a fast start gave way to a disconcertingly disjointed display – during which Lincoln more than held their own for long periods – would not have dispelled the doubts that had crept in during recent weeks.

Ademola Lookman found the net via the unexpected route of his head 11 minutes in, as Everton's early pressure and slicker passing told. Spreading the ball across the pitch, the Blues eventually worked the ball wide the over-lapping Baines who curled a cross to the back post where, unmarked, Lookman looped a header over the goalkeeper and over the goal line where the covering defender couldn't keep it out.

Two minutes later it was 2-0 and Everton were flying. Another nicely worked move saw Gylfi Sigurdsson find Dominic Calvert-Lewin in the area. He played Bernard in behind the last man and the Brazilian lifted the ball expertly over Josh Vickers.

After that, the impetus suddenly and inexplicably left the Blues' game, and Lincoln started coming forward. John Akinde had been giving Kurt Zouma plenty of problems early on, not least when the Frenchman gave the ball away in the middle of the park and was then "skinned" by the burly striker as he tried to ward him off. But it was Mina's cheap foul that handed the Imps a free-kick opportunity from which they scored.

The dead ball picked Jason Shackell out free in the six-yard box and while Jordan Pickford repelled his point-blank header, the rebound fell straight to Michael Bostwick, who converted from close range.

For the next half hour of the match, Everton struggled to rediscover their rhythm, even after Silva had attempted at half time to address the lack of control in the middle by replacing the disappointing Davies with Gomes. This was a match that Sigurdsson, Idrissa Gueye and Bernard, all of whom had played in World Cups, should have been absolutely bossing from start to finish, and for the likes of Davies, Calvert-Lewin and Tosun, it was a chance to really shine.

Of the younger players drafted into the side, Lookman was the only one who made a strong case in patches for a regular first-choice berth, and only Baines lived up to his billing as a former international and Premier League star.

Still, in the cup, the final score is always paramount and, in that respect, what mattered was the Blues being in the hat for the next round. While this wasn't the dominant performance Evertonians would have hoped for, both Silva and Marcel Brands would have added more information and context to their plans for further strengthening the squad during the January transfer window or over the summer.

Final score: Everton 2-1 Lincoln

***

13 January 2019: Everton v Bournemouth

Ever since the Roberto Martinez fairy-tale turned sour, somewhere between the Europa League defeat in Kiev in March 2015 and the consecutive home defeats to Leicester and Stoke the following Christmas, Goodison Park's atmosphere had periodically been a topic of debate among Evertonians.

Where the library-like milieu that away fans liked to mock was concerned, there was often a push-pull between those who felt it was incumbent on the crowd to generate the atmosphere from the off and those who put the onus on the team to excite the fans. Then, of course, there was the altogether more concerning toxicity that was prevalent on occasions under Martinez and Ronald Koeman. That was brought into sharper focus by midfielder Nikola Vlasic when he spoke of Everton's players being paralysed by fear.

There might not have been outright fear to this point among the Blues' ranks by January 2019, but the psychology had been off kilter since the derby defeat at Anfield in early December, and concerns over Everton's home form since. While there may have been a consensus that Marco Silva was going to need time and a good deal of patience to rectify the problems sown during the two regimes that preceded him and the interim Sam Allardyce tenure, it was fairly obvious that supporters were disappointed with how yet another season was coming off the rails.

Under those circumstances, it probably wasn't surprising that there was an air of uneasiness about the place when what was an important game against Bournemouth kicked off. With no home wins since late November and on a run of just one Premier League win in eight since then, the importance of three points wasn't lost on anybody.

By the time the hour mark approached, however, roused by an additional common enemy — the villain of the piece wearing black — and an improving, more robust and committed display by the players, Goodison was a good deal more animated; and, half an hour later, the Evertonian collective was celebrating a victory. An ugly victory that masked some continuing issues, but a victory which fans hoped would inject some confidence into the Blues' veins.

Silva had routinely asked for more aggression from his team, and he got plenty of it even if, spurred on by seething injustice at one of the most inept refereeing displays seen at Goodison in quite a while, André Gomes threatened to cross the line on more than a few occasions.

Having been harshly yellow-carded when he reacted to the latest in a litany of bafflingly poor decisions by Anthony Taylor, the Portuguese dangerously toed a tightrope in the closing stages and was fortunate not to see red.

Ultimately, though, Taylor's horrendous refereeing provided the focal point that roused the Goodison faithful from that uncomfortable silence that had enveloped most of the ground as Everton laboured through a fairly torrid first half hour. Where Bournemouth, a side on a run of 10 defeats from 13 coming into the game and five losses on the bounce away from the Vitality Stadium, were zipping the ball around comfortably the Toffees struggled to string three passes together in the face of the visitors' pressing.

All the openings in the first quarter of an hour were created by Eddie Howe's team, the best of them falling to David Brooks when played into a one-on-one situation with Pickford, but he struck his shot off the post, with Goodison erupting in boos at referee Taylor for failing to bring the play back for an obvious foul on Kurt Zouma.

It was the first of many baffling and infuriating decisions by the official who ratcheted up Evertonian ire when he awarded Adam Smith a free kick for falling into Gomes on the edge of the box. Pickford was equal to it, pushing Junior Stanislas's free kick behind.

Everton, who had been passed off their own patch for 30 minutes, gradually came to life and by the hour mark had taken the lead with a goal fashioned by Lucas Digne. The Frenchman drove to the by-line and, going away from goal, he expertly hooked a cross to the edge of the six-yard box where Zouma powered home his first Everton goal.

Bournemouth were unbowed, though, and an often bad-tempered affair remained nervily close until stoppage time and when one last boot downfield from Jordan Pickford was collected by Lookman who he held up long enough for substitute Dominic Calvert-Lewin to arrive about 16 yards out and stroke the winger's pass into the net with a wonderfully composed finish.

It was a reminder of what the young striker could do. Calvert-Lewin had struggled to show the consistency required of a first-choice starter but it was clear he could produce clinical moments like that one and chip in with important goals.

What remained to be seen was what effect this result would have on Everton's performances from then on, and whether it was a fillip that could get them back to playing the way they were pre-Anfield. The lack of passing options, an over-reliance on getting the ball wide for crosses into the box, and the misunderstandings that are often clear between the midfield and the two central forward players, all continued to be concerns and challenges for Silva to resolve.

Final score: Everton 2-0 Bournemouth

***

26 January 2019: Millwall v Everton

Everton's army of away supporters never disappoint. They turn up in their thousands for every game, and deal with whatever life throws at them. On a visit to London for an FA Cup Fourth Round tie against Millwall, it was bricks, bottles and blades, as sections of the home supporters ambushed the Blues' fans on their way to the New Den.

One Evertonian, Jay Burns, was slashed in the face, and received life-changing injuries.

As Jonathan Humphries, Crime Reporter for the *Liverpool Echo*, wrote: "Jay Burns made the trip to East London on Saturday but never made it to Millwall's ground, The [New] Den, after being caught up in a mass brawl in Hawkstone Road, Southwark, at around 4.45pm. Mr Burns, 29, told the *ECHO* the group of Everton fans he was travelling with were 'not looking for trouble' and were being escorted by police when they were attacked by another group. Mobile phone footage shows a man in a flat cap appear to make a slashing motion towards Mr Burns, who then staggers backwards clutching his face.

"He was rushed to hospital where he required over 25 stitches to a wound stretching from beside his right eye down to his chin. He told the *ECHO*: 'I just don't understand why people carry knives to a football match.'

"The fight ahead of the game was not the only incident of violence on the day. Coaches carrying Everton fans were pelted with bricks and bottles near The Den, smashing windows."

On the pitch, Everton were turfed out of the FA Cup by the Championship side, amid fury at an obvious handball goal and familiar frustrations over the team's inability to defend set-pieces.

Marco Silva's side twice led in a tie played in sodden conditions at and occasionally torrential rain, but squandered their advantage on both occasions, before one more silly foul handed the Londoners the chance to win the tie from a free kick.

Silva and Everton were livid that Jake Cooper's controversial goal, which levelled the contest at 2-2, was allowed the stand — despite this being a televised match, the Football Association had elected not to employ Video Assistant Referee technology — but it couldn't mask the Blues' attacking shortcomings, nor their galling weakness at defending high balls into the box.

An unsurprisingly poor game didn't see its first shot on target until the 43rd minute when Richarlison gave Everton the lead. André Gomes' pass found Richarlison with space to shoot from outside the area and his slightly deflected shot squirmed under goalkeeper Jordan Archer with two minutes left of the regulation 45 in the first half.

Millwall were level less than two minutes later, though, when Everton failed to deal with a free kick. Cooper nodded forward for Lee Gregory and the striker looped a header over Jordan Pickford and into the net.

Everton were better in parts in the second half but had only a scuffed Sigurdsson shot to show for their efforts before Cenk Tosun replaced Dominic Calvert-Lewin with 25 minutes to go. The Turk had been on the field for seven minutes before he notched his third goal of the season. Sigurdsson played him in between two defenders and Tosun tucked his shot inside the far post to make it 2-1.

A sloppy free-kick conceded by Lucas Digne set the home side up for an immediate reply, however. Everton's defence were beaten easily in the air again and though Pickford saved the first shot well, the rebound hit Cooper on the arm and bounced over the line. Referee Michael Oliver consulted his assistant to confirm the decision, and the goal stood despite Everton's vociferous protests.

The Blues were heading for a replay until another ill-advised transgression in a dangerous area by Digne led to a stoppage-time winner.

Once again, Millwall prevailed as they swung the ball in. There were more blue home jerseys than visiting white shirts in the six-yard box going for the second ball, and Murray Wallace pounced to consign Everton's Wembley hopes to the bin for another year.

Silva would point to the injustice of the second goal, but the problems in all areas of the pitch that showed no signs of abating were what lay behind a performance that yielded just three shots on target and precious little of the control that is expected of a Premier League side playing against lower-division opposition.

The painful defeat effectively ended Everton's season in late January, and increased the scrutiny of the manager and several of the Blues' expensive but under-performing players.

Final score: Millwall 3-2 Everton

***

7 April 2019: Everton v Arsenal

Following their FA Cup exit, Everton's form under Marco Silva could be best described as inconsistent .

A 1-0 away win against Huddersfield was followed by three consecutive defeats: against Wolves, Manchester City and Watford. Respite came through a 3-0 away win against Cardiff and a hard-fought 0-0 draw against Liverpool at Goodison Park. Another defeat, this time 3-2 away to Newcastle, preceded two consecutive 2-0 wins, against Chelsea and West Ham that lifted the Toffees back into the top half of the table.

With another home game against a "Top 6" side in the offing, the key question was once again, could Everton attain some of the consistency that had eluded them all season?

Prior to the visit of Arsenal in early April 2019, it had also been over two years since an Everton side earned three successive clean sheets. But thanks to a solitary Phil Jagielka goal and a laudably resilient performance against a team looking to leapfrog their neighbours, Tottenham, into third place, Everton saw off the third London team in a row without Jordan Pickford's goal being breached.

Pickford's wild punch dropped straight to Aaron Ramsey early in the second half and might have been punished on a different day but, thankfully, the Welshman volleyed over. Then apart from a couple of tame efforts on his goal, Pickford's role mostly centred around his distribution from the back which was, pleasingly, hugely improved.

Instead, the focus was, rightly, on a Blues display under-pinned by determined and impressive defending, phenomenal work-rate throughout the side and the hit-and-miss nature of Everton's counter-attacking which, if they could get right, would make them a seriously dangerous team.

The Blues had taken just 10 minutes to make the breakthrough via the somewhat unlikely source of Phil Jagielka, a player who wasn't even supposed to be on the pitch. Silva had named an unchanged XI but, with Michael Keane unable to shake off the effects of a virus, the club skipper stepped into the team and was on hand to tuck home what would prove to be the winning goal.

There was a note of controversy in the game's assessment afterwards, with some observers of television replays suggesting that Lucas Digne had stepped over the touchline in delivering one of his tomahawk throw-ins but it was rightly deemed legal by the officials as Jagielka flicked it on and then profited from a fortunate ricochet when Dominic Calvert-Lewin's header fell to him in front of goal and he couldn't miss.

From then on, it was a question of Everton suffocating the visitors with tireless closing down, remaining on the front foot for most of the first half, but just lacking the killer instinct to extend their lead, as their overall performance warranted.

As the game opened up later in the second half, a slew of opportunities were created for Everton that they just couldn't convert into further goals. Bernard, Gylfi Sigurdsson, Richarlison and Dominic Calvert-Lewin all spurned decent chances.

Meanwhile, at the other end, Arsenal attempted to find an equaliser as full time approached, but Everton saw the game out with a flurry of late substitutions.

This could and should have been an even more handsome victory, but Silva's men had found turning those quick transitions and interceptions into goals a challenge all season. Everton racked up 23 shots over the 90 minutes but only six on target and while good goalkeeping by Bernd Leno was partially responsible for the home side only scoring once, poor ball control and decision-making also prevented this from being a hiding for an Arsenal team that hadn't travelled well all season.

Having at times looked so bereft of answers this season, Silva finally looked as though he was finding his feet again at Goodison Park, with some real signs of progress. As galling as the defeat at Newcastle had been, that second-half collapse at St James' Park (and, perhaps, 45 shaky minutes before half-time against Chelsea) stood as an aberration in a six-match sequence that had yielded four wins, a goalless draw in the Merseyside derby, and progress back up the table. The Blues were back to within a point of seventh place and looked to have established a platform on which Silva and Marcel Brands could build in the summer.

Final score: Everton 1-0 Arsenal

***

13 April 2019 Fulham v Everton

Everton could really be beyond parody at times. An "Everton, that" phenomenon had become a running joke on social media for years, a product of the relentless mediocrity and fallibility that had plagued the club for the past three decades, and it was made for days like this one.

Given that Fulham came into this game with their relegation back to the Championship confirmed, without so much as a point from their previous nine Premier League matches and with just one clean sheet to their name all season, Evertonians might have asked themselves if there was there anything more nailed on than what played out at Craven Cottage.

Credit went to Scott Parker and his team. Relieved of the pressure of a battle to avoid to the drop, Fulham were energetic, physical and became increasingly confident once it became apparent that the visitors were having a day to forget.

After a first half in which they had given the Blues a couple of scares, Marco Silva needed to deliver a similar half-time team talk to the one that spurred the second-half display against Chelsea a few weeks earlier, and which had ignited what looked like a strong charge to finish in seventh place.

Instead, the home side came out from the half time interval and immediately scored. Everton then descended into the irredeemably awful display that fans had hoped had been consigned to the history of a frustrating 2018/19 season.

For the hosts, it was all about Ryan Babel and Aleksander Mitrovic, with the Serbian striker rattling the crossbar and forcing a point-blank reaction save from Pickford, while the Dutchman set up Tom Cairney to score within 30 seconds of the start of the second half.

He then galloped away into oceans of space behind Everton's leaden-footed back line to dink the ball over Pickford and make it 2-0 with 21 minutes to go.

There was ample time for Everton to summon some kind of reaction, but against the second-worst team in the Premier League their response was pitifully bad, with players seemingly unable to even control a routine pass and even three changes from Silva failed to improve the fare. From an attacking perspective, there was almost nothing of note to report from the Toffees' 100-odd minutes of "action" – against a defence that had already been breached 76 times to that point in the season, Everton managed just one shot on target.

The depressingly familiar tendency for Blues teams to descend into maddening disarray lived on, regardless of the occupant of the technical area. Eradicating it would be one of Silva's big challenges.

Final score: Fulham 2-0 Everton

***

"It was a disappointing result," Silva admitted afterwards. "We didn't perform the way we want or the way we expect.

"We knew before the match and we spoke in the dressing room before how difficult it is to play here always. For us, it's not important that they were just relegated — they always put big pressure on the player with the ball.

"It wasn't a good game for us at all — I think they were more aggressive than us and faster than us."

***

21 April 2019: Everton v Manchester United

Atonement for the debacle at Craven Cottage came the following weekend as Everton powered their way to an impressive 4-0 drubbing of Manchester United. It was arguably Everton's best result for two years and it was the kind of performance that hinted at what could be under Marco Silva, with another transfer window under his belt and the chance to build on a 2018/19 season that would finish in very positive fashion.

Not since they had hammered Manchester City by the same scoreline in January 2017 had an Everton team looked so strong against "big six" opposition and they set the tone early by pegging United back for long periods before taking the lead in the 13th minute.

Lucas Digne's long throw-in was knocked on by Dominic Calvert-Lewin and Richarlison swivelled onto it to slam the opening goal into the roof of David de Gea's net.

Marcus Rashford went close on what would be a rare attack for United when he fired over after collecting a ball over the top of the home defence, but Everton broke away nine minutes later and Sigurdsson drilled an excellent shot into the bottom corner from 30 yards.

With Michael Keane back in central defence alongside Kurt Zouma and Morgan Schneiderlin slotting into midfield seamlessly in place of the suspended André Gomes, Silva's side were in dominant mood, hustling United out of their stride and forcing errors.

Silva withdrew Richarlison with a rib problem a few minutes into the second half, but his substitution in favour of Walcott didn't halt the momentum established by Everton, who extended their advantage in the 56th minute.

Sigurdsson's attempted shot deflected behind, and when De Gea punched the resulting corner clear, it fell to Digne, who rapped it back past the Spaniard with a crisp first-time effort from 25 yards out.

De Gea was stranded again in the 63rd minute when the Icelandic star sent Walcott away and the substitute finished with aplomb, guiding the ball into the far corner.

Final score: Everton 4-0 Manchester United

***

The fine victory against Manchester United, secured in brilliant Easter sunshine at Goodison, moved Everton back into 7th place on goal difference; but, after a goalless draw at Crystal Palace, a comfortable 2-0 win over Burnley, and an entertaining 2-2 draw at Tottenham – where they almost pulled off a win to end the campaign on a high – Silva's men had to be content with finishing in 8th.

Despite being pegged back late on in North London, the season had ended in hugely encouraging fashion. It meant that Everton fans could consign some really poor form over the winter months to the history books and hope there would be an injection of more genuine quality over the summer.

Question marks remained over the futures of loanees Kurt Zouma and Andre Gomes, but there was clear evidence of a structure, a plan and a process about Silva's work at Goodison that pointed the way to a more stable and competitive future for Everton.

Unfortunately for the Portuguese and the Blues, it turned out to be anything but.

2019: Bramley-Moore Dock stadium visuals revealed

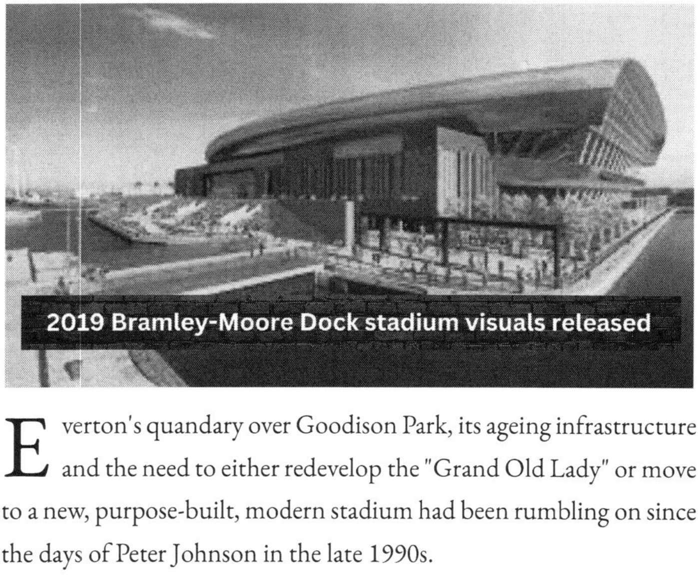

Everton's quandary over Goodison Park, its ageing infrastructure and the need to either redevelop the "Grand Old Lady" or move to a new, purpose-built, modern stadium had been rumbling on since the days of Peter Johnson in the late 1990s.

The dream of a waterfront home had died with the collapse of the Kings Dock proposal in 2004; and what many Evertonians felt was a potentially disastrous move to neighbouring Knowsley was avoided when the Destination Kirkby project was killed off by local opposition; whilst a plan to develop a ground on Walton Hall Park in 2012 had never really got off the ground.

Farhad Moshiri's arrival as major shareholder and chief benefactor in 2016 had finally allowed the club to get a new stadium project moving forward, and on 25 July 2019 Everton unveiled the first visuals of their proposed new stadium at Bramley-Moore Dock, at a special presentation on the eve of the second phase of its public consultation into the scheme.

Architect Dan Meis was in attendance at a special event for supporters that coincided with the release of artist's impressions and a brilliant CGI fly-through of the new ground.

Around 1,000 invited supporters at the Titanic Hotel, along with the Chief Executive Denise Barrett-Baxendale and chairman Bill Kenwright, gave Dan Meis a standing ovation. The structure would feature a floating roof above a brick facade, designed to embrace the unique waterfront location in Liverpool's north docks.

It was said that the design of the stadium celebrated the club's history, and the architect's aim was to try to replicate the best characteristics of Goodison Park while improving on it, with modern facilities to meet the expectations of Evertonians.

The brickwork on the exterior would pay homage to the famous Archibald Leitch latticework at Goodison Park – and supporter experience would be at the forefront of shaping the fan plaza.

Additionally, the club planned on investing more than £55 million to preserve, restore and celebrate the heritage assets at Bramley-Moore Dock. The site had been inaccessible for many years and had sat behind locked gates, while the Everton scheme aimed to bring the dock into productive use and open up the area for the public to appreciate its heritage.

Working with local and national heritage bodies, Everton had committed to saving and restoring the Grade II listed hydraulic tower. It was anticipated that they would use the tower all year round.

The water channel would also be maintained, to keep the integrity of inter-connecting docks. Other historic features, such as cobbles, capstones and tramlines, would be kept, as would the dock walls under the stadium.

In embracing its future, the club had also planned how to care for its past. Goodison Park has been a cultural icon of the city for almost 130 years and a Legacy Project was initiated that planned on delivering health and wellbeing facilities, education amenities, business start-up facilities, community retail, a youth zone, homes – including sheltered housing for the elderly – and a permanent tribute to Goodison Park through green space, using the area of the famous pitch's centre circle.

The future still looked promising, and Farhad Moshiri's vision for Everton had never looked brighter. However, just one day later, the Club announced that Jon Woods and Deputy Chairman Keith Harris were leaving the Board of Directors, saying the changes had come about following a period of "review and strategic planning".

Dr Harris had been charged with leading Everton's plans to relocate to a new stadium Bramley-Moore Dock. It was also announced that CEO Denise Barrett-Baxendale would oversee the work of Stadium Development Director Colin Chong, and take responsibility for the new stadium project — including the delivery of a community-led legacy at Goodison Park — with Sasha Ryazantsev responsible for finalising the funding for the schemes.

2019: CHANGES TO SILVA'S SQUAD, ON AND OFF THE FIELD

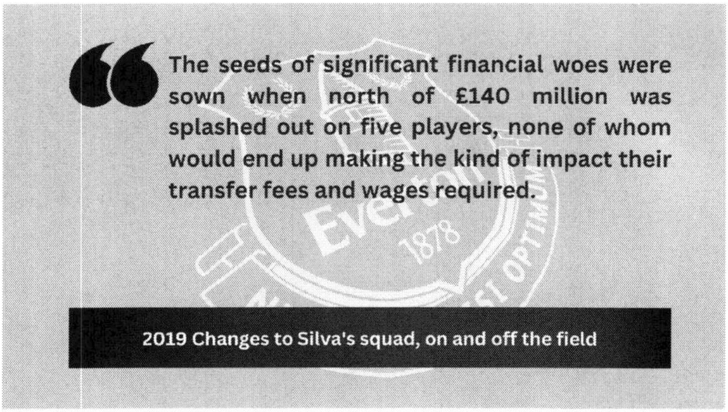

The close season is often a time of change in football and the summer of 2019 was no different at Everton, where within three weeks of the final game of the season, surprise news arrived on 1 June, when the club confirmed that Assistant Manager Joao Pedro Sousa had left the club to take up a managerial role in his native Portugal.

Marco Silva's Number 2 had accepted a two-year contract to coach at newly promoted Famalicao.

Sousa had worked with Silva at each of his five most recent clubs, including Everton, and the pair were also teammates at Trofense during the late 1990s. His departure was unwelcome news for the young Everton manager.

***

Three weeks after that, Everton confirmed the first of their summer signings aimed at further strengthening Silva's squad to support a push towards the top six in 2019/20. In all, six players would come in before the unusually early transfer deadline on 8 August (for one season the Premier League tried closing the summer window before the start of the season) but, with central-defensive stalwart Phil Jagielka leaving on a free transfer after 12 years with the Toffees, it was the signing the club didn't make that, arguably, came back to haunt them.

Furthermore, the seeds of significant financial woes were sown when north of £140 million was splashed out on five players, none of whom would end up making the kind of impact their transfer fees and wages required.

Following the arrival on goalkeeper Jonas Lössl on a free transfer, André Gomes was acquired for £22 million in a deal struck with Barcelona. The Portuguese midfielder signed a five-year contract and made permanent his switch from the Nou Camp after a successful season on loan at Goodison Park in 2018/19.

"I know the Club made a massive effort to sign me and I'm very happy and thankful to them," Gomes told evertonfc.com at the time. "I said during the year that I felt part of a family and that is the most important thing to me.

"Last year was a really good experience for me. I just wanted to feel part of something special and I found it here. It was good for me in that moment and right now, after signing for Everton, it's even better.

"I always got massive support since day one. I'm really happy to have this badge on me right now.

"I want to give all the fans my best because I think they deserve the best. I have to thank Marco and Marcel, too, because they made a really massive effort for me to be here."

Following his impressive form for Valencia and on the international stage for Portugal, where he was in the team that won the 2016 European Championships, Gomes had joined Barcelona in a big-money deal in 2016 that was worth €35 million up front and included another €20 million in appearance-related add-ons.

He made just 29 starts in all competitions for the Liga giants, being used more as a substitute than a first-team regular as his much-vaunted move turned sour. Linked strongly with a move to Tottenham in the summer of 2017, Gomes would end up staying at Barcelona. He had been open about the psychological toll his poor form was taking, and he welcomed the chance to join Everton on loan a year later.

A hamstring injury, suffered during Barcelona's pre-season trip to the United States, prevented him from making his Blues debut until October. Thereafter, he quickly established himself as a vital member of Marco Silva's team and formed a strong partnership with Idrissa Gueye in central midfield.

***

On 15 July, Everton completed the signing of 29-year-old Fabian Delph from Manchester City in a deal initially worth £8.5 million pounds, by agreeing a three-year contract that would keep him at Goodison Park until 2022.

"I'm hungry," he said after the deal was announced. "I don't like losing. I see myself as a winner. I'm at an age now where I am probably one of the most experienced players, so hopefully I can help my teammates here to do better.

"I'm really happy to be here. I'm going to give absolutely everything — nothing less than 100 per cent.

"Every time I have played against Everton, whether it was home or away, straight away the first thing that comes to mind when you see the fans is passion, Everton fans seem to know football, seem to understand it, it seems to be in their blood and they really back the team."

Having initially come to prominence at Leeds United. Delph had been linked with a move to Everton ten years earlier after he had helped the Yorkshire club gain a promotion from League One. He eventually signed for Aston Villa and became a full England international during the latter stages of his time there.

Despite verbally committing his future to Villa in the summer of 2015, Manchester City tempted Delph away with an £8 million move as they sought to bolster their squad. He made 89 appearances in all competitions for them, scoring five times.

Originally deployed in his natural central midfield role, he had played more recently as a left-back, to cover for Benjamin Mendy who sustained a long-term injury.

Delph had battled injuries of his own, however, in recent years but, with him being available for a cut-price fee a year before his contract expired at the Etihad Stadium, Marcel Brands and Marco Silva imagined the value in adding his versatility to their midfield options.

***

Early in August, Everton tied up the £23 million transfer of Jean-Philippe Gbamin from FSV Mainz 05. He also penned a five-year contract to become the fourth new face of the summer and was followed a few days later by the 19-year-old Italian striker, Moise Kean.

Both players fitted the profile that Brands and Silva were now principally targeting – young, exciting and with potential sell-on value down the road if they were successful at Goodison.

Ademola Lookman, a £10 million acquisition made by Steve Walsh in January 2017, had fitted the same bill but had struggled to settle on Merseyside, and was sold to RB Leipzig for a fee rising to £22.5 million in between the arrivals of Delph and Gbamin.

Gbamin, 23, had broken into the Lens first-team in 2013 after spells with Aire-sur-la-Lys and U.S. Saint-Quentin Blessy's youth setups.

Mainz had brought him to the Bundesliga in 2016 as a promising France U21 international, but he switched his international allegiance to Ivory Coast, the country of his birth, shortly afterwards, for whom he had won 11 caps to date.

Gbamin was intended to be the replacement for Idrissa Gueye, who had just joined Paris Saint-Germain, but he could supposedly also operate at centre-half if needed. He would wear the No. 25 jersey.

"It's a big moment with a lot of emotion and now it's on me to prove on the pitch why they bought me," Gbamin said.

"I'm excited because Everton is a great club here in England with a big history and ambition, so I didn't think for more than a moment — I wanted to come here."

***

Moise Kean, meanwhile, was drafted in from Juventus in a deal that was officially undisclosed but said to be worth £25.1 million.

The Blues won the race for the highly rated teenager, fending off reported interest from the likes of Arsenal and Manchester United, and he signed a five-year contract after completing a successful medical.

The Serie A club would have first option on Kean should Everton decide to sell him in the future but there was no buy-back clause in the deal, negotiated to be paid in three instalments, that would rise to £27.5 million if appearance-related add-one were triggered.

"I am very proud and honoured to wear the Everton shirt. I will give my best to this team," Kean said on evertontv.

"I was convinced to sign because Everton is a club looking to the future and so am I.

"I know about the size of the club. It has big ambition and I will work very hard to help us fulfil what we want to achieve.

"I am used to winning and I want to bring this winning attitude to the team. I hope I will be very good on the field and bring the fans joy."

After the signing, Marco Silva, said: "A striker was one of our priority signings this summer.

"Moise is strong, fast, with many good qualities as a striker and he is just 19 years old. He has talent, and he is ready to work, ready to improve our squad and gives us different solutions."

***

As July was drawing to a close, Marco Silva had publically stated that Everton needed to sign five more players before deadline day if the club were, in his words, to do "better than last season".

Gbamin and Kean filled two of those spots but the manager also reportedly wanted a centre-back to replace the departed Jagielka, a winger, and a new right-back and admitting that a shortage of options in that position had forced him to "risk" playing Seamus Coleman in two pre-season friendly games in Germany that summer.

Asked if he thought it possible for Everton to complete their business in less than two weeks, the manager said: "It should be if you really want to be competitive and to do better than last season. Because, at the end of the day, it is what we want to do: do better than last season."

***

This transfer deadline day was Thursday 8 August. As usual, there was lots of last-minute activity and speculation in the media with Everton known to be targeting a wide player and a centre-half as the window entered its final 24 hours.

The French full-back, Djibril Sidibé, became the sixth Everton signing of the summer when he arrived on loan from AS Monaco for the season, but the Blues had been unable to persuade Chelsea to part with Kurt Zouma who had excelled during his loan spell with the club the previous season.

With the benefit of hindsight, it was clear that Brands and Silva had put too many of their eggs in a Zouma-shaped basket, and were left with few options to bolster their defence as time ran out.

An approach to sign defender Chris Smalling was reportedly knocked back on deadline day by Manchester United but, otherwise, the speculation was dominated by the search for a winger, one that became more urgent after Everton were foiled in their attempts to sign Wilfred Saha from Crystal Palace.

Farhad Moshiri had made no secret of his admiration of the Ivory Coast attacker and the Blues were believed to have offered as much as £52 million for him. Palace, who would have to pass on 25% of any fee on to Manchester United, would not lower their asking price, said to be around £70 million, even after the player handed in a transfer request. With 90 minutes to go before the deadline, word came through from Selhurst Park that Zaha was not leaving the club under any circumstances.

That left Moshiri and Everton to scramble in the waning minutes of the window to try and agree a deal with Arsenal for Alex Iwobi. In between, Steven Bergwijn of PSV Eindhoven had been floated as a potential alternative but it was Iwobi who re-emerged as an option with just 15 minutes to go before the 5pm cut-off.

It would later emerge that Iwobi was on a boat in Dubai when the call came through from Marco Silva sounding him out over a potential move to Goodison Park, but he and his potential new club faced a race against time to get the paperwork filed on time.

"We told them it was an emergency, like we needed to spin the boat [around] and get back quick, because we were in the middle of nowhere," Iwobi would later recount. "I have to give props to the driver because I don't know how he sped back to get us back in time to try and sign the documents."

In the end, Everton were able to submit a deal sheet to the Premier League almost within seconds of the deadline and successfully completed the transfer for an initial fee of £28 million rising to £35 million depending on appearances.

On balance, Iwobi's move to Merseyside was not the success all concerned hoped it would be. The winger would struggle for consistency for his first couple of years as a Toffee, and it would take another Londoner, Frank Lampard, to draw the best out of him just when Everton needed it most in order to stay in the Premier League. Eventually Iwobi would return to London, after a move to Fulham late in the 2023 summer transfer window.

2019: Blues Keep Faith in Marco Silva

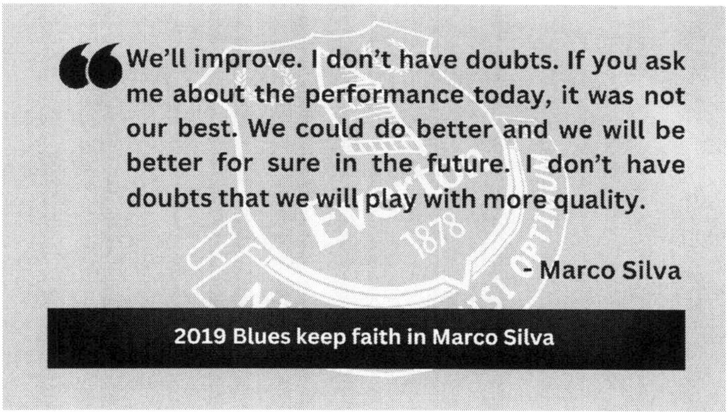

The way in which Everton finished the 2018/19 season, with just two defeats in 11 games and with impressive home victories against Chelsea and Manchester United that helped secure an eighth-place finish, had engendered real optimism for Marco Silva's second season in charge.

Though there was concern over the failure to sign a centre-half to cover the loss of Phil Jagielka and loanee Kurt Zouma, there as cautious excitement about the new signings the club had been able to make during the close season.

***

17 August 2019: Everton v Watford

The first home game of 2019/20 was against Silva's former club, Watford. After the disappointment of the opening day's 0-0 stalemate at Crystal Palace the previous week, this felt like one of those games Everton needed to win if they were to improve on last season's 8th place finish.

Seeing Goodison Park in full voice with 38,000 blue-and-white flags waving as the blaring siren gave way to Z-Cars, and Everton then taking an early lead, it felt as though a more convincing result was in store than ultimately proved to be the case. But a win was a win; three points are three points.

It could easily have ended in an irritating draw, and the Blues had contrived to throw away two points or more on so many occasions in recent years that it would have come as little surprise if they had. Certainly, when there didn't seem to be much of a central midfield, with André Gomes looking like he was playing with the benefit of pain-killing jabs and Jean-Pierre Gbamin fading after an impressive start, or when Watford launched their aerial bombardment in the last quarter of the game, you couldn't help but sense a dreaded equaliser in the offing.

But this was an Everton team that, stretching back into last season, had now kept 10 clean sheets in its last 13 Premier League matches and hadn't conceded a goal at home since the beginning of February. Despite the departure of Zouma, Michael Keane had simply picked up where the Chelsea man had left off the previous season, and Yerry Mina was quickly converting the doubters with two towering displays to start 2019/20. And in Jordan Pickford, Silva had inherited a player capable of preserving winning positions with his bravery, presence of mind and sheer shot-stopping ability... even if that sometimes meant keeping the ball out with his face!

If a solid defensive foundation appeared to be in place the fluidity and potency of the attack looked like it would take more time. Richarlison and Gylfi Sigurdsson, in particular, had yet to pair their industry off the ball with effectiveness on it. Dominic Calvert-Lewin, full of running and work-rate himself, still didn't look like the best fit for Silva's current system; the 22-year-old didn't have a shot during his 72 minutes on the field whereas his replacement, Moise Kean, quickly showed that he might already fit the profile, and could have scored twice, which really would have put the seal on the afternoon.

Thankfully, while chances were at a premium, Bernard proved to be the difference on the day. The little Brazilian had taken his time to adjust to life in England but against Watford, he showed signs of his growing confidence.

The match was just 10 minutes old when Lucas Digne swept a sublime ball down the left channel for Bernard to chase. The No. 20 cut inside, showing all the signs of looking to play in a teammate, but instead fired an early, low shot inside the near post and past Ben Foster before the goalkeeper could react.

So far, so good for Silva's men, who were looking a great deal more inventive than they had been at Selhurst Park the previous weekend. As the only player among the new signings to be making his home debut, Jean-Philippe Gbamin was in the spotlight. He was given plenty of the ball and showed in consistent flashes over the first half hour that he could be both a physical but also enterprising presence in the midfield's heart.

Watford posed a regular threat from set-pieces and they came close to cancelling out Bernard's goal midway through the first half when Craig Dawson's header come back off the post, and the second period didn't start in encouraging fashion for the home side, either.

Former Goodison favourite, Gerard Deulofeu, accelerated between Digne and Richarlison and knocked the ball into the path of Troy Deeney by the penalty spot, but Pickford was off his line quickly and took the shot squarely in the face to preserve the clean sheet.

Everton still remained the more dangerous of the two sides in attack, especially following Kean's introduction with 18 minutes left, and the tide turned back in their favour. With the Hornets chasing the contest late on, Bernard sent Kean clear but the young Italian blazed a shot high and wide from around the edge of the box and screwed an even better chance an inch the wrong side of the upright in stoppage time.

Had it gone in, it might have taken the roof off Goodison, but there was plenty from the teenager to suggest that he would prove to be a very exciting addition to the team. Deceptively powerful, he showed superb strength against some large defenders and proved he could turn on the jets as well when presented with space in front of him.

In the end, the one goal was enough. That kind of resilience could only stand Everton in good stead while the new boys bedded in. Four points, two clean sheets, and with none of the summer acquisitions yet fully embedded in the team, it represented a pretty good start to the new season.

Final score: Everton 1-0 Watford

***

Afterwards, Marco Silva said he was sure that Everton would play better but he was pleased his side had seen out an important victory.

"It was not our best performance, for sure," he said. "We played really well [for] the first 30 minutes, but even when we weren't doing so well in the game, the fans were always behind the team and supporting the players.

"I think we deserved the three points. Of course, it's always a tough game in the Premier League but we created more chances to score.

"We'll improve. I don't have doubts that we will play with more quality."

***

On 27 August Everton confirmed that their new midfielder, Jean-Philippe Gbamin had damaged a quadricep tendon in training and was expected to be out for at least eight weeks.

The club's statement indicated that they would be consulting experts in Europe for possible advice on how best to rehabilitate the injury. Sadly for Gbamin and the club, this would turn out to be the first in a series of major injuries for the player.

***

1 September 2019: Everton v Wolverhampton Wanderers

The second away game of the season had seen Everton give a debut to new signing, Alex Iwobi, who came on as a second-half substitute. Frustratingly, the Blues squandered many chances, eventually going down 2-0 to a spirited Aston Villa side.

The midweek Carabao Cup game away at Lincoln had been far more positive. Goals from Lucas Digne, Gylfi Sigurdsson, Iwobi and Richarlison were enough to secure a place in the 4th round, in a 4-2 win.

Back on home turf, where they were on a five-match winning streak going back to the end of the previous season, for Sunday afternoon kick off against Wolves, they entertained the Goodison crowd to a high-scoring match against Nuno Espirito Santo's side.

Had this match ended 2-2, as it looked like it might with 15 minutes to go, Evertonians would have gone into the international break feeling somewhat deflated.

Five points from a possible 12 would have felt like a poor return from the relatively comfortable opening set of fixtures to the new season, but seven points and 6th place heading into the first enforced two-week hiatus of the campaign had a much rosier look to it.

Everton were still reeling to a degree from the debacle at Villa Park nine days prior and Silva needed both a reaction and a strong performance from some key individuals. And in Gylfi Sigurdsson, Andre Gomes and Richarlison, in particular, he would have seen three players who responded in pleasingly strong fashion, while also getting some telling contributions from another trio making their full Premier League debuts.

Alex Iwobi scored with his second header in the space of four days. Moise Kean played a vital role in the opening goal and Fabian Delph helped coordinate things in the middle with the energy and combativeness that was so sorely lacking in the matches against Crystal Palace and Villa. If he could stay fit, the £8 million acquisition from Manchester City looked as though he could prove to be the steal of the summer.

Not that it was all plain sailing, of course. Wolves twice pegged Everton back with goals that were poorly defended. Sometimes the Blues' central midfield was a little too porous and in the first half especially, the visitors were getting behind the fullbacks with worrying ease. But, having twice lost the lead, this was a test of character and resolve that Silva's boys passed, even in the face of some typically one-sided refereeing from Anthony Taylor.

The biggest headlines deservedly belonged to Richarlison, a player who was perhaps fortunate to keep his place in the team after the opening three matches of the season. Silva had enough faith in the young Brazilian and was rewarded as he got the hosts off and running inside five minutes of kick-off.

Conor Coady miscued a back-pass to Rui Patricio, the keeper's attempted clearance struck Kean and fell invitingly into the path of Richarlison who fired a shot that bounced off the ground and looped up into the goal.

It was a lead that would last just four minutes, though. Lucas Digne failed to deal with a high ball down Wolves' right flank and Adama Traoré took it off him and burst to the byline, out-stripping the Frenchman for pace again as he powered inside before fizzing it low across the face of Jordan Pickford's goal. Seamus Coleman could only block its path and Romain Saïss prodded home the loose ball to level the match.

Everton were back in front just three minutes later. Richarlison hooked an excellent pass down the line for Sigurdsson and he whipped an equally impressive ball into the middle where Iwobi was on hand to steer a header past the goalkeeper.

In contrast to the previous home game against Watford, this was an open, entertaining and often breathless encounter between two attacking sides. Everton came out of the half-time break still willing to push to extend their lead but, having dealt with the threat from the visitors fairly well, they succumbed meekly in the 75th minute when Willy Boly flicked a throw-in to the back post and Raúl Jiménez stole in untracked by Digne to head in the second equaliser of the game.

That could have been another of those pivotal, confidence-draining moments, but Everton would be back in front for good when Digne and Richarlison underlined the precious value of quality when they combined beautifully with 10 minutes left.

The Frenchman appeared to be going nowhere, closer to the corner flag than the penalty area but he cracked a superb cross in from the byline that Richarlison met with a towering leap over Boly that he guided past the keeper's fingertips and inside the far post.

3-2! Goodison was bouncing at three well-earned points that lifted Everton above three of last season's top six heading into the international break. More than that, in contrast to this same fixture in 2018/19 where the Toffees were played off their own park, it showed just how good Silva's team could be when they had their best players firing on all cylinders.

Final score: Everton 3-2 Wolves

***

21 September 2019: Everton v Sheffield United

How the pendulum swings! No sooner had Marco Silva and Everton sent a signal that the blue touch paper might have been lit on their fledgling season with the hugely encouraging victory against Wolves, than they followed it up with the huge disappointment of a 3-1 away defeat at Bournemouth.

In his latest pre-match press conference, the manager had spent his time with the print media fending off the notion that his team were in an early-season crisis. Yet, come the final whistle at Goodison Park following an utterly dreadful performance against Sheffield United, the Portuguese's dishevelled hair and flustered countenance betrayed a man who could be under no illusions about the mess he and his team were now making of the new campaign.

After finishing 2018/19 so promisingly, Everton were arguably better placed than most to start the new season strongly and help set the early pace in the Premier League. A favourable start against two newly promoted clubs and three that had "bottom half" written all over them should have provided the ideal platform to do so. The proverbial door to the top six was open; instead, there was now mounting evidence that the Blues had probably already scuppered their hopes of finishing among those coveted positions come May.

As it turned out, it wasn't too early for such doom-laden prognostications following an utterly dire display. Sheffield United won 2-0 with just two shots all game and only one on target (Yerry Mina inadvertently scored a first-half own goal) with a performance that their manager, Chris Wilder, described as their worst with the ball so far this season.

Everton had 70% of the possession but — stop us if you've heard this before — did almost nothing with it, forcing just three meaningful saves from Dean Henderson, none of which were taxing of the Blades' goalkeeper.

The most worrying aspects of the whole match, however, were the set-piece defending, the galling lack of character and attacking punch in the Blues' side, particularly in the second half, and the desperate moves made by Silva to salvage something from the game.

Eyebrows were raised when Alex Iwobi, arguably one of the most effective Everton players in recent games, was dropped to the bench to accommodate Bernard, while the manager persisted with two holding midfielders against a limited attack. Moise Kean's return to the starting XI was less surprising, given Silva's desire to bed him in at home, but by the end of 90 minutes the hosts had a five-man forward line, just three defenders and not much of a midfield to speak of, after Morgan Schneiderlin and Seamus Coleman were withdrawn in the second half.

As the Toffees chased the game in the final quarter of an hour, it was not surprising that John Lundstram was able to capitalise on the space. He slipped Lys Mousset in, to double the lead and kill the match with a clinical finish past Jordan Pickford. That Everton failed to muster a chance worthy of the name in the ensuing 11 minutes plus five of stoppage time told you everything you needed to know about a team going nowhere.

Final score: Everton 0-2 Sheffield United

***

Speaking after the defeat, veteran midfielder Fabian Delph said that Everton's players needed to shoulder their share of the blame for the dire reverse against Sheffield United.

"The manager always ends up coming under a lot of pressure, but us players need to have a good look in the mirror and look at each other," admitted Delph.

"I hate losing. I have three little girls and cannot let them win anything. I'm a nightmare.

"But you get your frustration out. You speak about the game individually to people and collectively. Now we focus on Sheffield Wednesday [in the League Cup].

"We weren't good enough. We planned well all week, and it didn't click. It is a big club with a lot of history and we expect more from ourselves.

"The fans always turn up and they have made their feelings clear."

***

3 November 2019: Everton v Tottenham Hotspur

Following that alarming loss, Everton steered themselves into the League Cup Quarter Finals with wins over Sheffield Wednesday at Hillsborough and Watford at Goodison Park, but had slid worryingly down the Premier League table in the interim with defeats to Burnley,

Manchester City and Brighton – although the loss the Seagulls on the south coast was an especially cruel one. The Toffees had largely been spared, to that point, of any controversy by the recently-introduced system of Video Assistant Referees. But, having played well against Brighton and come from behind to lead 2-1 in the second half, their efforts were derailed by an astounding recommendation by VAR Lee Mason. He proposed the on-field referee award the hosts a penalty, when Michael Keane inadvertently stood on the foot of Aaron Connolly. Neal Maupay converted the resulting spot-kick to level the game at 2-2, Everton never recovered and a miserable afternoon on their part was complete when Lucas Digne put through his own net in stoppage time.

By the time Tottenham came to Goodison Park in early November, it was feeling like a 'must-win' match. But not only were the Toffees denied all three points, they would lose a first-choice midfielder in André Gomes to an horrific ankle injury as well.

Two teams struggling for form and sitting in the bottom half of the table before kick-off played out a first half depressingly bereft of quality, made worse by typically horrendous officiating from referee Martin Atkinson.

Richarlison had Everton's brightest moments before half-time when he spun on Digne's low cross in the 32nd minute but fired straight at Gazzaniga in the Spurs goal and later rolled Davinson Sanchez before lashing over.

The second period had begun in the same vein until the match came to life with an hour gone. First, Richarlison finished a smart move by latching onto Digne's cut-back but was foiled by a good save by the Tottenham keeper.

Then, a costly mistake by Alex Iwobi in his own half allowed Spurs to take the lead. The former Gunner passed straight to Son Hueng-Min, who released Dele Alli to turn inside his marker and drill a shot past Pickford to make it 1-0.

Everton tried to push in response, almost prompting Ben Davies to turn the ball into his own net. A lengthy VAR check looked like it might hand the home side a spot kick after Alli handled the ball in his own box, but, controversially, no penalty was awarded.

The contest then turned from frustrating and fractious to sombre in the 78th minute. Son, aggrieved not to have been awarded a free-kick in Everton's half, chased Gomes down as the Portuguese advanced down the hosts' left flank and impetuously lunged in from behind.

Gomes collided heavily with Aurier and was left prone in unmistakable distress near the touchline, with the horrified reaction of supporters in the Family Enclosure nearby leaving the television audience in no doubt that the midfielder had suffered a terrible injury.

Under advice from the VAR official, Anthony Taylor changed Son's initial yellow card to a red and the Spurs forward, wracked by tears at the extent of Gomes's condition, walked down the tunnel. Meanwhile, Silva prepared a double change that saw Gylfi Sigurdsson and Dominic Calvert-Lewin come on, with Tom Davies the other player to make way.

Calvert-Lewin came close to equalising when he headed an excellent Sigurdsson cross over, but it was Tosun who finally made the breakthrough with 97 minutes on the clock to ensure that the spoils were shared.

The result kept Everton in 17th place, one above the relegation zone, and still searching for the consistency expected of an expensively assembled side.

Final score: Everton 1-1 Spurs

***

Afterwards, Cenk Tosun described how he had tried to comfort Gomes whom, it would transpire, had sustained a dislocation fracture to his ankle following Son's reckless tackle. Insult would be added to that injury a couple of days later when the South Korean's red card was downgraded to a yellow.

"Everybody is so sad inside," Tosun said. "Some players, they nearly cried.

"[André] was in shock. His eyes were open so big. He was crying, shouting, and screaming. I just tried to hold him and speak to him; I tried to tell him to stay calm. We couldn't understand him. He was the one who had got the injury.

"It will be a tough time for Andre, but sometimes in football, these injuries happen.

"I just hope and pray he comes back stronger after his surgery. We will give him the motivation he needs. My goal is for him, the point is for him. If we had a few minutes more, we would have won it for him."

The circumstances of the horror injury to Gomes, one that looked at the time as though it might cost him a year of his career at least, were just a part of a match that was officiated badly by Atkinson and ruined by yet more VAR controversy. Taylor was called upon in Stockley Park to review three potential penalty incidents, all three of which were deemed not to be fouls, even though there was clear contact on Richarlison by Aurier for one and an even more obvious handball by Dele Alli in another.

The Dele incident, subsequently explained by the Premier League as not being a penalty because Yerry Mina's presence supposedly caused Alli to handle the ball, took three minutes of review by VAR before a decision came back to Atkinson, further undermining the credibility and usefulness of a tool that had failed Everton on two successive weekends.

"It is really tough for us to talk about what has happened on the pitch," said Marco Silva, who accepted a dubious penalty decision by VAR that went against Michael Keane in Brighton the previous weekend. "What I want to tell you, all of us love football and we play for our fans and I am 100 percent sure they didn't like what they saw this afternoon."

On Gomes, Silva said he was waiting to learn of the extent of the injury but photographs of the aftermath of Son's tackle left no doubt that he had suffered an awful injury.

"He's gone to hospital. Our medical staff are in control. This is a bad moment for us and our team — this was [about] more than a football game. We will give all support to André and his family."

As it turned out, Gomes would make a stunningly rapid recovery and, remarkably, he was back playing again just 112 days later.

***

23 November 2019: Everton v Norwich

Everton had followed up the draw against Tottenham with an away win at Southampton. Yet, at the halfway stage of a home match against newly-promoted Norwich City in late November, Evertonians were feeling as though they were stuck in a familiar pattern: just biding their time for Theo Walcott to be substituted around the 70-minute mark; for Alex Iwobi to come on like a fortnight previously to make some telling contribution that made a mockery of his selection among the substitutes; for Gylfi Sigurdsson to finally be deployed in the No.10 role; or for Marco Silva to throw on Dominic Calvert-Lewin either in place of, or in addition to Cenk Tosun.

Mostly, though, it felt like the Everton fraternity was simply marking time until Silva's time was up, and the Board put a merciful end to what was looking increasingly like a failed tenure. After the Norwich game, there was a sense that timescale had compressed dramatically.

Many Blues expected Silva to pick up three points against a Canaries side who came into the match rock bottom, then to eke out a few points from a daunting December programme, and limp his way to May where, maybe, the Everton hierarchy would make a bold decision to replace him with someone more experienced and more qualified.

Yet, there was an urgency about the managerial situation at Goodison, with the team in danger of spiralling out of control in a manner evoking the death throes of he Ronald Koeman and Roberto Martinez reigns. Indeed, there was a very "last days of Martinez" feel to this match, after Norwich took a second-half lead and the dread set in that, not only would Everton not recover but, just like Sheffield United did in September, the Canaries would complete the job with a late second.

That they did, and it triggered a chorus of loud boos and a rapid emptying of the stands, as disgusted fans poured out into the streets around Goodison amid a crushing sense of collective déjà vu, while many of those who remained to the bitter end made no secret of their feelings.

That Everton always provided accommodating opposition for any team or player struggling through a poor run is the stuff of gallows humour and social media meme, but after two wins and a draw since the frustrating events at Brighton last month, there can't have been many Blues who foresaw what unfolded today.

Norwich had arrived on Merseyside without an away win, with just a single goal on their travels since they regained promotion, and a stench of the doomed about them. But they matched Everton in a dull first half and by full-time, they had run rings around a desperately poor Toffees outfit, carved them open to score their first in the 55th minute, added a somewhat fortunate but predictable second in stoppage time and were just a Teemu Pukki goal from putting the cherry on top of the "Everton, That" cake.

It was that bad – so disorganised, passionless, lethargic and lacking in leadership – that even if they had rescued a point, it wouldn't have been enough to dampen the growing sense that Silva's week-to-week case for remaining in the post needed to come to a definitive end.

Final score: Everton 0-2 Norwich

***

4 December 2019: Liverpool v Everton

This fixture had become so painful as the years stretched on after Everton's last win on Liverpool's soil in 1999 that by the time Roberto Martinez had overseen two 4-0 defeats at Anfield, many Evertonians had developed a self-protective numbness to the derby. A certain level of defeatism and realism in the run-up to the game helped Blues fans cope with the agony of defeat and no one really gave Everton a chance when they crossed the Park in early December 2019 with manager Marco Silva under mounting pressure.

Whether this latest drubbing at the hands of the old enemy was as bad as feared or simply just depressingly predictable probably depended on who you asked, but at the base level, it felt as though Silva had failed the Blue faithful.

The injuries to his three preferred central midfielders continued to provide somewhat mitigating circumstances but where Silva arguably erred was in persisting with Gylfi Sigurdsson in midfield alongside Tom Davies, rather than restoring Morgan Schneiderlin, a player more used to playing in a withdrawn role in front of the back four, to the team.

Just as he had against Leicester on the preceding Sunday, a match that also ended in defeat for Everton, Davies struggled with the demands of covering more than just his usual duties alongside the Icelander, who was anonymous for long stretches even by the holographic standards he had set that season. It made for a vacuous midfield compounding a high defensive line that Liverpool ruthlessly exploited.

Given the reds' form and reputation, and the calamity that had recently befallen Everton in the final half hour at the King Power Stadium, at the very least one might have expected a compact and concentrated performance during the first half; one designed to nullify the Liverpool attack. Instead, the Blues were cavalier in the early going and, just as they had been by the Foxes the previous Sunday, were undone with depressing ease by fast transitions and then balls over the top that were so simple in their conception, it was a wonder how Silva's defence was still being caught out by them.

Sadio Mané should have completed a hat-trick, but far from learning from the error, Silva persisted with the high line, and was probably fortunate to escape Anfield without an even bigger deficit. Klopp's side quickly showed that all they had to do was catch Everton on the counter-attack, or ruthlessly exploit a ponderous and shambolic back line with long balls behind the defence to tear up the Portuguese's game plan.

They took all of six minutes to get the humiliation underway. Mané and his precision pass caught Michael Keane flat-footed and Jordan Pickford in no-man's-land off his line, allowing Divock Origi to take it past him and roll the ball into the empty net.

Ten minutes later, it was 2-0. Mané carried the ball to the edge of the Toffees' box and waited for Xherdan Shaqiri's run across him before slipping it into the path of the Swiss who cut it past the stranded Pickford. Cue remonstrations between Mason Holgate and Sidibé and earnest conversations between Keane and Davies.

To their credit, Everton didn't immediately fold, and they were back in the contest within just four minutes. A short corner routine almost broke down, with a poor ball by Sidibé, but the ball broke to Davies, he slid it to Alex Iwobi who drove the ball into the box where it came off the sliding Dejan Lovren and Keane knocked it over Adrian to make it 2-1.

Four minutes after that, Iwobi sent Calvert-Lewin away with a beautiful slide-rule pass but the striker was barged over by Virgil van Dijk just as he was pulling the trigger. If there was a VAR check, Everton would never have got a decision off Martin Atkinson, so play continued.

Unfortunately, what could on another day have been a turning point in the contest in favour of Everton's, prefaced a third goal for Liverpool. Once again, it was galling in its simplicity. Lovren looked up and sent a missile over the top behind Keane and Holgate, which Origi controlled and then steered high into Pickford's net.

That prompted an early change from Silva, who hooked Sidibé, who had been dreadful, and threw on Bernard; moved Holgate to fullback; and pushed Richarlison further forward alongside Calvert-Lewin.

But when an Everton corner was cleared, a rampant Liverpool sped away to score their fourth. Mané turned inside Iwobi in his own half and sent Alexander-Arnold away into a two-on-one situation. The young right back waited for the Senegalese to arrive before teeing him up for a tidy side-foot finish inside Pickford's right-hand post.

If there had been a beacon of light for Everton on an otherwise bleak and harrowing evening, it was that their two Brazilian lads never not lost their heart or desire. They combined to great effect in first-half stoppage time to send the visitors into the dressing room with some hope. Played down the left by Lucas Digne, Bernard despatched a left-footed cross towards the penalty spot and, throwing himself at it between the two centre-backs, Richarlison sent the ball flying past the goalkeeper into the net, off his shoulder.

It wasn't until the last 10 minutes that what had been a typically fractious derby opened up again. Despite a one-on-one chance for Kean against Adrián, it was the Reds who added insult to injury with a fifth goal in the 90th minute. Firmino twisted and turned Holgate near the by-line, cut it back to Gini Wijnaldum who sent an early shot through three Blue jerseys and inside the far post.

With his hands dug into his pockets, Silva had spent much of the second half with an expressionless demeanour, perhaps knowing that his team was struggling its way to another defeat. It had been men against boys for much of the match and it resulted in another psychologically damaging defeat.

Final score: Liverpool 5-2 Everton

***

Silva would rightly point to injuries to key players, cite awful officiating and injustice by VAR and bemoan some pretty rotten luck, but the scale and nature of this defeat unfortunately underscored that in a very Martinez way, Silva was struggling to prove that he could learn from his mistakes.

Amid reports that the Board of Directors would imminently discuss the manager's future by conference call, the axe was expected to fall swiftly. Whom they would bring in to replace him would be just as important as the decision to put Silva out of his misery. And those decisions would say a lot about the state of play in the boardroom, and just how much sway Marcel Brands now had.

2019: Silva sacked after 5-2 mauling at Anfield

> “Everton’s players were reportedly asked to stay behind after training to be addressed by the owner, and at 7.00 pm the first report emerged via the BBC claiming that Silva had been sacked and would not be in charge against Chelsea on that weekend

2019: Silva sacked after 5-2 mauling at Anfield

The morning after the debacle at Anfield, and amid fevered media speculation that Marco Silva would receive his marching orders, Everton’s owner Farhad Moshiri was photographed leaving Runcorn train station before travelling to the club’s training complex at Finch Farm. He was joined by Sasha Ryazantsev, his representative on the Board, and chairman Bill Kenwright for what bore all the hallmarks of the executioner coming to end Silva’s time as manager.

Just a week earlier, following an interview by Director of Football, Marcel Brands, in which the Dutchman had stressed the club was going to stay united behind the manager, it appeared as though the Portuguese would be given more time to turn things around. But the nature of the derby defeat, in which Everton conceded four first-half goals for only the second time in the Premier League era, combined with the supporters' reaction, might have forced Moshiri's hand.

In truth, Silva had been clinging onto his role for weeks, lurching from damaging defeats to brief periods of apparent stability. However, successive defeats to Norwich City, Leicester and Liverpool proved to be the final straws for the club hierarchy who felt compelled to act.

Everton and their manager had left the field at Goodison to boos at the end of the 2-0 reverse to the Canaries, the third time this season that Silva's side had lost to a newly-promoted side without registering a goal. And, despite a promising showing against the Foxes, a weakened reds team had humiliated them in the Merseyside derby.

Those results had left the club sitting in the relegation zone, having lost nine of their opening 15 games of the Premier League campaign; a miserable return from what was, until that week, a relatively comfortable run of fixtures. Silva left the club with an overall win percentage of 36%, lower than Ronald Koeman's 40%, below Roberto Martinez's 38%, and a shade under the 37% managed by Sam Allardyce.

On a strange day at Finch Farm, Everton's players were also reportedly asked to stay behind after training to be addressed by the owner. By 7.00 pm the first report had emerged via the BBC, claiming that Silva had been sacked and would not be in charge against Chelsea on that weekend.

Indeed, sacked Silva was; 18 months into his three-year contract. First-team coach Duncan Ferguson was appointed in a caretaker capacity to take charge of the clash with the Londoners at Goodison

Park, while a club statement confirmed that Everton would look to appoint a new permanent manager as a quickly as possible.

Billed as potentially the next Jose Mourinho, Silva had been an ambitious hire by Moshiri who had pivoted from the experience and more staid style of Koeman and Allardyce to what he hoped would be a more dynamic style under a young, innovative coach.

But in Silva, many Evertonians had found echoes of Martinez's reign as boss, with an undercurrent of stubbornness against changing formations and defensive vulnerabilities that frequently cost his side points. In the wake of the miserable game at Anfield, few were left in doubt that Moshiri had needed to act.

2019: Big Dunc's Blues beat Chelsea

> Anyone who was at Goodison Park when Duncan Ferguson took charge of his first match as stand-in manager would have been in no doubt of the level of anxiety coursing through the crowd, given the outpouring of emotion and relief that greeted what happened that day.
>
> **2019 Big Dunc's Blues beat Chelsea**

In the years following his departure from Goodison Park, Marco Silva would lead Fulham back to the Premier League and rebuild his reputation as one of the most promising young managers in the game by achieving a top-half finish in the Cottagers' first season back in the top flight. As Everton lurched from one managerial crisis to the next, it would prompt much discussion about the culture at the club and the root causes behind so many failing coaches.

Even back then, there was a feeling that Evertonians might look back on the start of December 2019 and wonder – as they did two years previously when the club lifted itself clear from relegation danger during the transition from David Unsworth to Sam Allardyce – what all the panic was about.

But after the humiliation of the Merseyside derby, Everton sitting in the relegation zone for the second time in the space of two years, and with a daunting set of fixtures looming in the run-up to Christmas and into the New Year, there was still an understandable sense of foreboding among supporters.

Indeed, anyone who was at Goodison Park when Duncan Ferguson took charge of his first match as stand-in manager would have been in no doubt of the level of anxiety coursing through the crowd, given the outpouring of emotion and relief that greeted what happened that day.

7 December 2019: Everton v Chelsea

Duncan Ferguson had taken his first press conference as interim boss at Finch Farm the day before, where he expressed the pride he would feel standing in the dugout as manager of the team he represented with such passion as a player during two stints in the 1990s and early 2000s.

"It'll be an incredibly proud moment for me," Ferguson said. "Everybody knows how I feel about the club and I'll be emotional, nervous, excited and obviously looking for a positive result."

The 47-year-old admitted that he wasn't entertaining thoughts of taking on the managerial role at Goodison Park on a full-time basis, expressing that he didn't feel ready, and he repeatedly stressed during his presser that the focus was all about the match against Chelsea.

The Everton hierarchy had tasked Ferguson with rousing the players following Silva's dismissal and a damaging defeat in the Merseyside derby, and he admitted that while the team was going through a difficult time, sending a positive message would be really important.

"It's not nice for a manager to lose his job," the Scot said. "We all felt for him, everybody at the club supported him as best we could and it's unfortunate that he's lost his job but results determine that, don't they?

"[The reaction from the players has been] mixed as you can imagine .... but we've got to try and pick them up now. That's the great thing about football — there's always another game."

Away from the cameras and behind closed doors with the press journalists, Ferguson betrayed a little more emotion and explained that his message to the players would be one around the need to acknowledge the gravity of the situation facing the club and to give everything for the badge.

When asked whether Everton falling into the bottom three had hurt the players as much as it did him, Ferguson said, "Is that possible?" Well, we all hope it is, don't we? That is the kind of message we gave the players. We have to bleed for this club. We have to bleed on that pitch.

"I am looking forward to the team talk. Rallying the troops, no? There is not a lot you can do in this situation, a short period of time. You keep the message simple.

"There will be a rallying cry to get blood and thunder, but we also have to be sensible because we know how good Chelsea are. They can hurt you on the counterattack, so we need a good defensive balance and then take it from there.

"I believe in this squad. I believe they can turn it around and I believe that is what we will do. I have my ideas. I know what I am going to go with. My message is clear."

Everton badly needed a result against Chelsea; one point would have done in the circumstances but three would have been priceless. And cometh the hour, cometh the Talisman – wearing Howard Kendall's watch, it would later be revealed – to inspire from a hitherto listless and directionless team a performance of high intensity, desire and determination that was matched by a raucous and then rapturous Goodison Park.

The team sheet, featuring the much-maligned Gylfi Sigurdsson, Morgan Schneiderlin, Theo Walcott, and Dominic Calvert-Lewin - a player who hadn't scored since October – was not greeted with much enthusiasm. Yet the trust instilled in them by Ferguson was returned tenfold.

In a pleasing and long-overdue break from Silva's reliance on a lone — and all-too-often isolated — striker, Ferguson deployed Richarlison up front with Calvert-Lewin and the difference in terms of the latter's game was significant. Both players were involved in the opening goal, a well-worked move that Richarlison started by collecting a pass from his strike partner and laying it off wide to Sidibé, who still had plenty of work to do before whipping in a perfect cross for Richarlison to meet in the middle with another unstoppable header. A goal straight from the playbook of Big Dunc, the player.

With fresh instructions from Ferguson at the break, Everton emerged from half-time with the same sense of purpose that had served them so well in the first period, and they doubled their lead just four minutes after the restart. Kurt Zouma, back at Goodison for the first time since his loan spell with the Toffees ended in May, could only slice a loose ball into the air.

Calvert-Lewin jostled with Andreas Christensen as it dropped, got a fortunate bounce off Zouma that took it beyond the defender and had time to weigh up his shot before steering it beyond Kepa to make it 2-0. Ferguson, who had leapt down the touchline in unbridled joy for the first goal, went galloping out of his technical area again, this time scooping up a ball boy, as he celebrated what felt like a massively important second goal.

Chelsea were back in it within three minutes, though, thanks to an accomplished finish by Mateo Kovacic. Frank Lampard's side attacked down their left flank and when Digne could only sweep a cross as far as Kovacic, the Croatian guided a controlled first-time shot past the unsighted Pickford and inside the post to make it 2-1.

Sensing that his team might need bolstering in midfield, Ferguson withdrew Richarlison with 20 minutes to go and introduced Tom Davies, a decision that did not sit particularly well with the Brazilian.

Christensen had too much space to advance into in the 79th minute and he pinged one narrowly off target from distance. A minute later, Holgate, another particularly impressive performer on the day, blocked Mount's volley and Pickford tipped Azpilicueta's shot over from the rebound as Chelsea continued to press for an equaliser, but it was to be Calvert-Lewin's day.

Kepa's pass out from his area missed Zouma and was intercepted by the alert Walcott, who tucked a beautiful pass between two Chelsea players and into Calvert-Lewin's path. He back-heeled it to Davies who couldn't quite dig it out from under his feet, Kanté blocked the loose ball and it ricocheted nicely for Calvert-Lewin to stretch out a boot, knock it through the legs of both Azpilicueta and the keeper and into the empty net. Lady Luck, who had utterly abandoned Silva, smiled on the Blues.

It was not clear how long Ferguson would remain in charge at Goodison. If he was to be given the responsibility of overseeing the next few games or even asked to stay on in the role until the end of the season, it was hoped that future results would not tarnish what was a magical day for him and a match that will live long in the collective Evertonian memory. The way he spoke after the game, you got the feeling he would have loved to take this match and result back home with him, put it on the mantlepiece if he could, and just be happy with that for the time being.

More than a few supporters questioned the wisdom of appointing Ferguson, a first-team coach about whose abilities fans knew very little, to the job of taking up the reins from Silva with the team in such dire need of a pick-me-up. But he answered the call in typical "Duncan" fashion — with a passion and hunger that left no player on that team in doubt of what it means to represent Everton Football Club. The reaction that he and a bear-pit crowd inspired in the players could not have been understated.

His influence spurred the Blues to a massive victory that smashed through the wall of worry that had surrounded the club and its supporters as they viewed a pre-Christmas schedule with dread. A trip to rejuvenated Manchester United next would test the team to the limits, but there was no question that a performance of this ilk would have struggling Arsenal quivering in their boots back at Goodison in a fortnight's time, and there was renewed hope for the looming League Cup Quarter-Final tie against Leicester as well.

Final score: Everton 3-1 Chelsea

***

After the final whistle, Duncan Ferguson was revelling in what he described as an "incredible experience" at a bouncing Goodison Park but he insisted that he wasn't thinking about becoming permanent boss.

"It was incredible today!" Ferguson beamed to *BT Sport*. "Honestly, I've felt nothing like it in my life. It was unbelievable. What an atmosphere.

"I know we had to defend a lot and probably sit back and keep in a good shape and pick a time to break. I think we did that well. We kept our shape well and, as you can see, it was a 4-4-2 screening their two holders. I thought we did that well, and we pressed the ball well when it went wide.

"I thought all the players were absolutely fantastic."

Asked if he was looking beyond the events of the day, towards the next few matches or even contemplating putting himself forward for the role permanently, the 47-year-old quipped: "I'm just looking to get home for a lie down, I think!

"No, I'm not looking too far ahead at all, to be honest with you. I was just looking at this game and that is it. We're just savouring the moment. It's three fantastic points for us, that's the main thing.

"I think they (the hierarchy) saw how enthusiastic I was on the touchline, but it's one game, it's one result."

In his post-match press conference, he joked with the media, "I don't think I could go through it again, to be honest with you!

"Listen, it was just one game at a time for me. I was asked to come in and I'd never turn down Everton Football Club, but I'm also realistic. It was a game. I'm made up and delighted for the fans. Three points is massive for us."

***

A week after the Chelsea triumph, Ferguson held onto the managerial reins for a tough away fixture at Old Trafford, and his side came away with a deserved 1-1 draw before entertaining Leicester City in the last eight of the Carabao Cup. Everton bravely rallied back from being 2-0 down to the Foxes after just half and hour, with Tom Davies pulling one back before Leighton Baines smashed home a stunning strike in stoppage time to force a penalty shootout. Unfortunately though, Baines was one of two Blues players to see spot-kicks saved and the visitors went through.

Meanwhile, talk of who would become the club's next permanent manager was rumbling on in the background. The broad consensus was that Ferguson was too raw and inexperienced for the role and Vitor Pereira, a name that would surface again much further down the line, quickly ruled himself out of the running by committing his future to SIPG Shanghai.

For a while it seemed as though the most likely successor to Marco Silva was none other than David Moyes who was unemployed at the time, having been overlooked for a permanent role at West Ham in favour of Manuel Pellegrini. The Scot would later describe how close he came to coming back on board as the Toffees' manager that month – all the pieces were being put in place for that after Moyes' interview in Germany with "the people who run Everton." Then, at the last minute, Farhad Moshiri saw an opportunity to land an unexpectedly big fish.

The day before the League Cup Quarter-Final against Leicester, Everton had moved to dampen what seemed to be bizarre speculation that coaching legend Carlo Ancelotti had committed to become the club's next manager.

The Italian, one of the most decorated head coaches in European footballing history, had just been sacked as manager of Napoli and was on the market, but the Blues released a statement asserting that, despite reports the Italian had agreed a deal to succeed Marco Silva, no firm contract offer had been made to Ancelotti.

Everton's statement read: "In the 11 days since Marco Silva left the club, the Everton Board have been working to recruit a new manager - and has held meetings with a number of candidates. We can confirm that thus far no contract offer has been made, and no candidate has chosen to withdraw from the process."

Everton playing coy might have been because Ancelotti still had to return to Naples to complete the details of his severance from the Serie A club, but media reports, both on the Continent and in Britain continued to suggest that he was set to become the next incumbent of the Goodison Park hot seat.

Sky Sports News and their sources in Italy claimed that Ancelotti, having been persuaded to join by Moshiri in a telephone conversation, had already travelled to England and agreed a deal in principle with

Everton. Incredibly, within days the Italian would be in the Directors Box at Goodison next to his new bosses.

2019: Carlo Ancelotti is Blues' surprise Christmas present

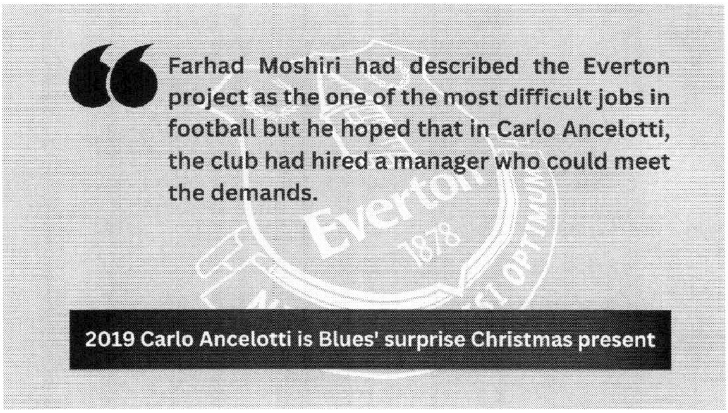

Just hours before they were due to face Arsenal at Goodison, just four days before Christmas, Everton confirmed what had become one of football's worst-kept secrets: Carlo Ancelotti was the club's new manager, succeeding Marco Silva following his dismissal from the role on 6th December and the Italian's departure from Napoli.

Ancelotti signed a four-and-a-half-year contract and became the third permanent appointee under Farhad Moshiri's reign at Goodison Park, following the high-profile capture of Ronald Koeman in 2016 and the protracted pursuit of Silva that led to the Portuguese being hired in May 2018. Previously, they had installed controversial coach Sam Allardyce on an interim basis after sacking Koeman only 18 months into the job, having achieved Moshiri's goal of avoiding relegation in 2017/18.

Ancelotti, meanwhile, had had his contract ended by Napoli, despite leading them to the second place in the Italian top flight the previous season, and securing their passage to the knockout phase of the Champions League just before he was fired. It had ended a difficult relationship with the Serie A club's chairman, Aurelio De Laurentiis, one that had made a parting of the ways at Stadio San Paolo seem inevitable.

The then 60-year-old coach – who had infamously been fired by Chelsea in a corridor at Goodison following a league game against Everton in 2011 – had begun talks with Everton's hierarchy five days earlier, and reports emerged that evening that Ancelotti had agreed a deal in principle .

Negotiations had continued, amid rumours Everton were prepared to make Ancelotti one of the highest-paid coaches in Europe. There were also reports he was seeking assurances from Moshiri and his board that there was scope for investment to upgrade the team.

He would officially take charge on Boxing Day when the Toffees faced Burnley at home, which left the reins in Duncan Ferguson's hands for the Premier League clash with Arsenal. It meant Ancelotti would watch on from the stands, near to the Gunners' own newly-appointed head coach, Mikel Arteta.

It had also been agreed that Ferguson would stay on at the club as one of the new man's assistants, alongside Ancelotti's son, Davide.

Ancelotti was one of the most successful managers in the game and his appointment represented an impressive acquisition for Everton and another statement of intent by Moshiri. The Everton gig was the Reggiolo-born coach's 10th managerial role, having helmed some of the biggest names in European football, including Juventus, AC Milan, Paris Saint-Germain, Real Madrid and Bayern Munich.

He had won 15 major trophies in his 24-year career, was one of a select few to have already won the Champions League three times, and had won league titles in four different countries.

The day's match against the club from North London almost seemed like a sideshow, and the dull goalless draw that played out seemed to reinforce that notion.

Final score: Everton 0-0 Arsenal

***

Farhad Moshiri had described the Everton project as the one of the most difficult jobs in football but he hoped that in Carlo Ancelotti, the club had hired a manager who could meet the demands.

The Blues' majority shareholder was speaking with Jim White of *TalkSport* at Goodison Park after the draw with Arsenal and he spoke of his gratitude to Duncan Ferguson for restoring the passion to Everton's game while also explaining how he felt Marco Silva struggled to cope with the pressure brought on by the supporters' expectations.

With the appointment of Ronald Koeman in 2016, Moshiri felt he was hiring a man capable of fitting into the "Hollywood" of managers that he felt the northwest of England had become, with Jurgen Klopp in place across the park, together with Pep Guardiola and Jose Mourinho in Manchester.

While Ancelotti certainly fitted that bill more than Koeman, the Iranian-born billionaire distanced himself from that description in his chat with White:

> "We've had managers from Wigan, Southampton and Watford and they've all had their impact, but we've invested heavily in a group of players. They're all internationals, so we think they could benefit from someone of this pedigree. It has nothing to do with 'Hollywood' really. You know, we've rediscovered Everton in the past two weeks. I've had my most enjoyable time with Duncan and we're really grateful to him. This is the club and I think we just need to keep this; that is the most valuable aspect of Everton, not Hollywood. This passion, celebrations of fans and the manager together. Carlo is a real football man and we hope with Duncan next to him we keep the passion, and we build on it.

> Everton is a very difficult job in football because you're two home losses from being disowned by fans. It's very hard and what we've noticed for younger managers is that it's difficult to cope. Because you have the bad runs, but I think the fans don't give you any

time and the strength of Goodison is the passion of the fans and once you lose that it's very difficult. I think Silva was a very talented coach and when the gods of football aren't kind to you, what can you do? You know, we lost six points through VAR, he loses 70% of his midfield but I think a good general is a lucky one, that's the thing. I think this is one of the most difficult clubs. We don't have the financial base but the fans' expectations are huge so I think this mismatch somehow needs to be resolved. So we've put a lot of money in to give the club a platform to match the fans' expectation and sometimes it's just too much for a young manager so we hope that an experienced manager can cope and deal with it better."

***

26 December 2019: Everton v Burnley

If Marco Silva was reclining somewhere watching this game with his slippers on he might have been nodding ruefully in the second half, as Everton struggled to break down a Burnley side who had brought their most defensive of game plans to Goodison Park for Carlo Ancelotti's first game in charge.

As the contest ticked towards the 80-minute mark, the visitors had failed to register a shot on target but the hosts, who had enjoyed almost 70% of the possession overall, had still failed to break the deadlock. As for so much of the Portuguese's tenure, Everton were dominating the ball but struggling to find the inspiration and penetration in the final third and it was all very reminiscent of the previous regime.

There was, however, a fluidity to the Blues' system, one which alternated between 3-4-3 with Djibril Sidibe in a more advanced right-midfield role and Seamus Coleman tucking into the back line, and a more conventional 4-4-2. Besides an assurance about their possession of the ball overall, there was also greater positional dynamism in Everton's midfield which allowed Bernard, in particular, to drift into the middle and Richarlison to drop back into the hole, creating the space and opportunities for the Blues to break Burnley's lines in quick transition in a manner that wasn't always the case under Silva.

With a bit more decisiveness and composure in advanced areas, it might have yielded an earlier goal, but there were embryonic signs of the flexibility and ideas that Ancelotti could bring to the team. As it was, just when it looked as though the Italian was realising first-hand the shortcomings of the side he had inherited, everything came together with 10 minutes to go.

Sidibé received the ball on the right flank and the Frenchman delivered another of his telling crosses that Dominic Calvert-Lewin met with a gloriously old-school diving header that bounced in off the far post to hand Ancelotti his first three points as the Toffees' boss.

Though the lead was a narrow one, Everton never really looked to be in any danger of giving up the points in the closing stages and they comfortably held out for the win that lifted them into 13th place and within three points of their next opponents, Newcastle, who were sitting in 10th place. Ancelotti described it as the perfect first game and while it was short on genuine thrills and entertainment, few

Blues would argue given the wider context of the season and the key absentees in the squad, particularly in midfield.

Final score: Everton 1-0 Burnley

***

28 December 2019: Newcastle United v Everton

Within six days of Carlo Ancelotti taking his first training session as Everton's new manager, he already had six points on the board and, depending on what happened with other teams, the Blues could have had the comfort of starting 2020 in the top half of the Premier League table.

That felt like an awfully far cry from how Evertonians were feeling on the 5th of December following a third successive defeat, and humiliation in the Merseyside derby that had left the club sitting in the relegation zone with three more of the "big six" still to play in successive games.

Duncan Ferguson, of course, had played his part, rousing a squad depleted of personnel and morale to a win and a draw before Farhad Moshiri landed one of the biggest fish possible as Marco Silva's successor.

It was very early days but the contrasts between the vastly experienced Italian and a comparative managerial novice were already clear, not least in terms of tactical shifts and game management, both of which elements lay at the heart of a 2-1 victory at St James's Park.

It was hard not to draw the distinctions between this result and the corresponding fixture on this ground last season. On both occasions,

Everton were winning 2-1, with 25 minutes to go but where, in March, Silva's side collapsed in the final 10 minutes and lost a match they had been leading 2-0, this time Ancelotti's charges held on in disciplined and increasingly assured fashion to secure the points.

Aside from the first couple of exchanges, Everton dominated the first 25 minutes, hogging almost 70% of the ball, and a spell of pressure that began in the 10th minute eventually told.

Gylfi Sigurdsson's direct free-kick cannoned back to him off the defensive wall, his shot on the rebound deflected off a defender and fell to Dominic Calvert-Lewin in front of goal, and he picked his spot beyond Dubravka to give the Toffees the lead.

It was a mostly professional away performance, particularly after Calvert-Lewin had slid the ball home to put Everton back in front after Fabian Schär had cancelled out his first-half opener.

With a win that had given Everton 11 points from a possible 15 since Silva's departure, things were certainly looking up for the Blues as they looked ahead to 2020. And after 22 shots on goal to add to the 21 they registered against Burnley, there was no shortage of attacking endeavour in the team now.

Ancelotti rightly pointed out afterwards that his team could and needed to play better football. It disappointed him with the way they ceded the initiative back to Newcastle in the first half, but he was justifiably pleased with his return of maximum points so far.

The trip to Manchester City on New Year's Day and an FA Cup date at Anfield would pose altogether more difficult challenges, but Evertonians would travel to both games with a good deal more confidence that their side could produce something away from home.

There was a long way to go with some key parts of the side that the new boss would eventually want to improve, but the way things were going, there was hope it would be a happy New Year after all.

Final score: Newcastle United 1-2 Everton

***

In January, 2020, for anyone wondering how Everton could fund further investment in Carlo Ancelotti's squad and simultaneously finance a new stadium, news that billionaire businessman, Alisher Usmanov, was pondering greater involvement at Everton was timely.

Usmanov's name had already come up in reports suggesting he had personally spoken with Ancelotti to assure him of financial backing for improving the squad, and he admitted that he was considering increasing his investment in Everton, including the possibility of buying naming rights in the club's new stadium.

By this point, the Uzbek-born tycoon had sold his 30% stake in the Gunners after the London club's owner, Stan Kroenke, confirmed he had no interest in letting him onto the Board of Directors at the Emirates.

Usmanov said in an interview with the *Financial Times* in December 2019 that he would think seriously about increasing his exposure at Everton beyond the current sponsorship deals with USM Holdings and Megafon if Moshiri wants him on board:

"Yes. With great pleasure, if he asks. I am thinking about my investment in this club. I cannot reject Arsenal. I will not leave them as a fan. But if I join Everton, then I will wear an Everton shirt, because I am a professional. They are going to build a new stadium. Why not the USM Arena? It is not obligatory for me to participate myself. I could just sponsor them."

***

5 January 2020: Liverpool v Everton

Carlo Ancelotti had only been in his post for 12 days when he took his new side across Stanley Park for an FA Cup Third Round tie against Liverpool, and it seemed that not even the venerated Italian was immune to the malady that so often afflicts Everton teams at Anfield.

Gutless. Spineless. Witless. Hapless. It was a case of choose your adjective on a harrowing night. Everton's long-suffering fans had witnessed some pathetic performances at Anfield in recent years, but this one, against a Liverpool team featuring nine changes and stuffed with inexperienced kids, took the proverbial biscuit.

Everton turned in a second-half display so bereft of fight, quality, spirit and urgency that it left fans wishing they could throw half the players out the club immediately. Sadly, as the imminent financial accounts would show, the club was counting the significant cost of almost four years of horrendously expensive and just plain poor recruitment that would no doubt require Ancelotti to use all four-and-a-half years of his contract to fix.

The second 45 minutes was indescribably bad from a group of players who, it was felt, couldn't provide much worse than some of the dross they had already served up that season. Whether through fatigue, or a simple sense of the futility that had embodied this fixture for Everton for two decades, they appeared to just give up.

For so much of this increasingly dejecting match, the team full of youngsters was the one playing with all the composure while the one with four players 30 or older and packed with internationals was struggling just to do the basics. And it was a reliance on the basic, later abandoned, that had served them so well in the first half hour of the game when they had gone close to taking the lead.

A low drive from around the penalty spot from Dominic Calvert-Lewin was perhaps too accurate, in that he put it down the middle and Adrian saved with his feet. Mason Holgate latched onto a whipped free-kick from Gylfi Sigurdsson, but he planted a free header straight at the goalkeeper. And when Theo Walcott cut the ball back from the by-line for Richarlison, he too was denied by the goalkeeper's foot.

With Liverpool failing to trouble Pickford, it felt as though it was only a matter of time before Ancelotti's men made the breakthrough but the tide started turning in the second half and Everton gradually disappeared from the contest. Pickford pushed out a bouncing, speculative effort from Divock Origi before Curtis Jones produced the moment of magic that the match had been sorely missing, particularly from those in blue jerseys.

The 18-year-old collected Origi's pass after good hold-up play by the Belgian and he sized up a shot from the edge of the area that he curled over Pickford's despairing fingertips and in off the underside of the bar.

The effect on Everton, with all the experience in its ranks playing in front 8,000 expectant supporters, was utterly demoralising, because Ancelotti's men appeared to lose all belief and any remaining ability to string together a series of passes.

Ultimately, Everton's failure to put a single effort on target in the final hour of the match was a damning indictment of the performance, and of the players who plumbed new depths of awfulness.

Just four games into his new job, Ancelotti would have had his eyes opened to the problems that existed in this squad, and the amount of work that would be required to turn it around. So early in his reign, this one wasn't on the manager; this was squarely on a group of players who had largely escaped the worst of the criticism and allowed Marco Silva to carry the can, but now had nowhere left to hide.

Final score: Liverpool 1-0 Everton

***

1 February 2020: Watford v Everton

Although Carlo Ancelotti had begun 2020 with successive away defeats, to Manchester City in the Premier League and Liverpool in the FA Cup, he stabilised Everton's form over the following month with three wins and two draws that lifted the Blues into the top half of the table for the first time since the previous September.

Two of those points had slipped away in almost comical fashion at Goodison against Newcastle in late January when Everton, leading 2-0 going into stoppage time, somehow contrived to draw 2-2 as the Magpies netted two quick goals in the 94th and 95th minutes.

However, they would make amends three days later with a thrilling victory at Watford with their own last-gasp goal.

It was rare that Theo Walcott completed 90 minutes in an Everton shirt by that stage. Indeed, before this match, he hadn't managed it since the final day of the previous season at Tottenham — also the last time he had scored — and had it not been for Fabian Delph's dismissal in the 72nd minute of this game at Vicarage Road, it's possible he would have been hooked again well before the end.

Such are the quirks of fate that meant that Walcott, a rival to Delph for the worst performer in blue on the day, remained on while Dominic Calvert-Lewin was sacrificed. That enabled the introduction of Michael Keane to shore up the back, and Walcott was there in the final minute of regulation time to score a dramatic winner that capped an equally stunning Everton comeback from 2-0 down.

If Carlo Ancelotti's men needed to get the final minute of that recent Newcastle 2-2 draw out of their system, this certainly did the trick and they exorcised a few other demons, not least Marco Silva's failure to engineer victory from a losing position during his stewardship of the team. The last time an Everton side had come back from being down prior to this had been in December 2017, and the last time they'd overcome a 2-0 deficit away from home was under Roberto Martinez when they beat West Bromwich Albion in 2015.

This Everton team also didn't tend to score from corners and yet, thanks to Yerry Mina goals that came around like buses, they bagged two and then stymied Watford enough when they were a man down to allow for the counter-attack that led to Walcott becoming the unlikely hero of what was ultimately an unforgettable afternoon.

Gerard Deulofeu created the opener for Watford by bringing the ball out of the air deftly laying it to Adam Masina who had driven forward, completely untracked by Walcott. He fired a shot into the ground, past Pickford's left glove and inside the far post to score. Of course, his first ever goal for the Hornets.

A dreadful error from Delph led to the hosts' second when he gifted the ball straight to Troy Deeney outside his own penalty area and the striker paused before playing Roberto Pereyra in to drive a shot past Pickford three minutes before half-time.

Just as they had done at West Ham a fortnight previously, however, Everton pressed in the dying phases of the first half and were rewarded when Yerry Mina met a flighted corner from Lucas Digne, the ball dropped to Holgate who couldn't force it past the man on the line, but it finally broke nicely back to Mina who prodded home.

That would end up being more than just a fillip to take into the dressing room because two minutes later, Everton would score from their second corner after Pereyra had blocked Digne's attempted cross. Sigurdsson took the honours this time from the opposite side and he swung his delivery over everyone except Mina who easily stepped in front of Craig Cathcart to plant a downward header into the unoccupied side of Foster's goal to make it 2-2.

Suddenly the whole complexion of the game had changed and with fresh instructions from Ancelotti ringing in their ears, the Blues emerged for the second half with much more intensity and tempo about their game. However, despite the overall improvement from Ancelotti's men, chances were few.

The prospect of victory appeared to evaporate in the 71st minute, however, with the latest of Delph's bone-headed lapses in judgement. The midfielder had Etienne Capoue safely up against the touchline and going nowhere, but elected to tackle him and ended up chopping him down to concede the free kick. As stupid as the supposedly experienced midfielder's challenge was, it was a ridiculously soft decision by referee Craig Pawson to book him but, in making the challenge, Delph had given the officials a decision to make, one heavily influenced by Capoue's theatrics and the urging of Watford's players and the crowd, and it ended with Everton finishing the game with 10 men.

Ancelotti sacrificed Calvert-Lewin for Keane, moving the excellent Holgate into midfield alongside Schneiderlin and the move proved inspired, giving Everton the defensive solidity to hold Watford at bay before they pinched all three points at the death.

Masina couldn't bring Holgate's defensive header from Mariappa's long throw under his spell, and Kean nipped it off his toe into the path of Richarlison who raced off down the left while his strike partner and Walcott sped forward with to his right. The Brazilian delayed until he got within 10 yards of the box before slipping it in to Moise Kean who, depending on your point of view, either missed his kick or helped it on to Walcott arriving at the back stick in time to steer home a composed finish.

The release of emotion, perhaps pent up from that frustrating conclusion to Everton's last game, was palpable as all the players and substitutes mobbed Walcott near the corner flag in front of the delirious away fans.

Indeed, this was the perfect, albeit slightly mad, antidote to the utter emptiness with which Toffees fans greeted the final whistle against Newcastle. Whereas that draw with the Magpies had seen Everton throw away two points at the end of arguably their best performance of the season, this time they first looked to have retrieved a point from a seemingly lost situation, and then they grabbed all three just when it looked as though a draw would have to be enough, even after being reduced to 10 men.

It meant that they would finish the weekend in at least 10th, and, at most, just four points off fifth place with a series of fixtures against last season's top six to come that presented real opportunities for further upward progress. If this was the Ancelotti effect, long may it continue!

Final score: Watford 2-3 Everton

2020: COVID-19 GRIPS FOOTBALL

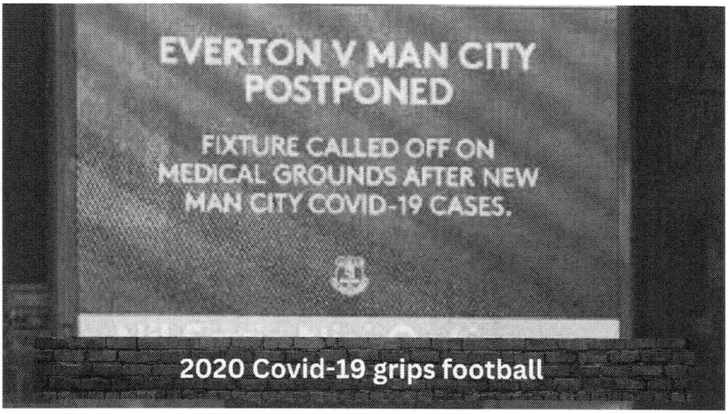

On 11 January, 2020, the Chinese National Health Commission notified The World Health Organisation that they had identified a new type of rapidly-spreading coronavirus, SARS-CoV2. The world was about to be turned upside down.

By 31 January, Italy had flagged that its first infections had occurred, in two tourists from China. Spain reported its first cases the next day. The U.K. saw its third case confirmed on 6 February, with the patient having visited Singapore.

Throughout February and early March, the number of cases of this mysterious new virus reported around the world increased exponentially. Deaths followed cases. Dramatic scenes of Emergency Departments at full stretch filled our TV screens hourly.

The UK government was relatively slow to implement restrictions on large gatherings. Sporting and cultural events, including football, continued into March. Everton drew 1-1 with Manchester United on 1 March in front of a packed Goodison Park, followed by an away game at Chelsea on 8 March.

The Cheltenham Festival took place from 10th to 12th March, attended by 150,000 people. Meanwhile, Liverpool hosted Atletico Madrid on 11 March, with thousands of Spaniards flying into the city for the Champions League match.

Despite the spread of the coronavirus, and the fact that the rest of Europe's major leagues had either been suspended or scheduled to go ahead behind closed doors, the Premier League released a statement saying that the full programme of matches would go ahead on the weekend of 15 March.

The situation quickly changed, however, when Arsenal manager Mikel Arteta and Chelsea players Callum Hudson-Odoi both tested positive for the virus and both squads went into "lockdown", prompting an emergency meeting of the Premier League and EFL. The Premier League then issued a statement, initially suspending English football until 4th April, which read:

"Despite the challenges, it is the Premier League's aim to reschedule the displaced fixtures, including those played by Academy sides, when it is safe to do so. In this fast-moving environment, further updates will be provided when appropriate."

Premier League Chief Executive, Richard Masters added: "Above all, we wish Mikel Arteta and Callum Hudson-Odoi speedy recoveries, and everyone else affected by COVID-19. In this unprecedented situation, we are working closely with our clubs, Government, The FA and EFL, and can reassure everyone the health and welfare of players, staff and supporters are our priority."

The suspension of all Premier League, EFL and top-level women's football in England meant the friendlies against Italy and Denmark, scheduled for 27 March and 31 March respectively, were also shelved.

In addition, Everton closed Goodison Park, Finch Farm and their headquarters at the Royal Liver Building once an un-named player went into self-isolation after exhibiting symptoms suggestive of coronavirus or influenza. In statement, the club said:

"Everton Football Club can confirm that one member of the Everton first-team squad reported a high temperature last night and is now undertaking a period of self-isolation for seven days. In line with Government guidelines no other players are self-isolating at this stage but the Club's USM training facility has been closed as a precaution and staff, including players, have been advised to stay away from all Club sites until further notice."

***

By 24 March, there was a mounting acceptance among Premier League players they would have to play to empty stadiums if any attempt to conclude the 2019/20 season by June 30th was to be successful.

That was the date by which UEFA had said that Europe's domestic leagues needed to have played their remaining fixtures but, with the COVID-19 crisis still unfolding, there were fears that the new 30 April timeline set by the Football Association for the resumption of matches would come too soon.

Certainly, with Prime Minister Boris Johnson having only just moved the country into a "suppression" phase of the virus contagion, by mandating that citizens stay home except to conduct essential errands and business, and experts predicting that the U.K. could be as hard hit by the coronavirus as Italy and Spain, there appeared to be little chance that fans would assemble under one roof again only five weeks later.

While *The Mirror's* back page screamed, "No Fans, No Way!" amid claims the players would revolt if asked to play behind closed doors, a report by David Ornstein for *The Athletic* following conversations with PFA deputy chief executive, Bobby Barnes, suggested the players were taking a realistic view towards the need to finish the current season and were increasingly aware that they wouldn't be playing in front of people.

Barnes admitted that, at the outset, there was significant opposition to the idea of empty stadiums, but the financial realities of the situation would ultimately hold sway.

"I've been speaking to players — including two or three very high-profile Premier League players more or less on a daily basis — and the conversations I had with them at the outset were based around not wanting to play behind closed doors, if at all possible," Barnes explained.

"I said to them, 'Look, none of us, in an ideal world, want to play in front of empty stadiums. Football is about fans. But the reality is that, for the vast majority of the players, particularly at the highest level, television money funds their income and there are contracts that have to be adhered to. In order for us (the PFA) to be able to protect those players in terms of securing their salaries... if that's the only offer we have on the table to complete the season, then that is what it will be'.

"The players get it. They understand the alternative. Quite frankly, if we're going to get the season finished in a timely fashion so that we can even consider starting next season, we've got to be open to all options.

"If it means playing behind closed doors has to happen in order that contracts are protected, fixtures fulfilled and commercial deals honoured, then I think we've all got to come together and accept we've all got to sacrifice to try and find a solution for the industry as a whole."

Britain, together with most of the developed world, was soon in full lockdown, and Carlo Ancelotti said that he believed football, like so much of the world, would emerge changed from the Coronavirus crisis when things eventually returned to some sense of normality.

The Premier League entered its third week of forced shutdown as the COVID-19 pandemic continued to sweep across Europe, with the United Kingdom still on a depressingly upward curve in terms of positive cases and deaths from the virus. Meanwhile, the timeframe for when football could return kept getting moved further out.

Speaking in an interview with *Corriere dello Sport,* Ancelotti insisted he wasn't concerned with when matches could resume, but he admitted that, financially, the game will necessarily 'downsize', amid the predicted economic fallout of a severe global recession.

"I'm certain we're all going to have to get downsized, starting with football," the Italian said. "Today's priority is health to limit the contagion. Everything else is secondary.

"When you start again when you finish, the dates, the promises, the hopes... believe me, I don't care in this moment and [that is] the last of my thoughts.

"The initial idea was to restart in May, but it's out of the question that we can do it. I hear talk of salary cuts, suspension of payments. They seem to me to be untimely solutions.

"Soon the economy will change, and at all levels, television rights will be worth less. Players and coaches will earn less, tickets will cost less because people will have less money. Let's prepare for a general decline."

In the media, there was soon talk of players needing to defer salaries and agree potential wage cuts, as football of all levels grappled with the effects of lost income and the unknown duration of the shutdown.

***

By the end of April, a plan was starting to come together. English clubs were discussing plans that could see the 2019/20 season restart on 13 June, albeit behind closed doors as the nation remained in the coronavirus's grip.

By that time, the Premier League had already been shut down for over six weeks. The COVID-19 pandemic which, according to Government figures, had already claimed the lives of over 20,000 Britons, made the prospect of playing top-level football matches unthinkable.

With the threat of millions of pounds of default payments due, because of lost broadcast revenue, the top-flight clubs committed to finishing the campaign rather than voiding it entirely. Yet there was still little scope for holding matches, even without fans in attendance given the testing requirements of players and the estimated two to three hundred people needed on site at each game.

UEFA were pressuring each of its member leagues to furnish them with plans by 23rd May, for either completing or cancelling the current season.

According to *The Mirror*, the Premier League had scheduled the middle of June as a date on which matches might resume, with the season running into August if necessary to clear the backlog of 90-odd fixtures.

English Clubs met again to discuss “Project Restart” in further detail. In the meantime, France effectively called an end to the season, after their government ruled out any matches, even behind closed doors, being held until September.

It was 10 June before they finally made the decision to allow the derby game to be played at Goodison Park on 21 June behind closed doors, with a 7.00 pm kick off.

That followed weeks of speculation, by Liverpool City Council’s ground safety advisory group, after most local entities (the police, the mayor, the clubs) had expressed their support for the game going ahead at Goodison Park.

The Goodison derby had been on a list of fixtures which the United Kingdom’s football policing lead, Deputy Chief Constable Mark Roberts of South Yorkshire Police, said local forces had requested to be played at a neutral venue.

However, Merseyside Police appeared to contradict DCC Roberts by saying they were happy to police matches in Liverpool. Then, at a meeting of the council’s Safety Advisory Group, they gave Everton approval to play their remaining home games at Goodison Park after reassurances they could manage the conditions outside the ground.

Councillor Wendy Simon, Deputy Mayor of Liverpool and Chair of the Ground Safety Advisory Group (GSAG) said: "A lot of factors have been taken into consideration, especially the safety of the players, match officials and staff in attendance. We are confident the measures in place will allow matches to be held behind closed doors without any detrimental impact to all concerned and recommend to the city council that the safety certificate [for Goodison Park] be amended to allow this to happen."

***

21 June 2020: Everton v Liverpool (Behind Closed Doors)

On 17 June, after a 100-day hiatus caused by the COVID-19 pandemic, the Premier League finally restarted the 2019/20 season. Four days later, the two Merseyside clubs played their first games since the campaign had come to an abrupt halt in March when they met behind closed doors at Goodison Park.

For those less than enthused about the prospect of the Premier League returning to empty stadiums, perhaps the only thing capable of stirring the Blue blood for Everton's first match back was that it was a derby. And if the Toffees' record in this fixture had long since beaten the optimism out of Evertonians, there was always that flicker of hope in the heart (based on the law of averages, if nothing else) that Everton could finally beat Liverpool for the first time in a decade.

For a heart-stopping moment in the 80th-minute of an often tedious match, it looked as though the Blues might have done it, too.

A driving run from Richarlison, a cheeky heel-flick goal-wards from Dominic Calvert-Lewin pushed into the path of Tom Davies and, with the far corner of the goal beckoning, the young midfielder tucks a shot past Alisson Becker.

Ordinarily, a packed Goodison Park would have held its collective breath, ready to erupt in jubilation. As it was, Evertonians up and down the country and across the globe froze on their sofas as Joe Gomez got a crucial deflection on the shot, diverting it onto the post. Just when Everton needed a touch of luck to end a sorry Merseyside derby record, it didn't arrive.

But as the cliché goes, you make your own luck and in football, that means creating enough chances to increase the odds of fortune falling in your favour. Everton didn't really do that, even though they came out of the game having carved out the better opportunities to win the contest.

Under normal circumstances it would have been more frustrating, but emerging from a three-month suspension of the season with no competitive action since that harrowing defeat at Chelsea in March, the performance from Carlo Ancelotti's men had to be taken in context. This goalless Goodison derby, the third in a row, was played out between two rusty-looking teams, often with the feel of a pre-season friendly or exhibition game.

With Europe already slipping away prior to the lockdown, this last quarter of the season was always bound to be one of further discovery for Ancelotti and, by blooding Gordon and deploying Iwobi in a different role, he was learning more about the capabilities of his squad.

The boss would take heart from an impressive defensive display, even allowing for some early sloppiness in distribution, but the team remained uncomfortably short of quality in attacking midfield, something that would hopefully be addressed in the summer.

Final score: Everton 0-0 Liverpool

***

27 July 2020: Everton v Bournemouth (Behind Closed Doors)

Between the derby game on 21 June and the final game of the season, Everton had languished in mid-table. There were wins against Norwich, Leicester and Sheffield United, draws against Southampton and Villa, as well as defeats against Spurs and Wolves. The players had adjusted to playing in eerily quiet stadiums and on an accelerated schedule that crammed nine games into a little over a month, and the season would be concluded by 27 July. With the final game being a home match against Bournemouth, there was an opportunity for Carlo's men to sign off in style.

At an empty Goodison Park, another weak and uninspiring performance and a fifteenth Premier League defeat of the campaign condemned Everton to their lowest league finish since 2004. Hardly a fitting occasion for one of the finest players of the modern era to bow out and yet a result entirely in keeping with this wretched season.

Leighton Baines came on as a 70th-minute substitute, made one last goal-denying tackle and then called time on his magnificent career after the game. He would leave the Blues having never won a trophy, but departed with the adoration of Evertonians everywhere.

Baines would not be a part of what came next at Everton (at least not in a playing capacity), but in some ways he might have felt like he was better off out of it; because unless Carlo Ancelotti could effect more than just the "evolution" he promised, there was more frustration to come with this collection of players.

In the final reckoning of this match, one that condemned Bournemouth to relegation despite them recording the league double over Everton for the first time in their history, the only positives came from a trio of youngsters: Jarrad Branthwaite, deputising again for Mason Holgate, again exhibited poise and cool beyond his tender years; Anthony Gordon came off the bench to inject the urgency that had been lacking up to that point; and Moise Kean showed some lovely touches and distribution while also notching his second goal in Royal Blue with a simple tap-in late in the first half.

In his post-match interview, Ancelotti explained he had told the players who would remain that summer, that they would need to show more motivation next season. If finances were to be as tight as many expected, the Italian would not be in a position to replace almost all of his midfield, sign a new goalkeeper and fill the other roles that badly need attention. But if he and Marcel Brands were able to add some genuine quality in key areas, it would help. Whether it would be enough to build a bridge to the top six in 2020/21 remained to be seen, and much would depend on Ancelotti's own managerial talents.

"I want a better team," he told the press. "We want a better team. We will have a better team. I want to see more fight."

Once again, Everton would go into a vitally important transfer window, with long-term irrelevance beckoning if they couldn't get it right.

Final score: Everton 1-3 Bournemouth

2020: Allan, Rodriguez and Doucouré sign for Don Carlo

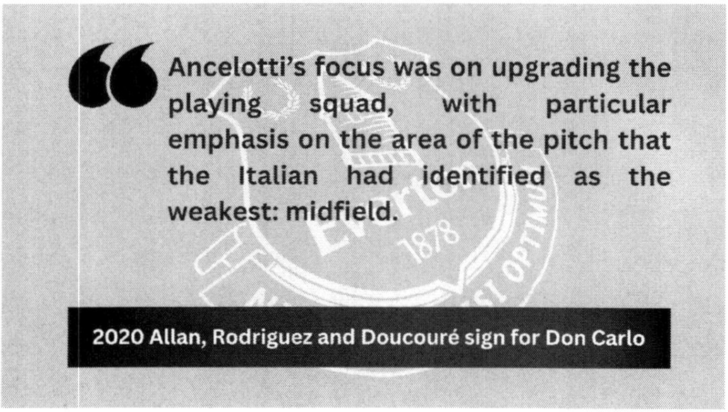

The delayed finish to 2019/20 meant that the calendar for the following season had to be pushed out accordingly. The new Premier League campaign would kick off on 13 September and the transfer window, which usually closed on or around 1 September, was shifted so that the new deadline would fall on 5 October.

At Everton, where Carlo Ancelotti was preparing for his first full season in charge, all the focus was on upgrading the playing squad, with particular emphasis on the area of the pitch that the Italian had identified as the weakest: midfield.

The veteran, Fabian Delph, had made just 13 league starts as he battled with a succession of soft-tissue injuries, while Jean-Philippe Gbamin, the highly-anticipated addition from Mainz a year earlier had had his first season in England wrecked by a thigh tendon tear, and then by a ruptured Achilles. In their absence, that limp conclusion to the campaign underscored the galling lack of drive, guile, imagination and presence in Everton's midfield.

Ancelotti had seen enough and it probably didn't take much persuading on his part to prompt Marcel Brands into making a sizeable change in his recruitment policy, by advocating the need to sign some players capable of making a genuine and immediate impact, even if it meant acquiring talent at the upper end of the age range.

The result was the arrival of three significant signings in the space of three hectic days, a week before the new season was due to kick off.

***

Brazilian midfielder Allan Marques, one of Ancelotti's most dependable players during his time at Napoli, came in for £21 million. The price was half of what Paris Saint-Germain had offered Napoli for the 29-year-old in 2019 before that proposed deal collapsed. Since then, it had been Allan's desire to link back up with his former boss, Carlo Ancelotti, and he got his wish when he signed a three-year contract and joined compatriots, Richarlison and Bernard on Merseyside. He would wear the number 6 jersey.

"It is a real pleasure to sign for Everton. I am immensely happy to be here," he told evertontv. "It is a club with a rich history in the Premier

League, has real ambition, and then there is Professor Ancelotti. He has done everything possible to bring me here.

"It is the size of the Club and the name of the coach, which means you don't think twice about coming to Everton."

Allan promised to add strength to that part of the team and more of a box-to-box presence than anyone currently at the club. While not a prolific goal scorer — he had scored 16 times in 212 appearances in all competitions for Napoli — he could get forward, reportedly had a good turn of pace, and offered both strength and technique on the ball.

***

Just two days later, Everton confirmed the signing of James, the Colombian star from Real Madrid in a deal that, it was eventually revealed, cost the club almost nothing by way of an up-front fee. In what was a potential coup for the club, the 29-year-old linked back up with Carlo Ancelotti, the man who made him the fourth-most expensive player in world football in 2014 when he signed him for Real from Monaco for £63 million and then brought him to Bayern Munich on loan for two seasons starting in 2017.

Indeed, Ancelotti helped to persuade James to join him at Goodison Park, vouching for him personally and making several phone calls to him to describe the project he is working on with the Toffees.

Rodriguez signed a two-year contract, with the club, keeping the option of a third.

"I am really, really happy to be at this great club, a club with so much history, and here with a manager who knows me really well," he told evertonfc.com. "I'm looking forward to achieving great things here — and winning things, which is what everyone's aim is. I've come here to improve, to get better. I've also come here to help the team to win, to play good football — entertaining football.

"I'm convinced, with Carlo and his technical staff, we can achieve big things, and one of the big reasons [I signed] was the presence of Carlo Ancelotti. I have enjoyed some great times with him previously at two different clubs. That was a massive reason to come here.

"I'm a winner... a real winner. I like to win things and I'm convinced we can have a great season. I know we have a very talented squad, full of top players, and, I think, with the additions we're making during this transfer window, it's going to make us even stronger."

***

The next day, Abdoulaye Doucouré left relegated Watford to join the Toffees for an initial £20 million, although a further £5 million in appearance-related add-ons would eventually bring the transfer closer to £25 million.

It was believed that Brands had long had his eye on the Frenchman and, based on Doucouré's comments following his unveiling as an Everton player, the feeling had been mutual.

"I have been waiting a long time to come here and now it has happened so I am very happy," Doucouré told evertonfc.com. "I had some interest from other clubs, but from the beginning, when Everton showed an interest in me, I told my agent to focus on Everton.

"It was the only club I wanted to join. Everton has a big history in English football and it is a good club for me to have a step up in my career. I am very happy now to be an Everton player and very excited for the future."

"I can bring my energy - I am a powerful player, I can run a lot, all the game. I can add goals as well. I will try my best to score goals and help the team.

***

Almost overnight, Everton's midfield had been completely overhauled, with indisputable power, tenacity, physical presence, flair and a bona fide playmaker added to the ranks. A disjointed mid-section that had ambled its way through the final weeks of 2019/20 with the lackadaisical Gylfi Sigurdsson, the faltering Tom Davies, the ill-fitting Alex Iwobi, the half-fit André Gomes and the timid Bernard, now had plenty of options and much-needed competition for places.

With a total outlay of over £60 million that summer, once young defender Ben Godfrey had been added to the ranks in a £20 million move from Norwich City, Director of Football, Marcel Brands, was under pressure to recoup transfer funds before the transfer deadline.

However, while the club were reportedly willing to listen to offers for a few first-team regulars and fringe players, they only managed to collect £1.8 million for Morgan Schneiderlin who left for Nice, and Fraser Hornby who joined Stade de Reims for the same fee. Otherwise, those players who left did so on free transfers, with Sandro Ramirez, Oumar Niasse, Cuco Martina and Luke Garbutt departing alongside goalkeeper Maarten Steklenburg and academy graduate Kieran Dowell.

As such, it had been an expensive close season. When the expenditure on incoming transfers was added to the estimated £12 million a year being paid to Ancelotti and the club-record salary for James – that was variously reported to have been between £150,000 and £250,000 a week - it represented a big gamble by Farhad Moshiri.

In many ways, it was the last roll of the dice for the Everton owner; a sizeable bet placed on the managerial abilities of Ancelotti and his ability to fashion a winning side from the players he had inherited and those who had arrived in the summer.

For a few heady weeks early in the season and again after Boxing Day 2020, it looked like the gamble might pay off. Evertonians might have been restricted to following their team from their own homes but they were imbued with a rare sense of optimism as Ancelotti's new-look side began the campaign in electric form.

***

As ever, things were also moving off the pitch as Farhad Moshiri and the Board of Directors sought to push forward on the issue of Everton's new stadium. In late August, the club had announced they would submit a revised planning application in September, which would include architectural and design changes to the proposed structure at Bramley-Moore Dock.

The club's original planning documents had been submitted to Liverpool City Council in December 2019, with a decision expected sometime in 2020. Although the application had been made just before the outbreak of the COVID-19 pandemic, Everton insisted their plans, which were very much in line with the Government's "build,

build, build" mantra aimed at stimulating an economic recovery, had been moving on apace.

The changes to the plans for Bramley-Moore Dock would trigger an additional review of the planning application which they expected the Council to complete by December this year, and which would probably involve a delay a start of construction of the project until at least April 2021.

Everton also confirmed key members of the project team.

Laing O'Rourke had been chosen as the contractors for the proposed build, and they had selected Pattern to be the technical architects. Buro Happold and Planit-IE were to be enroled as engineering consultants and landscape architects, respectively.

Colin Chong, Stadium Development Director for Everton Football Club, detailed the changes and the new path forward in a lengthy blog on the club's website.

However, objections to the club's proposed new stadium had been made to Liverpool City Council by Historic England and the International Council on Monuments and Sites (ICOMOS), a heritage body acting on behalf of UNESCO.

Historic England, together with ICOMOS, advocated the Government should review the proposals because of their concerns over the impact of Everton's plans to infill the dock could have on what was a UNESCO World Heritage Site and Conservation Area. Similar concerns were raised by the Victorian Society.

As it turned out within months, the club's proposed development had proved to be enough for UNESCO to strip Liverpool's historic waterfront of the World Heritage status it had enjoyed since 2004, with the new stadium deemed to be the final straw for the UN's heritage body who, *The Guardian* reported in July 2021, blamed their decision "on years of development for an 'irreversible loss' to the historic value of its Victorian docks."

Among the changes that had been proposed by Everton to their original planning application were the inclusion of a river-facing plaza on the west side of the ground and the removal of the multi-storey car park.

Additionally, the West Quay would now become the car park with spaces for disabled supporters, with the solar panels originally planned for that location now moving to the stadium roof. The brick façade was to be simplified to make Archibald Leitch lattice work patterns more obvious.

The club stressed they did not expect that the changes would create any additional expense for the project, which was then estimated to cost around £500 million, with construction expected to be financed by private investment.

2020: Ancelotti's Blues off to a flyer. Second by Christmas

2013 — the last time Everton had won away at a "big six" team; 2012 — the last time Everton had beaten Tottenham; 2008 — the last time Everton had won on Tottenham's home turf. All three unwanted statistics tumbled on the opening day of the 2020/21 season, and while there was a discussion to be had around the extent to which the absence of fans reduces home advantage, it would take nothing away from the Toffees' performance, the magnitude of the result, or the transformation the team had undergone since the same fixture just seven games previously.

***

13 September 2020: Tottenham Hotspur v Everton (Behind Closed Doors)

This was night and day from that miserable display in early July when a pretty awful Spurs edged an utterly dreadful Everton thanks to a Michael Keane own goal. A defeat that effectively ended any notion of the Toffees sneaking into a European qualification place had been attributed on fan website, ToffeeWeb, to "a black hole of a midfield, one devoid of guile, imagination and drive, where the first instinct was to go backwards because of an inability to play through an opposition press." In the first game of the new season, they found victory through a completely revamped mid-section, with three new signings making stellar debuts in royal blue.

From front to back, this was an Everton that looked hungry, determined but also finally confident in its own ability thanks to the new boys, and they dominated the early exchanges. Mourinho admitted in his pre-match press conference that on the back of their transfer business, he now considered the Blues genuine rivals for the top six but even he might have been surprised by the way Ancelotti's men set about controlling the ball, at least until Spurs finally got to grips with them to a degree as the first half wore on.

Everton should have been a goal up after a quarter of an hour, but Richarlison ignored Dominic Calvert-Lewin – free in the centre waiting for a tap in - went for glory and sliced an off-balance effort well off target.

Spurs then broke at speed in a two-on-two situation where Dele Alli could have slipped Kane in for a clear chance on goal but also went for it himself, and Pickford reacted brilliantly to push his shot over the crossbar. Later, Matt Doherty, played a one-two with Kane, latching onto the latter's scooped ball over the top and aiming a shot for the far corner of the goal but Pickford was equal to it, making an impressive save with his foot to divert the ball away to safety.

For Everton, Allan was efficiently going about his business closing down spaces, winning the ball, and handing it off with the minimum of fuss and Abdoulaye Doucouré was covering ground, claiming second balls, driving forward with purpose but was also alert enough to put in an excellent stretching tackle to stop Lucas Moura from racing away for the hosts.

James Rodriguez, meanwhile, was oozing class with every silky touch and pin-point accurate cross-field pass and he would create more chances in a game than any Everton player had for two years.

The goal, when it came, though, was not from the cultured boot of Rodriguez or the mercurial Richarlison but emphatically from the head of a man about whom questions had been raised at the tail end of last season when he failed to score at all during the nine games of "Project Restart". When Richarlison was fouled wide on the left and Digne whipped the ball behind the defence, it was Calvert-Lewin who rose powerfully and purposefully in the image of his Finch Farm mentor, Duncan Ferguson, and despatched an unstoppable header high into Lloris's goal. It was a thumping finish worthy of any Everton No.9 and a well-deserved winning goal.

Ancellotti had promised that his Everton team would be more competitive in his first full season in charge and his players delivered on that pledge in spades. Combative, resilient but also confident and composed, they bossed this match and were more than deserving of the points, despite Jose Mourinho's churlishness.

This was just one match at the start of a long season and Evertonians were more than accustomed to disappointment, heartbreak and false dawns but this felt different — the effect of a top-class manager stamping his will and class on a team with targeted acquisitions and a touch of magic. If this was to be the platform from which this side got better as the new players settled in and attained full match fitness, then these could be the beginnings of exciting times at Everton... if so, the Blues hadn't half earned them!

Final score: Spurs 0-1 Everton

***

Afterwards, Ancelotti expressed his satisfaction with Everton's impressive win, saying that the players did exactly what was expected of them.

"Unbelievable," Ancelotti said. "The game was good. The game was what I expected from the team. I know it was not easy, but I thought the new [players] brought energy, brought quality and the others supported really well.

"So the performance was brilliant. We had some difficulties in the beginning, but we were comfortable on the pitch."

Asked if it surprised him at how quickly his new signings had bedded in, Ancelotti smiled, "Players that are able to play football don't need a lot of time to adapt. James knows very well what he has to do, and Allan and Doucouré are the same.

"I told them to show their quality and I think they did. I think we have a good combination in midfield — we have quality in Gomes and James, we have Allan [who does really well] in possession, and we have Doucouré who can work box-to-box.

"Last season, we had a lot of players with quality on the ball, but in football sometimes you have to play without the ball."

***

19 September 2020: Everton v West Bromwich Albion (Behind Closed Doors)

2020 might have felt like an interminable year, but it hadn't been all that long ago that Everton, under Sam Allardyce, ranked rock bottom in the Premier League for attacking prowess: 20th for shots taken, 20th for shots on target, 20th for chances created, and 20th for chances created from open play.

While there was always the feeling that Farhad Moshiri would choose to get his over-arching dream back on track by binning one of the most unpalatable managerial appointments in the club's history at the end of 2017/18, nothing was guaranteed. It was that uncertainty which had made for sobering times for Evertonians.

Fast forward two-and-a-half years and the outlook at Goodison Park had been transformed. In between, Marco Silva's tenure did come to an unsuccessful end, but he was at least responsible for buying Richarlison. Now, thanks to Carlo Ancelotti and three astute signings over the summer, Everton were an entirely different proposition from an attacking perspective.

It was hard to overstate the importance that a primarily defensive acquisition such as Allan had been to the side, but it was James Rodriguez, a player who promised to be a goldmine of assists for the Blues, who predictably grabbed the headlines.

In his first two games as an Everton player, the Colombian magician had created more "big chances" than André Gomes, Tom Davies, Fabian Delph and Morgan Schneiderlin had created in all of the previous season combined. He weighed in with an assist on his first Premier League appearance at Goodison Park against West Brom, scored what Evertonians hoped would be the first of many goals in royal blue when he put the Toffees ahead on the stroke of half-time, and underscored the size of the coup Ancelotti and Marcel Brands effected when they brought him from Real Madrid.

And it was Dominic Calvert-Lewin who stood to benefit most from the transformation in midfield. The 22-year-old ensured that the lion's share of the limelight was his this time by grabbing his first hat-trick, to bury a spirited Baggies outfit as Everton ran out 5-2 winners and temporarily topped the Premier League table for the first time in three years.

Although the Baggies levelled the game at 2-2 early in the second half through an admittedly brilliant Matheus Pereira free-kick when they were playing with only 10 men following Kieran Gibbs's dismissal in first-half stoppage time, Everton's irresistible attacking options eventually prevailed.

Richarlison's header from a 54th minute free-kick by Lucas Digne was pushed away by the keeper but Michael Keane was on hand to tuck away the rebound.

Eight minutes after that, Everton scored arguably the pick of their five goals on the day when James knocked a perfect ball over the top to Richarlison who prodded in on past the keeper and Calvert-Lewin slid in to toe it over the line and make it 4-2.

Calvert-Lewin wrapped up his hat-trick when he met a Rodriguez corner with the back of his head and sent it flying in past the stranded Sam Johnstone.

Including the 3-0 midweek win against Salford in the Carabao Cup, it was now three wins out of three in all competitions and a brief stint at the top of the Premier League to mark a terrific start to the new season for Ancelotti and Everton.

Things would get better, too – at least until a controversial Goodison derby temporarily derailed Everton's excellent start.

Final score: Everton 5-2 West Bromwich Albion

***

30 September 2020: Everton v West Ham United (Behind Closed Doors)

After a 5-2 win against Fleetwood in the cup, and a fine 2-1 away win at Crystal Palace in the league, Everton booked their place in the last eight of the Carabao Cup for the second year running as Dominic Calvert-Lewin grabbed his second hat-trick of the nascent season to propel the Toffees to another handsome win over the Hammers.

Ancelotti had named another strong line-up, keeping his in-form strike force intact, but this time adding James Rodriguez for his cup debut and Allan in midfield alongside Gylfi Sigurdsson and Fabian Delph. Niels Nkounkou and Jonjoe Kenny continued as the full-backs with Lucas Digne putting in another impressive display at centre-half partnering Michael Keane.

Keane had impressed over the first few games for his defensive work but it was his peach of a ball over the top that set Calvert-Lewin up for his first goal of the evening. The striker pulled the defender's pass over the top out of the air with jaw-dropping control and then stroked the ball past Darren Randolph to make it 1-0 with 11 minutes gone.

Everton had barely had time to set themselves for the second half before West Ham were level. Attacking straight from kick-off, the Hammers worked the ball forward, and it ended up at the feet of Robert Snodgrass in too much space and he whipped a shot past Pickford from 20-yards.

The home side's response was emphatic, however, and they restored their lead when Richarlison again terrorised the visitors' back line by running at them and then across the edge of the box, where he unleashed a shot that deflected off Declan Rice and flew past the keeper.

Then, following a short corner, substitute Alex Iwobi curled a shot off the right-hand post and Calvert-Lewin was in the right place at the right time to tuck home the rebound.

And the shoo-in for an England call-up completed his hat-trick six minutes after that. Rodriguez was involved again as Sigurdsson slipped 'DCL' in behind the defence with just Randolph to beat, which he did with calm aplomb and a tidy left-foot finish. It was Calvert-Lewin's eighth goal of the season already and it capped another strong performance from Ancelotti's men.

The newfound confidence in the side was again in evidence. Where Everton teams of recent years might have crumbled after giving up the lead, then losing key members to injury and, perhaps, struggled to a draw and had to survive the lottery of penalties, Ancelotti's 2020/21 edition simply carry on undeterred and score again themselves.

After a strong showing over their first three rounds in the cup, Everton had a break until the third week of December when the quarter-finals were scheduled to take place. At least five of the other seven sides left in the competition were from the Premier League, four of them from the so-called 'big six', but injuries permitting, the way they were currently playing, the Toffees would fear few sides.

Final score: Everton 4-1 West Ham

***

Once again, Ancelotti was really pleased with what was his team's sixth straight win in all competitions to start the season.

"[It] was a very good performance. We did well and [we have] good momentum, we have focus, we have motivation and we keep going and winning, which is really important.

"We have to pay attention because [other] games can be more difficult [and] we don't have a lot of time to recover and prepare for the game against Brighton, but I hope we can [produce] a repeat performance."

That fixture against the Seagulls at Goodison Park just four days later ended up posing little problem for Ancelotti's men. For the fourth time in seven games, they scored at least four goals, with James Rodriguez grabbing a brace in a 4-2 win that put Everton in dreamland – top of the Premier League heading into the first international break.

Despite not being able to witness any of their team's early-season successes in person, Evertonians were in ebullient mood heading into the Goodison derby. As the catchy 1980s song 'Spirit of the Blues' was used in more and more memes on Twitter and Instagram, a groundswell movement eventually propelled the song to Number 1 on the UK iTunes charts as more and more fans bought digital versions of the track.

The phenomenon carried over into the following day, with 'Z Cars' climbing to the No.2 spot followed by the 1985 FA Cup song 'Here We Go' at No.3. The recently-released film 'Howard's Way' about the glorious 1980s side also ascended to No.1 on the iTunes Movies charts. 'Spirit of the Blues' would become the club's unofficial anthem over the next years, and the soundtrack to two desperate struggles against relegation.

***

Just six days before hosting Liverpool at Goodison, news emerged that Everton's neighbours from across the park, together with Manchester United, were driving a radical overhaul of the Premier League power structure. A one-off, £250 million rescue package and hugely increased ongoing funding for English Football League clubs, in exchange for a reduced Premier League and consolidated voting power among England's biggest clubs, were among a raft of proposals in a 'Revitalisation' document that was revealed by *The Telegraph* and given public backing by EFL chairman, Rick Parry.

Amid the onset of the COVID-19 pandemic, which was triggering a financial crisis in football, particularly in the lower reaches of the English professional football pyramid, Manchester United and Liverpool were working with Parry on what they dubbed *Project Big Picture*, one that had the potential to reshape the finances of the game.

Under their proposals, the Premier League, the most lucrative sports league in the world, would see a reduction to 18 teams, with automatic promotion from the Championship for two clubs each season and the next three best-placed teams playing off with the 16th-placed Premier League club to determine which gets a place in the top flight.

The League Cup and Community Shield would be scrapped, allowing for greater participation of England's top clubs in an expanded UEFA Champions League. It was also proposed that the distribution of broadcast revenue be altered, with one portion based on performance in the league on a rolling three-year basis.

The existing system of parachute payments to clubs dropping out of the top division would stop, with 25% of the Premier League's TV income distributed among clubs across the second to fourth tiers instead.

In exchange for these measures designed to safeguard the future of the domestic game, the Premier League's nine longest-serving clubs — the so-called 'big six' of Arsenal, Chelsea, Liverpool, Manchester City, United and Tottenham, plus Everton, West Ham and Southampton — would get greater voting power, with a majority of six required for certain decisions, including, for example, the power to approve or veto takeover bids for clubs.

The Premier League itself came out against the proposals, saying that while it supported, "a wide-ranging discussion on the future of the game, including its competition structures, calendar and overall financing ... in the Premier League's view, several individual proposals in the plan published today could have a damaging impact on the whole game and they were disappointed to see that Rick Parry, Chair of the EFL, had given his on-the-record support."

Parry told *The Telegraph*: "What do we do? Leave it exactly as it is and allow the smaller clubs to wither? Or do we do something about it? And you can't do something about it without something changing."

Three days later, *Project Big Picture* was slapped down by a majority of the top flight's other clubs and unanimously declared a non-starter during a meeting of the 20 Premier League clubs. Instead, the League resolved to undertake a wide-ranging 'strategic review' that would seek to implement the key measures, particularly those relating to a greater share of the money to the EFL.

According to *The Guardian*, Everton CEO, Denise Barrett-Baxendale, demanded an apology from Liverpool and United, which was denied by the clubs' representatives, Tom Werner and Ed Woodward.

***

17 October 2020: Everton v Liverpool (Behind Closed Doors)

If the directors of Everton and Liverpool had been allowed to mix at an appropriate social distance before and after the derby match, it was possible the atmosphere in the Goodison boardroom would have been a little frosty.

On the field, it was clear you could take the fans out of the derby but you seemingly could not take the 'derby' out of this historic local rivalry, with this edition seeing four goals, an almost obligatory red card — 88 minutes after Jordan Pickford could have received his marching orders — and a last-gasp intervention from VAR's hair's-breadth rulers. In a fixture that so often failed to deliver the greatest exhibition of football from both sides, there were plenty of talking points and drama to chew over.

Everton came into the game with a 100% record and greater optimism of ending their miserable record in this fixture than they had done for many years, but they didn't do themselves justice. For long periods, there was just too much of the 'old Everton', the one that struggled to beat the opposition press, relied too heavily on Pickford's boot to launch 'attacks' and lacked the crisp, clinical passing of the like that Liverpool used to race into a very early lead.

With players possessing the ball-moving qualities of James Rodriguez, Allan and André Gomes — and certainly given the start they'd made to the new season — Evertonians were expecting more from their team, especially in the first half where they struggled to contain a reds side operating near their peak.

When Everton were fleetingly sublime, unsurprisingly it was James who was at the heart of it, but the Colombian had a mixed performance himself (which, when you consider he was still probably the best player in Blue on the day, was quite something), while Richarlison, like Yerry Mina displaying the effects of trans-Atlantic travel on the Thursday, was peripheral until he took centre stage late on.

But if the feeling was that Adrián was a weak link in the reds' side and that the loss of Virgil van Dijk being forced off with an injury within the first 10 minutes gave the Blues another big advantage, the hosts didn't end up taking full advantage. Apart from having to pick the ball out of the net and denying Dominic Calvert-Lewin prior to the first equaliser, the Spanish keeper wasn't sufficiently worked by Everton.

Instead, the home side finished the match with 10 men after Richarlison's deserved dismissal. They also played a Get Out of Jail Free card in stoppage time when Pickford, who had kept his side in it with an impressive display, almost threw a point away. Jordan Henderson's goal – another potential heart-breaker for Blues supporters – was, however, ruled out for marginal offside.

If there were fears that Everton would take the brunt of Liverpool's response to the 7-2 battering they had taken at Villa Park before the international break, they were realised right at the start of this contest. Jürgen Klopp's side came flying out of the traps and were ahead inside three minutes.

A rapier-like move through the hosts' midfield ended with the ball being played out to Andrew Robertson wide on the left and he centred hard and low for Sadio Mané to slam the ball high into the goal with a first-time finish.

Sensing blood, the Reds came forward again in the fifth minute and when Virgil van Dijk threatened to meet a ball to the back post, a knee-high tackle by Pickford cleaned him out. With the whistle having already gone for offside and Pickford's 'tackle' deemed serious foul play and not violent conduct, there was no scope for VAR to review the incident and either award a penalty or send the goalkeeper off.

It was a massive let-off for Pickford, and Everton then gradually settled and equalised with 18 minutes on the clock. Calvert-Lewin collected a ball down the right-hand channel and stung Adrian's palms with a powerful drive from the angle. James took responsibility for the resulting corner and deposited it into the six-yard box, where Keane connected with a strong header through the keeper's gloves.

That should have been the cue for the Blues to slow things down a bit and play their game a bit more, but the passes just weren't hitting their mark and, all too often, the midfield was bypassed by Pickford's long kicks forward.

Then, with half an hour gone, Everton lost an important player of their own when Seamus Coleman suffered a recurrence of the hamstring problem that had prematurely ended his game against Brighton last time out. Ben Godfrey replaced him, and acquitted himself very well on what was a baptism-by-fire debut.

Thiago Alcântara fired narrowly wide, Mané sliced a shot off target, and Calvert-Lewin's side-foot touch slid past Adrian's post as the two sides traded blows late in the first half but it was all square at the half-time interval.

The second period started in similar fashion to the first, with the visitors driving forward and seeing efforts from Fabinho and Henderson fly over the crossbar but Everton found some rhythm of their own and James was at it again with another quite brilliant cross. Richarlison dived to meet but his header came back off the post before the Colombian star had an effort of his own diverted away from goal by the keeper.

It was Liverpool who took the lead again in the 72nd minute, though. Mina cut out a cross from the right but only presented it on a platter for Salah, who took an instinctive snap-shot that spun beyond Pickford's dive and inside the far post.

And 2-1 almost became 3-1 five minutes later. Joel Matip lost his marker in the box at a corner and headed towards the top corner, but Pickford pawed it out the air superbly to deny the defender before parrying a stinging Salah shot over the bar.

Everton hit back again, however, nine minutes later as James and Digne combined to serve up the second equaliser for Calvert-Lewin. Rodriguez, who had ghosted over to the left flank, fed the Frenchman down the line and his deep cross hung up perfectly for Calvert-Lewin to meet it with one of his amazing leaps and then steer his header back across the keeper.

"Now win it," was the collective refrain from Evertonians watching on screens across the world over but Richarlison effectively killed the Blues' hopes of taking all the points with a dreadful and needless challenge on Alcântara in the centre-circle.

The incident almost proved to be even more costly because Liverpool tried to press home their numerical advantage in the last few minutes, and looked to have claimed victory with yet another sickening stoppage-time winner. They played Mané in down their left and he cut the ball back into the centre for Henderson, whose side-footed effort looked routine enough for Pickford to palm away. Instead, the ball spun off his glove and over the line, but Liverpool's celebrations were cut dead by Video Assistant Referee, David Coote, who adjudged that Mane's shoulder had been beyond the last defender.

It was a huge slice of fortune for Everton, but then the Blues had been due some derby luck after years of dodgy refereeing decisions and last-gasp winners. Reds fans would have felt aggrieved at VAR and moaned for months that Pickford should have received his marching orders after just five minutes; but after years of refereeing injustice in Merseyside derbies — Dirk Kuyt's flying kick on Phil Neville; Steven Gerrard's two-footed lunge on Gary Naismith; Joleon Lescott getting assaulted with no repercussions; Luis Suarez's histrionics in getting Jack Rodwell sent off; and even cynical a kick out at Allan by Robertson that went unpunished in this game — Evertonians wouldn't be losing any sleep.

Despite being well below the best of what they had shown to that point in 2020/21 season and never seeming to get out of second gear, Everton had grabbed a draw against what Klopp described as his side's best away performance of his tenure. The spirit of a side that knew the meaning of how to come twice from behind was admirable and hugely encouraging.

That was definitely something to build on for Ancelotti, but it was a relief that the next tortuous derby wasn't until February, when the Blues would slay two hoodoos at once.

Final score: Everton 2-2 Liverpool

***

By December 2020, ten months into the pandemic, the decision was taken to allow a limited number of spectators, sufficiently spaced out for their protection, to attend Premier League matches in certain cities designated as Tier 2 or better in terms of COVID-19 restrictions.

That meant that for three matches that month, 2,000 Everton fans were drawn by lottery for the home games against Chelsea, Arsenal and Manchester United. It would be another five months before more supporters were allowed back into top-flight stadiums, and even then they were capped according to coronavirus protocols.

Since the fractious Merseyside derby in mid-October, the Toffees' form had suffered due to James Rodriguez struggling with an unspecified groin injury, as a result of being pole-axed by reds defender Virgil van Dijk, and Richarlison's three-match ban following his sending off for fouling Thiago Alcântara. Having won all seven of their opening fixtures in all competitions, Everton registered a victory in just one of the next seven and had fallen to ninth place following a dismal 1-0 home reverse to Leeds United and a 1-1 draw at Burnley.

By the time Arsenal came to town, back-to-back wins over Chelsea and Leicester had vaulted Ancelotti's side back up to fifth; and by the time the final whistle had blown on their last match of the calendar year, against Sheffield United at Bramall Lane, Everton were in second place and primed for a tilt at finally qualifying for the Champions League.

***

19 December 2020: Everton v Arsenal (2000 spectators)

A year into their respective managerial tenures, Carlo Ancelotti and Mikel Arteta found themselves in very different positions. Everton, heading into Christmas, were sitting in the top three, while Arsenal languished towards the bottom of the Premier League table. The visitors' early approach showed their lack of confidence, as the two teams sized each other up in cagey fashion for a quarter of an hour before the first real moment of excitement presented itself from the unlikely boot of Michael Keane.

The centre-half strode forward as space opened up ahead of him and unleashed a swerving missile of a shot that bent agonisingly within a whisker of the post from thirty-plus yards out.

Seven minutes later, Alex Iwobi, playing against his old club, capitalised on more space afforded him by Arsenal to whip the ball in from the right where Calvert-Lewin got a glance on it with his head and it flew in off Rob Holding for what would go down as a 22nd minute own goal.

Arsenal responded and received a route back into the contest when Tom Davies clumsily felled Ainsley Maitland-Niles as he tried to collect a loose ball. It provided referee Andre Marriner with an easy decision to award a penalty. Nicolas Pépé assumed responsibility for the spot-kick and calmly slotted it past Jordan Pickford to make it 1-1.

With Allan out injured, the manager had asked Davies to step into the breach, and whilst he had a decent enough first 45 minutes, he was emblematic of a lack of creativity from the Blues that largely characterised their performance. It was a display crying out for the invention of someone like James Rodriguez and, in the second half, someone like Bernard; but in the Colombian's absence, the onus fell in Alex Iwobi and Richarlison, both of whom popped up now and then with decent contributions without ever really stamping their authority on the game.

Importantly, in the absence of any consistent imagination or attacking ideas, Everton fell back on the industry of Calvert-Lewin and their threat at set-pieces to reclaim the lead. The striker's overall work-rate deserved a goal, and he almost got it on the stroke of half-time when he tested Bernd Leno with an excellent left-footed strike from the edge of the box that was heading for the top corner until the keeper finger-tipped it behind.

From the resulting corner, Gylfi Sigurdsson delivered the ball to the near post to meet Mina's run and the big Colombian defender steered a header impressively on goal and past Leno at his near post for his second goal of the campaign.

Old habits seemed to die hard for Everton in the second half and it made those dogged and professional games, where Everton got themselves ahead and then dug in to protect what they held, nerve-wracking to watch. Evertonians of any vintage remember all too well how often their side would try to sit back against opposition teams down the years and inevitably concede to toss away points; but they were now having to get used to the pragmatism and game-management of Ancelotti, a man not averse to finishing a match with seven defenders on the pitch in the interests of seeing out a match.

The second 45 minutes against Arsenal were not a comfortable watch but by the end, the Gunners were banging their heads against the same brick wall that had confronted Chelsea and Leicester in the preceding week. It said much for how far the Gunners have fallen despite their impressive cup form that Everton almost completely ceded the midfield battle in the second half and only fleetingly looked like being punished for it.

Arsenal came close to wiping out their hosts' lead for a second time early in the second half when David Luiz hit the crossbar and it needed a save from the returning Jordan Pickford in the closing stages to ensure that Ancelotti would toast a third successive victory. Hardly a performance to set the pulse racing but the win was paramount and the fact that it was secured without the team playing especially well in an attacking sense – not to mention without three of its best and most creative players – boded well. With just two shots on target, Everton were a model of efficiency as they climbed into second place in the Premier League.

Final score: Everton 2-1 Arsenal

***

Following what was a third successive win for the Toffees, Phil McNulty, Chief football writer at the *BBC*, wrote of a result that:

"Capped a superb week for Ancelotti and Everton after wins against Chelsea and now Arsenal at Goodison Park, flanking a midweek victory at Leicester City.

"And as Ancelotti took the acclaim of the 2,000 fans inside Goodison Park, especially those on the Gwladys Street, the 61-year-old's status was confirmed.

"If Ancelotti had plotted out a week to mark his first year, three months of which were without action as football went into lockdown because of the Covid-19 pandemic, then this would have been his perfect script.

"Everton were left in 15th place after that draw with Arsenal last December, Ancelotti sitting a few seats away from Arteta in the directors' box on that freezing lunchtime.

"And how glad Moshiri and Everton must be that the cards fell neatly into place in those decisive days when both they and Arsenal were seeking a new manager, the Gunners having sacked Unai Emery.

"Ironically, Arteta had supporters of his own inside Everton's boardroom and his appointment may well have been warmly welcomed by supporters, while Arsenal were linked with Ancelotti because of his global stature and his previous success in the capital with Chelsea, where he won the Premier League and FA Cup double.

"Arsenal went with the rookie with roots at Emirates Stadium while Everton pushed for Ancelotti - both clubs satisfied with the outcome.

"Ancelotti, typically, refuses to get carried away. He has seen it all and knows rough times may still be around the corner as he contemplates Wednesday's EFL Cup quarter-final against Manchester United at Goodison Park.

'We did very well in our last few games - brilliant performances and fantastic results,' he said. 'We showed more consistency. This season we started well, then we had a difficult moment, but right now I'm really pleased. The position in the table is really good. But as I said last week, it is not the end of the season. We have to keep fighting but this was a top, top performance.'

"One year on, Everton and owner Moshiri have every right to be elated at the acquisition of a man regarded as managerial royalty."

***

At the club's AGM on 14 January 2021, a major topic was the planning application review for the club's proposed new stadium at Bramley-Moore Dock, which had been delayed by the pandemic; but Professor Barrett-Baxendale expressed her confidence that the impact would not be unduly detrimental to the timeline which called for the first spade to go into the ground that year.

"Liverpool City Council's public consultation period closed in October and the club is confident of securing a successful planning determination very soon, with the potential to commence construction on-site shortly thereafter," she told shareholders.

"While the Club awaits the determination of a planning application, we continue to pursue a range of funding opportunities, including senior debt, alternative sources of equity and subordinated debt.

"Phase two due diligence is currently being conducted to support the funding process, including direct research with supporters to help shape what match days will look like at the new stadium."

***

10 February 2021: Everton v Tottenham Hotspur (Behind Closed Doors)

Perhaps occupying the dizzy heights of number two position in the league had caused a collective team nosebleed. Certainly results after the Arsenal game had been mixed. A home defeat against Manchester United in the Carabao quarter final, was followed by the Boxing Day away win in Sheffield, and by a New Year's Day home defeat against West Ham. The next seven games included 4 wins, 2 draws and another home defeat, this time to Newcastle.

The next match at Goodison saw Everton drag themselves into the last eight of the FA Cup, with a gutsy, if defensively suspect, display and a dramatic extra-time winner in a back-and-forth, goal-laden thriller against Spurs made famous by Carlo Ancelotti's gloriously nonchalant reaction to his side scoring to go 5-4 up.

It was Spurs who had came out of the traps with more purpose and within three minutes of the kick-off, Everton's zonal marking system had utterly failed with Davinson Sanchez rising unchallenged to nod home a corner from the Tottenham left.

Hugo Lloris tipped a Dominic Calvert-Lewin effort onto the post as the home side found their attacking belief and after Yerry Mina headed a corner wide 10 minutes before the half-time break, Everton sparked a burst of three goals in seven minutes when Dominic Calvert-Lewin hammered in his 18th of the season and 50th for the Toffees, via Lloris's gloves.

Two minutes later, Digne's headed lay-off from Sanchez's awkward header was heel-flicked neatly to Richarlison by Calvert-Lewin and the Brazilian, finally looking like his usual self, took a touch to his right before drilling through a defender's legs and into the bottom corner from 20 yards to make it 2-1.

Five minutes after that, when Pierre-Emile Højbjerg accidentally clipped Calvert-Lewin's heels as the striker went to collect a pass inside from the left flank. Referee David Coote had no hesitation in pointing to the spot and, after a check by Video Assistant Referee, Chris Kavanagh, Sigurdsson stepped up to roll home the resulting penalty.

That should have seen the Toffees into the interval with a two-goal cushion, but an awful lapse in concentration from Mina allowed the ball to slip by him in the box and Eric Lamela was on hand to clip it past stand-in keeper Robin Olsen deep into injury time.

Everton's slender 3-2 lead felt more precarious when, just nine minutes into the second half, Calvert-Lewin had to be withdrawn with a recurrence of his recent hamstring problem and Richarlison moved into a central attacking role.

Indeed, it was an advantage that would last only a couple of minutes longer and once again it was schoolboy defending at a corner from the same side as before that was the Toffees' undoing. Sigurdsson kept his attentions on Sanchez and not the ball, which meant it was the Colombian who tracked it and, holding off the Everton man, stuck out as a leg to stab it home and level things up at 3-3.

If the pendulum had swung toward Spurs, Richarlison would ensure that the hosts landed the next blow. Sigurdsson played him in nicely between the lines and the Brazil international powered past his man before lashing a superb left-footed shot across the keeper and in off the far post from a tight angle.

With 82 minutes gone, however, Everton's defence was breached again, following yet another corner. Olsen's glancing fist on the ball ended up with Lamela again, his shot headed off the line by Abdoulaye Doucouré, but when Son Hueng-min collected the loose ball on the far side and bent a cross to the back post, substitute Harry Kane was there, unmarked, to head in from close range.

Once more, with their deeper bench and their tails up at having made it 4-4 to force extra-time, Spurs might have felt the momentum was with them, but it was Everton who grabbed the deciding goal that finally broke Spurs's resilience – and it was one worthy of settling any tie. Bernard played a ball inside to Sigurdsson. He controlled it and then chipped deftly over the defence for the little Brazilian to track and then half-volley sweetly past Lloris with his left foot.

On the sidelines, cameras caught Ancelotti nonchalantly sipping his tea in his technical area as the Blues' bench celebrated behind him.

Perhaps he couldn't feel confident that the ninth goal of the contest would be the last; or maybe it was emblematic of his generally calm demeanour. Either way, he had steered Everton into the last eight.

Final score: Everton 5-4 Spurs

***

In other news, two days after that mad-cap Spurs game, Ancelotti's Crosby home was burgled by masked thieves who were disturbed by his daughter, but not before they had taken off with a safe.

A report in the *Liverpool Echo* partially substantiated a rumour that had began on WhatsApp and quickly spread to social media that the intruders had held the Everton manager up at knife-point. However, Ancelotti, who had regularly expressed how much he enjoyed living in the area, was not at home.

Merseyside Police said: "two men wearing balaclavas and black waterproof clothing perpetrated the crime." They reportedly gained entry to the property and removed the safe. When they noticed Ancelotti's daughter, they fled the scene.

The Police later said the safe, which had been forced open, was found dumped in a car park off Runnells Lane, near Masefield Road, in Thornton.

It was later rumoured the harrowing incident played an important role in the Ancelotti family's decision to prematurely leave Merseyside.

2021: Liverpool 0-2 Everton

> “This time it was different, and it was over. It was finally bloody over. 21 years and five months since Everton last won at Anfield, the most depressing sequence of results in the club's 143-year history ended as Carlo Ancelotti's team beat Liverpool 2-0.
>
> **2021: Liverpool 0-2 Everton**

When Kevin Campbell scored a fourth-minute winner in the Merseyside derby in September 1999, little did he know that it would be more than two decades before Everton would win again at Anfield. The Toffees' record since the turn of the 21st Century, on the ground they had called home until the 1892 split that led to Liverpool FC's formation, had been depressingly torrid. The more years that passed since their last victory on the Reds' turf, the more anguished the fixture became.

20 February 2021: Liverpool v Everton (Behind closed doors)

The psychology behind the fixture appeared to trump the law of averages, but in February 2021, 22 years of pain finally came to an end as Carlo Ancelotti oversaw a precious victory on the other side of Stanley Park.

For far too long, Campbell been the last man to score an Everton winner at Anfield. That accolade now went to the warrior-like Richarlison, the player who fired home unerringly in the third minute to send Everton on their way to a cathartic, misery-ending victory. Gylfi Sigurdsson's late second merely ensured that the points in a Derby would go the Blue side of Merseyside for the first time in over a decade.

To outsiders, the spontaneous outpouring of emotion at the final whistle, the jubilant hugs, clenched-fist bellows and boisterousness in the changing room may seem curiously excessive, but they were a visceral illustration of how much this meant to Everton's players and staff, and not just a local like Tom Davies or the long-haulers like Seamus Coleman and Duncan Ferguson. Newcomers like Ben Godfrey, James Rodriguez and even Ancelotti himself had also grasped the importance to the club and its supporters of banishing this rotten hoodoo.

In the end, it didn't take a fantastic attacking performance, but as expected against the defending champions, it required a resolute defensive stand and some heroics from Jordan Pickford.

That last part was gloriously poetic. Everton's goalkeeper has been the subject of some shameful media scrutiny and criticism over what happened in the Goodison derby last October; hysteria that continued right up to kick off this evening. But he responded with a man-of-the-match display, playing behind a defensive unit that could probably all have laid claim to that accolade, such was their individual and collective effort.

Mason Holgate had had an inconsistent season but was immense, as were Michael Keane, Godfrey, Coleman and Lucas Digne, who left everything out on the pitch in terms of effort and desire. This was a towering display by Everton's rear-guard that began at the front, but which was founded on discipline and shape throughout the team against a notoriously dangerous Liverpool attack.

It needed to be, because the Blues often made it more difficult for themselves than need be with some poor ball retention and it was no surprise that in the final reckoning they had just 28% of the possession. It didn't matter, because they were more than good enough at the back.

The tragedy, of course, was that no fans were there at Anfield to see it. Two decades of Blues had gone across Stanley Park and suffered either valiant draws or painful defeat, but the hope now was that with the hex gone, Evertonians would savour victory at Anfield in person some day soon. Until then, Blues just had to drink the feeling in.

Final score: Liverpool 0-2 Everton

***

On 25 February, Carlo Ancelotti told *The BBC* he hoped he could extend his time at Everton beyond the terms of his existing contract, saying he would like to still be there when the club moved into its new stadium in the autumn of 2024.

The Italian had signed a 4½-year contract when he became Everton manager in December 2019, which meant his existing deal would expire at the end of what looked at that stage like it would be the Toffees' last season at Goodison Park.

Everton's proposed new ground on the banks of Mersey was being reviewed by the Secretary of State following a unanimous vote by Liverpool City Council to approve the extensive planning application for the project. If all went well, the Blues hoped to kick off the 2024/25 season in their new home.

Ancelotti had spoken before of his desire to stay longer than his original contract and he reiterated that, saying: "I would like to stay as long as possible.

"I would like to be there when the new stadium will be opened. It will be a good achievement for me, of course.

"I think to finish the contract in 2024 you did a good job and when you did a good job, the contract will not be stopped in 2024, it will continue."

Meanwhile, speaking of more immediate concerns at his press conference regarding Everton's ambitions this season, Ancelotti said:

"For us, it will be really important to play in Europe next season and it means a step forward for the players, a step forward for the club. In my opinion, we don't have to look at the table. We have to play game by game and see where we are at the end of the season. We have to work hard, because it will not be easy, because a lot of teams are involved there, but I think we can compete until the end.

"The result [against Liverpool] was really good, and the performance was also. We [have] showed we can compete in some games and now I think we have to look forward because we have a home game and our run in the last period was not good. If we want to fight for European positions, we have to improve our form at Goodison."

2021: BMD PLANNING PERMISSION RECEIVED

On 23 February 2021, just three days after the success at Anfield, there was more good news for the Blues. Everton's planning application for its new 52,888-seat stadium at Bramley-Moore Dock was approved unanimously by Liverpool City Council, taking the club a major step closer to realising its plans to move from Goodison Park. Following a recommendation from the Council's Planning Officer last week, the local authority convened a special Planning Committee Meeting composed of 11 councillors to approve the proposals,

which were originally submitted in December 2019 before being updated in September 2020.

The Blues' CEO, Denise Barrett-Baxendale, and Stadium Development Director, Colin Chong, were both in attendance to outline the club's case for the project, which they expected could bring £1.3 billion worth of revenue to the area and create 15,000 jobs. Colin Chong had been steering the project since the departure of Keith Harris from the Board of Directors in July 2019.

The club's vision for the redevelopment of Goodison Park in Walton also got the green light.

Barrett-Baxendale said in an email to supporters: "The planning consent from the City Council means that our application will now be referred to the government — a standard procedure for an application of such scale. The government will have an initial 21 days to review the plans and make its decision.

"Once that process has concluded - and provided it is a positive outcome - we can press ahead with the plans we have developed over the last few years.

"I am sure you are aware of how important a new stadium will be for us - providing the state-of-the-art facilities befitting of an ambitious Premier League club — as well as the important role it can play in boosting our local economy at a time when it's never been more needed.

"The project, which will be one the most significant infrastructure projects our city has seen in many years and one of the largest single-site developments in the country at this time, will provide a £1.3 billion boost to the local economy and deliver more than 15,000 jobs."

"If we achieve the final planning approval, we have all worked so hard for, then we will be in a position to complete our funding arrangements and confirm our schedule for the build process at Bramley-Moore Dock."

Chairman Bill Kenwright said: "Whilst today is just one more step in our long journey, it is a very important one. Farhad [Moshiri] and I would like to thank Denise and Colin and their dedicated team for the extraordinary hard work and commitment that has got us to today.

"We are also enormously grateful to the many organisations and tens of thousands of individuals across the city region who have given us their feedback, ideas and support along the way. It's been a good week for Everton and Evertonians."

The project still faced objections from UNESCO, however, who insisted that the stadium "would have a completely unacceptable major adverse impact on the authenticity, integrity and outstanding universal value" of what is part of a designated World Heritage site. They were urging Secretary of State for Housing, Communities and Local Government, Robert Jenrick, to call the project in for full scrutiny, which would delay any final decision from Westminster, but it never came to that.

***

The good news regarding the stadium was followed by the announcement that Farhad Moshiri had taken up a massive new share issue.

New shares worth £200 million were issued to him in exchange for new cash injections and the conversion of old loans into equity.

Everton received £50 million of new money from the majority shareholder, which came on the back of an injection of £50 million in November.

Moshiri's input of £100 million in cash came in combination with the conversion of existing loans into share equity, thought to be around £100 million.

In total, 100,000 new shares in Everton FC were created, 66,667 of which were issued to Moshiri at that time, which increased Moshiri's ownership stake in the club to 93,698 shares, representing 92.16% of the 101,667 shares issued to that point. Bill Kenwright's shareholding remained at 1,750 but it reduced his stake to 1.72%.

***

A month later, on 26 March, Everton's plans to develop a new stadium at Bramley-Moore Dock were finally given the green light after the club's planning application received government approval.

The Secretary of State for Housing, Communities and Local Government, Robert Jenrick, had asked for more time than the statutory 21-day review period to assess the plans but he and his department agreed with the LCC that the Bramley-Moore Dock project would provide a boon to the city of Liverpool and the Merseyside area.

The club's first step, ahead of starting construction that summer, would be to purchase the site from Peel Holdings for £22 million and confirm Laing O'Rourke as the preferred contractor to move ahead with a final construction schedule.

The exact details of how the estimated £500 million development would be funded were yet to be finalised, but Everton owner, Farhad

Moshiri, had already committed to sourcing private investment and sponsorship in preference to a public funding model involving the Council that was initially floated.

***

By the middle of June 2021, Everton had begun preliminary inspection work at Bramley-Moore Dock in anticipation of construction work on the new stadium beginning later in the year, with the first project being the filling in of the dock itself.

The *Liverpool Echo* reported that specialist firm Boskalis Maritime would send a boat out onto the Mersey to carry out various checks on the dock and its hidden contents.

Their team would conduct a survey of the bottom of the dock and check for any potential hazards like unexploded devices from the Second World War – they would find around a dozen – while also assessing the condition of the dock wall ahead of the infilling operation.

The *Echo* report also suggested that other work would include a survey of microbiological organisms present in the water and the recovery of panels and materials installed to better understand the local climate, with construction work set to start in late summer or the autumn.

2021: EVERTON JOIN FIGHT AGAINST EUROPEAN SUPER LEAGUE

Whereas the final two decades of the old English Football League Division One had produced nine different champions, the 20 years after the formation of the Premier League in 1992 saw just five teams win the title. It was an illustration of the increasing dominance of the domestic game's major honours by a small group of elite and monied clubs, and it extended to that same group's grip on England's four Champions League qualification places.

That situation ensured that the millions of pounds of broadcast and participation revenue, which naturally grew the longer teams remained in Europe's elite club tournament, was consistently going into the coffers of these same clubs, widening the gap between England's 'haves' and 'have nots' and reducing competition within the Premier League.

It also had the effect of heightening the jeopardy for clubs that failed to qualify for the Champions League in a given season – their spending, wage bills and commercial arrangements were all predicted on dining at Continental football's top table. With the quartet of clubs once dubbed the "Sky Four" (due to the satellite broadcaster's focus on England's most powerful clubs, Arsenal, Chelsea, Liverpool and Manchester United) having extended to the so-called 'Big Six' with the addition of Manchester City and Tottenham in the 2010s, it meant two of these teams would miss out on qualifying each season.

When Leicester City upset the apple cart in 2016 and romped to their first title as 5000-1 outsiders, three of the six finished outside of the Champions League places, a precedent that many observers believe was part of the impetus behind the spectacular hubris of the notion of a breakaway European Super League of 12 clubs from Europe's 'Big Five' Leagues.

England's Big Six, along with AC Milan, Atletico Madrid, Barcelona, Inter Milan, Juventus and Real Madrid suddenly announced on 18 April 2021 that they would be the founding members of a new competition that would directly challenge UEFA's Champions League.

Three more clubs were expected to join the competition for its inaugural season, which ESL signatories said was "intended to commence as soon as practicable", possibly as early as 2022/23. They proposed offering five further places each year to qualifying teams, in an effort to blunt FIFA's objections to 'closed shop' leagues.

The concept, a cynical attempt to further consolidate more earning power in the hands of a dozen or so of the Continent's most powerful clubs was met with swift condemnation and a revolt by supporters horrified at the implications for England's domestic leagues, the oldest in world football.

Within hours, the Premier League had issued a statement saying the six member clubs would face expulsion if they elected to take part in the Super League, in what a spokesperson described as "a proposal that attacks the principles of open competition and sporting merit which are at the heart of the domestic and European football pyramid."

A joint statement by the Football Association, UEFA and the Premier League said that they were "united in our efforts to stop this cynical project" which was "founded on the self-interest of a few clubs, at a time when society needs solidarity more than ever. This persistent self-interest of a few has been going on for too long — enough is enough."

UEFA and FIFA, football's global governing body, warned that they would ban any player who took part in such an unsanctioned league from appearing in the World Cup and European Championships.

The European Club Association, the body which represented 246 leading clubs in Europe, joined in the near-universal denunciation of the plan and reiterated its commitment to revamping the Champions League instead.

Reportedly led by the American owners of Liverpool and Manchester United and chaired by Real Madrid president Florentino

Pérez, the ESL was to be backed by JP Morgan bank. They would supposedly put up £3.5 billion to launch the league and pay each of its member clubs €350 million just for participating.

Former Manchester United defender Gary Neville voiced his disgust at the breakaway and called on the respective leagues to come down hard on the rebel 12.

"It's pure greed; they're imposters," Neville said. "The owners of Manchester United, Liverpool, Chelsea and Manchester City, they are nothing to do with football in this country.

"Manchester United, Arsenal, Tottenham aren't even in the Champions League. And they want a God-given right to be in there? They're an absolute joke.

"The time has come now to have independent regulators to stop these clubs from having the power base. Enough is enough."

***

Everton's owner, Farhad Moshiri, branded the ESL proposal as "preposterous arrogance" and on 20 April joined the call from the Premier League's other 14 clubs for disciplinary measures to be taken against the rebel six.

Meanwhile, in a statement from the Everton Board of Directors and an email to supporters from CEO Denise Barrett-Baxendale, the club outlined its commitment to the football pyramid and principles of open competition and sporting merit.

The messages from Everton came as reports suggested that at least two of the English six were wavering in their commitment to the controversial new venture.

The Guardian claimed that "a well-placed executive at another club approached to join the breakaway league" said that Chelsea and Manchester City, the last two clubs to commit to the Super League on Saturday, already had second thoughts following the fierce backlash to the plan, particularly in England.

The Telegraph, however, said that according to their sources, legally the ESL clubs now could not reverse course without being sued for billions of pounds because of the "binding agreements" they signed.

The following day, opposition to the Super League continued, with FIFA president, Gianni Infantino finally breaking his silence by saying that, "there is no doubt whatsoever of FIFA's disapproval of this," but while he warned that, "concretely, ... you cannot be half in or half out of [European football]," he stopped short of threatening action against the rebel clubs.

U.K. Prime Minister, Boris Johnson, meanwhile, offered "unwavering support" to the football authorities in their fight against the Super League and, in a statement from 10 Downing Street, said it, "was clear that no action is off the table, and the government is exploring every possibility, including legislative options, to ensure these proposals are stopped."

Moshiri, who sold his stake in Arsenal before his business partner Alisher Usmanov did the same after failing to gain entry to the North London club's board under their owner, Stan Kroenke, spoke to *TalkSport* where he voiced his disgust at the betrayal of the Premier League:

> "Every facet of this is against the very idea of British football. Football clubs are community assets, they

> belong to fans and their communities. This just takes much of their romance away. It just makes it a money game — it's not football any more. This is six clubs attacking the very heart of the Premier League, and I think they should be disciplined."

The statement from Goodison Park, meanwhile, urged their rival clubs to withdraw the proposals for the breakaway league that "[disenfranchised] supporters across the game — including their own — by putting the very structure that underpins the game we love under threat. Moshiri continued:

> "The backlash is understandable and deserved — and has to be listened to. This preposterous arrogance is not wanted anywhere in football outside of the clubs that have drafted this plan. On behalf of everyone associated with Everton, we respectfully ask that the proposals are immediately withdrawn and that the private meetings and subversive practises that have brought our beautiful game to possibly its lowest ever position in terms of trust end now. Finally we would ask the owners, chairmen, and Board members of the six clubs to remember the privileged position they hold — not only as custodians of their clubs but also custodians of the game. The responsibility they carry should be taken seriously. We urge them all to consider what they wish their legacy to be."

Later that day the 'rump' of 14 Premier League clubs convened in a meeting led by the League's chairman Richard Masters and issued their statement afterwards that said: "The 14 clubs at the meeting unanimously and vigorously rejected the plans for the competition. The Premier League is considering all actions available to prevent it from progressing, as well as holding those shareholders involved to account under its rules."

In a separate memo sent to the 14 clubs, Masters reportedly wrote: "This venture cannot be launched without English clubs and we call upon any club contemplating associating themselves or joining this venture to walk away immediately before irreparable damage is done."

By that same evening, the controversial breakaway Super League all but collapsed, as Manchester City formally withdrew from the ESL, followed by Chelsea, Arsenal, Liverpool, Manchester United and Tottenham.

As fans clogged the road at the players' entrance at Stamford Bridge ahead of Chelsea's Premier League match against Brighton, the London club had seemingly become the first to lose its nerve.

The *BBC* were first to report that Chelsea were preparing the paperwork to withdraw, but City were the first to provide official confirmation later in the evening. Sources at Chelsea suggested that extricating themselves from the binding contract they signed was complicated, but it was little surprise that the two clubs believed to have been the last two of the 'Dirty Dozen' to sign up were the first to bail.

Shortly before 11pm U.K. time, the two north London clubs, and both United and Liverpool, confirmed their intention to walk away from the Super League, with only Arsenal offering an apology in their statement to supporters.

The Super League company itself refused to give in, announcing that the launch would be delayed and reshaped.

A statement read: "Despite the announced departure of the English clubs, forced to take such decisions due to the pressure put on them, we are convinced our proposal is fully aligned with European law and regulations, as was demonstrated today by a court decision to protect the Super League from third party actions. Given the current circumstances, we shall reconsider the most appropriate steps to reshape the project, always having in mind our goals of offering fans the best experience possible while enhancing solidarity payments for the entire football community."

The dominoes would fall in Europe as well, however, and when the dust settled, just three clubs – Real Madrid, whose president Florentino Perez had been the primary driver behind the original proposal, Juventus and Barcelona – were still clinging to the ESL idea.

Few in the game were under any illusions that the "hydra" of a European Super League had been killed off forever, but the furore did help usher in a new format for the Champions League that would take effect in 2024/25 and which was designed to not only increase the money earned from participating by increasing the number of games, but also gave richer clubs a greater chance of qualifying each year.

To its critics, it would simply be a watered-down Super League, while the cynics surmised that the Continent's most powerful interests would always get their way somehow.

2021: Everton: European hopefuls to mid-table obscurity

> "It was sobering, pretty humiliating and, perhaps most alarmingly, not all that surprising; the final ignominious chapter in a season that promised so much but ended on perhaps as flat a note as it could for a team that sat in second place in the Premier League on Boxing Day.
>
> **2021 Everton: European hopefuls to mid-table obscurity**

Back on the field, Everton had slipped steadily down the league table and further away from European qualification; and at the heart of it was their dreadful home form. While the absence of crowds had no doubt helped the Toffees rack up a record-equalling 11 victories away from home, their results at Goodison Park consistently undermined their bid to finish in the top four.

While not helped by injuries at times to key personnel like Allan and Abdoulaye Doucouré, or the fact that James Rodriguez had become an increasingly unreliable presence in the side as he battled a niggling calf problem, it was still a conundrum that Carlo Ancelotti couldn't solve despite all his experience and coaching ability.

Relegation bound Fulham came to L4 and won, followed by Burnley who stunned Everton 2-1, before Aston Villa and then doomed Sheffield United also left Goodison with all three points before the end of the season.

***

19 May 2021: Everton v Wolves (6,068 spectators)

With hopes of Champions League football long gone, the best the Blues could hope for was a spot in the new Europa Conference League. Their opponents for the final home game of the season were Wolves.

This was not a good performance, but it was enough to earn the Toffees their first home win since the start of March, and it was fitting that Richarlison bagged the winner.

Evertonians had mused that few players feed off the energy of a crowd more than the mercurial Brazilian, and the way he rose to the occasion of supporters being let into Goodison for the first time since December seemed to bear that out. Quiet in the first half, Richarlison scored a terrific headed goal just two minutes into the second and, by the end, he was looking very much like the player Blues fans had come to love since he joined from Watford three years earlier.

Given how tentative and typically ponderous Everton had been in their build-up play, it was perhaps not surprising that the winner came from a set-piece. The fans in attendance had been desperate to see James Rodriguez in the flesh but were left wanting when the

Colombian withdrew from the squad due to "fatigue". The team lacked creativity without him.

But in his absence, Gylfi Sigurdsson provided the energy in the press even if he wasn't as productive when Everton had the ball, and it was his corner that served up the winner. The Icelander's out-swinger was placed perfectly for Richarlison to leap highest and guide his header into the far corner.

Sigurdsson went close to sealing it either side of a penalty claim for handball by Wolves against Doucouré, first with an attempted curler that hit the stanchion on the right side of goal, and then with another effort searching out the same corner that took a nick off a defender on its way behind.

But after months of misery on their home soil, Everton had ended their campaign of fixtures at Goodison Park on a high and with a victory that meant they could still qualify for the Europa Conference League if they bettered Tottenham's result on the final Sunday of the season.

The failings at home against the likes of Leeds, West Ham, Burnley, Fulham, Newcastle and Sheffield United – where just a point in each would have meant Champions League qualification would still be possible heading into the final day – would forever hang over this strange pandemic-affected season, but Ancelotti would have learned plenty about these players and what he needed to push for in 2021/22.

Final score: Everton 1-0 Wolves

***

Ancelotti had shown that he and Marcel Brands were aligned over what Everton would have to do in the transfer market over the summer in order to improve the squad, and he laughed off the notion that the club might be sanctioned over financial fair play rules, in view of the failed Super League.

Just like the previous year, the Italian appeared committed to making impactful signings in the close season but there has always been assumption that Everton would need to offload fringe players first in order to remain within UEFA's Financial Fair Play regulations and the Premier League's own profit and sustainability rules.

Fans expected outgoings when the current season ended, with Moise Kean topping the list of players who could be sold but Ancelotti, somewhat naively as things turned out, said the club would not need to wait for sales to come to fruition.

"The Premier League has to solve different problems than the financial fair play of Everton [because of] the fact that six teams wanted to go in [to] the Super League," he told print journalists following his pre-match press conference in front of the broadcast media yesterday afternoon.

"First of all, they have to take care of this and then, maybe, they can have a look at Everton. But we are going to look at ourselves.

"If they looked at us, with the problem they had with the top six that wanted to join the Super League, that would be funny. Of course, we will take care of our financial aspect, but we can buy without selling players this summer for sure."

"We're all agreed on the plan. We have to improve the squad and there is no doubt we are totally focused on this," Ancelotti continued.

"We are totally agreed, from the manager, the club and the technical director, Marcel Brands."

***

23 May 2021: Manchester City v Everton (10,000 spectators)

In what Blues fans hoped wasn't a portent of what was coming the following season, Everton wore their 2021/22 black away kit at the Etihad Stadium for their final attempt to secure European football for the 2021/22 season. But it was less The Black Watch and more the death watch as they extinguished the last breaths from European-qualification hopes that had been on life support for a few weeks and had effectively died a week previously with a horrible home defeat to Sheffield United.

Manchester City, true to their exacting manager's footballing philosophy, were merciless. Pep Guardiola eschewed any notion that his mind and those of his players was on the looming Champions League Final against Chelsea. He named an almost full-strength line-up, watched them tear the Blues apart, and still had plenty of time to bring on the departing Sergio Agüero for his triumphant swan song. Just as they were for Arsenal's title party in 1998 and Leicester's in 2016, Everton were obliging guests who laid down the welcome mat and got trampled amid the revelry.

It was sobering, pretty humiliating and, perhaps most alarmingly, not all that surprising; the final ignominious chapter in a season that promised so much but ended on perhaps as flat a note as it could for a team that sat in second place in the Premier League on Boxing Day.

So much seemed possible heading into the New Year, not least because Carlo Ancelotti was fashioning his side into one of the most effective away from home. Increasingly, the formula was a simple one centred around discipline, hard work and the deployment of the low block, in the expectation that the Toffees could pinch a goal on the break or from a set-piece and then dig in for the points.

Aided by the lack of home supporters, it worked an impressive number of times; which is why it was curious that the Italian chose a game away at the newly crowned Champions, who had fans in the stands for the first time since February last year, to abandon the tactics that had served him so well to this point.

By his own admission Everton tried to play further up the pitch and take the game to City and while it was laudable in their pressing need to win to have any chance of making the Europa Conference League, in retrospect it was puzzlingly naïve.

The visitors had some bright moments in the early exchanges but the floodgates opened in the 11th minute when Kevin De Bruyne's run into an ocean of space in front of Everton's defence went untracked and he had the time to pick his spot with a typically excellent finish inside the far post.

Three minutes later, Michael Keane tried to dribble through a clutch of City players near the halfway line and the hosts pounced, with De Bruyne picking out Jesus who easily turned Mason Holgate and fired home to make it 2-0.

A potential route back into the game for the Toffees arrived ten minutes before the break, though, in a moment of controversy where Everton felt that Ruben Dias should have seen red for denying Richarlison a goal-scoring opportunity.

The Brazilian raced onto a through-ball and was caught by the Portuguese defender's slide-tackle and then clattered by Ederson, with referee Michael Oliver electing to only yellow-card Dias.

Gylfi Sigurdsson stepped up to take the penalty but placed his shot at the ideal height for the goalkeeper and Ederson pushed it away, while Richarlison's shot from the rebound was charged down by a recovering defender.

Phil Foden made it 3-0 eight minutes after half-time with another impressive finish after Abdoulaye Doucouré's loose pass was cut out on in the centre-circle and City attacked quickly.

Ancelotti sent on Alex Iwobi for Doucouré and then Bernard for Sigurdsson, but neither player made much impact. Instead, it became the Agüero send-off party as Tom Davies became the latest player to be dispossessed cheaply in his own half and Agüero navigated his way around Holgate before guiding the ball into the far corner with the outside of his boot with 20 minutes left.

Six minutes after that, Everton's misery was complete. Fernandinho crossed from the right for Agüero, who had positioned himself inside the 10 yards of space between Godfrey and Keane and the Argentine steered a header beyond Pickford's reach to make it five.

In the final reckoning, even had Everton pulled off the improbable against a City side that existed in another universe to its own, it wouldn't have mattered, anyway. Displaying a good deal more spirit and enterprise than has been in evidence from the Toffees in recent weeks, Tottenham Hotspur came back from 2-1 down to beat Champions League hopefuls Leicester 4-2 at the King Power stadium, securing a spot in the inaugural Europa Conference League.

For Everton, the wait to play Continental football again would have to wait at least another year, but of more immediate concern was the way what seemed, as recently as March a hugely promising season had unravelled so dramatically, with Ancelotti seemingly powerless to do anything about it.

Final score: Manchester City 5-0 Everton

***

Richard Jolly, writing in *FourFourTwo*, on May 26, asked the question on the lips of so many of the club's fans:

Everton: How did things go so wrong this season for the Toffees?

His answer made sombre reading: "Carlo Ancelotti's Everton went from European hopefuls to mid table obscurity in a pitiful 2021. [The Man City result] was the heaviest defeat of Carlo Ancelotti's coaching career and, indeed, the heaviest suffered by any manager with three European Cups in his trophy cabinet.

"The juxtaposition between Ancelotti's past and his present has rarely felt as clear as during Manchester City 5 Everton 0. This time, the silverware being celebrated on the pitch was not anything Ancelotti won. His side had the carrot of European football - but were thrashed by a team with nothing to play for and recorded his lowest league finish of any full season in charge anywhere.

"The sight of Everton in 10th underlines the way this season was a missed opportunity and not merely because it is logical to assume that Liverpool and Chelsea will be stronger next season and thus the bar for a top-four finish will be set higher.

"Everton got historic wins away at Arsenal, Tottenham and Liverpool, triumphed at Leicester and West Ham for good measure and finished two places lower than they did under Sam Allardyce in 2018 and Marco Silva in 2019. Their four major signings – James Rodriguez, Allan, Abdoulaye Doucouré and Ben Godfrey – all succeeded to some extent, but the season concluded with the tone-deaf Colombian tweeting pictures of himself on a plane bound for the Copa America when Everton's destiny was still to be determined. 'Tiredness' was an inadequate reason for missing important games.

"It was a campaign when, even when Everton got some things right, others went horribly wrong.

"Everton ended the campaign without a regular system or a style of play. Ancelotti switched shape intelligently at times, adapting to the rotating cast on the treatment table, but it also betrayed Everton's inability to find a settled 11. It felt damning that, in the end, they were better when they had less of the ball and when less was expected of them.

"Everton were prisoners of their past, Ancelotti encumbered by previous poor signings like Alex Iwobi and Bernard, lumbered with an imbalanced squad that contained too many midfielders and yet, because of their injuries, too few at times; but they were also architects of their own failure. Too many games felt a failure of mentality, leading Ancelotti to use the word "unacceptable" after the Sheffield United game. Seamus Coleman was often more scathing; the captain may be in decline but his own attitude was invariably beyond reproach.

"His frustration stemmed in part from the awareness he will not have many more chances to accomplish something seismic. Everton will not have many better ones. Ancelotti was brought in to elevate them to the next level, not to see them finish below a promoted club, plus their former manager, David Moyes. He showed a sure touch in 2020. Yet Everton's demoralising 2021 meant even an eminently amenable man seemed irritated. One of the season's achievers ended up among its underachievers".

***

For Evertonians, who would spend the coming days wondering whether the summer would bring some positive signs, what happened next was a real shocker.

2021: ANCELOTTI LEAVES EVERTON IN THE LURCH

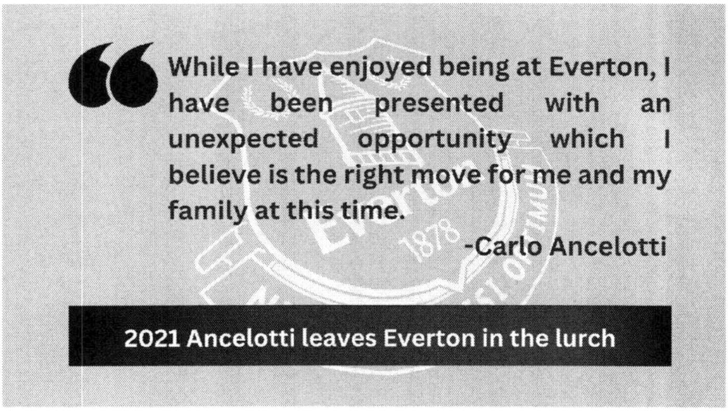

Gone! Less than 18 months after he joined Everton as a surprise managerial appointment to succeed Marco Silva, Carlo Ancelotti abruptly left Goodison Park to return to Real Madrid, the club that sacked him six years previously.

Only weeks earlier, the Italian had been talking in terms of extending his contract to enable him to see the club into their new stadium, so the Blue half of Merseyside was stunned by reports that broke in the late afternoon on 31 May, that the Italian was being lined up to replace Zinedine Zidane at the Bernabeu. Events moved quickly, to where Ancelotti was confirmed as Real manager that evening.

It left Everton having to put their summer transfer plans on hold and scramble to draw up a shortlist of candidates to replace Ancelotti, with the likes of Eddie Howe, David Moyes and Nuno Espirito Santo among the early names being linked.

Zidane's decision to step down at Madrid had been on the cards as the 2020/21 season drew to a close and it sparked rumours that Ancelotti might be among the candidates to replace him; suggestions the Italian had laughed off during his final pre-match press conference of the season ahead of the Manchester City match.

The lure of Madrid proved too much for the 61-year-old, however, and after firm contact was made with his representatives, Ancelotti came to a final agreement that saw him sign a three-year contract at Real, which was reportedly worth less than half per year than he was earning at Everton.

One wondered what impact the burglary of Ancelotti's home in Crosby had had on the willingness of his family to stay longer on Merseyside. Certainly, they were unlikely to come across the same problems when living within a luxurious, gated-community, in the salubrious part of Madrid that would become their new home.

"While I have enjoyed being at Everton, I have been presented with an unexpected opportunity which I believe is the right move for me and my family at this time," Ancelotti said once the club confirmed he had left for Madrid.

"I would like to thank the Board of Directors, the players, and the Evertonians for the tremendous support they have all given me during my time at the club.

"I have complete respect for everyone associated with Everton and hope they can achieve the exciting opportunities they have in front of them."

***

Meanwhile, Everton's board of directors held an emergency meeting to discuss the club's next steps.

Just 24 hours after the news of Carlo Ancelotti's departure had rocked the club, the Blues were reportedly set to open talks with former Wolves boss Nuno Espirito Santo after installing him alongside David Moyes as a preferred candidate to replace the departed Italian.

The Portuguese had left Wolves last month after four years in charge and had been in discussions with Crystal Palace about succeeding Roy Hodgson at Selhurst Park.

Sky Sports claimed Nuno would be the first candidate to be interviewed by the Everton hierarchy.

David Moyes, who was still expected to accept a contract offer from West Ham, had come close to being re-appointed as the Toffees' boss 18 months ago but had been pipped to the post by Ancelotti. Former Leipzig boss and onetime candidate to replace Moyes in 2013, Ralf Rangnick, was also thought to be in the frame.

In the interim, Josh King, who had been curiously under-used by Ancelotti, was one of five confirmed departures on 4 June, together with Muhammed Besic, Yannick Bolasie and Theo Walcott, all of whom were released from the first-team squad.

But incoming transfers had to be put on the back burner while the search for Everton's new head coach dragged on to the end of the month. The appointment when it finally came, was as controversial, divisive and destructive as any in the club's history.

2021: MOSHIRI: BENITEZ IS A PROVEN WINNER

> Rafa has managed clubs with big expectations and won some of the biggest trophies in the game. He's a proven winner. We are confident that his winning mentality will bring success to us at Everton.
>
> - Farhad Moshiri

2021 Moshiri: Benitez is a proven winner

On 30 June 2021, after days of speculation, Everton finally announced former Liverpool manager Rafael Benitez as Carlo Ancelotti's successor, a little over four weeks after the Italian had abruptly left the club in the lurch to return to Real Madrid.

Benitez arrived at Everton's Finch Farm training ground ahead of the official confirmation that a deal with the club had been finalised, despite a vociferous outcry from a significant section of the fanbase who continued to react with shock and horror at how he could be the new Everton boss.

Because of his long association with the reds and comments he once made about the Blues after a Merseyside derby in 2007, Benitez's arrival was highly contentious for a section of the Everton fanbase. Banners protesting the Board of Directors' decision appeared outside Goodison, and someone left a reprehensible one near his Caldy home, with a threatening message warning him not to sign on with the Toffees.

Everton's majority shareholder, Farhad Moshiri, pushed through the appointment despite the protests, stating that Benitez was the best candidate to bring success to the Blue half of Merseyside – or, at the very least, to keep the club on an even keel.

In a curious twist of fate, Benitez had become Ancelotti's immediate successor for the second time in his career — the Spaniard replaced the Italian at the Bernabeu in 2015. He also became Moshiri's fifth managerial appointment in as many years, starting with Ronald Koeman's much-vaunted appointment in June 2016.

He signed a three-year contract with Everton and became the first man in the modern era to have managed both Merseyside clubs, having coached Liverpool between 2004 and 2010. He brought fitness coach and long-time associate Paco De Miguel with him to the club, while Duncan Ferguson, Leighton Baines and goalkeeping coach Alan Kelly remained in their existing roles.

"I am delighted to be joining Everton," Benitez said. "Throughout this process, I have been greatly impressed by the ambition shown by the senior representatives at the Club and their desire to bring success to this historic club.

"I believe this is a club that is going places. I'm determined to play a big part in helping this great club achieve its ambitions."

In a statement lacking his usual effusiveness, Bill Kenwright, said: "Rafa Benitez is joining Everton Football Club at an exciting time. On behalf of the Board of Directors, I wish him well in achieving success for our football club - success our supporters long for and deserve."

Moshiri's rationale for hiring Benitez was likely based on his previous success as a manager – as well as his affinity to Merseyside, where he still lived with his family – although by the time he arrived at Goodison Park it had been eight years since his last trophy.

Following an unremarkable, injury-affected playing career between 1978 and 1986 Benitez moved into management in 1993 with Real Madrid's B team. Spells at Valladolid, Osasuna, Extremadura and Tenerife followed before he joined Valencia, where he emerged as a noteworthy coach by twice winning La Liga while also guiding Los Murciélagos to a UEFA Cup triumph in 2004.

Those achievements caught the attention of Liverpool who hired him to replace Gérard Houllier, and in his time across Stanley Park he won the FA Cup and reached two Champions League finals, beating Ancelotti's AC Milan in Istanbul in the first in 2005.

The reds regarded the 2009/10 season as a campaign of decline and Benitez left Liverpool in the summer, when he joined Inter Milan to replace Jose Mourinho. While he won the Supercoppa Italiana and the FIFA World Club Cup, they dismissed him just six months into the job as the reigning Serie A Champions slumped to 6th place under his stewardship.

Two years later, he became interim manager at Chelsea, where he ignored supporter discontent at his appointment to guide the Londoners to a Europa League triumph 6 months later.

Benitez returned to Italy to take the reins at Napoli where he won the Coppa Italia. Then came a brief tenure at Real Madrid, where he managed James Rodriguez. That was followed by three years at Newcastle United. Brought in late in the 2015/16 season, he could not keep the Magpies in the Premier League, but he remained with the club and secured an immediate return to the top flight.

His final season on Tyneside was a middling one, dominated by reports of a testy relationship with owner Mike Ashley and disagreements over transfer policy. Though he was loved by Newcastle's fans, his contract was allowed to expire in 2019, and he took up the invitation to try his hand in China with Dalian Professional, an assignment that was curtailed by the COVID-19 pandemic and Benitez's desire to return to his family on Merseyside.

***

On the Everton FC website, the club published an interview with the owner under the headline: FARHAD MOSHIRI: WHY WE WANTED RAFA.

In it, the club's owner explained that Benitez had "stood out as the best candidate," fulfilling the remit of, "a manager with experience of managing at the highest level, who has a strong track record of delivering success, who can work within our structure and who fully buys into our vision for the future.

"We want to be playing in European competitions and challenging for silverware at home and abroad - so it was vitally important we have a manager who has been there and understands what it takes to achieve that level of success.

"Rafa has managed clubs with big expectations and won some of the biggest trophies in the game. He's a proven winner. We are confident that his winning mentality will bring success to us at Everton.

"I know that the last few weeks have not been an easy time for our supporters, so I'd like to thank them for their patience throughout this process. Hopefully now we can come together and be confident about our plans on and off the field. There are some exciting times ahead and I hope the supporters know that they have my full commitment in terms of delivering our ambitions."

***

Another shock announcement came on 20 July, when Everton confirmed they had suspended a first-team player pending an investigation by police.

A brief statement by the club said that they would continue to support the authorities with their inquiries and would not be making any further statement.

The bulletin from the club came in the wake of a report by the *Daily Mail* that a Premier League club had suspended a 31-year-old player because of inquiries by police.

The player in question, who wasn't ever named in the British press for legal reasons, would eventually have his contract terminated and never again played for the Toffees.

***

Later that day, desperate for some good news, Everton announced the acquisition of Andros Townsend on a free transfer from Crystal Palace, the first signing of Rafael Benitez's tenure as the Blues' manager. The 30-year-old winger agreed a two-year contract that would run through the end of June 2023, bringing to an end a five-year spell at Selhurst Park while renewing his association with Benitez who managed him briefly at Newcastle United in 2016.

Townsend explained that reuniting with his old boss and the prospect of playing for a "massive and ambitious" club like Everton meant he could not turn down the chance to sign when it came up.

"I think everyone knows what Everton is. It's a massive football club, it's very ambitious, a club which has been trying to get back to where it belongs into Europe and beyond," Townsend told evertontv. "I'll be doing all I can to help the Club do that.

"Everton is a massive football club and has big ambitions next season. As the old cliché goes, it was a no-brainer.

"Rafa is very experienced. He does a lot of work on the tactical side on the training pitch. He leaves no stone unturned. But more importantly, he's a great man, a great man-manager, and he's always talking to you. I'm sure he will be very successful here."

***

Then, hot on the heels of signing Andros Townsend, Everton confirmed the signing of Asmir Begovic as goalkeeping cover for Jordan Pickford over the coming season for an undisclosed fee and on a 12-month contract from Championship side Bournemouth.

***

Just two days later, Everton completed another signing with the confirmation of the capture of winger Demarai Gray from Bayer Leverkusen.

The Blues activated a clause in the former Leicester City player's contract and landed him in a deal with around £1.7 million. Gray signed a three-year contract that would keep him at Everton until 2024, but there was an option for the club to extend it by a further year.

"I'm delighted to be back in the Premier League at such a big club and I'm excited to play with the team and get to work," Gray told evertontv. "Speaking to the manager and Marcel Brands, I had a really good feel for the Club and I feel this is a place where I can continue to develop.

"The manager, with his ambition and what he has won in the past, is important and we'll look to push forward and compete with the top clubs. I think a club of this magnitude has all the potential to be right up there.

"I want to push on, be a pivotal player in the squad, and help the team score goals and assist goals," Gray continued.

"I'm a speedy, tricky winger. I enjoy running with the ball. I like to play anywhere along the front three and I feel like I can be dangerous in all areas."

***

Having been linked with many strikers, and in need to sign more firepower, Everton completed their fifth signing of the window on transfer deadline day with the acquisition from Dalian Professional of Salomon Rondon, who linked back up with former boss, Rafael Benitez. The oft-mooted transfer happened ahead of the 11pm transfer deadline, after the Venezuelan striker ended his contract in China.

Remarkably, the 31-year-old, who signed a two-year contract with the option of a third, was the only addition to the Blues' squad on a day that looked as though it was going to be hectic, but ended up being a damp squib.

***

Though there was disquiet among large sections of the Everton fanbase, concerning the appointment of Benitez, the club continued to make progress on the stadium project and it was soon confirmed that the start date for construction work at Bramley-Moore Dock would be Monday, 26 July, 2021. Main contractors Laing O'Rourke would immediately begin the first phase of the project to build the club's new 52,888-seater stadium.

That was the day the club took possession of the site from Peel Holdings and the enabling works to prepare the dock site in readiness for the build could begin.

Work would include the repair and preservation of the Grade II listed dock wall, stabilisation of the old hydraulic tower, the development of welfare facilities for Laing O'Rourke construction staff, the preparation for demolition of existing non-listed structures, and raking of the dock floor. Pipework would also be installed, needed for infilling of the dock.

Bill Kenwright, said: "We are thrilled to be able to confirm that construction work will commence on our new stadium later this month. This will be a momentous day in the history of the Club and is testament to the ambition and financial commitment of Farhad and the determination and talent of Denise and her executive team at the Club.

"Like every Evertonian, Goodison Park has been a massive part of my life but in moving forward we could not have found a more fitting nor more glorious site for our new stadium — one which will both honour our history and celebrate our magnificent future."

Meanwhile, Everton's Chief Executive, Denise Barrett-Baxendale, commented: "This moment will rank as one of the most important in the Club's history as it symbolises a new era for Evertonians, an era which will see our supporters, their children and their children's children supporting their team in one of the finest stadiums in world football.

"This project presents such an exciting future for our club and is a clear demonstration of our owner's commitment and ambition."

***

On the eve of another new season, and with the team under the control of yet another new manager, Evertonians finally hoping to see James Rodriguez in the flesh at Goodison Park were disappointed to hear the Colombian was not in the squad.

Like Moise Kean, James had been training away from the rest of the first-team squad in what they presumed to be a precaution. However, Rafael Benitez said some of his players were quarantining in line with COVID-19 protocols, with Rodriguez among them.

Rodriguez had been using the video community Twitch to interact with his fans over the previous couple of weeks and had given little sign his future belonged at Everton.

Against a backdrop of media talk that Rafael Benitez had apparently told him he didn't suit the Spaniard's plans for the team, James claimed that he simply wanted to play where he was wanted.

He cast doubt on his participation in the season-opener against Southampton when he said on his channel: "There is a game on Saturday... but I don't know. I don't think I'll play. Everything can happen until the end of the month. Soccer always changes fast," he concluded.

If he was successful, it seemed like Evertonians would never get the chance to see Rodriguez play for their team in person. Certainly, supporters wouldn't see him play against Southampton.

Benitez said in his pre-match press conference that he had spoken with James and that the club would do its best to find the right solution for him.

"I have had my conversation with him and he knows my idea," Benitez said. "Now, he is not available, so not an issue for tomorrow. We will discuss with every single player with their agents to find the best solution."

Kean, meanwhile, had reportedly made it known that he wanted to leave the club before the transfer deadline, and had removed all photographs from his time at Everton from his Instagram feed.

A permanent move to Paris Saint-Germain, where he had spent the preceding season on loan, did not look to be on the cards after the French giants refused any other arrangement than another temporary spell, having just signed Lionel Messi from Barcelona.

***

14 August 2021: Everton v Southampton

Meanwhile, Benitez began his reign with a rousing season-opening victory over Saints, as Everton welcomed a practically full house back to Goodison Park for the first time in almost 18 months.

Buoyed by a positive reception for Benitez from the fans, Everton made a positive start but were undermined by a horrendous error by Michael Keane midway through the first half. The defender, playing alongside Mason Holgate with Yerry Mina on the bench because of his lack of pre-season activity following a delayed return from the Copa America, was caught dallying on the ball inside his own half and was robbed by Che Adams. Adams prodded it forward to release Adam Armstrong, who made no mistake, lifting the ball past Jordan Pickford and into the top corner of the goal.

Benitez's half-time talk and a tactical shift that swapped the positions of the two centre-backs and switched Demarai Gray to the left with Richarlison moving into the centre did the trick, however, in spurring his charges into more purposeful action. Gray won a 47th-minute corner that was only cleared as far as Townsend. He nodded a looping header back towards the six-yard box where Richarlison stole in behind the static Mohammed Salisu and stabbed it into the roof of the net.

That ignited the home crowd, but it would take another half an hour for the next goal to arrive as Southampton responded in what was an even encounter until 15 minutes from the end. Despite a couple of nervy moments claiming aerial balls from a flurry of Saints corners, Pickford didn't have a save of note make after denying Armstrong in the first half.

Instead, it was Alex McCarthy who was picking the ball out of the back of the net following a wonderful strike by Doucouré. Operating much closer to the opposition box than was the case in the latter stages of Carlo Ancelotti's tenure, the Frenchman was involved in the build-up to the goal when he fed the ball out to Seamus Coleman on the right flank.

The Irishman's scooped pass found recent substitute Alex Iwobi, who headed it back to Doucouré just inside the area. He took one touch to turn his marker and then unleashed a fabulous effort into the top corner to make it 2-1.

That became 3-1 in the closing stages and Iwobi was involved again. Picking up the ball on the right from Richarlison, he then threaded a perfectly weighted pass between two defenders and the Brazilian whipped a peach of an early cross to the six-yard box where Calvert-Lewin stooped to force a diving header into the net, to set the seal on a superb afternoon for Everton.

It was a performance wholly at odds with the team's struggles at home under Benitez's predecessor and a victory earned by playing to the Blues' strengths as a side. The previous season's games in an empty home stadium were too often a story of capitulation and attacking ineptitude, but against Southampton, the character and response from the team was exactly what was required.

They owed much to Richarlison, who was excellent in the second half and a driving force in attack, but both new signings played important roles and the new boss got his tactics right on the day.

True football was back with the return of a ground full of supporters who enjoyed a stirring victory that would, for the time being, banish the cloud of pessimism with which many fans approached the 2021/22 season.

Final score: Everton 3-1 Southampton

***

The positive start to the season under Benitez continued with a creditable 2-2 draw at Leeds, followed by a 2-1 away win at Huddersfield Town in the Carabao Cup, and another impressive 2-0 win away at Brighton.

Unfortunately, the win on the south coast in which Dominic Calvert-Lewin had notched his third goal in four games to start 2021/22 would be his last until January 2022, by which time Benitez was on the brink of losing his job at Everton.

The striker, who had been so impressive during Ancelotti's only full season and become the long-awaited replacement for Romelu Lukaku by default, suffered a serious quadricep tear that would not only sideline him for a significant portion of the season but would trigger a series of soft-tissue complaints for months afterwards.

***

13 September 2021: Everton v Burnley

Everton returned home after their win over the Seagulls for some Monday night football where they came from behind for a second successive home game to sweep Burnley away at Goodison Park, which was bouncing by the end of what had threatened to be a frustrating evening under the lights.

The Blues had toiled through a disappointing first half, playing with a five man defensive formation under Rafael Benitez for the first time, and fell behind early in the second half to a Ben Mee header, a goal that evoked painful memories of a string of home defeats under Carlo Ancelotti last season.

Rather than wallow in impending defeat, however, Everton responded in almost immediate and irrepressible fashion, scoring three goals in six mesmerising minutes – the pick of them coming like a rocket off the boot of Andros Townsend – and coming close to adding a fourth soon afterwards, but Abdoulaye Doucouré's effort was ruled out for offside.

The equaliser arrived within seven minutes of Mee's opener, just as Benitez was preparing his first change in order to alter the course of the contest. A short-corner between Lucas Digne and Demarai Gray ended with the latter firing disappointingly into a defender but the Blues kept the ball, worked it to Townsend on the opposite flank and he whipped a perfect cross onto the head of Keane who just had to guide it past the stranded Pope to make it 1-1 on the hour mark.

Five minutes later, the game was turned on its head in the same manner Everton had flipped it on Southampton a month ago on the opening day. Andros Townsend cut back inside off the flank with a couple of touches and then unloaded a quite magnificent left-foot shot from 30 yards out that crashed into the top corner, leaving Nick Pope with no chance.

Just over a minute later it was 3-1, as Burnley's attack following the restart broke down in Everton's area. Townsend knocked the loose ball to Doucouré, who spotted Gray's run through space in the centre-circle and released him with a perfect pass that allowed him to bear down on keeper and bury it past him in front of the ecstatic Park End.

The hosts threatened to turn it into a rout and there was a late cameo for another new signing, Salomon Rondon, but Everton were content otherwise by that stage to see out their second 3-1 home win of the campaign and move joint-top on points in the Premier League table.

Final score: Everton 3-1 Burnley

***

21 September 2021: QPR v Everton

If Rafael Benitez had made a surprisingly impressive start to life as Everton boss, leading the Toffees to a fourth-place berth by mid-September, the wheels would come off in spectacular fashion, starting with a 3-0 defeat at Aston Villa and then the club's almost customarily premature exit from the Carabao Cup.

Indeed, an Evertonian of any pedigree knows there was nothing shocking about the result in a third round tie at Queens Park Rangers which once again saw the club out of the League Cup before autumn had officially begun.

Everton have never won the competition, and it's highly unlikely they ever will; not just because the Carabao Cup is under threat from the burgeoning international calendar and calls for the fixture list in England to be pared down, but also because the perennial down-playing of the tournament by playing weakened sides means that successive Everton managers are always playing with fire.

Benitez was the latest to get burned.

The rationale for making wholesale changes to the team for cup fixtures is well-established, of course. It's an opportunity to rest your stars and give some game time and a chance to impress for fringe or younger players against the calibre of opposition that Everton should beat regardless of which mix of the first-team squad is out there.

Benitez's impulse to rest some key players was justifiably strong. He was already without Dominic Calvert-Lewin, Richarlison and Seamus Coleman (although none of them had played in the previous round at Huddersfield) and could ill-afford to lose any more ahead of Premier League matches against Norwich and Manchester United.

The bigger inquest really surrounded the paucity of Everton's squad and the disastrous recruitment decisions that had left the squad so shallow in terms of quality. Nevertheless, whenever you make wholesale changes, you leave yourself wide open to the danger of being picked off by a lower-division side and on this occasion it came at the hands of Queens Park Rangers and the lottery of a penalty shoot-out.

Still, given that six of the 11 that started at Loftus Road had been in the line-up at Huddersfield in the previous round, where his charges still squeaked through despite going down to 10 men in the second half, the Spaniard might have expected better than the dreadful fare Everton served up for much of this contest.

He was let down badly, particularly by the centre-half pairing of Ben Godfrey and Mason Holgate who struggled to cope with veteran striker Charlie Austin before improving in the second half, and a limp midfield duo of André Gomes and Tom Davies that contributed to QPR enjoying, at one stage, 70% of the ball... against a Premier League team!

If Benitez was relying on a repeat of the Huddersfield tie, the early knockings might have comforted him but it only took 18 minutes for Everton to fall behind. The porous nature of Everton's below-strength midfield and right flank, where Jonjoe Kenny offered little resistance, underscored QPR's first meaningful attack. Chris Willock twice made a mug of Davies before finding Ilias Chair, who knocked it to Sam McCullum. When Asmir Begovic could only palm his cross straight to Austin, the striker simply nodded into the empty net to make it 1-0.

Digne had the Toffees level within 12 minutes, though, when QPR's offside trap was sprung by a delicious ball over the top by Townsend, that picked out the run of the Frenchman who calmly side-footed it home first time.

Parity lasted just four minutes, however, as Everton's soft centre showed again. This time it was Chair who swung the ball in from the Rs' left and Austin capitalised on the yard's worth of space afforded by Godfrey by rising above him and glancing a header inside the far post.

With their manager's half-time team talk no doubt ringing in their ears, Everton got the early goal they needed once the second period resumed. Gomes scuffed a corner to the near post, Holgate knocked it across into the mix in front of goal, where Townsend converted from close range to make it 2-2.

That should have provided the platform from which Everton won the game, but they lacked the requisite cutting edge or drive in midfield.

Benitez hooked Gomes and introduced both Abdoulaye Doucouré and Demarai Gray but there was never enough cohesiveness or penetration about the team to enable either to fashion or score a winner... although the Frenchman probably should have had a penalty in the 74th minute when he appeared to be tripped in the box.

Once it had gone to penalties, Everton's League Cup curse took over, manifesting itself in the worst spot-kick of the shoot-out from Davies who invited Dieng to save it at full-stretch and set Dunne up to be the hero with QPR's eighth successful kick.

Once again, the aftermath to an early League Cup exit was dominated by recriminations over the manager fielding a much-changed side. Gary Lineker had quipped before the previous round that, "the Carabao Cup is where a bunch of teams enter a competition and Manchester City win it at the end," and there was more than element of truth about the futility of this tournament where teams like Everton were concerned.

By the same token, though, progression through each round narrowed your odds, and for a club like Everton – trophy-less for what would be 27 years by the time the finals of the domestic cups came around the following spring – could they not put their best foot forward in every round and do everything possible to win a piece of silverware? The 3,000 fans who packed the away end on a Tuesday night in London deserved much, much better.

Final score: QPR 2-2 Everton (Pens 8-7)

***

More bad news was to follow. James Rodriguez finally left Everton in a permanent transfer to Al Rayyan of the Qatar Stars League for a fee that was officially undisclosed, but reported to be around £7.2 million.

It ended James's one-year association with the Toffees that began in a hail of publicity and some scintillating early performances, but which ultimately became a constant source of frustration as the player battled injury during the 2020/21 season, with many also questioning his commitment to the Everton cause.

The departure from Goodison Park of his mentor Carlo Ancelotti in June seemed to signal that Rodriguez's time with the Blues would also be cut short; but there was a point when the summer transfer deadline passed in England and he could not find another club, where it looked as though he could yet stay.

The suggestions in the media were that with Benitez unable to see a role for him in the team, Everton kept pushing James to find an exit to a country where the window was still open, so they could get some or all of his reported £200,000-a-week salary off the books.

Indeed, though Benitez had tried claiming that, "It's always up to the player; in the end he has the final decision," the manager had hinted earlier in the month of September that the former Galactico's exit was required as Everton worked towards remaining within the Premier League's Profit & Sustainability limits.

"We are talking about a special situation for this club," the Spaniard said after the Carabao Cup defeat to QPR, "[With] the financial fair play rules, we have to manage everything in the best way we can."

As he parted ways with Everton having never experienced the magic of Goodison at its most passionate, the Columbian wrote on Instagram:

"I ... want to thank Everton fans. A pity not to have played in Goodison Park with you. It would have been very nice. I always tried to give my best, and I always wanted to win. That is my mentality. I wish you all the best."

***

23 October 2021: Everton v Watford

Everton moved on from the cup defeat to QPR to register a 2-0 home win against Norwich, and began October with a 1-1 draw with Manchester United at Old Trafford. Those results put them in good spirits for the visit of West Ham to Goodison on 17 October, but an Angelo Ogbonna goal for the Hammers in the 74th minute decided the match and sent the restless crowd home frustrated. The defeat saw the Blues slip to 8th in the league.

The following Saturday, there was an opportunity to atone, when Watford were the visitors to Goodison. What unfolded was quite the opposite and it was an early harbinger of poor performances and results to come under Rafael Benitez as a former player, perhaps with a point to prove, ran riot.

In the expectation of a busy summer of transfer business, few had questioned the decision by Everton to let Josh King go at the end of 2020/21. The Norwegian international had shown flashes of promise off the bench in his few months with the club after arriving from Bournemouth in January, but Carlo Ancelotti has largely overlooked him and he failed to make a single start under the Italian. If he wasn't going to play, better to release him and sign someone more to the manager's liking.

Ancelotti left Goodison Park at the start of June, of course, and following an alarmingly austere summer, Everton effectively ended up trading King for Salomon Rondon, a player whose limitations were already obvious, and who once again proved to be utterly ineffective up front for the Blues. King scored a hat-trick as Everton fell apart in the final quarter of an hour.

Benitez's team were utterly shambolic, particularly in the closing stages as Watford players poured through their midfield and defence on the way to a four-goal assault in the space of 13 minutes. It was an absolute horror show, evocative of some of the worst collapses in a recent club history littered with embarrassing and gutless capitulations.

Michael Keane and the 2021/22, post-COVID version of Ben Godfrey made for an awkward and susceptible-looking pairing at the best of times, but against Watford, with both players turning in often shocking performances, it looked like a doomed partnership.

Yerry Mina had been a big miss against West Ham the previous weekend, and he proved to be again, side-lined as he was by a hamstring complaint. With Abdoulaye Doucouré and Dominic Calvert-Lewin also missing, Everton proved that without those important components of their metaphorical spine, they had no real spine at all.

In Doucouré's absence, Tom Davies looked to have stepped admirably into the breach by grabbing an early goal. Anthony Gordon fed Demarai Gray and when he crossed low into the six-yard box, where Davies arrived to slide home from close range to score his first goal in over two years, in only the third minute.

The Toffees' good work was undone, however, by another failure to deal with a set-piece. A free-kick, whipped in from the right near the corner flag, came off Ben Godfrey's head and dropped to King, who was free to prod it into the gaping net.

Disconcertingly, the goal visibly drained much of the Blues' early belief and it would be a while before they rediscovered some of their mojo. What should have been the turning point of the contest came just past the hour mark when Richarlison, absent for the past few games with a knee injury, came off the bench to score within three minutes of his introduction. The Brazilian ghosted into space to connect with Keane's clipped ball into the box and launched himself to guide a header past Ben Foster and send Goodison into rapture.

With 16 minutes left, Keane could have killed the contest but crucially planted his header off a free-kick the wrong side of the post. Just four minutes later, Watford were level again. Sloppy play by Davies forced Keane to put the ball behind and the resulting delivery found Juraj Kucka, who bulleted a header past Pickford.

King's second goal turned the game on its head at 3-2, and any chance of Benitez's charges getting something from the contest evaporated three minutes from the end of the regulation 90. Godfrey failed to clear his lines as three Everton defenders got in each other's way and the ball was poked through to King who side-stepped Keane and slotted past the keeper to make it 4-2.

And Everton's misery was complete in added time, as Emmanuel Dennis took advantage of an AWOL defence to stroke home Watford's fifth in front of rapidly emptying seats.

So, just as in the previous year, Everton had seen a flying start to the season massively undercut by injuries to key players and the poor recruitment that had left the squad so thin. All of that capped with questionable decisions from a manager whose "honeymoon" was well and truly over. What began as a campaign infused with optimism that the wily, experienced Spanish campaigner could navigate a squad – lacking in depth, but blessed by sufficient quality when everyone was fit – to an improved final placing on those achieved in recent seasons, was supplanted by fears that the Blues' chief focus should be on getting to 40 points as soon as possible.

Back-to-back defeats at what is supposed to be Fortress Goodison ratcheted up the pressure on Benitez to find the solutions to his team's inability to defend set-pieces, and to plug a large, Doucouré-sized hole in midfield with the winter transfer window still over two months away.

Final score: Everton 2-5 Watford

***

Since overcoming Norwich in late September, Everton's form had slumped, with the team registering two draws and six defeats in the ensuing eight games and falling from 5th to 14th place in the Premier League in the process.

They had undoubtedly struggled in the absence of players like Richarlison, Abdoulaye Doucouré, André Gomes, Dominic Calvert-Lewin and Yerry Mina, but all but two of those team members were now back fit so the excuses were starting to run out.

The latest of those disconcerting defeats had been a humiliating 4-1 home defeat against the manager's former club, Liverpool. For those stalwart Evertonians, watching on glumly at a rapidly emptying Goodison, while 3,000 away fans sang merrily about Rafael Benitez, it felt like the final straw.

Farhad Moshiri had been pushing back against speculation that Benitez could be sacked, though, by expressing his belief that the Spaniard would turn things around at Everton in the coming weeks.

The Toffees' owner and the Board of Directors came under fierce criticism from the club's fans after the derby mauling and there had also been calls for Benitez to be fired after a miserable run of just two points from the last 24 available.

In a text exchange with *TalkSport* host Jim White, however, that the Scot read out on air, Moshiri blamed injuries for Everton's abysmal form:

> "Football is about crisis one day and glory the following day. Rafa is a good manager and underperformance is largely due to the injuries. Next two weeks, we will get to a full squad and, in the meantime, results will improve. Rafa needs time to have his mark on the squad. He will be supported to add depth to the squad. Managers need time."

***

Supporters, however, were growing ever more frustrated and concerned. A collection of fan groups on social media called for Evertonians to leave their seats in the 27th minute of the televised clash with Arsenal on 6 December.

Dubbed "27 Minutes For 27 Years", the initiative signalled to the club's hierarchy the frustration Evertonians felt at the club's lack of progress, and the team's shocking run of results in recent weeks. Form the fans put down to poor player recruitment.

Since the release of initial hashtag and social media announcement, the campaign leaders published the full rationale for their initiative and the goals they hoped to achieve.

They said: "The #27minutesfor27years was to be a campaign highlighting Everton's longest peacetime trophy drought, 27 years in May 2022 since club captain Dave Watson lifted the FA Cup at Wembley. Why 27 minutes for 27 years? It was designed to bring attention to the majority shareholder Farhad Moshiri who despite investing approximately £685 million since February 2016 (£450 million into the club, £100 million into the Bramley-Moore stadium and £135 million approx. in buying existing shares) had not seen an improvement in the club's fortunes with multiple managerial appointments, a weakened and less competitive first team squad and declining performances on the pitch."

In a message to supporters, the group expanded on their aims, and there was a call to action for all attending the next match at Goodison Park:

> "**The Campaign:** Monday 6th December, Everton vs Arsenal, Goodison Park. At the 27th minute fans supporting this campaign to leave their seats as a visual representation of the need for change at Everton. The

campaign respects individual decisions to leave their seats for 5 minutes, until half time or for the remainder of the match. The campaign is a bringing together of supporter groups, fan organisations and individual supporters. Its sole purpose is to engage Farhad Moshiri and promote changes in the running and management of the club. Something that can only be addressed by the major shareholder. The individuals supporting the campaign continue their support of the football club and are fully committed to supporting the players on the pitch to better performances and results.

The campaign welcomes and acknowledges his financial commitment to the club. However, the campaign draws attention to the governance and management of the club during these last 6 years. The campaign recognises that without investment and fresh recruitment in the board and executive teams the prospects of a change in fortune in the club remains slight. The campaign recognises that the fans' emotional investment and financial commitment to the club are totally aligned with Farhad Moshiri's investment. We seek the same outcome, a better return for both our investment. We call on Farhad Moshiri as major shareholder to make the management changes necessary to see an improvement in performance. We call on

> Farhad Moshiri to communicate in future through official club channels. We call on Farhad Moshiri to engage, meet and discuss fan concerns with the fans. The campaign will seek the widest possible support across the fanbase and is committed to maintaining the campaign until such a time as Farhad Moshiri engages and agrees to the changes necessary to resolve the club's decline." – #27MinutesFor27Years Campaign

***

6 December 2021: Everton v Arsenal

Arsenal, who had travelled to Merseyside in good form and had designs on moving back into the top five, began the game well and played the more impressive passing football without really threatening Jordan Pickford's goal.

Halfway through the first half, it was Everton on the attack. Gray flashed a dangerous ball across the face of Arsenal's goal, just as the clock was about to tick into the 27th minute marker when the #27MinutesFor 27Years campaign had called for fans to leave their seats. With most eyes still focussed on action on the pitch, a smattering of disillusioned Blues left their seats and walked out. Watching on from the Directors Box, Bill Kenwright and Denise Barrett-Baxendale would have been relieved that the spectacle was not more dramatic.

The game came alive, just before the interval when Richarlison was fouled outside the box. From Townsend's free kick, Richarlison thought he had put the Blues ahead with a typically excellent header. Sadly, the VAR adjudged him to have been fractionally ahead of the last man as he leaned forward to make his run to meet the ball.

Two minutes later, and well into injury time, Everton were undone at the back. Kieran Tierney got beyond Seamus Coleman to centre for the untracked Martin Ødegaard and he side-footed home from close range.

Everton were undaunted, however. They had the ball in the net for a second time shortly before an hour's play had elapsed. Allan passed to Doucouré, who picked out Richarlison to drill it past Ramsdale and wheel away in vindication. But, once again, VAR returned an even more agonising hairline verdict.

With Goodison burning with a sense of being hard done-by, Benitez brought André Gomes off the bench and Everton dug deep to turn the match on its head in thrilling fashion.

In the 79th-minute, Gomes' shot rebounded off a defender to Gray just outside the box. He attempted a delicious curling shot with his instep that cannoned back off the face of the crossbar to the waiting Richarlison, who looped it deftly over the stranded goalkeeper to finally get his goal.

Then, as the game moved into stoppage time, Gray took centre stage by firing home an Exocet missile from 25 yards to complete a stirring comeback.

The hard-fought win was Everton's first since late September and arrested a slide of six defeats in seven games to lift the club up to 12th place in the table, ahead of back-to-back away games in the capital against Crystal Palace and Chelsea. Was there still a chance that Benitez' team could turn things around?

Final score: Everton 2-1 Arsenal

2021: Everton Director Ismailov Steps Down

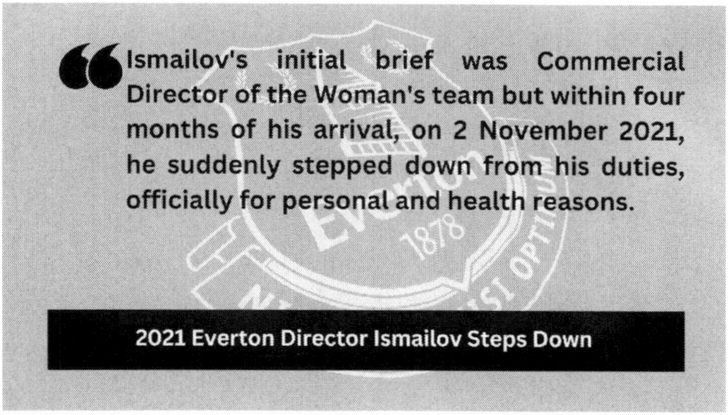

If there was a regular criticism of Farhad Moshiri's reign at Everton, it was that the Board of Directors under the British-Iranian businessman hadn't been augmented either in size or capability under his leadership. So it was a surprise when the club announced the departure of Sasha Ryazantsev in August 2021, and indicated it was part of a reorganisation of the Board which also saw Grant Ingles appointed as Chief Finance Officer.

Ryazantsev had joined the Everton Board as the Owner's Representative in 2016. He then became the Club's first Chief Finance and

Commercial Officer in 2018, and was also appointed as Managing Director of Everton Women in 2020. He had seemingly performed well, at least in public, and his sudden departure fuelled speculation that some heavyweight external talent was incoming.

Instead, the vacuum was filled by 25-year-old Sarvar Ismailov, the nephew of Alisher Usmanov. Ismailov was made a Director of the Club Board and Moshiri's Executive Representative. He had initially joined Everton in 2019 as Global Commercial Consultant, before becoming Everton Women's first Sporting and Commercial Director and a member of the Everton Women Strategic Leadership Team in 2020. It was confirmed that Ismailov would retain his role at Everton Women and will also remain on the Club's Stadium Board – a post he took up in 2019. It was hoped he would bring some fresh ideas to the boardroom. But more significantly, it also hinted, perhaps, at greater involvement from Usmanov himself.

Within four months of his Board appointment, on 2 November 2021, he suddenly stepped down from his duties, officially for personal and health reasons.

Three weeks later, Ismailov was charged by Westminster Magistrates' Court with GBH for an incident that occurred in London on 11 June 2021. Together with his brother Sanjar, Ismailov, he was accused of causing grievous bodily harm to Edmond Krasniqi at a flat in Hyde Park Gate.

According to *BBC News,* Sanjar Ismailov was further charged with causing actual bodily harm to model Astrid Fajcsi.

It was the kind of publicity all concerned could have done without.

A month later, Daniel Sandford of *BBC News* reported that: "The case against former Everton director Sarvar Ismailov has been dismissed due to a 'lack of evidence'. Following a three-week adjournment, Westminster Magistrates' Court heard the case had been discontinued. No further details were given in court by the Crown Prosecution Service. But a spokesman later said: "We have a duty to keep all cases under review and on further consideration we decided this case no longer met our legal test. It has therefore been discontinued and we have written to the complainant explaining our decision."

In July 2022, Joe Thomas in the *Liverpool Echo* reported that: "Former Everton director Sarvar Ismailov has been sanctioned by the British Government. Ismailov, a nephew of already-sanctioned Russian oligarch Alisher Usmanov, was today named among a list of new figures to be hit with action. The sanctions follow the Russian invasion of Ukraine. In a statement, the Foreign, Commonwealth and Development Office said: 'Also sanctioned today are Sarvar and Sanjar Ismailov, nephews of major Russian oligarch Alisher Usmanov who has close ties to the Kremlin. Both Sarvar and Sanjar have significant interests in the UK, it is believed that they own homes in Highgate and Hampstead Heath.' Both men had their assets frozen. Their father, Gulbakhor Ismailova, was sanctioned in April 2022.

***

In other news, the panel commissioned with performing a fan-led review of Football Governance published its findings and recommendations on 25 November 2021.

The Fan Led Review of Football Governance had resulted from three crisis points: the collapse of Bury FC, the COVID-19 pandemic, and the attempt to set up a European Super League (ESL) in April 2021.

The panel was chaired by Tracey Crouch, Conservative MP and former Minister of Sport, and included Everton CEO and recently-named 'Business Woman of the Year for 2020,' Denise Barrett-Baxendale.

Their report included some far-reaching recommendations, which sought to wrest overall control of English football from the Premier League and its six dominant members. Their 10-point plan said:

1. To ensure the long-term sustainability of football, the Government should create a new independent regulator for English football (IREF)

2. To ensure financial sustainability of the professional game, IREF should oversee financial regulation in football.

3. New owners' and directors' tests for clubs should be established by IREF replacing the three existing tests and ensuring that only good custodians and qualified directors can run these vital assets.

4. Football needs a new approach to corporate governance to support a long-term sustainable future of the game.

5. Football needs to improve equality, diversity and inclusion in clubs with committed EDI Action Plans regularly assessed by IREF.

6. As a uniquely important stakeholder, supporters should be properly consulted by their clubs in taking key decisions by means of a Shadow Board.

7. Football clubs are a vital part of their local communities, in recognition of this there should be additional protection for key items of club heritage.

8. Fair distributions are vital to the long term health of football. The Premier League should guarantee its support to the pyramid and make additional, proportionate contributions to further support football.

9. Women's football should be treated with parity and given its own dedicated review.

10. As an urgent matter, the welfare of players exiting the game needs to be better protected — particularly at a young age.

Subsequently, it became known that the Premier League was ardently opposed to the appointment of an independent regulator for English football. It would remain to be seen whether Denise Barrett-Baxendale's participation in the panel and Everton's very "anti-ESL" stance would have negative consequences for the club.

2021: Moshiri backs Benitez. Brands resigns. Digne sold

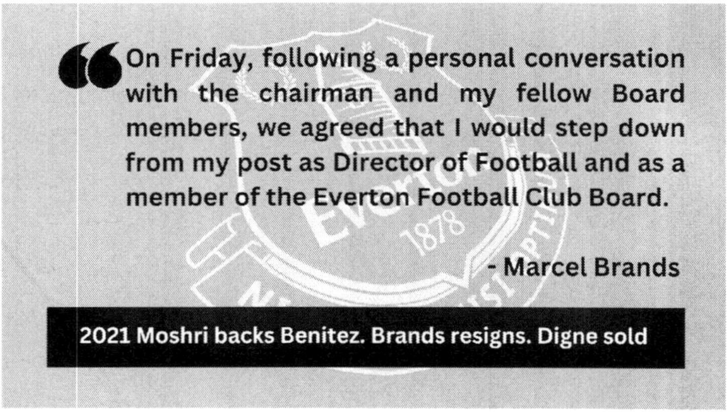

The evening of 1 December 2021 had been one of anger and frustration at Goodison Park. Everton had just been trounced 4-1 by Liverpool, suffered the ignominy of reds' fans taunting them with chants hailing Rafael Benitez, and supporters were demanding action. Boos and chants of "Sack the Board" rang out at the final whistle and Marcel Brands was accosted by one irate supporter as he left the Directors Box who admonished the Sporting Director for the poor quality of the playing squad.

In what was interpreted by some as Brands suggesting there was plenty of blame to go around, he responded by saying, "It's not just the players, is it?"

Within two days, the 27 Minutes for 27 Years campaign had called on fans to stage a walk-out protest during the Arsenal game on 6 December, as a means of highlighting the urgent need for change at Boardroom level.

Two days later, the club announced that Brands' 3½-year stint as Everton's Director of Football was over after he agreed to leave the club by mutual consent because of a clash of visions for the future of the club.

Shortly before midnight on 5 December, Everton finally confirmed media reports that started earlier in the day with *The Mirror* claiming that the Dutchman, who had only signed a new three-year contract in early 2021, had agreed to leave the club with immediate effect.

The Blues' hierarchy had come under mounting pressure for the club's declining fortunes. Though many of the problems that led to Everton being unable to spend more than a paltry £1.7 million over the summer in the transfer market pre-dated Brands' arrival, he was seen as part of the issue.

However, given the opaque nature of the club's structure and general lack of communication on the division of responsibility, it was never clear how much power Brands ever had for player recruitment and the hiring of managers.

In a statement, Brands explained his departure:

> "On Friday, following a personal conversation with the chairman and my fellow Board members, we

> agreed that I would step down from my post as Director of Football and as a member of the Everton Football Club Board. This decision has taken some time and some consideration and was one of the most difficult I have faced in my career. The Board and I agreed that there is a clear difference in the vision and direction for this beautiful club and, with that in mind, the decision was taken. I want to thank everyone in the club who I have worked closely with over the last three and a half years. There are a lot of talented people at Everton with huge passion and commitment to move the club forward, both on and off the pitch. I want to wish all of the squad every success, and I am convinced that there is enough quality to improve the current situation quickly. It has been an honour for me to work at this fantastic club and I wish everyone associated with Everton the very best for the future."

Though reports suggested that Rafael Benitez would take on full responsibility for player recruitment, Everton's own statement pledged a "strategic review" of operations on the playing side:

> "A strategic review of the football structure will now take place, which will inform the best model for the Club to proceed with in the long-term. In the meantime, the Owner and Board of Directors will continue to provide our manager, Rafa Benitez, with their full support."

It was also rumoured that Chief Executive Officer, Denise Barrett-Baxendale had been "seeking alternative employment" for some time, and might have been the next board member to move on. It turned out that she would remain in her post for another 18 months, by which time things would become a good deal worse.

2022: Benitez sacked after defeat at Norwich

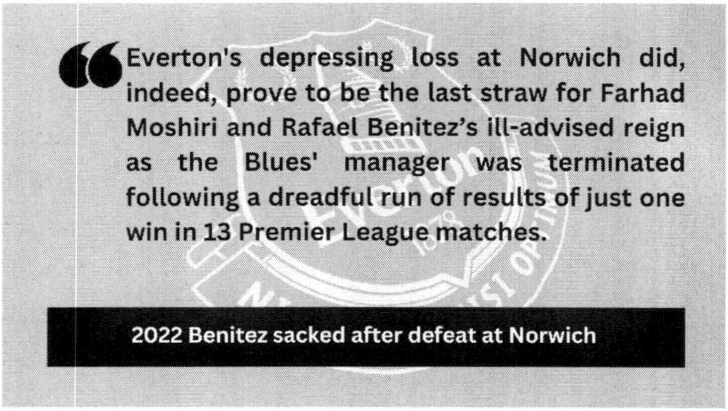

It would have been nice to say that an Everton defeat to a Norwich City side that had comfortably been among the worst in the top flight all season - who came into this match on a six-match losing streak, and who hadn't scored a Premier League goal for seven weeks - was unthinkable but it really wasn't.

15 January 2022: Norwich City v Everton

Indeed, any Blue would have been well aware that there was no better team to face than this version of Everton when you've not won for ages and can't score for, well, toffee. And Rafael Benitez's side were all too obliging, handing the Canaries their first league win since Dean Smith's first match in charge in mid-November.

Benitez had proven incapable of producing results at Everton since the last time they met Norwich in September and beat them in comfortable, if rather unconvincing, fashion at Goodison Park. Since then the Spaniard had overseen just one victory in the Premier League, one inspired and secured by the individual brilliance of Demarai Gray and Richarlison as they turned the match against Arsenal on its head a month earlier.

Rather than act as a springboard, that adrenaline-fuelled, crowd-backed triumph over Mikel Arteta's vastly improved Gunners proved to be an aberration in what had become a miserable sequence of nine defeats in 12 games under Benitez; games blighted by mystifying team selections and formations, even allowing for absences from injury and positive COVID-19 tests.

This match was no exception and by the time it had ended, few could have been left with any doubt that Benitez's time as Everton's boss was over. Certainly, Farhad Moshiri would finally be compelled to act with the Toffees in a tailspin and sinking towards the relegation zone.

Benitez did at least dispense with his bizarre five-man defence, overly staffed by full-backs, and opted for what looked, on paper, to be 4-4-2 at Carrow Road. It ended up with Salomon Rondon operating almost as an awkward and baffling number 10 behind Dominic Calvert-Lewin.

Calvert-Lewin himself had been a welcome returnee to the team after sitting out the narrow win at Hull City in the FA Cup the previous weekend, but there were long stretches of this contest where it was easy to forget he was playing, such was Everton's impotence as an attacking force.

Indeed, apart from some early probing forays by Demarai Gray and the occasional threat posed by Anthony Gordon, Everton didn't really pose much danger to Norwich's goal until Richarlison came on as a second-half substitute to score a spectacular goal that, sadly would be forgotten, given the result.

Credit went to Norwich for a spirited performance where they capitalised on Everton's mistakes and defended doggedly to prevent the Toffees from salvaging a draw in the closing stages, but the story was all about Benitez and his team's incomprehensibly bad form.

The deadlock was broken in the 16th minute, when Josh Sargent's cross came in from the Canaries' right and Michael Keane stuck out a leg that diverted the ball past Pickford to give the hosts the lead.

They were two goals to the good almost immediately. Everton were trying to attack at one end when Seamus Coleman sold Anthony Gordon short with an attempted pass that was intercepted by Brandon Williams who strode forward and calmly threaded the ball to Idah to fire past Pickford.

When Benitez finally made moves to change his approach with his two substitutions, it took Richarlison just six minutes to make his mark. A corner from the Blues' right was cleared, but Everton kept the ball and when Tim Krul failed to get purchase on a punch from Mykolenko's deep cross, it sat up invitingly for Richarlison to overhead-kick it cleanly into the top corner from near the penalty spot.

What should have been the catalyst for an all-out assault on the Norwich goal failed to spark much more attacking penetration from the Toffees, however, as Norwich defended in numbers and dealt with the slow-tempo play in front of them.

As ever, Benitez deflected all the criticism for this latest defeat onto the shoulders of the players, blaming them for making mistakes while commending them somewhat for a more purposeful second-half display. It was true that he couldn't really legislate for Keane's clumsy own goal or the sloppy distribution that led to Norwich's second and his players had more than enough time to claw things back to at least earn a point.

Yet they looked utterly lost under a manager who seemed clueless how to get the best out of them, or set them up to win matches in the Premier League. The feeling was that Benitez's time at Everton had been up for a while. That Farhad Moshiri had waited so long to end the farce merely sacrificed precious points and prolonged the fans' frustration.

Many of the club's irate travelling fans aimed chants of "you're getting sacked in the morning" and a now-familiar banner imploring the former Liverpool boss to "Get out of our club" was unfurled in the away section before and during the game. Within 48 hours, they would get their wish.

Final score: Norwich 2-1 Everton

***

16 January 2022: Benitez Sacked

Everton's depressing loss at Norwich did, indeed, prove to be the last straw for Farhad Moshiri and Rafael Benitez's ill-advised reign as the Blues' manager was terminated following a dreadful run of results of just one win in 13 Premier League matches.

The decision to part ways with the Spaniard was, apparently, made at an emergency board meeting, and they made an official announcement after an agreement on compensation was reached by both parties.

The writing had arguably been on the wall for Benitez since that chastening evening of the Goodison derby at the start of December and the 1-0 defeat at Brentford that had preceded it, and where the travelling Everton supporters had first made their displeasure with the Spaniard known.

However, the early-warning signs had emerged in September after Calvert-Lewin sustained his serious injury that side-lined him for four months, when Benitez' gamble of playing a weakened side at QPR failed, and when his side collapsed in that horrible 5-2 home defeat to Watford.

Between a come-from-behind win over Burnley in mid-September and the calamitous loss to Norwich, Benitez presided over just two League victories. He had been pointing for weeks to a debilitating injury list — the squad was certainly down to the bare bones because of injured players and positive coronavirus tests — but he could not escape criticism for poor tactics, player selection and game-management, not to mention his team's frustrating passivity, particularly in the first-half of matches.

In a form table encompassing matches since week eight of the season, Everton were sitting rock bottom, and looked to be heading for a desperate fight for survival given the team's inability to pick-up points under his watch. There was an argument for his dismissal after the embarrassment of the Goodison derby but whether Moshiri simply wanted to give him as much time as possible or was trying to avoid sacking another manager, he let the situation drift until mid-January.

By then, it felt as though Benitez had lost the confidence of the players and any lingering support from the fans, particularly after he had frozen out key first-team player, Lucas Digne. The impasse had eventually forced the French left-back out of the club altogether. Digne signed for Aston Villa in early January 2022, further weakening the Toffees' squad and strengthening the feeling that Moshiri had afforded Benitez and his ego too much power.

***

The board's list of candidates to replace Benitez reportedly included Wayne Rooney, who had been impressing as Derby County boss, Niko Kovac, Rudi Garcia and Roma manager Jose Mourinho, although the Portuguese reportedly took himself out of the running, as did Brighton head coach Graham Potter. Vitor Pereira, never too far away when there was a managerial vacancy at Goodison, was also said to be in the mix. Meanwhile former Derby and Chelsea head coach, Frank Lampard, indicated he would prefer to assume his next post in the summer and with the benefit of a pre-season to prepare.

Suddenly Roberto Martinez emerged as the 'clear frontrunner' and the wheels appeared to be turning quickly on that front, until the Belgian FA, who wanted Martinez to lead their team at the World Cup in Qatar later in the year, blocked his departure.

In the interim, Duncan Ferguson, an outside bet for the full-time role himself, retook the reins. He had led Everton to a thrilling 3-1 win over Chelsea in front of a raucous Goodison crowd in December 2019 following the departure of Marco Silva. There was no doubt he would relish the opportunity to manage the team again when Aston Villa came to town.

***

22 January 2022: Everton v Aston Villa

Evertonians had no doubt envisaged this match going differently. An expectant Goodison Park crowd was ready to back Duncan Ferguson and the players to the hilt for 90 raucous minutes. Meanwhile, by posting some long-overdue communication with supporters from Farhad Moshiri via email ahead of the match, the Everton hierarchy no doubt felt that they had blunted one of the 27 Years Campaign's chief gripes ahead of a more unified atmosphere around the club.

By the end of the clash with Aston Villa, their most feared outcome had occurred, and the post-match protests by supporters aiming their ire at the owner and the Board of Directors felt as justified and as urgent as ever. Not that any immediate change off the pitch could address the very real near-term threat of relegation. The Blues had found themselves in a mess created by many years of mis-management; but those in charge's next act — the appointment of a successor to Rafael Benitez — would have a huge bearing on whether this famous old club remained in the Premier League after that season.

You had to feel for Ferguson at the final whistle. There wasn't a soul who doubted how badly he would have wanted to lift the gloom around Goodison a little by guiding Everton to a badly needed win. That "lightning in a bottle" first match as caretaker boss against

Chelsea a little over two years prior was always going to be hard to replicate, but the Scot clearly felt that a repeat of the passion and the high-octane, more direct football that delivered that famous win would be enough on this occasion.

Unfortunately, Ferguson came up against a Villa team that was reaping the benefits of having made their own managerial change early in the season, and of savvy recruitment in a squad that balanced silk with steel. Everton had plenty of the hard stuff themselves, but little of it was constructive and when the intensity of their spirited start inevitably abated, they didn't have sufficient guile to fashion a vital goal.

It was supremely ironic that one of Benitez's most controversial acts (sanctioned, of course, by the club) – namely the sale of Lucas Digne to Villa just days before he they fired him – should come back to haunt the Blues. It was Digne who provided the assist for the game's only goal by Emiliano Buendia from a corner in first-half stoppage time.

Employing a less refined, more direct approach than the visitors, Everton had hoped to make the most of Dominic Calvert-Lewin's aerial prowess and Richarlison's own physical attributes but the pair got little change from Tyrone Mings and Ezri Konsa, particularly in a first half where the Toffees failed to register a shot on target.

It took the introduction of Anthony Gordon, a surprise omission from the starting XI, for Everton to carve out their first genuine goal-scoring opportunity of the contest after just a couple of minutes on the field. Gordon whipped a ball in from the right that Richarlison could only steer high and wide of goal. Three minutes later Ben Godfrey sent a brave header goal-wards, but Tyrone Mings headed off the line.

That was as close as Everton would come to scoring, and with this latest defeat they were now very much in the thick of a battle to avoid relegation – a notion that was unthinkable just a year before, when they had Carlo Ancelotti at the helm and were sitting in fifth place.

The belief that this team was too good to go down wasn't misplaced. It had been stripped of its most creative elements over the previous few months, but there was still talent there if they could harness it under the right system and remain as motivated as they were against a highly-organised Villa side.

Things would probably hinge on the Blues' best players remaining fit, however and the club hopefully making a move to bolster central midfield before the transfer deadline. More than anything, the hierarchy needed to make one of the most important decisions they've ever had to make in terms of a new manager. This was a team crying out for a fresh approach from new eyes, but it would be an appointment that the club could not afford to get wrong.

These were harrowing times to be a Blue, and a hugely important month in the football club's history lay ahead.

Final score: Everton 0-1 Villa

***

After the match, Duncan Ferguson couldn't hide his sadness at not being able to deliver three desperately needed points on his return to the touchline as caretaker boss this afternoon against Aston Villa.

The result, coupled with wins for teams below them that weekend, left Everton hovering precariously above the relegation zone with just one League win in 14 games.

"I think I got a reaction from the players," Ferguson said afterwards. "The first half we were not quite on it. The second half, they had a good go at it and they gave me everything. I could not fault their effort.

"I am on the floor. I am gutted. I was kicking every ball. I am sick for the fans. I was desperate to get the win. I feel for them because I am one of them. It's a bad moment for me."

A couple of hundred Evertonians remained behind in the stands after the final whistle to protest the failings of the Board of Directors and owner Farhad Moshiri. Before kick off, a plane trailing a banner calling for Bill Kenwright to stand down had flown over the stadium and was captured by television cameras.

The interviewer asked Ferguson for his thoughts on the protests.

"The fans, for me, can protest and they can say what they want," he said, "because it's their club at the end of the day, and they have the right to support in any way, shape or form they want. I know how sick they are, believe me. I'm gutted as much as them."

***

As had been the case when Ronald Koeman was sacked, and again when Carlo Ancelotti left, there did not appear to have been a coherent succession plan at place at Everton when Benitez was terminated. 10 days after the Spaniard's dismissal, there was still no clear candidate to replace him; although a shortlist appeared to have three names on it.

One of them, Vitor Pereira took the unusual step on 26 January of pitching his credentials for the Everton job with a live phone call with *Sky Sports*, as the club's search for a new manager verged on farce.

Interviewed by Bill Kenwright nine years previously as a potential successor to David Moyes, the Portuguese's name resurfaced on most occasions that the Goodison hot seat became available.

A journeyman manager since leaving Porto in 2013, Pereira was a controversial candidate with supporters because of his chequered record that includes that short stint with 1860 who were relegated from 2. Bundesliga under his stewardship. He also had a couple of unspectacular stints with Fenerbahçe, won titles in Greece and China, but had no extensive experience or demonstrable success in any of Europe's top five leagues.

Nonetheless, he emerged as the favoured candidate to succeed Rafael Benitez with reports in the media that Everton might announce him as the new Blues boss before the end of that week.

However, amid a backlash from supporters that included graffiti on a wall at Goodison Park against Pereira's appointment and in favour of Frank Lampard, the *Daily Mail*'s website claimed that the 53-year-old was considering withdrawing from the running.

In his conversation with *Sky*, Pereira said he felt his interviews with Everton officials had gone well, and he had laid out what he felt he could bring to the role. He also defended his performance at 1860 Munich five years earlier and implored supporters to look at his overall record.

"I've had more than one interview with different people," he explained. "I think they were enthusiastic about what I proposed to them — an intense, pressing game with possession. We need to give confidence again to these players, to approach the fantastic supporters again.

"I think the first decision from the manager in the club is to bring again the organisation, the way to press and the intensive game I saw a few years ago. To me, to watch at Goodison, to show other teams. Goodison is a fortress, and it's difficult to play.

"They have other candidates. I understand this is the time for decisions. They have told me to wait for the decision and to be calm. They are grateful for interviews and that was all.

"In my opinion, some of the critics are not for me because they do not know me very well. They do not know my work or me personally. I have worked in a lot of countries and at different levels. I've got several titles. I understand the feeling of the supporters because in the last few years they didn't get results.

"Of course, this is the first time in my career that I see this kind of things," he continued, regarding the graffiti at Goodison. "Never in my career have I seen these comments. My CV speaks for itself. I think these [criticisms] are not directly [aimed at] me. It's something to do with [the environment]. I don't take this as a personal attack.

"This passion is the power of the club. The spirit of the supporters can change the game. The passion in football can be on a positive side or a negative side. What a manager should do is bring the positive side.

"If you look at the top managers in the world, we have titles in different countries. Teaching young players. I started my career with 8 years in Porto. In Munich, it was a very difficult money situation. They were relegated because of the money, the money to pay the players. You must look at the titles I've won. You must look at the positives.

"I have built my career with passion, organisation, competence. This is what I can offer to the club. I give 100% of me, football for me is 24 hours. This is my life, my passion. All of my career I have worked under pressure. The pressure is to be at the best level.

"I still want the job, of course. Now it's a club decision. I will move forward with my life. If they want me, they must call me."

***

Another protest against the Everton board by disgruntled fans took place that evening, next to the Dixie Dean statue at the gates of Goodison Park.

Hundreds of fans assembled outside the ground after a tweet was sent out alerting supporters of the proposed action.

Chants of "sack the board!" were accompanied by ironic banners reading "No Status No Optimism" and "School of Silence."

The criticism came against the backdrop of mounting frustration with Everton's owner, Farhad Moshiri, and the Board of Directors for what the fans perceived to be their shambolic stewardship of the club which had left the Blues hovering above the relegation zone and searching for yet another new manager.

Though not organised by the 27 Years Campaign, the group lent their support to the protest and planned to be in attendance. It followed similar protests in the stands after the defeat to Aston Villa, and a display of banners outside Everton's headquarters at the Royal Liver Building.

2022: Moshiri increases Blues shareholding to 94.1%

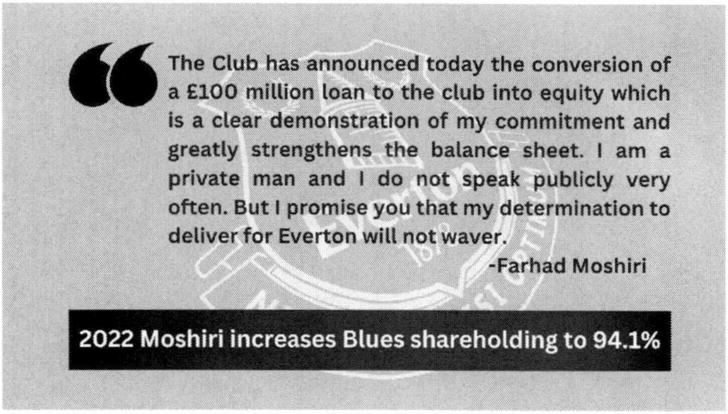

In a personal letter sent to all Official Everton Members and season-ticket holders on 21 January, 2022, Farhad Moshiri announced he had further increased his ownership commitment to the club by converting an additional £100 million in loans to equity in Everton shares. The move increased his majority shareholding in the club to 94.1%.

In the lengthy letter, one that represented rare direct communication with supporters from the Monaco-based billionaire, Moshiri recognised the poor run of recent results that had led to the sacking of

Rafael Benitez and put himself firmly behind Duncan Ferguson, while also referring to the strategic review underway into the footballing side of the club and the search for a new manager. Moshiri's letter also trumpeted the creation of a Fan Advisory Board which was underway in concert with Everton Stakeholder Steering Group (ESSG) and which, with the separate news that the Board intended to amend the Articles of Association so that the commitment to an Annual General Meeting of shareholders was removed, looked as though it would become the prime method of engaging supporters over the long term.

Moshiri's communiqué read in part:

> "I understand the frustration felt by everybody who loves Everton because of our inconsistent form in recent seasons, despite significant investment in the playing squad, The money that has been spent since 2016, not just on the playing squad but also on key projects including our new stadium, demonstrates my commitment to Everton. I write to you to assure you that my commitment remains strong and focused. The Club has announced today the conversion of a £100 million loan to the club into equity which is a clear demonstration of my commitment and greatly strengthens the balance sheet. I am a private man and I do not speak publicly very often. But I promise you that my determination to deliver for Everton will not waver. The strategic football review that is cur-

> rently ongoing will ensure we have the best model in place moving forward. I am working closely with the Chairman and the Board as part of that strategic review - and I can assure you the recruitment process for a new manager is aligned to that. It is vital we appoint a manager that fits the structure we are putting in place and so, whilst we are keen to make an appointment as quickly as possible, we will work together to ensure it is the right candidate to deliver the success we all crave." – Extracted from Farhad Moshiri's Open Letter, 21 January 2022

Meanwhile, chairman Bill Kenwright rejected the core message of protest groups like the 27 Years Campaign and The Originals that the Board was the problem at Everton.

A group of fans had remained behind in the Gwladys Street and Park End stands after the 1-0 defeat to Aston Villa to demand changes at boardroom level at the club.

The frustrated Blues supporters blamed the club's owner, Farhad Moshiri and the members of the Board that included Kenwright and CEO Denise Barrett-Baxendale for the situation that had left Everton facing severe spending restrictions because of the Premier League's profit and sustainability rules, searching for yet another manager, and hovering above the relegation zone following the Rafael Benitez's disastrous tenure.

In mobile phone video shared in a tweet that was later deleted, Kenwright was barracked by fans in Goodison Road after the Villa match with calls of "let go if you love the club" as he made his way to his car. The chairman stopped to confront some of his critics and hear their pleas.

Kenwright agreed that the team's form this season had been "horrible" but when challenged that fans have had to endure 27 years of misery without a trophy, he retorted:

> "It hasn't been 27 years, has it? We've had some good times."

To another fan, he argued that changing the Board "is not the answer."

***

On 28 January 2022, the long-standing requirement that Everton Football Club Company Ltd shall call an Annual General Meeting of shareholders was cut from the Articles of Association provided to Companies House.

For many years, the AGM had been the means by which small shareholders (numbering around 200 people) could express their opinions and concerns about how the club was being run.

But things came to a head with a raucous AGM in 2007 when Bill Kenwright found himself strongly challenged over issues with the previous failed stadium venture known as Destination Kirkby. Kenwright took the unilateral action to suspend AGMs for the next 7 years, denying the small shareholders any voice.

Resolute action by the Everton Shareholders Association forced an Emergency General Meeting in 2013, at which AGMs were reinstated, and had been operating normally until the COVID-19 pandemic, with the AGM in January 2021 being held virtually.

Because of continuing COVID restrictions, the club canvassed shareholders that November for future AGMs to be held virtually if necessary. Several vocal shareholders who saw it as a further limitation to the expression of shareholder opinions met this with resistance.

While publication of Everton's Report and Accounts for 2020/21 was delayed and the expected timing of an AGM for 2021 came and went, the club took an executive decision on AGMs, sending a written resolution to Companies House dated 24 January 2022, rescinding Item 10.1 of the Articles of Association, which read:

10.1: Once in every calendar year, the company shall call a general meeting

However, the rest of Section 10, dealing with Notices of General Meetings, remained in place, suggesting that meetings could be called in the future. They subsequently filed the revised Articles of Association at Companies House.

Instead of AGMs, the club said it was working with selected fan groups already associated with the club — through the Everton Stakeholder Steering Group (ESSG) — to put in place a Fan Advisory Board by the end of the season, as well as instigating some supporter representation at board meetings.

2022: Moshiri praises new manager, Frank Lampard

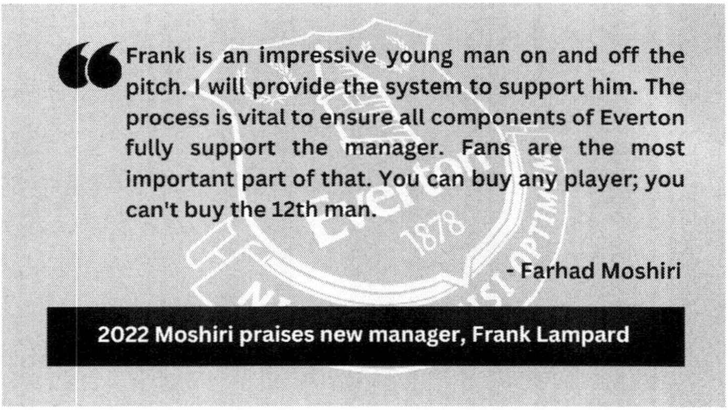

Vitor Pereira's bizarre on-air telephone call with *Sky Sports*, where he had publicly stated his case to become the next Everton manager, had caught many at the club off-guard. That, in combination with supporter sentiment appearing to coalesce around Frank Lampard, may well have taken Pereira out of the running for the position.

Five days later, and more than two weeks after Rafael Benitez had been fired, Everton officially unveiled Lampard as their new head coach, after he had signed the final paperwork on a 2½-year contract.

The then 43-year-old became the sixth managerial appointment since Farhad Moshiri had come on board as the club's major shareholder in 2016.

The makeup of Lampard's backroom had also taken shape, with Joe Edwards handed the role of Assistant Manager, Paul Clement First Team Coach and Chris Jones coming on board at Finch Farm as Head of Performance.

Though rumoured he might step away, Duncan Ferguson remained on the coaching staff, as did goalkeeping coach Alan Kelly. Lampard also offered a coaching position to his former Chelsea teammate Ashley Cole.

"It is a huge honour for me to represent and manage a club the size and tradition of Everton Football Club," a beaming Lampard said at his unveiling as the new boss. "I'm very hungry to get started. After speaking to the owner, chairman and the Board, I very much felt their passion and ambition. I hope they felt my ambition and how hard I want to work to bring it together.

"You can feel the passion Everton fans have for their club. That will be hugely important. As a team — the competitive level that the Premier League brings and the position we are in the table — we certainly need that. It's a two-way thing. I think Everton is a unique club in that you can really understand what the fans want to see. The first thing they want is fight and desire, and that must always be our baseline.

"My first message to the players will be that we have to do this together. We'll try to do our job and I know the fans will be there backing us."

A playing legend at Chelsea where he had a glittering career and established himself as one of the best midfielders of his generation, Lampard had cut his coaching teeth at Derby County whom he led to the final of the EFL Championship play-offs, just falling short of promotion to the Premier League in his first season in charge when the Rams were beaten by Aston Villa.

It was enough, however, to persuade his old club Chelsea to hire him in the summer of 2019 where, in his first season there, he guided the West Londoners to fourth place in the league and into the FA Cup final where they lost to Arsenal.

Despite huge investment in players in the summer of 2020, his second season at Stamford Bridge proved to be more challenging, and with Chelsea sitting outside the Champions League places he was sacked by the notoriously trigger-happy Roman Abramovich and replaced by Thomas Tuchel the following January.

Lampard had been out of work for just over a year when he joined Everton but, according to those close to him, had been keen to get back into management, and had used the time off to reflect on his two previous roles while expanding his coaching knowledge.

He assumed responsibility for a Toffees team that had won just one Premier League match in 14 games and had plummeted from the European qualification places in September to sit just four points above the relegation zone with 18 games left.

The club had moved in the background to address the most pressing issue Lampard would face, namely significant problems in central midfield where Abdoulaye Doucouré, Tom Davies and Fabian Delph were all side-lined for at least a month, by agreeing a loan deal with Manchester United for Dutch midfielder Donny van de Beek who would be the first signing under the new manager. Just before the transfer deadline, the Blues also added fallen Tottenham star Dele Alli to the squad in a complicated deal.

Two young full backs who arrived at the club prior to Lampard's appointment were Nathan Patterson from Glasgow Rangers, in a deal that could ultimately be worth £16 million, and a replacement for the outgoing Lucas Digne by the name of Vitalii Mykelenko, who joined from Dynamo Kiev for a fee reportedly worth £18 million.

Lampard would take charge of training for the first time on Monday 1 February 2022, with the FA Cup Fourth Round tie against Brentford his first assignment at the weekend, before a crucial trip to Newcastle in the Premier League.

Moshiri appeared rarely at USM Finch Farm, but he arrived along with Bill Kenwright to welcome the new boss. The Everton owner called on Everton's fans to give new manager Frank Lampard "that Goodison feeling" and suggested that bringing in a man that supporters could unite behind might be the most important move the club would make this month.

Among the 27 Years Campaign's biggest gripes had been a lack of footballing expertise in key areas of Everton's hierarchy, particularly after Marcel Brands had left both the club and its Board the preceding month. However, striking legend Graeme Sharp had been promoted to the boardroom earlier in January, and there were rumours that Tim Cahill would be appointed to head up a new technical department at Finch Farm, after Moshiri confirmed the Australian was very much involved in the negotiations to bring Lampard in as manager.

"We ensured a lot of expertise went into it," Moshiri asserted. "We had Graeme Sharp, with his vast football experience on our board. Tim Cahill was advising me personally and attending all the interviews. He did very diligent, serious work.

"Our chairman is very important. We are keeping the chairman as long as we can. He manfully fulfils his functions, and I really appreciate what the chairman does."

***

5 February 2022: Everton v Brentford

In contrast to Rafael Benitez's aloof and somewhat dispassionate demeanour, Frank Lampard brought welcome enthusiasm and warmth to Finch Farm and his energy was welcomed by supporters based on the fragments of video of training sessions that were disseminated by the club over its social media channels in the first few days of his tenure.

Telling his players to "enjoy the ball", Lampard offered the promise of a young and hungry manager who could not only transform the mood of a dispirited camp in the short term but might also lay the foundations for a more progressive and successful style of football than had been in evidence under his predecessor.

That feeling was bolstered by his first match in charge as his reign began with a flurry of goals and a first win as the Blues swept Brentford aside to progress to the fifth round of the FA Cup.

The new manager oversaw what would be Everton's biggest win of the season as Yerry Mina, Richarlison, Mason Holgate and Andros Townsend all found the net, rendering Ivan Toney's second-half penalty meaningless.

Lined up in a 3-4-3 formation and exhibiting a more settled passing style and more confidence with the ball at their feet overall, Lampard's side made all the early running in this all-Premier League tie and Mina made the breakthrough from a 30th-minute corner. Demarai Gray swung a dead ball in from the left and Mina won the match-up with his marker to power home a header from six yards out.

The second half was less than three minutes old when Everton doubled their lead. Allan picked the ball up in midfield, chipped it deftly into the path of Richarlison and the Brazilian forward took advantage of the goalkeeper's decision to rush to the edge of his box by knocking it calmly into the open net from 18 yards out.

Brentford responded when Christian Nørgaard picked Ivan Toney out with an excellent defence-splitting pass. The striker smartly left his foot in as Pickford slid across to close him down and referee Michael Oliver pointed to the spot.

Toney sent Pickford the wrong way with his penalty and halved the visitors' deficit, but it would take Everton just eight minutes to restore their two-goal cushion. Gordon's cut-back found Gray, but his shot deflected behind and from the consequent corner, the Blues scored their third.

Once again it was Gray the taker, and when Bech Sorensen got a head to the ball under pressure from Mina, he could only knock it into the path of Holgate, who nodded inside the far post to make it 3-1.

Two late substitutes helped Everton put the gloss on Lampard's day with the Toffees' fourth in stoppage time. Alex Iwobi touched Cenk

Tosun's clever ball inside on to Andros Townsend in the box and the winger had time to pick his spot and whip a shot past the keeper.

It was a perfect start for the new boss, the biggest margin of victory in a first match in charge for an Everton manager since WJ Sawyer, 104 years earlier, and safe passage to the next round.

Final score: Everton 4-1 Brentford

***

Afterwards, Frank Lampard thanked Everton's fans for the terrific reception they had given him, not only for his first match in charge, but all week since his appointment as the club's new boss.

The media asked Lampard afterwards for his thoughts, both on how the team performed and what pleased him most after just a few days' training under the new regime.

"It was the things that we'd talked about in the week and worked on," he said. "I know the players have been through a tough time results-wise, and that knocks confidence.

"So, when you ask certain things of them, like being brave on the ball, and trying to play through the lines like they did for the second goal, that makes me really happy.

"I certainly won't be getting carried away with one win in the FA Cup. We've got big games coming again, particularly in the League as we know, so it's important that the players keep level-headed about it. But there's so many things from today that we can take as positives and take them forward."

Lampard's arrival had given an enormous lift to a fanbase that had felt hugely let down by the hierarchy's decision to appoint Benitez, and four months of dire football under the Spaniard once his initially good start had fallen away.

Goodison gave Lampard a rousing welcome and also applauded the new signings, Donny van de Beek and Dele Alli onto the pitch at half-time, for which the manager expressed his gratitude.

"I can't thank the fans enough for the support I've had before this," he said. "Today was something very special and something I'll never forget.

"Coming to this club last week in difficult times... they've given me messages, the feeling in the city for the last week since we've been here and then the reaction they showed [in the ground] today... that means a lot to me so I thank them for that.

"But what means even more is when they support the team. When we are trying to play, there'll be moments after today when we're trying to do things and sometimes passes may go astray or people are trying to do some different things on the ball...

"But that's the way I want us to go and so we need their support and we absolutely got it today."

***

12 February, 2022: Everton v Leeds

Everton's post-1980s history may have been mostly barren, but Goodison Park has witnessed some truly memorable occasions in that time — the quarter-final victory over Newcastle on the way to the 1995 FA Cup triumph, the vital win over Manchester United under

David Moyes to press the Blues' Champions League qualification hopes 10 years later, impressive home triumphs over United and Arsenal during Roberto Martinez's first season in charge, and the 4-0 thumping of Manchester City under Ronald Koeman, for examples.

In terms of sheer visceral emotion and roof-raising atmosphere, however, many have come in the face of adversity; when Everton's players have needed the unbridled, raucous passion of their fans and the famous Goodison 'bear pit' to help drag them over the line. The 4-4 draw against Liverpool in the FA Cup in 1991 required that the Toffees come back from a goal down four times; Duncan Ferguson's first goal in that famous derby came at a very low ebb for the club, as did his first win as a caretaker manager 25 years later; another famous night under the lights against Fiorentina began with the team 2-0 down from the first leg in Italy; and the two skin-of-our-teeth scrapes against relegation in 1994 and 1998 took place with the Goodison roar behind them. It's proof positive that when the chips are down, Evertonians rally around their side and they would prove it over and over in 2022 and 2023.

Though there were still 17 games to play and 51 points still on offer coming into this fixture against Leeds, there was a feeling that Everton could enter a death spiral of shattered confidence and a horrible losing habit if they were beaten in this game. Their fantastic fans brought their flags, their banners and their voices, and the players responded in spades to ease the immediate threat of relegation battle with a magnificent victory.

There were smatterings of desperation, exasperation and trepidation and helpings of determination, inspiration and motivation all channelled into a super-charged, high-octane performance played out against a deafening Goodison Park atmosphere. This was the Arsenal home game of two months prior cranked up to 11; individual brilliance from that evening augmented by a front-to-back display of unity, cohesion and maximum effort. This was irrepressible front-foot dynamism, high-press intensity and final-third productivity. This was Everton.

Having endured the end of a short-lived honeymoon at St James's Park on the previous Tuesday, when the Toffees had gone down to a 3-1 defeat, Frank Lampard needed a big performance form this new team.

His selection – which left Dele Alli on the bench, dropped Alex Iwobi into the starting XI for only his eighth League start of the season and his first since mid-December, and deployed Jonjoe Kenny as an emergency left-back – was bold but paid off handsomely as the players, in the manager's own words, "delivered".

There were stories of redemption written through this pulsating victory. Iwobi was terrific throughout, tracking back and harrying Leeds players out of their stride in the press, giving and going with teammates and putting in his best performance yet in a Blue jersey.

Kenny, a player on whom the club had given up – his continued presence at Everton only because of a lack of willing suitors - was stellar, operating out of position on the left side of defence. Raphinha, a man looking for this fourth goal in as many games against Everton, was rendered so peripheral that he had to be substituted at half time. The Cruyff turn Kenny executed down by the Leeds penalty area was just further proof that the hometown boy wasn't phased by the weight of the occasion or his unfamiliar role.

In the centre of a defence stripped of arguably its two best members, two players who have had their critics this season rose to the occasion. Michael Keane turned in a rock solid defensive display and stepped into Yerry Mina's set-piece scoring role at the other end. Mason Holgate, at fault for Newcastle's equaliser the previous Tuesday, was composed and assured.

Donny van de Beek, meanwhile, was imperious in the double-pivot alongside Allan, turning in a full-debut display that made his treatment at Manchester United over the past 18 months seem utterly mystifying. Coming deep to collect the ball, an integral part of the press and provider of a "pre-assist" for Everton's opening goal, the Dutchman made an instant impression.

Then there was Seamus Coleman, the long-serving captain who appeared to be at a loss somewhat at the club's latest bout of chaos, and whom many questioned could handle a third game in the space of a week. The Irishman rolled back the years with a swashbuckling display that was epitomised by some committed defensive work at the back and a tenacious 10th-minute diving header on a memorable afternoon.

It was a fine move, too. Coleman began a neat passing exchange that saw Anthony Gordon touch a lovely ball inside two defenders for Van de Beek and when Dominic Calvert-Lewin couldn't quite divert the Dutchman's low cross home under pressure from a defender, the ball sat up invitingly for the skipper to crash it home with a lunging header ahead of Mateusz Klich on the goal line. The importance of the goal, what it meant to him and the catharsis of the moment etched onto his face as he wheeled away towards the Main Stand in clenched-fist celebration.

Everton doubled their lead when Richarlison's determination won them a corner on the right and some clear work on the training ground paid dividends. Gordon swung the set-piece in beautifully as a conga line of blue shirts prepared for its delivery and Keane battled his way to meet it with an unstoppable header.

Unable to maintain the furious pace of the first 45 minutes, the Toffees, understandably, sat off a little in the second half and focused on containing their opponents, which they did with aplomb for long stretches. They restricted the Yorkshiremen to one wayward Dan James effort and a rising Rodrigo shot that would never trouble Pickford's goal and then wrapped up the scoring when Allan laid the ball off to Richarlison. The latter Brazilian danced along the 18-yard line and fired a low shot that crept inside the far post via Gordon's heel, with the goal ultimately awarded to the young winger who had, again, been superb throughout.

With relief having already poured off the stands following the killer third goal, the final whistle was met with jubilation and full-throated renditions of "Grand Old Team" and "Spirit of the Blues" as the players and their new manager milked the applause of a top-class display and massively important victory.

Lampard reiterated afterwards that he was just getting started and the Blues weren't out of the woods yet. But if ever they needed to prove that they were too good to go down, today was the day. Indeed, with a more inspiring figure in charge, together with a team of forward-thinking coaches and more results like this, Everton could start looking forward to a brighter future rather than nervously over their shoulders. And they could do it having reclaimed a lot of their identity as a club.

Final score: Everton 3-0 Leeds.

Man of the Match: The 12th Man

2022: Russian invasion of Ukraine changes everything

> Following a statement that 26 individuals with close ties to Vladimir Putin and the Kremlin would be subject to measures, Usmanov's assets in the EU were frozen, and he was barred from travelling through any member state.
>
> **2022 Russian invasion of Ukraine changes everything**

In comparison with the terrible acts of warfare Russia has inflicted on the Ukrainian people, beginning with the invasion of its neighbour on 24 February, everything else pales into insignificance. However, that was also the day everything changed in Farhad Moshiri's grand plan for Everton.

Just four days later, Alisher Usmanov, the Uzbek-born tycoon who co-owned two of Everton's biggest sponsors, found himself on the list of Russian oligarchs being sanctioned by the European Union. The United Kingdom and United States would soon follow, as the international community levied an unprecedented series of economic and trade sanctions against Russia.

Following a statement that 26 individuals with close ties to Vladimir Putin and the Kremlin would be subject to measures, "In respect of actions undermining or threatening the territorial integrity, sovereignty and independence of Ukraine", Usmanov's assets in the EU were frozen, and he was barred from travelling through any member state.

Usmanov, a Russian citizen who at one time was Britain's richest resident with an estimated £20 billion fortune, was named specifically as a "pro-Kremlin oligarch with particularly close ties to ... Putin. [He] was referred to as one of Vladimir Putin's favourite oligarchs ... [who] actively supported materially or financially Russian decision-makers responsible for the annexation of Crimea and the destabilisation of Ukraine" and "actively supported the Russian government's policies of destabilisation of Ukraine".

Usmanov offered a response in writing in which he said:

> "On 28 February 2022, I became the target of restrictive measures imposed by the European Union. I believe that such decision is unfair, and the reasons employed to justify the sanctions are a set of false and defamatory allegations damaging my honor (sic), dignity and business reputation. I will use all legal means to protect my honour and reputation. I hereby suspend the exercise of my duties as the President of the International Fencing Federation, effective immediately until justice is restored."

According to *The Athletic* at the time, Moshiri, who had always insisted that his investment in Everton was entirely independent of Usmanov, declined to comment on the situation. However, almost immediately, Everton suspended their sponsorship arrangements with three of their key sponsors. Not long afterwards, the club announced that Farhad Moshiri was severing his links with USM Holdings, the Russia-based conglomerate he helped found with Usmanov.

This was a hugely significant move for Everton and it would have lasting and profound implications for Moshiri and the football club he owned.

USM Holdings – the conglomerate that Everton owner Farhad Moshiri chaired and of which Usmanov owned a 49% stake – sponsored the club's Finch Farm training complex and had purchased a £30 million first option on the naming rights for the new stadium at Bramley-Moore Dock. Its subsidiary MegaFon was a key matchday sponsor at Goodison Park and, along with Yota, sponsored Everton Women.

A statement from Everton read:

> "Everyone at Everton remains shocked and saddened by the appalling events unfolding in Ukraine. This tragic situation must end as soon as possible, and any further loss of life must be avoided. The players, coaching staff and everyone working at Everton is providing full support to our player Vitalii Mykolenko and his family and will continue to do so. The Club can confirm that it has suspended with immediate effect all commercial sponsorship arrange-

> ments with the Russian companies USM, Megafon and Yota."

All signage relating to MegaFon was removed from Goodison Park overnight and Everton Women played their next fixture against Aston Villa with blank jerseys after the same company's logo was dropped from their kit.

2022: KEVIN THELWELL APPOINTED AS NEW DIRECTOR OF FOOTBALL

> Following a rigorous search and recruitment process, Kevin was the standout candidate to become our new Director of Football. He brings quality, experience and an outstanding track record for developing young players.
>
> -Bill Kenwright

2022 Kevin Thelwell appointed as new Director of Football

On 25 February 2022, the day after the dreadful news concerning Russia's invasion of Ukraine, but prior to the termination of the club's most important and lucrative sponsorship deals, Everton announced the appointment of Kevin Thelwell as the club's new Director of Football. It was almost three months since Marcel Brands had left the role following a disagreement over the strategic direction of the football club.

For 12 years, Thelwell had held the same position at Wolves having been promoted from Head of Football Development and Recruitment after originally joining the Midlands club from Derby County in 2008 as academy manager.

In 2020, he made a switch to the United States where he assumed the role of Head of Sport at New York Red Bulls. Former Blues favourite, Tim Cahill, may well have played a role in facilitating Thelwell's move to Everton.

As a player, Thelwell represented Northwich Victoria, Winsford United and Congleton Town in a semi-professional capacity after coming through the ranks at Crewe Alexandra and serving an apprenticeship at Shrewsbury Town.

Thelwell had earned his FA/UEFA and FAW/UEFA Advanced Licences and the UEFA Pro Licence, before completing a B.Sc (Hons) degree in Sport Science at Warwick University and fulfilling the role of Director of Coach Education for all of Welsh football. He was arguably more qualified on the football and coaching side than the other candidate who was heavily linked with the Everton job, Steve Hitchen, formerly of Tottenham Hotspur.

According to a statement on evertonfc.com, Thelwell would report directly to the Board of Directors, "acting as the strategic lead for recruitment and all the club's football departments, including First Team, Academy, coaching, sport science, medical services and analysis."

Upon taking the role at Finch Farm, Thelwell said: "I'm so pleased to be joining Everton and to have the opportunity to play a part in the club's ambitious journey. I'm greatly looking forward to working with Frank and the players, and to helping the owner and board achieve their long-term footballing objectives.

"The Owner, the chairman and the CEO all presented compelling reasons for me to join this great club and I am really excited to have the opportunity to work with them all and to move Everton forward. I can't get wait to get started."

Bill Kenwright said of the man credited with identifying and bringing in the likes of Diogo Jota, Ruben Neves, Adama Traore and Leander Dendoncker to Wolves: "Following a rigorous search and recruitment process, Kevin was the standout candidate to become our new Director of Football. He brings quality, experience and an outstanding track record for developing young players."

***

On 12 April, six weeks after Kevin Thelwell's arrival, the club announced that David Unsworth would leave his position as Everton's Academy Director and Under-23s manager, to pursue his ambition of becoming a first-team head coach elsewhere.

Unsworth was originally appointed as Everton's assistant Under-21 manager in 2013 following roles in the Championship, including as assistant manager at Preston North End and Sheffield United.

He progressed into his last role of Academy Director and Under-23 manager and enjoyed success, winning the Premier League 2 title in 2016/17 and 2018/19 the Premier League 2 and Premier League Cup double in 2018/19.

He had also twice taken caretaker charge of Everton's first team — first, at the end of the 2015/16 season and then for 8 games in 2017.

In terms of player development, Unsworth had overseen progression to the first team of several young players, including then regular first-team players Tom Davies, Anthony Gordon, Jonjoe Kenny, Mason Holgate and Dominic Calvert-Lewin.

Unsworth described how hard it would be to leave the club he has represented as a player and coach for 30 years:

"This has been one of the hardest decisions I have had to make in my career," he said. "Everyone knows what Everton means to me.

"However, to give me the best chance of achieving my aspirations and becoming a first team manager, I believe now is the right time for me to move on."

Bill Kenwright said of Unsworth's impending departure: "Since coming back to Everton, Unsie has shown everyone what he is — a great coach, a great Evertonian, and a winner.

"While we're sad to see someone with his talent and love for the club moving on, we completely understand and respect his decision."

It was also announced that former player John Ebbrell would take charge of the Under 23s until the end of the season, as changes initiated by Thelwell at Finch Farm began to roll out.

2022: Everton reveal massive losses for 2020/21

On Tuesday afternoon, 29 March 2022, Everton published their accounts for the financial year ending June 2021, showing losses of £120.9 million on turnover of £193.1 million, the highest losses in the club's history.

Coming on the heels of a record loss of £139.8 million in 2020 and a further £111.8 million in 2019, these amounted to £395.4 million over four seasons, an eye-opening illustration of the financial lengths to which Farhad Moshiri had chased the dream of seeing the Toffees playing in the Champions League. The club would later explain the mitigating circumstances behind these losses, such as COVID and the early-stage costs of building its new stadium at Bramley-Moore Dock.

Indeed, the losses were said to include at least £170 million attributed to the impact on the club of the COVID-19 pandemic, with £103 million of that figure coming in the 2020/21 financial year.

Salaries had risen from £164.8 million to £182.6 million, pushing the club's wages-to-turnover ratio up from an already-high 89% in 2019/20 to a staggering 95% in 2020/21.

Only a financial injection in the form of two share issues by Moshiri — of £100 million in 2020/21, and a further issue of £97 million in January 2022 — had stabilised the club's finances, with Everton reporting current net debt of £58 million.

With top-flight clubs in England restricted to losses of £105 million over a three-year period, on paper than put Everton significantly outside the bound of the Premier League's 'Profitability and Sustainability' rules.

However, having maintained a constant dialogue with the Premier League since the summer of 2021 – discussions that included oversight and sign-off by the league of incoming transfers – the club were insistent that the latest accounts complied with the financial fair play regulations. It believed its accounts were fully compliant, due to allowable deductions for unforeseen losses attributed to the pandemic, continued investment in the new stadium at Bramley-Moore Dock, Everton's women's team, and the club's official charity, Everton in the Community.

Commenting on the accounts, Evertonian and finance expert Paul the Esk wrote:

"The club is caught in a perfect storm of underperformance on and off the pitch whilst funding capital projects, having too big a cost base, and having little idea as to how to grow its commercial income. From a financial perspective, the club is entirely dependent on Moshiri's willingness and ability to keep funding extraordinary losses.

"From a regulatory perspective, i.e., profitability and sustainability, the club is suggesting that, such is the level of COVID-related contributions to losses (£170 million in two years) that the club remains compliant with the Premier League rules. The club has confirmed, as reported here that discussions have been ongoing for a considerable period with the Premier League. The warning signs for the club are there for everyone to see. We have an individual who is prepared to fund these losses, but equally the same individual must be held responsible for allowing the existing board and management teams to perform in such an unsatisfactory manner.

"We are a shadow of the club Moshiri inherited despite his financial backing. He has to address this through bringing in a competent board to run the club without his involvement. A continuation of a deteriorating performance can only result in non-compliant losses and probable relegation despite the progress at Bramley-Moore Dock. This set of accounts can bring no comfort to any Evertonian and should bring no satisfaction to Moshiri."

2022: Everton beat Palace to secure Premier League status

> “The celebrations went on long after the final whistle, only this time the Goodison pitch was a high-decibel mass of jubilant Evertonians; a chorus of relief and joy following an evening of high drama and true Blue spirit.

2022 Everton beat Palace to secure Premier League status

Against a backdrop of all the off-the-pitch developments surrounding Alisher Usmanov, the loss of Everton's key sponsorship deals and the club reporting record losses, team manager Frank Lampard and the players were fighting a battle to preserve the Blues' top-flight status.

The consequences of Everton falling out of the Premier League were potentially disastrous. This was a fact no one seemed to understand better than the club's beleaguered but indefatigable fanbase, who were doing something unique in the history of football over the final few, emotion-fraught weeks of the season.

If the atmosphere at Goodison Park during the emphatic win over Leeds in February had set a new bar for the kind of support and energy that could be transmitted from the stands of the Old Lady to the pitch, the Toffees' fans would find new levels as the weeks went on and victories remained depressingly hard to come by.

Following the Leeds match, Everton had lost four straight games in the Premier League, against Southampton, Manchester City, Tottenham and Wolves, and had struggled to overcome non-League Boreham Wood in the FA Cup Fifth Round. They sat 17th in the table when Newcastle United, resurgent under Eddie Howe and new ownership from Saudi Arabia, came to town.

***

17 March 2022: Everton v Newcastle United

Defeat for the Blues at home to Wolves the previous week seemed to have sapped the morale from the supporters but, perhaps grasping the gravity of a situation that meant even a draw would have done little for the club's parlous position, Evertonians shed their nerves at kick-off and dragged the players through 90-odd minutes of fire, brimstone and controversy. There was even the bizarre interruption of an anti-oil protester, cable-tying his neck to one of the posts early in the second half, to what ended up as one of the most important results and most memorable games in the club's history.

The crowd seemed to live every throw-in, every tackle, every refereeing decision, practically every kick of what was, in truth, an ugly game of football played against the backdrop of gnawing anxiety leading up the game so tangible you could have cut it with a knife. Even as the odds stacked up against the Blues — the loss of Donny van de Beek and Jordan Pickford to illness before-hand, being deprived of kicking towards the Gwladys Street in the second half, and then the infuriating circumstances behind Allan's red card — the fans maintained the volume.

And then... sweet, blessed relief as Alex Iwobi pivoted from being a ceaseless bundle of industry chasing black and white shirts around the park, to the scorer of what was, in truth, a lovely goal and one worthy of settling any game.

In a purely footballing sense, Everton offered desperately little. Newcastle, with the benefit of having had Howe in the job longer than Lampard and with some savvy recruitment having beefed up what was a woeful side prior to January, were more composed and penetrative over the 90 minutes. Yet they came up against the bristling intensity of a Blues team that responded to the urgency of the moment through sheer commitment.

The Magpies didn't shrink from the ferocity of the atmosphere in the way that Leeds seemed to; indeed they gave as good as they got in what was a very physical contest that straddled the line between legal and not. So it was fitting that referee Craig Pawson, having cultivated a permissive stance over the course of the game, only booked Allan for his cynical and late tackle on Allan Saint-Maximin with nine minutes left of the regulation 90.

His decision, however, at the prompting of Video Assistant Referee Stuart Attwell sitting a couple of hundred miles away in Stockley Park, to upgrade that yellow card to red was shocking, and it simply ratcheted up the fury in the crowd, while simultaneously under-cutting what little chance Everton seemed to have of getting the victory they so badly needed.

Newcastle had been denied the chance to make their numerical superiority count by dogged Everton defending by all nine remaining outfield players, and by goalkeeper Asmir Begovic who denied Willock with another good save at his near post.

Then, after future Magpie Anthony Gordon was denied a penalty when barged over in the box, enter Iwobi, the unlikely hero of the hour, a player whose only previous league goals in a Blue jersey had come at Wolves in each of the last two seasons and who was, perhaps, only in the starting XI because of Van de Beek's absence.

Seamus Coleman, who was back to his tenacious best in this game, won a full-blooded challenge against Saint-Maximin, bouncing off the French winger in the centre-circle and moving the ball quickly forward to Iwobi.

The Nigerian glided inside Dan Burn, left him for dead and found Dominic Calvert-Lewin on the edge of the box. He composed himself when it looked like his first touch might have got away from him before turning and laying a lovely reverse pass into Iwobi's path who slotted across the keeper and into the far corner to send Goodison wild.

On the sidelines, Everton's management team erupted, with Lampard admitting afterwards that he might have broken a bone in his hand in the process while the Goodison crowd, which had fought every moment along with the players all night, turned into a mass of limbs.

In the final reckoning of a rollercoaster season, this would prove to have been a vital victory.

Final score: Everton 1-0 Newcastle

***

The win over Newcastle may not have had a transformative effect on Everton's results but it did demonstrate once again to the Toffees' supporters the power of Goodison and the huge role that Evertonians could play in hauling their club away from the trapdoor to the Championship. Frank Lampard's side faced three away games over the ensuing 3 weeks and lost them all, bombing out of the FA Cup at the Quarter-Final stage with a miserable 4-0 defeat at Crystal Palace, one that that had the manager questioning whether his players "had the bollocks" for the fight, and going down to defeats at West Ham and relegation rivals Burnley.

The loss at Turf Moor had been particularly demoralising given that Everton had come back from conceding an early goal to lead 2-1 at half-time, only to then lose 3-2 to an 85th-minute Maxwel Cornet goal. The result closed the gap between the two clubs to a single point in the table with nine games to go. By the end of April 2022, after beating doomed Watford at Vicarage Road by two late goals, Burnley were sitting level on points with Leeds and five above the Toffees who were in the relegation zone.

With third-place Chelsea next up at Goodison, the situation was starting to feel desperate. But Evertonians refused to be bowed and, spurred on by an initiative from supporters groups, they crammed the streets around the stadium before kick-off and filled the air blue with smoke canisters to give the team coach a rousing welcome.

That energy flowed into the stands and fired up the team ahead of a match that, like the one against Newcastle, produced indelible moments, images and a single goalscoring hero. This time it was Richarlison who scored the game's only goal a minute into the second half and celebrated by raising a billowing blue "flare" aloft as he celebrated a vital goal that lifted Everton to within two points of safety with five matches of the season left.

Sent on their way by a unique coach send-off by fans at Finch Farm, a first away win since way back in August 2021 was secured at Leicester City thanks to a stunning volley by Vitalii Mykolenko, the Ukrainian full-back who had been signed to replace Lucas Digne in January, and a winner from centre-half Mason Holgate. All Everton needed to do to virtually guarantee their survival was to beat Watford, a team that was on a club-record 11-match losing run, in their next match; if not, Brentford at home offered another chance to put the issue of relegation to bed.

Unfortunately, a lethargic contest at Vicarage Road ended 0-0 and after a devastating 3-2 home defeat against the Bees four days later, Everton were likely entering the Last Chance Saloon in their last fixture of the season at Goodison against Crystal Palace. Because looming on the final day was a trip to Arsenal and no one of a Blue persuasion wanted to travel there needing anything by way of points.

It called for one last push of passion and energy, blue smoke and thunderous renditions from the Everton catalogue of chants; a collective summoning once more of emotion and devotion; and the use of the power of Goodison Park and all its history to drag this club out of the mire and preserve its Premier League life.

***

19 May 2022: Everton v Crystal Palace

For a third successive home game, fans lined the streets outside Goodison Park to usher the team coach towards the players' entrance and turn the air blue. It was the most vociferous welcome yet for Frank Lampard's team, and the hope was that it would be enough to propel Everton to the three points that had eluded them at Watford and against Brentford in the preceding nine days.

By 8:30pm, the Grand Old Lady was a murmuring shell as Evertonians contemplated a relegation battle going right to the wire at The Emirates four days later, with all the uncertainty and danger that would entail. Everton were 2-0 down at half-time to Crystal Palace following a fairly dreadful first 45 minutes, with many of those lessons from a chastening season seemingly unheeded, as a two-man midfield featuring the struggling André Gomes had been overrun by Patrick Vieira's confident charges, and the Toffees' infamous vulnerabilities at set-pieces were exploited by Jean-Philippe Mateta.

To add insult to injury, another one of those dangerous tackles that were supposed to have been outlawed by the Premier League failed to yield a red card for Jordan Ayew, and the forward would pop up just two minutes after his ugly challenge on Anthony Gordon to bundle in a goal that was horribly reminiscent of Gary Ablett's almost comical own goal against Wimbledon 28 years ago.

But, just like that "That Game" in 1994, the Toffees – more Goodison Gang than Crazy Gang – refused to lie down. Over 45 minutes that are now irrevocably woven into Goodison folklore, amid an atmosphere that somehow surpassed those that had stunned neutral observers in the preceding weeks, they dug down deep and pulled off a thrilling comeback victory. Win number 1,878 in England's top flight... as if written in the stars.

On this occasion, thanks largely to the transformative introduction at half-time of Dele Alli and a decisive switch, from 3-5-2 to 4-3-3, it was enterprising and smooth. Mostly, it was scrappy and ugly; direct, uncompromising, and uncultured football tailored to the desperation of the stakes. Yet it was spirited, visceral and, by the end, pure Everton, as a classic diving headed goal scored by a No.9 in front of the Gwladys Street secured a quite remarkable 85th-minute winner.

This was a night that Dele, a largely forgotten January addition who had remained an enigma after leaving Tottenham, and Calvert-Lewin, a player who had struggled to recapture anything close to his 2020/21 form, joined the ranks of the redeemed.

This was vintage Calvert-Lewin: all committed running, prodigious leaps, flick-ons and chest lay-offs before the decisive lunge to meet Demarai Gray's curling free-kick and bury a header past Jack Butland to spark pandemonium in a stadium that was rocking to its foundations.

Behind him for 90-plus minutes was a cast of tireless heroes, most prominent among them Richarlison and Michael Keane who had scored the goals to bring Everton back from the dead to 2-2, Alex Iwobi who never stopped from start to finish, and veteran captain

Seamus Coleman who atoned for a first-half error to roll back the years to play a vital role in a game for the ages in L4.

And on the sidelines, Lampard got to reprise those fist-pumping, bulging-vein celebrations that marked his arrival at Everton, but this time knowing that he had completed the first part of the massive job he undertook back in January.

Everton had started in the frenetic and adrenaline-charged fashion that had characterised their performances recently under Frank Lampard but in the 21st minute it was 1-0 to Patrick Vieira's side who went ahead. And it came in all-too familiar circumstances for Everton's supporters. André Gomes fouled Jeffrey Schlupp on Palace's left flank and when Eberechi Eze swung the resulting free-kick into the box, Mateta easily got in front of his marker to plant a header past Jordan Pickford from a central position in front of goal.

10 minutes before the break, Ayew doubled Palace's lead amid calamitous defending from Everton. Pickford only parried Mateta's cross away from the goal out to Wilfried Zaha. The 'keeper then got a hand to the Ivorian's bouncing first-time shot. Tragically, the ball span onto Ayew's head. It was he who bundled it over the line, as Mykolenko desperately tried to keep it from going in.

Gomes had once again struggled in a midfield that was being overrun by Vieira's men, prompting Lampard to send Dele out to warm up during the half-time break. The former Spurs man had made sporadic appearances until then, but his impact in the second half was seismic and it was the foul on him that led to Everton pulling a goal back in the 54th minute.

Mykolenko swung in a deep free-kick. Mason Holgate headed it back into the danger area, where Keane took a touch before guiding a lovely left-foot finish into the far corner of Butland's goal.

Demarai Gray replaced the willing but flagging Anthony Gordon to re-inject some pace and verve to the Toffees' attack, Palace briefly rallied, requiring another match-winning contribution from Pickford who batted Mateta's shot behind with a raised glove, and then Everton regained their footing. With 15 minutes of an increasingly bruising contest to go, they were level.

Coleman turned inside his man and clipped the ball to the back post, Dele's cross-shot was knocked back to Richarlison, and the Brazilian dug it out from under his feet before scooping it past Butland with the help of a slight deflection off a Palace leg.

And then, with five minutes of the regulation 90 to go, Everton completed their amazing recovery after Zaha dragged Coleman down, setting up a free kick for Gray to line up on the Blues' right flank.

The winger arced the ball behind the Palace defence and Calvert-Lewin threw himself at it, powering a wonderful diving header home. Goodison erupted and a small, ill-advised invasion of the pitch by ecstatic fans ensured stoppage would stretch beyond seven agonising minutes.

Everton hung on, though, as the home faithful cheered every throw-in and free-kick earned before referee Anthony Taylor blew his whistle and charged towards the tunnel as the stands emptied onto the pitch in unbridled joy at survival achieved.

As they did after the wins over Chelsea and Leicester, the celebrations went on long after the final whistle, only this time the Goodison pitch was a high-decibel mass of jubilant Evertonians; a chorus of relief and joy following an evening of high drama and true Blue spirit.

Police and stewards formed an arc around the dugouts within which the players stayed after fans had mobbed them, some held aloft on the shoulders of supporters. Arm-in-arm, they chanted along with the crowd from the Goodison hymn book and eventually Lampard made his way through bowels of the Main Stand to emerge triumphantly in front of the Directors' Box to bask in adulation.

In his post-match interview, the manager once again struck all the right notes, acknowledging that while Everton hadn't won anything, the supporters' celebrations were an out-pouring of emotion from a fanbase that has gone through a horrible year, looked square in the face of relegation from the top flight for the first time in 68 years, and emerged with their proud membership of the elite intact. And they'd done it all together.

Final score: Everton 3-2 Crystal Palace

***

After the match, Richarlison said Everton's incredible comeback against Crystal Palace, that ensured Premier League survival and ended a turbulent campaign, was one of the highlights of his career.

"The invasion of the crowd was something I had never witnessed in my career," he told *Globo Esporte*. They were all very distressed, worried about the situation, and in the end, it was a relief for everyone to win and escape relegation. It was all very exciting.

"It was one of the most special games of my career. A moment I will never forget. We went through a very difficult situation during the season. There was nothing calm during the year and what remains is the learning of all of us, because a team like Everton can no longer be in a situation like this."

No doubt feeling the effects from the jubilation that had followed the dramatic events of win over Palace, Everton travelled to the Emirates for their final fixture of 2021/22 and were soundly thrashed 5-1. Those Evertonians who had made the trip were in celebratory mood, however, and treated it as a day out and a way to decompress from a frustrating, stressful and emotional season that they hoped would not be repeated for a very long time. Years of costly mistakes and the lack of a clear-eyed strategy and vision for the playing side of the club had nearly cost Everton their place among the elite.

Not all the players who came across with Frank Lampard to the away section, to thank the fans for their unprecedented levels of support, would be around for the reconstruction of the squad that needed to be undertaken. Changes would be demanded at higher levels of the organisation as well.

The Blues had found collective strength in adversity; but would the warnings from 2021/22 be heeded?

2022: Moshiri Apologises in Letter to Supporters

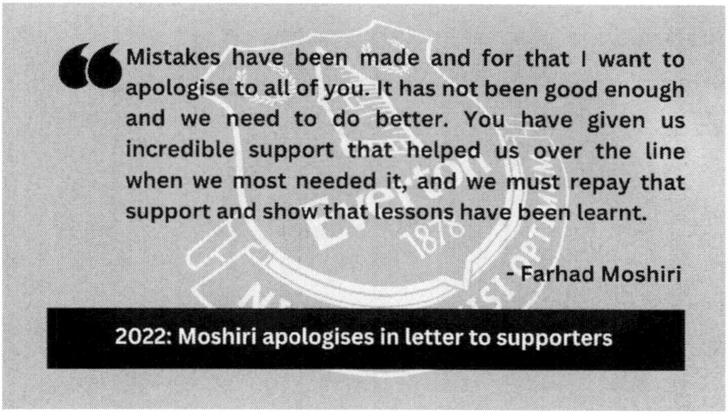

Still under fire from supporters angered by Everton's close call with relegation, Farhad Moshiri, wrote to supporters on 8 June to apologise for the mis-steps that had culminated in a traumatic struggle to stay in the top-flight in 2021/22, and to pledge that the club would do better.

The Iranian-born businessman had been in *de facto* and now *de jure* control at Goodison Park since 2016 and had ploughed historic levels of funds into the club, chiefly on the recruitment of players, many of whom failed to make the grade or improve the team's fortunes.

The massive expenditure, combined with compensation payments to sacked managers and the big hit to revenues that came from the COVID-19 pandemic, had left Everton with historic losses and hamstrung by the Premier League's profitability and sustainability rules.

A mis-matched squad of players proved incapable of dealing with injuries to key players and struggled badly under the management of controversial hire Rafael Benitez, which left the club in danger of being demoted from the top flight by the time the Spaniard was sacked in January. His successor, Frank Lampard, eventually steered the club to safety, thanks in huge part to unprecedented backing from Everton's fans, which had enabled the hierarchy to consider mistakes made and to plan for a more sustainable approach. Moshiri wrote:

> "Mistakes have been made and for that I want to apologise to all of you. It has not been good enough and we need to do better. You have given us incredible support that helped us over the line when we most needed it, and we must repay that support and show that lessons have been learnt. I am committed to securing the future success of the Club by delivering a fully funded stadium that will underpin our status as a leading Club. Of course, the stadium alone will not help us achieve our objectives and we are committed to not making the same mistakes again including how we have not always spent significant amounts of money wisely. During the 2021/22 season, the Board led a strategic review of our operations which included looking at working practices, our recruitment

> process and the whole structure of our footballing operation in order to clearly identify the causes of our under-delivery on the pitch. Many of the learnings have already been implemented."

Moshiri cited the appointments of Frank Lampard and Kevin Thelwell as examples of the new way forward, and he concluded his letter by mentioning the tremendous response from club officials and the fans to Russia's invasion of Ukraine, and the support shown to Vitalii Mykolenko, as well as a planned friendly against Dynamo Kyiv to raise funds for the war-torn country, before signing off with a note of thanks to Evertonians for their unwavering support:

> "Thank you for everything you did to support your Club so brilliantly during such a challenging season. You did not deserve the frustration and fear that the season brought. Your incredible support is never taken for granted and together we move forward."

***

The consequences of the mistakes to which Moshiri admitted, both potential and real, would continue to be felt going forward.

Earlier in May 2022, it was revealed that Leeds United and Burnley had written a joint letter to the Premier League accusing Everton of breaching 'Profitability and Sustainability' rules and asking for an independent commission to investigate Everton's financial situation within six weeks of their correspondence.

The two clubs, embroiled in a battle to avoid the last relegation slot, threatened to start legal proceedings and bring about a claim for substantial damages against Everton and the Premier League, after the Blues reported combined losses of £370 million over the preceding three years. According to the Premier League's P&S rules, a club could lose a maximum of £105 million over a three-year period. Should there be a breach, a club could face sanctions – including possible points deductions for serious breaches.

Everton had responded by saying: "We have worked so closely with the Premier League to make sure we are compliant, and we are comfortable we have complied with the rules. External auditors have told us what we can and cannot claim against the pandemic. If they want to take legal action, then they can do so by all means."

***

Later in the summer, one of the heroes of the preceding season left the club as Everton urgently moved to offset the operational losses incurred in the 2021/22 financial year with the £50 million sale of Richarlison to Tottenham.

Richarlison had, inevitably, become the subject of transfer speculation linking him with a move away from Goodison, and a recent change of agents sparked suggestions he was preparing to leave after four years with the Toffees. Everton's failure to challenge for European football in 2021/22 would prompt him to seek a club that could offer him a better opportunity to in the Champions League. From the club's perspective, his value would significantly reduce their financial deficits and may yet avoid them falling foul of Premier League rules. It was the trade-off for losing a key player and a gamble that Richarlison's goals and general contribution would not be missed too much during the forthcoming season.

2022: KENYON CONSORTIUM FAIL IN BLUES TAKEOVER BID

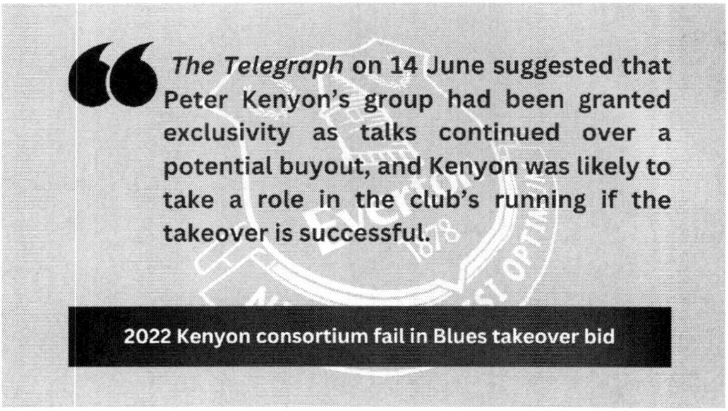

Six years after he had first bought into the club, and with his project at arguably its lowest ebb in that time, media speculation began that Farhad Moshiri would listen to reasonable offers to either buy out his 94% stake-holding in Everton entirely or just a portion of the club.

Moshiri's estimated net worth had reached as high as £2.9 billion at one stage but had taken a hit following Russia's invasion of Ukraine, the resulting personal sanctions against his business partner Alisher Usmanov, and the general impact of the war on USM Holdings.

June, 2022 saw the first concrete reports indicating he was ready to sell up, with *The Telegraph* claiming that Peter Kenyon, the former CEO of Manchester United and Chelsea, was reportedly spearheading a consortium intent on taking over Everton. The consortium, which included the chief executive of Minneapolis-based Talon Real Estate, Maciek Kaminski, and American entrepreneur John Thornton was being advised by investment specialist Michael Klein, along with the U.S. law firm Weil, Gotshal and Manges.

According to the report, the group were already in talks with the Blues' majority shareholder and that the discussions, which initially centred around financing the stadium at Bramley-Moore Dock, had developed into a proposal to buy the entire club outright. While still said to be in the preliminary stages, *The Telegraph* suggested that heads of terms – the first step towards a sale agreement – were already in place, signalling the intent by both parties to progress.

It was said Moshiri valued Everton at over £500 million, a figure that included the club's debts, but *SportsMail* said that Kenyon's consortium was only offering £400 million at that stage.

Furthermore, Kenyon and his partners were apparently seeking assurances that Everton would not be subject to any action from the Premier League, either through a heavy fine or points deduction in relation to breaches of Profit and Sustainability rules. The club had consistently maintained they remained compliant and had comfortable headroom regarding the League's financial regulations.

In his recent letter to supporters, Moshiri had reiterated his pledge to deliver a fully funded stadium, with the rest of the estimated £500 million construction costs also expected to be funded privately. These costs would also have to be factored in by any buyer and would likely affect the price of any buy-out offer, which would, as a result, be the biggest stumbling block to any takeover deal.

Further updates from *The Telegraph* on 14 June suggested that Kenyon's group had been granted exclusivity as talks continue over a potential buyout, and that while Kenyon was likely to take a role in the club's running if the takeover is successful, it was Kaminski who was "providing the greatest financial weight behind the bid".

***

By the end of the month, however, the deal was dead in the water. The U.S.-backed consortium did not have its period of exclusivity extended beyond 30 June, and its bid to take the club did not proceed any further, with *The Athletic* reporting that Moshiri had walked away from the talks with the American investors having lost faith in their ability to fund the buyout and cover the cost of the new Everton stadium.

According to *The Times* and *The Liverpool Echo*, it was understood Moshiri would now be "moving on from discussions with Peter Kenyon's group." Meanwhile, Moshiri reportedly maintained his commitment to delivering the club's new ground at Bramley-Moore Dock, but would still entertain advances from investors who would help fund the stadium.

He also apparently intended to focus on strengthening Frank Lampard's' playing squad over the summer of 2022, following the sale of Richarlison to Spurs.

According to *The Athletic*, however, the Kaminski camp remained keen on extending their period of exclusivity to undertake full due diligence of Everton's accounts.

Liverpool Echo journalist Dave Powell passed on the Kaminski family's' stance via Twitter, saying:

"I'm told by [the] Kaminski group that their position hasn't changed and that 'paperwork was exchanged overnight' with regards to exclusivity extension. [The] group say the situation hasn't' changed despite reports to the contrary and that they remain 'the only show in town.'

If the deal was dead as suggested, the news came just days after reports suggesting that Kaminski had visited Merseyside, and that Maciek and his son planned to be installed as directors on Everton's Board while Kenyon was eyeing the role of Executive Chairman in place of Bill Kenwright. All the while, however, there was reported interest from other parties, perhaps from the Middle East and the Far East, although no concrete details were revealed.

2022: STRIKER-LESS EVERTON IN DREADFUL START TO NEW SEASON

> “We need to make sure [we’re not back in a relegation fight come March] for those supporters who are travelling down every single [game] to watch us play in Bournemouth or Newcastle or wherever it may be. We’ve got a lot of learning to do and we’ve got to do it quickly.
>
> \- Conor Coady

2022 Striker-less Everton in dreadful start to new season

By the summer of 2022, few Evertonians were under any illusions as to the difficult conditions under which their club was operating. That Richarlison's transfer to Tottenham had gone through on the final day of Everton's 2021/22 financial year was indication enough that the Blues had needed to sell to satisfy Premier League Profit and Sustainability rules. Given those constraints, whether, and to what degree, the club would be able to replace the talismanic Brazilian was a different question.

It was a situation compounded by Dominic Calvert-Lewin's ongoing injury problems which were very much in line with the adapted cliché: sometimes it feels like if it weren't for bad luck, Everton would have no luck at all. The club, under Farhad Moshiri's stewardship, had rightly been criticised for poor recruitment decisions and profligacy in the transfer market, but it was also cursed by a succession of serious injuries that had robbed the Blues of key — or potentially key — players for long periods.

James McCarthy's and Seamus Coleman's double leg breaks, Yannick Bolasie's torn ACL and meniscus, André Gomes's sickening ankle fracture dislocation, Jean-Philippe Gbamin's thigh and Achilles woes, successive knee injuries to Cenk Tosun (not a key asset, of course, but a saleable one) and, more recently, Dominic Calvert-Lewin's quad tear, all of these formed the bulk of a sorry list of serious injuries to have befallen Everton players over the past few years.

***

6 August 2022: Everton v Chelsea

The season opener against Chelsea was a chance to see whether Everton's fortunes were about to improve. Alas, it was not the case.

Yerry Mina had been available for less than half of the games for which he was eligible since arriving from Barcelona in 2018, due a frequency of his injuries that had become almost tragically comical over the past 12 months. A £27 million signing and arguably Everton's best centre-half, through no fault of the club's, he played in just 11 of 38 Premier League games in 2021/22. And, after "crocking" himself again in the season opener against Chelsea, he would make just seven more starts.

Then there was Ben Godfrey, who had battled COVID and a torn hamstring, worked his way back to full fitness and was rewarded with a starting role for this game, only to break his leg inside ten minutes. The footballing gods were evidently amusing themselves at Everton's expense.

At least in Godfrey's position, Frank Lampard had replacements on whom to call, and against Chelsea he drafted in Mason Holgate, who continued the run of good form he had had since the new manager took charge at the end of January.

Up front, of course, Lampard was pitifully short on options: with Richarlison sold to Spurs in June, Calvert-Lewin missing, and Ellis Simms out on loan, he didn't even have Salomon Rondon as an alternative. That left him trying to fashion a forward line geared for pace on the counter-attack against a superior opposition and, rather than deploy Dele Alli as a false nine, he plumped for Demarai Gray and Anthony Gordon as the two most advanced forwards, with Dwight McNeil making his debut in support.

Predictably enough, the Toffees struggled in attack without a genuine focal point and, with neither Gray nor Gordon renowned for their consistency of end product in the final third, they carved out few clear-cut scoring opportunities. And as if to remind Goodison of the large DCL-shaped hole in attack, some tempting deliveries into the box would go begging; particularly in the first half. You felt that, had the No 9 been there, Everton might have scored and won this fixture for a fifth successive season.

Ultimately, though, the contest was settled by one moment of clumsiness by the otherwise impressive Abdoulaye Doucouré, and a controversial penalty award.

Everton had been doing a decent job of keeping the visitors at bay and restricting them to half chances and dead-ball opportunities but their good work and that of Doucouré was undone deep into the time added on for Godfrey's injury. Raheem Sterling jinked into the box and was clumsily barged over by the Mali international, leading Craig Pawson to point to the spot.

Though Mina and Pickford did their best to put him off, Jorginho made no mistake with the penalty, sending the keeper the wrong way.

Doucouré had a shot from around ten yards out saved well by Edouard Mendy in the Chelsea goal early in the second half but, on the whole, the Blues struggled to create chances.

Thomas Tuchel's men, meanwhile, had resorted to delaying tactics and time-wasting. They barely threatened Pickford's goal until seven minutes from the end of the regulation 90 when Vitalii Mykolenko made a goal-saving intervention to prevent Sterling from putting the game to bed off Marc Cucurella's cross.

It was easy to dwell on the disappointment of a rare opening-day defeat — that was Everton's first loss in their first game of a new season for 11 years — and to miss the elements of this performance that were genuine cause for optimism.

The Blues' passing was crisper and more accurate than was the case the season before, and they played their way through the lines with a confidence and efficiency that was almost entirely absent by the time they sacked Rafael Benitez in January.

James Tarkowski had slotted right in and cut an assured, leader-like figure at the back; Nathan Patterson made a hugely promising Premier League bow, displaying some exciting attacking instincts while betraying some rawness against the trickery of Sterling; the defence faced a dizzying succession of corners but held firm where last season they would surely have conceded; and Alex Iwobi continued his unforeseen but massively welcome rebirth as a midfield play-maker under the new boss.

At first blush, and contrary to some neutral observers' dire prognostications, the 2022/23 edition of Everton didn't look doomed to another battle against relegation; however, the rest of August and what lay beyond would provide far more worrying signs.

Final score: Everton 0-1 Chelsea

***

After the match, it was revealed that Godfrey had fractured his tibia and would face months on the side-lines.

The Blues suffered a double blow in the game, with Godfrey's central-defensive partner Mina sustaining yet another injury, this time to his ankle, that would side-line him for a period of months.

***

With young defensive prospect Jarrard Branthwaite out on loan, it left Lampard with only three fit senior centre-halves. Two days later came the news that Frank Lampard and Kevin Thelwell had secured much-needed central-defensive cover with the acquisition of Conor Coady from Wolves on an initial loan deal, with an option to buy the following summer.

"I'll give absolutely everything, every day, for this football club," Coady told evertontv in his first interview:

"I feel privileged and lucky to be given this opportunity. We want to be sure we're going out and making supporters happy and improving the club at the same time.

"I'm someone who was desperate to come here, to play for this club. I know how big it is and I know the passion people have for Everton. It's an important day and a proud day for me to get it over the line.

"As soon as I heard the interest from the manager but also the Football Club itself, I really wanted to be part of it straight away. I'm over the moon to join.

"I've grown up around the city," the St Helens-born, former Liverpool youth player continued. "I know the Football Club, how big this club is and what it means to the fans."

Coady brought with him a wealth of Premier League experience, reliability and, like James Tarkowski who had been drafted in on a free transfer earlier in the summer, leadership qualities from having been captain at his previous club.

While Idrissa Gueye's slow-motion return to Goodison Park from Paris Saint-Germain continued, amid reports that the Senegal international was undergoing a two-part medical in France and was awaiting international clearance to travel to Merseyside, Everton landed their biggest signing of the 2022 close season in the form of Amadou Onana from Lille.

Having beaten off competition from David Moyes's West Ham, the Blues negotiated a £33 million deal involving a low up-front payment in return for additional appearance-related add-ons and a sell-on clause benefitting the French club.

Tall, rangy and still only 21, Onana was a recently-capped full Belgian international and widely regarded as one of the finest central prospects in Europe. As such, it was something of a coup for Everton, and Lampard was delighted to bring him on board.

Transfer deadline day saw Gueye's protracted return finalised for around £2 million and highly-rated young midfielder James Garner arrive for an initial fee of £9 million. Yet it was the lack of effective cover for Dominic Calvert-Lewin at centre-forward that remained a vexing issue for supporters.

Thelwell and his recruitment team had tried for weeks to strike a deal with Southampton for Che Adams but were put off by a lofty asking price, reported to be as high as £20 million. An approach to take Guinean international forward Serhou Guirassy on loan failed when Rennes insisted on a permanent cash deal instead and nothing came of rumoured interest in the likes of Samuel Chukwueze of Villarreal, Joao Pedro of Watford or Ben Brereton Diaz of Blackburn Rovers.

However, Everton almost pulled off one of the signings of the summer when they came to the brink of capturing Mohammed Kudus from Ajax Amsterdam. In what was, perhaps, one of those sliding doors moments in terms of Lampard's future at the club, a proposed loan deal for the exciting Ghana international looked to have all but been arranged when the Dutch club pulled the plug.

In parallel to their talks with the Toffees, Ajax were also negotiating the blockbuster sale of winger Antony to Manchester United for around £85 million and once that was agreed, they insisted they had no interest in losing both of their star attacking midfielders in the same transfer window.

Kudus temporarily went on strike and refused to train in an effort to force through a move to Goodison Park, but the matter was resolved at Ajax a few days later and Evertonians had to watch him turn heads at the World Cup in Qatar three months later, and wonder at what might have been.

In the end, the only forward who arrived at Everton was Neal Maupay from Brighton & Hove Albion in a deal worth a reported £12 million. Prolific at Brentford in the season they won promotion to the Premier League, Maupay had been less successful with the Seagulls where he was averaging a goal every four games, a far cry from what Everton needed.

Nevertheless, the Frenchman was, at least, a nominal striker who, it was felt, might be able to bring some of the qualities that Richarlison offered in terms of work-rate and generally being a pest in opposition penalty areas.

Nottingham Forest, who were in the midst of a record overhaul of their squad in preparation for their return to the Premier League after two decades in the second tier, had apparently agreed a reported £15 million fee with Brighton for Maupay. But once Everton's interest became known and Lampard spoke with the player personally to convince him to join his project at Goodison Park, the 26-year-old's mind appeared to be made up.

"Everton is a great club with unbelievable fans and I am so, so happy to be here," Maupay said. "It feels amazing.

"It was an easy choice for me when I started to talk with the club. I knew straight away I wanted to play for Everton and help the club to succeed."

Frank Lampard expressed his satisfaction at having added a much-needed attacking option to his squad, while he awaited Calvert-Lewin's return to fitness from his knee injury.

"We're delighted to bring Neal to Everton, a player of proven quality in the Premier League. We wanted to strengthen our attacking options and Neal provides a goal-scoring threat, as well as bags of energy and a fighting spirit that are vital to what we're building."

Much to the fans' chagrin, Everton had already played four Premier League matches without a recognised striker, with Lampard forced to mend and make do with Anthony Gordon and Demarai Gray as forwards. Infuriatingly, because of the late August Bank Holiday and a bizarre ruling that required player registrations to have been completed one full working day before the next match, it would be one more game before Maupay could come in.

The new signing was forced to watch from the side-lines as Everton took the lead at Leeds, but the Blues couldn't hold on to claim their first victory of the new season and had to settle for a draw.

***

18 September 2022: Everton v West Ham

No one had really wanted to put too much emphasis on one match, but with an international break coming up and an always tricky away game at Southampton looming on the other side of it, Everton really needed to beat the Hammers and earn their first win of 2022/23.

With defeats against Chelsea and Villa, and draws against Forest, Brentford, Leeds and Liverpool, three points were urgently needed. Another draw wouldn't have been catastrophic, of course, but to have completed a fifth of the season without picking up a victory would have been an unsettling return for the Blues in view of the previous season's close call with relegation.

As it was, they battled their way to a 1-0 victory, reversing the scoreline from the corresponding fixture the previous season, on the back of Neal Maupay's first goal for the club.

Everton didn't get much change from referee Michael Oliver but their luck held once more — an opposition player struck the post for the seventh time in four games but the ball again stayed out — and though there were a couple of other scares late on, they largely held the visitors at arm's length, with the defensive quartet of Nathan Patterson, Vitalii Mykolenko, James Tarkowski and, newly installed as deputy captain, Conor Coady excelling when it mattered in the closing stages.

Idrissa Gueye came into the starting XI for his first start since returning from Paris Saint-Germain and formed part of a midfield three that helped cancel out the visitors, but this wasn't a performance that would live long in the memory. Everton managed just two shots on target in the 90 minutes, both coming early in the second half and their forward play was often let down by the final ball. Indeed, neither side managed an effort on target until the stroke of half time, when Asmir Begovic comfortably caught a header from Kurt Zouma.

West Ham had the first chance of the second period when Pablo Fornals got to the byline and centred for Bowen, but he swept a first-time effort narrowly over. Soon afterwards, the lively Demarai Gray was involved in the game's only goal.

He knocked a neat pass inside to Alex Iwobi who then picked Maupay out on the edge of the penalty area. Having gathered the ball with a tidy first touch, the Frenchman fired a crisp shot wide of Fabianski and inside the near post to hand Everton the lead. He didn't know it then, but it was the only goal he would score for Everton all season.

The Londoners came very close to grabbing a point when Gueye lost the ball and Said Benrahma advanced towards goal before curling an effort around Begovic. The Bosnian keeper watched it bounce off the inside of his right-hand post and fly across goal before being cleared.

Begovic pushed Maxwel Cornet's shot behind and had to tip a sliced Jarrod Bowen cross over in stoppage time as the Toffees held out to claim three points that lifted them away from the bottom three.

As Lampard remarked afterwards, "there's a good feeling about the place."

The Blues still hadn't scored more than once in a game so far that season, and it looked as though goals would continue to be scarce, at least until Calvert-Lewin came back into the side. But the graft, the solidity and the character was there to suggest that the club could start looking upwards rather than over their shoulders.

Final score: Everton 1-0 West Ham

***

Three weeks before the 2022/23 edition of Everton v Crystal Palace, the club received a £300,000 fine for the two incursions onto the pitch by their supporters during the club's emotional win over the Eagles in May. Fans came onto the field in the 85th minute when Dominic Calvert-Lewin scored the dramatic winner at the Gwladys Street End, the goal that secured Everton's place in the Premier League, and then again in celebration after the final whistle.

Though there had been no physical altercations between supporters and opposition players, the Football Association cited 'threatening and violent behaviour from fans' as justification for the unprecedented financial penalty - a reference, perhaps, to the goading of Patrick Vieira that prompted the Palace manager to kick out at one individual fan.

Merseyside Police spoke to both Vieira and the supporter and, along with the FA, took no action over the incident. But, to show a strong hand in trying to crack down on pitch invasions, the game's governing body acted retroactively with a steep fine, after a hearing chaired by David Philipps KC – a lawyer who would later be selected to chair the Premier League's Independent Commission over Everton's alleged breaches of Profitability and Sustainability Rules.

The incidents at Goodison Park in May had been just one instance of fans pouring into the pitch after a game — similar incidents occurred at Nottingham Forest, with one supporter charged for assault for a head-butt on Sheffield United's Billy Sharpe, and at Manchester City, where home fans confronted opposition goalkeeper Robin Olsen.

***

22 October 2022: Everton v Crystal Palace

With November approaching, Everton had only managed three goals in their five matches at Goodison Park, but against Crystal Palace they doubled their home goals tally for the season in some style, putting three past their opponents for the second time that year.

There were many pleasing aspects to this performance: Dominic Calvert-Lewin was fit, firing and back among the goals; Anthony Gordon was demonstrating the marauding and tenacious form he had shown in the second half of the previous season; Seamus Coleman kept Wilfried Zaha in his back pocket; and Alex Iwobi was absolutely revelling again in his roving midfield role, weighing in with two assists – the second a delicious back-heel to present Dwight McNeil with the Blues' third goal.

After a seven-game unbeaten run had taken them to the brink of the top half at the start of the month, three successive losses, to Manchester United, Tottenham and Newcastle, had the potential to send the Blues into a bit of a tailspin. Coming into this game, the bottom three was looking ominously close again.

Lampard needed a big performance, back in front of a highly charged home crowd, and he got it with a high-intensity start that yielded an opening goal that was all down to Calvert-Lewin's physicality.

The 25-year-old dispossessed Luka Milivojević ten yards outside the Palace box. When Iwobi threaded the ball back to him, Calvert-Lewin took a neat touch past Marc Guéhi, then had the strength to hold the defender off before drilling a shot across the goalkeeper, Vicente Guaita, who couldn't prevent it from finding the far corner.

Palace were being kept very much at arm's length in the first half but Vieira's men came out of the half-time interval the more purposeful of the two sides. Everton re-asserted their dominance not long after the hour mark with a superbly-worked goal. It started with a goal kick in their own half, involved some confident passing out from the back and a lovely pass from Iwobi through the lines to Gray, whose pass to Amadou Onana found Mykolenko arriving in acres of space on the overlap.

Guaita got a hand to the Ukrainian's low shot but could only palm it into the path of Gordon, who had the simple task of knocking the ball into the empty net. The referee's assistant had raised his flag for offside, but a check by VAR resulted in what was clearly the correct decision — a second goal for Everton.

Dwight McNeil entered the fray in a 72nd-minute change and he took the invitation to drive at the Palace defence. He slipped a pass into the box for Iwobi, who deftly back-heeled it back into the winger's path and McNeil tucked it home to make it 3-0.

It was a lovely goal that underlined how good the side could be when it had its tails up and was in full flow. It wouldn't happen very often that season – all too often the Blues had been tentative and bereft of attacking invention – but what was the most complete performance under Lampard since the win over Leeds in February, had the potential to serve as a benchmark for future home matches, as the manager looked to take his side to the next level.

Final score: Everton 3-0 Palace

***

12 November 2022: Bournemouth v Everton

For a club that had become synonymous with false dawns, the handsome win over Palace and the slick nature of it proved to be yet another flash in the pan. No one knew it at the time, but it would be almost 12 months before Everton would once again score more than a single goal in a match at Goodison Park.

A dull but creditable goalless draw at Fulham had followed a week later, but when struggling Leicester came to Merseyside and left having collected three easy points with a 2-0 win, the alarm bells started ringing for the Blues' long-suffering supporters.

Worse was to follow with two trips to Bournemouth in the space of four days, one in the Carabao Cup and one in the Premier League, after which doubts started to solidify about Lampard's ability to steer the club clear of relegation for a second season.

The performance from a much-changed side in the cup-tie, against an equally under-strength Cherries side, had been abysmal. Yet there was hope that, when those first-choice players that were fit to play were reinstated for the second fixture between the two clubs at the Vitality Stadium, things would be a lot different.

They weren't. Far from making amends, the Blues left the south coast having been comprehensively beaten again by a Bournemouth team that hadn't won a league game in five attempts coming into the weekend, and who wouldn't taste victory again for another eight matches. Another chastening defeat meant the Blues were hovering above the relegation zone going into the six-week break for the 2022 World Cup.

A horrible mistake by Jordan Pickford gifted the Cherries the opener in the 18th minute. Dominic Solanke's cross was inexplicably batted into trouble by the England goalkeeper and Marcus Tavernier gratefully seized on the loose ball to knock it into the empty net.

11 minutes after that it was 2-0 as the Toffees failed to deal with a corner but then stopped to appeal for referee Craig Pawson to halt play for a clear head injury to Tarkowski. The official allowed play to continue, Pickford parried Phillip Billing's shot away, but when Tavernier put the ball back into the six-yard box, Kieffer Moore was there to power a header in from close range.

Everton didn't manage their first shot on target until the 40th minute, a fairly tame shot from Alex Iwobi that was comfortably gathered; while Maupay's appeals for a penalty in first-half stoppage time fell on deaf ears where Pawson was concerned.

The Toffees produced arguably their most dangerous moment of the contest shortly after half-time, when Amadou Onana laid the ball back to Idrissa Gueye who blazed over rather than work Travers in the Bournemouth goal.

But any hope that the visitors had of clawing their way back went out the window with 20 minutes left. Lewis Cook swung a free-kick into the Blues' box and with no one tracking the runner, they left Jaidon Anthony unimpeded to head powerfully past Pickford to make it 3-0.

The defeat left Everton going into the break for the World Cup sitting just two points off the bottom three. The manager's inability to find any consistency from his players, and the erosion of the defensive solidity that had been one of Everton's strengths earlier in the season, were the larger concerns looming over the team.

Final score: Bournemouth 3-0 Everton

***

Afterwards, Conor Coady was scathing in his assessment of how Everton had collectively performed at the Vitality Stadium, saying that it was "shocking."

"[I]t's nowhere near good enough from our point of view," the Wolves loanee said. "I don't want to speak about it, to be honest — the referee's done his job today and, whatever... Listen, we speak about referees after every game and I'm certainly not going to do that when we've put out a performance like that against Bournemouth.

"So, no, I'm not going to speak about the second goal. I'll speak about the performance and it was nowhere near good enough. It was nothing that represents an Everton team, that represents Everton Football Club, that represents our supporters; so one hard look in the mirror for everyone of us that plays for this football club."

Asked what the desperately poor team display was down to, Coady replied flatly: "Personal pride; standards; we have to set standards every day in training. It's not just about today; it can't be anything to do with the manager, his staff; it's nothing to do with that.

"It's up to us as players to have standards, to have personal pride in what we do every single day and we don't have that at the minute. So we have to make sure we have that because things like [today] are going to happen. So we need to look at ourselves long and hard... because it was shocking and nowhere near good enough.

"We've got to look at it because we've got a second half of the season where we have to be better, no matter what. We can't go into the second half of the season like that without a long talk in the dressing room in terms of what's going on and what needs to be done.

"[Bournemouth] wanted it more than us. [We're] massively short of where we need to be because this is Everton ... and we're not representing that as a team or as a club for the supporters.

"We need to make sure [we're not back in a relegation fight come March] for those supporters who are travelling down every single [game] to watch us play in Bournemouth or Newcastle or wherever it may be. We've got a lot of learning to do and we've got to do it quickly."

Referring to the uncomfortable scenes after the final whistle where those players who went over to the away supporters were booed by the Everton fans, Coady said:

"Today, for me, will take a lot of time to get over, if I'm being honest, because that feeling out there on the pitch at the end was absolutely horrendous. We need the supporters behind us, but how can we expect them to be when we're [playing like] that?"

2022: 27 Campaign writes to Moshiri demanding change

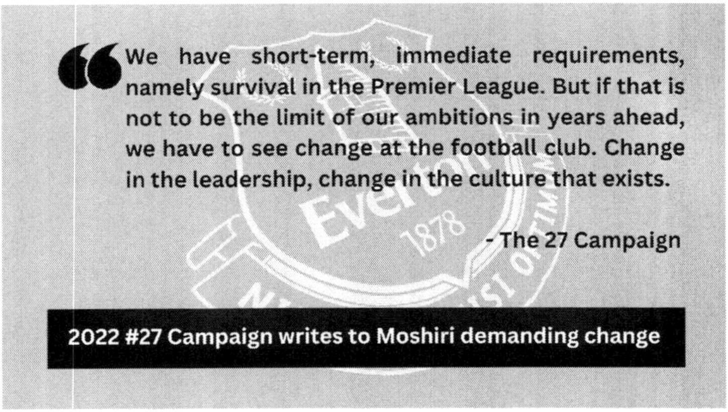

As the World Cup reached its Quarter Finals stage in Qatar, the 27 Campaign group released a second open letter to Farhad Moshiri, in which they outlined finances, ownership, leadership and direction as the main concerns that "directly relate to [Everton's] performance on the pitch" and which they wanted to see urgently addressed.

As part of that, the 27 Campaign (so-called because 2022 marked 27 years since the Blues had last won a trophy) was agitating for a change in the leadership of Everton – the group had highlighted a boardroom shake-up as one desired development they wanted to see happen – as well as a change in culture at the club.

The full letter read:

> Dear Mr Moshiri,
>
> **Change required:** Since our open letter in July 2022, we respected your request to all Evertonians to "judge you at the end of the (summer) window". We gave you the benefit of the doubt. We have continued to provide the manager, Frank Lampard, his team and the players, the very highest levels of support particularly on match days, home and away. A year ago, the 27 Campaign was formed to highlight the time since our last trophy win. Our actions, alongside other fan groups, then and since are driven by concerns as to the financing, ownership, leadership and direction of our great club. We believe that issues surrounding finances, ownership, leadership and direction directly relate to our performance on the pitch. Regrettably, given the absence of communications and any degree of change in the running of the club, we have in an open letter format, to ask you the following questions:

Finances: Other than the minimum statutory requirements, the club provides no information on its finances. On the back of constructing a new stadium, having extensive, continued losses, and profitability & sustainability issues, it is reasonable for shareholders and fans to expect regular updates on our finances. Our finances directly relate to our ability to compete. **Ownership:** Since the summer, messaging from the club has been confused. Is the club for sale? Are you seeking new investors to fund our working capital requirements? Other Premier League clubs seeking new investment or owners have appointed investment banks to handle their requirements. They have been clear with their communications. What is your intention, what are you doing, and when will you communicate it clearly? **Leadership:** In the near seven years since you acquired your initial shareholding, you have persisted in retaining the current Chairman and Chief Executive Officer. There is nothing in the club's governance, commercial, financial and indeed footballing performance, that suggests they warrant continued employment. As a result of huge losses and the squandering of resources, our competitive position declines on an annual basis in all respects. How can you justify their performance? **Direction:** What are your ambitions (if any) for the club?

The building of a new stadium, in isolation, will not cure the ills that have befallen Everton in recent years. So much more is required for us to be a competitive Premier League and ultimately European competitor once more. We have short-term, immediate requirements, namely survival in the Premier League. But if that is not to be the limit of our ambitions in years ahead, we have to see change at the football club. Change in the leadership, change in the culture that exists. You, as the majority shareholder, are the only person who can bring about that change. Surely you, with the financial commitment you have made, must recognise that change is necessary? With respect, we ask you to directly answer the questions put to you. Tell us what changes are to be made to change the direction the club is heading.

Yours Sincerely, The 27 Campaign.

***

26 December 2022: Everton v Wolverhampton Wanderers

Everton returned to competitive action, looking to set a very different tone to the one with which they went into the break for the World Cup in mid-November. They emerged from Boxing Day with a fourth successive defeat in all competitions, as the bottom club Wolves won this tense 'six-pointer' in stoppage time.

Julen Lopetegui picked up his first win as the Black Country club's new manager in his first game at the helm thanks to substitute Rayan Ait-Nui's last-gasp goal, while the Blues' boss, Frank Lampard, hustled down the tunnel with Goodison Park's frustrated boos in his ears at full-time.

Everton had their chances to put this game to bed long before a poor Wolves outfit caught them cold on the break in the final minute of time added on, but wastefulness plagued their attack, which was creating and scoring precious few goals.

Yerry Mina, playing instead of the ineligible Conor Coady, had settled the nerves of a shaky start by heading in what was Everton's first goal that came directly from a corner all season after just six minutes, glancing his header across Jose Sa and into the far corner of the goal.

However, Wolves hit back 15 minutes later with a corner routine of their own, as the ball was pinged to Joao Moutinho on the edge of the box. Rather than have a crack at goal, the Portuguese lofted a clever ball over a static defence where Daniel Podence arrived completely unmarked to guide it past Pickford and make it 1-1.

Everton's best chance of the rest of the contest arrived 11 minutes before the break when Idrissa Gueye made a fine interception and immediately threaded the ball through to Anthony Gordon in the box, where the young winger took one touch and tried to tuck it past Sa, but the Portuguese pushed his shot away one-handed.

Then, in the 42nd minute, a loose touch from Nathan Collins gifted possession to Maupay, but the striker fired another great chance straight at the keeper.

The onslaught for which the Goodison faithful were baying in the closing stages never came, with Lampard's charges continually recycling the ball in injury time rather than trying to play the percentages with a target man spearheading the attack.

There was a cruel irony, however, that as soon as they shed their inhibitions with one final attack and lost the ball on the edge of the opposition area, a sucker punch hit them hard. Wolves tore away on the counter-attack with numbers, Adama Traore centred and Rayan Ait-Nouri took a touch to set himself in front of goal before lashing it home.

It was a harsh and dispiriting end to a game that had been billed as must-win for an Everton side who would be in the bottom three when they travelled to the home of the champions, Manchester City on New Year's Eve.

The result also heaped more pressure on Lampard to solve his side's timidity and profligacy, and on Kevin Thelwell to bring in attacking reinforcements as a matter of dire urgency when the transfer window opened.

Final score: Everton 0-1 Wolves

***

That had been Everton's 4th defeat in eight home matches so far in 2022/23, a worrying trend for a team that had relied so heavily on results at Goodison Park to stay up the previous season. The grave concern for supporters who were looking for signs of progress having been made during the hiatus for the World Cup, were reflected by the frustrated reaction from the crowd at the end, a fact not lost on Lampard.

"I think the lads had all the right intentions, so for that I'd love the crowd to stick with them," the manager said afterwards.

"We saw what a positive it (Goodison Park) can be last year, so let's not come away from that.

"I'm in the dressing room with them, and I know they want to do the right thing. I'm not asking the players to play 100 passes in our own final third, but to be a bit braver on the ball. Good players want to play so I'd like that to get some backing as the reality is we haven't got Dominic (Calvert-Lewin) for the direct option. We have to take it on the chin. We are trying to improve off the back of where we last year and it will be baby steps."

***

3 January 2023: Everton v Brighton

If a surprise draw to close out 2022 at the home of the Champions Manchester City had ignited some optimism among the Toffees faithful, the first match of the New Year would plunge Evertonians to greater depths of concern.

A home clash with Brighton & Hove Albion under the lights at a sodden Goodison Park, turned into a footballing disaster, as the Seagulls humiliated Everton, first by carving them open in the first half to take the lead, and then by extending their advantage with three quick goals in the second half, each as concerning as the last.

There had been a contingent of supporters who felt that Lampard should have been sacked after the twin embarrassments in

Bournemouth before the World Cup, and their number grew following the dreadful display against Brighton. To make things worse, the Blues once again dropped into the relegation zone on the back of the result.

It was no surprise, then, given the rising tide of discontent that Everton's fans turned on the club's owner and board of Directors as they witnessed the astonishing collapse in the second half. The crowd loudly booed Lampard and his team at half-time and again at the final whistle, with chants of "sack the board" ringing out once again inside the Grand Old Lady.

Final score: Everton 1-4 Brighton

***

While reports in the immediate aftermath of the match claimed that no assurances had been given to Lampard about the safety of his position, within a couple of days it emerged that the club were planning to stick with him for the time being.

The Telegraph suggested that there was "a growing belief he was fighting a losing battle to keep his job" and, given that Everton hadn't won a game since confidently despatching Crystal Palace on 22 October and were now in the bottom three, the next three fixtures would be pivotal for both Lampard and, perhaps, the club's ability to avoid the drop this season.

Following talks with Director of Football, Kevin Thelwell, at Finch Farm and the club's Chief Executive Officer, Denise Barrett-Baxendale, it was decided that Lampard would take charge of the FA Cup tie against Manchester United at Old Trafford. The hope was that with a positive result against Manchester United, or at least, a promising performance, the manager might be able to imbue confidence among the board in his ability to take Everton forward.

Meanwhile, several Everton supporters groups, including fan websites like ToffeeWeb and the newly renamed NSNOW group, put their name to an open letter to the Blues' majority shareholder, Farhad Moshiri, calling on him to change the club's leadership.

The move came after a similar missive from NSNOW (then known as the 27 Years Campaign) appealing to Moshiri for greater communication around the governance of Everton FC and, in particular, the ongoing funding model for the club's new stadium.

That letter received no response from Moshiri's office, but the Brighton result had given the owners' critics greater impulse for action to be taken at the top of the club.

The latest letter from the supporters groups read:

> "To Farhad Moshiri
>
> The time to save our club from its continued decline is now. For too long, despite your investment, we have seen diminishing returns that now threaten our existence as a Premier League club. We the undersigned fan and social media groups call on you to make sweeping changes at Chair, Board and Executive levels. Bring in competent, experienced professionals

who can reverse our decline and make us competitive once more. The narrow window of opportunity you spoke of is all but closed. Act now, while we still have a chance. Change the culture of the club, change the Chair, Board & Executive. NSNO - our standard not just our motto."

2023: Insecure Board stays away from Goodison

Farhad Moshiri's response to the latest plea from the NSNOW campaign came two days before the latest 'must win' game to be played at Goodison Park – this one against Southampton, the newest incumbents of 20th place in the Premier League – and yet again he used the controversial medium of Jim White and *TalkSport* as the conduit to communicate his message to supporters.

A year before, he had informed White that he would no longer be calling him on air following pushback from fans who could not understand why he refused to use the club's official media channels to communicate with them. Now he was choosing, at perhaps his lowest point since coming on board as a major investor in 2016, to break that self-imposed exile.

On the phone call to the radio host, Moshiri defended his efforts as owner, gave Lampard the dreaded vote of confidence and, surprisingly, suggested that the sacking of previous managers like Roberto Martinez, Ronald Koeman, Sam Allardyce, Marco Silva and Rafael Benitez had all been driven by fan sentiment.

Asked if he thought Evertonians still had faith in him, Moshiri said "he hoped so," before reiterating his support for manager Frank Lampard and the need for continuity in the head coach role:

> "I put my money where my mouth is and that is the most an owner can do and I have done that. Some of the decisions we have taken is together with the fans, right? All the managers who have left have been driven by the fans, not me initially. I think you have got to stay with the manager to get the systems going, the players he brought in. I have a lot of faith in Frank that he will get it right."

On the likelihood of upcoming protests that weekend at the game against Southampton – demonstrations of discontent that were likely to have been intensified by Moshiri's decision to speak to *TalkSport* again – he agreed that:

> "Protest is a democratic right of everyone ... I think the feeling is well-known if you are communicating. But I would say the biggest thing is to support the team. So we need to give it and they will give it back to us."

One of the biggest bones of contention among many fans, and in particular the NSNOW movement, was the perceived lack of expertise in the boardroom. But the owner was unequivocal in his support of Bill Kenwright, Denise Barrett-Baxendale, and newer members like Grant Ingles and non-executive director, Graeme Sharp:

> "They have been there a long time. Some are new appointments but they are longstanding, they are dedicated, they are local and it is so important to keep the club in Liverpool and its roots in Liverpool. Those are the roots and the roots of the club. They love the club and they have been attending games under every condition, and it is just building a £760 million stadium that will be one of the best in the country [that] is an enormous challenge for a club. I think [the fans] need to acknowledge that [the directors] are going through a transformation and they are working extremely hard, and I have added to the board every now and again with support and we will do it again. You can't just make rash decisions. We have two big games, Saturday, and on the 21st (against West Ham), and that is the only focus."

Then, just three hours before Everton were due to kick-off against Southampton, the news broke that, in an unprecedented move, Everton's directors had been instructed by the club's security team not to attend the critical fixture at Goodison Park.

It came on the back of developments in the fans protest movement earlier that week, coordinated by NSNOW, who called for a peaceful sit-in at Goodison after the game against the Saints to show their concerns over the state of the club.

The order to the Board was apparently because of "malicious and unacceptably threatening correspondence" that had been received, along with "increasing incidents of anti-social behaviour – including targeted physical aggression - at recent home matches."

An unnamed Security & Safety Advisor said: "Following a thorough risk assessment, and in response to tangible threats received by the Club and intelligence we have gathered, the Club's board members have been told they must not attend today's fixture."

A spokesperson for the club added:

> "This is an unprecedented decision for Everton Football Club – never before has our entire Board of Directors been ordered not to attend a match on safety grounds. It is a profoundly sad day for Everton and Evertonians."

Merseyside Police later issued a statement saying no incidents or offences had been reported by the club.

***

14 January 2023: Everton v Southampton

Meanwhile, on the pitch against fellow strugglers, Southampton, the mess the Blues had become under Farhad Moshiri's ownership was laid bare once more, with Frank Lampard powerless to prevent his charges from slumping to what was their seventh defeat in eight games, despite taking the lead through the imperious Amadou Onana.

The Belgian, so impressive in defeat at Manchester United in the FA Cup eight days earlier, was brilliant again, and rewarded with a goal from a towering first-half header that should have been the platform from which Everton won the game. However, yet more calamitous defending saw the lead evaporate and the Toffees descend into crisis on and off the pitch.

Southampton, who came into the fixture on a two-game winning streak in the cups, one of them an impressive League Cup quarter-final victory over Manchester City, went close to capitalising on yawning gaps in Everton's back line, first when Mohamed Elyounoussi's shot looped towards the far post and dropped wide and then when Mohammed Salisu's header was parried by Jordan Pickford on the line.

Everton broke the deadlock, though, with seven minutes left in the half. Some neat footwork from Demarai Gray ended with his attempted cross being blocked behind. From the winger's corner, Onana fought his way through the crowd to meet the in-swinger, and planted a downward header home off Bazunu's glove.

It was his first goal for the club and a potential mood changer. If only Everton could have hung on, but they tossed the lead away with less than a minute gone of the second half.

A simple Adams flick-on past James Tarkowski found Ward-Prowse in plenty of space to draw a sliding block attempt from Ben Godfrey and then stroke the ball past the helpless Pickford to make it 1-1.

Everton briefly rallied, with a marauding run by Ben Godfrey allowing him to set Calvert-Lewin up just outside the box, but his shot took a vital deflection off a defender's out-stretched leg and smacked off the underside of the crossbar and away from goal.

Lampard tried to change the course of the game by throwing on Anthony Gordon for Seamus Coleman, but instead of making the difference at the Gwladys Street End he played an important role in Southampton's winner with a clumsy and needless foul on Che Adams that gave the visitors a free-kick in prime James Ward-Prowse territory.

With Pickford and his wall all at sea, the Saints Talisman simply picked his spot and drove the ball into the left-hand side of the goal as the goalkeeper stood rooted to the spot.

For the third time since Christmas, the players left the Goodison Park pitch with the frustration, ire and boos of the fans in their ears, before the demonstrations of disaffection with an absent board took centre-stage behind the Gwladys Street goal.

Everton urgently needed an injection of goals in the transfer market and a change of ideas in the dugout. Off the pitch, it was hard to see the wholesale shift in culture and leadership that was required coming in time to stave off relegation to the second tier for the first time in 72 years.

Final score: Everton 1-2 Southampton

***

Writing in *The Guardian* that evening, Jonathan Liew rather eloquently summarised the situation, with the sadness of an outsider all too aware of how far the giant that is Everton had fallen:

"I've been particularly enjoying the protest banners. Everton is a furious club right now, its fans and its ownership in open warfare, a mixture of rage and desperation and powerlessness. And yet for some reason all this anger seems to express itself in perfect, playful rhyming couplets. 'Everton were magic, Kenwright is tragic.' 'A football giant owned by a clown, all you'll achieve is taking us down.' 'A chairman who won't let go, an under-qualified CEO.'

"Only Everton fans, you feel, can capture an existential cry for help with the levity of a child's nursery rhyme. I don't propose to analyse the metre and scansion of the Everton banners in too much detail, but on some level I wonder whether the jauntiness of the medium is a subconscious counterpoint to the opacity and obfuscation of the Everton board, with their woolly "Official Statements", their anonymous briefings to favoured journalists, the intentionally imprecise messaging. You put out your press releases. We bring poetry. The natural instinct amongst many rival fans, and even some voices in the media, has been to poke fun at Everton's plight, chide their sense of legacy entitlement, deride their supporter base as delusional, demented, perhaps even dangerous. And as with any mass protest movement – and not to equate the aims of Just Stop Oil or Black Lives Matter with, say, the underwhelming signing of Neal Maupay in the summer – the focus invariably shifts towards the methods of protest rather than the substance of the protest itself.

"After the 2-1 defeat to Southampton on Saturday – a game the board did not attend citing vague and unspecified safety concerns – a small group of fans surrounded the cars of Anthony Gordon and Yerry Mina as they tried to leave Goodison Park. A little unsavoury, but essentially harmless. Perhaps so Mina, who grew up amid the barras bravas of Colombian football and has presumably seen much worse, looked so calm as he stepped out of his car to talk to fans and listen to their concerns. "Show us a bit of heart," one fan urges him. "All we want is passion. Show us a bit of passion. Start speaking up, lad, show them you're the man." There was a touching and curiously human quality to the whole exchange, one that really strikes at the heart of what Everton fans are really angry about. Because at its heart, this is not a protest about net spends or sporting directors or even league form. It's about hope and connection, the forlorn and obsolescent idea that a football club can still be an expression of its people, that those who run and administer it can still want the same things they do. What do Everton fans want? And can modern football even provide it? "The fans expect the best," reads another banner. Nil satis nisi optimum, the club motto from which one of the main protest groups takes its name, means "nothing but the best is good enough".

"You see the problem here. Everton had for a time one of Europe's best young strikers in Romelu Lukaku. Manchester United bought him for £75m. They had one of the world's finest managers in Carlo Ancelotti. Real Madrid took him. Gordon had half a good season before Chelsea started making eyes at him. What do we think happens to Amadou Onana if he starts tearing up the Premier League? Or Ben

Godfrey? Or Nathan Patterson? And these were the good decisions. But outside the game's VIP circle nothing good can ever last. For fans of smaller clubs, perhaps you make your peace with this fact sooner rather than later. But those one level removed from the elite, your West Hams and Aston Villas and Hamburgs and Sampdorias, are essentially trapped in a doom cycle from which there are only really two escapes: relegation or an autocratic benefactor. This isn't entitlement. It is simply the howl of a club and fanbase that, whether they make the right choices or the wrong choices, will simply never be allowed to grow. One of the interesting elements of this protest is how young the banner-wavers and slogan-shouters are. They're mostly young men in their 20s and 30s, some even younger. These guys aren't high on nostalgia. They're not pining for the days of Sharp and Sheedy. But they are slowly realising, perhaps for the first time, that the dream that was sold to them no longer exists, at least not for them. The game they were bequeathed by their parents, a thing of romance and aspiration, has been sold off and converted into crypto.

"There will be no trophies. There will be no famous Champions League nights at Bramley-Moore Dock. You will not get to see the world's finest players in an Everton shirt. You do not even get the giddy underdog rise through the divisions like fans of Brighton or Brentford or Wigan. Your owner is a billionaire who will never speak to you or attend a game, and if he wants to run the ship aground there is not a damn thing you can do about it. No matter how loudly you sing, no matter how many blue smoke canisters you let off, the limit of your ambition will always be top seven and occasionally signing someone promising from Burnley. Or, to put it in terms with which Everton fans will perhaps be more familiar:

"THREE DECADES OF FINANCIAL STRATIFICATION, HAVE MADE IT HARDER TO FIND GRATIFICATION. A REVIVAL OF EVERTON'S SUCCESS ON THE PITCH, WILL FOREVER BE THWARTED BY THE SUPER-RICH."

***

21 January 2023: West Ham v Everton

By the third weekend in January 2023, the situation at Everton appeared bleak. Following the loss at home to Southampton - the club's 10th game without a win – the Toffees sat joint bottom of the Premier League with the Saints and West Ham, the much vaunted search for a striker having turned up empty with just 10 days left of the transfer window. Frank Lampard was the proverbial 'dead man walking.'

As if to underline the gravity of the situation and the vulnerability of the manager's position, the Board of Directors, absent from Goodison the previous weekend because of security concerns, were all in attendance at the London Stadium for another 'six-pointer', this time against the Hammers. Not only that, but so too was Farhad Moshiri, who hadn't watched an Everton game in the flesh since October 2021.

That, surely, was Lampard's last chance to turn a tide threatening to wash away the Toffees' proud 69-year unbroken membership of the top flight in a league where, theoretically, any team could beat another on its day... any team, it seemed, except this Everton one.

Unfortunately, against the Hammers, with his 'executioners' watching on, Lampard's men turned in the display of a side crippled by a lack of self-belief, overseen by a manager who looked incapable of instilling any confidence in them or changing a game to rescue a losing situation.

Frustratingly, if Everton had started the game with the relative tempo they showed in the second period, they might have preyed on the tangible nervousness among the West Ham faithful in the opening stages. Both teams appeared frightened by their own shadows, but the visitors were at least looking fairly comfortable on the ball.

But that dominance of possession lacked any urgency, with Amadou Onana, so effective and purposeful the previous week against Southampton, disappointingly hesitant to drive forward.

Everton might have had a penalty when Angelo Ogbonna appeared to handle a cross from Gray with a quarter of an hour gone, but neither the referee nor Video Assistant Referee, Andre Marriner, felt it was worthy of being penalised as an infringement.

However, the Hammers got the encouragement they needed to come out of their shells as the half progressed and the opening goal came 11 minutes before the interval. The ball was chipped back into the Everton box following a West Ham corner, Yerry Mina and Conor Coady got in each other's way and Jarrod Bowen was on hand and fractionally onside to knock Kurt Zouma's flick-on past the keeper from close range.

1-0 became 2-0 three minutes before half-time when an attempted pass by Iwobi was cut out, the Hammers countered and Michail Antonio skipped past James Tarkowski's ill-advised lunge on the touchline. The burly striker centred past Coady and Bowen arrived to thump it home and claim his second goal of the afternoon.

Iwobi went very close to giving the visitors hope just before the interval, but his low drive took a decisive deflection off Declan Rice skidded wide off the outside of the post and Gueye's shot from 25 yards was tipped behind by Lukas Fabianski early in the second period.

Meanwhile, Pickford did superbly to turn Emerson's shot onto the crossbar in the 65th minute, and Nayef Aguerd headed over from the subsequent corner. Then Rice was inches away from making it 3-0 following a run down the left flank and a shot that just missed the far post.

Aston Villa's win at Southampton kept Everton from dropping to rock bottom in the division but without a win since October, no sign of one coming under the incumbent manager, and Lampard having now overseen the worst points return from the first 20 games of a season in Everton's history, his continued employment at the club seemed inconceivable.

Everton was a club gripped by apathy at the top, and agony and frustration among a helpless fanbase. But with things still so compressed at the bottom of the table, it was still not an irretrievable situation if the board acted decisively. A new managerial appointment would need time ahead of the visit of Arsenal, as well as help on the player recruitment side over the next 10 days.

The inevitable question was, 'who could do a better job than Lampard?' Sadly, with a run of results that now represented the worst record after 20 matches in the club's entire history, it became more a case of could anyone do any worse?

This Everton team looked bereft of everything apart from in goal — poorly coached with no confidence, no belief, no cohesion and no direction... except down.

Final score: West Ham 2-0 Everton

***

Afterwards, Farhad Moshiri and Bill Kenwright tried to beat a hasty retreat to their waiting cars outside the London Stadium but were intercepted by Gary Cotterill of *Sky Sports* who asked both men if Frank Lampard's time was finally up.

Neither could give the reporter a definitive answer but, perhaps suggesting that there would be better ways of delivering such news, the visibly harrowed chairman said: "It's been a bad run of results for us all but, no, I would never say such a thing to you." He added, it was "a bad time" for Everton and that "We just need to start winning games."

Moshiri offered little more, except to say:

> "I can't comment [on the question of whether Lampard would now be sacked]. It's not my decision."

The owner's response was taken by many as an indication that this would be a joint decision made by the Board, in concert with Director of Football, Kevin Thelwell, rather than a unilateral one made by Moshiri himself.

Less than two days later, 53 weeks after Rafael Benitez had been terminated, the axe fell again.

2023: Lampard sacked. Moshiri promises fans a new striker

> "Lampard's departure marked a sad end to a managerial tenure that held so much promise in its early days, and which reached its peak on an emotional night at Goodison in May 2022 when the Toffees secured their Premier League survival with the stunning come-from-behind win over Crystal Palace.

2023 Lampard sacked. Moshiri promises fans a new striker

Two days after the West Ham defeat, and in a decision made unanimously by Farhad Moshiri and the club's Board of Directors, Everton dismissed Frank Lampard from his position as head coach, less than a year into the role following a string of defeats and the club sitting in the relegation zone.

The 44-year-old had overseen just three Premier League wins all season, the worst 20-game sequence of results to start a season in the club's history, and failed to progress past the third round of either domestic cup competition.

Lampard's departure marked a sad end to a managerial tenure that held so much promise in its early days, and which reached its peak on an emotional night at Goodison in May 2022 when the Toffees secured their Premier League survival with the stunning come-from-behind win over Crystal Palace.

Fans had commended the former Derby County and Chelsea manager for the way he had tapped into the passion of the Everton faithful, and there had been high hopes that he could continue to develop not only his management skills but also the Blues' squad over the course of what was to be his first full season in charge.

However, having lost his best player, when Richarlison was sold to Tottenham Hotspur, Lampard was dealt another cruel blow just three days before the start of the 2022/23 campaign when Dominic Calvert-Lewin, a big miss for much of the previous season, suffered another serious injury and wasn't really able to recover full fitness for the entire season.

The failure on the club's part not to sign a reliable goal scorer of Calvert-Lewin's ilk, acquiring instead Neal Maupay from Brighton, further hampered the manager's attempts to build a winning side, even as it appeared he was making progress when Palace returned to Goodison Park in October and were swept aside with an impressive display that yielded a 3-0 win for Everton.

That was the last time Everton won under his stewardship and over the ensuing three months the club dropped from 12th place to 19th, with games running out to mount another great escape and avoid what would be a catastrophic drop into the Championship.

Everton would embark on the search for their eighth managerial appointment in ten years, and in the end, it came down to a choice between two wildly different candidates.

***

It would be a week until Everton unveiled the seventh managerial appointment of Farhad Moshiri's reign. In the meanwhile, a transfer window that, in the context of the desperate need for a reliable goal scorer, many fans had regarded as being potentially the most important in the club's history, was entering its final week without the Blues having signed anyone.

With the anticipated arrival of Arnaut Danjuma, on loan from Villarreal until the end of the season, it looked as though Kevin Thelwell had landed a player capable of providing much-needed attacking threat to a team that had scored just 15 times in 20 games.

However, having agreed personal terms, undergone a medical and completed most of the media duties associated with the unveiling of a new signing, a delay in the arrival of the paperwork from the Spanish club's end gave the Dutchman enough time to rethink his decision. In a stunning, last-minute U-turn, he opted instead to sign for Tottenham Hotspur.

***

On the same day, Everton released a video interview with Farhad Moshiri conducted by Jazz Bal, chair of the Fan Advisory Board, to address some of the key questions posed to that body by supporters. The discussion produced two headlines – first, that the owner promised in no uncertain terms that the club would sign a striker before the transfer deadline on 31 January; and second, his insistence that the club was not for sale but that he had been talking to top investors to bridge the funding gap on the stadium.

"I can't do it myself," Moshiri said. He added, "I want to bring top sports investors into Everton [to provide] more talent, and we are close to having a deal done. It's not selling the club at all, it's just bringing more expertise in terms of global sponsorship and commercial development."

Given that the interview had been recorded a week earlier, it was likely that Moshiri's confidence in making a striker signing was based on the positive discussions with the representatives of Danjuma and that player's willingness to sign.

The winger's *volte face* before heading for North London sparked a scramble in the transfer market to land either a centre-forward or a goal scoring, attacking wide player before the window closed. It proved fruitless. To the utter dismay of their supporters, Everton failed to bring in a single new face that January, leaving whoever was to take over from Frank Lampard worryingly short on firepower.

2023: Sean Dyche wins the two horse race

> I know about Everton's passionate fanbase and how precious this club is to them. We're ready to work and ready to give them what they want. That starts with sweat on the shirt, effort and getting back to some of the basic principles of what Everton Football Club has stood for over a long time.
>
> - Sean Dyche

2023 Sean Dyche wins the two horse race

Although the bookmakers and sports writers had reeled off a number of potential candidates to fill the void left by Frank Lampard's sacking, it quickly became apparent that the club had narrowed the search down to just two options with vastly differing styles – Argentine maverick, Marcelo Bielsa, and former Burnley boss, Sean Dyche.

On 26 January, it was reported Marcelo Bielsa had jetted in to England to hold talks with Everton, with the Board hoping to make an appointment by the end of the week.

Bielsa had been dismissed by Leeds almost a year previously after four years in charge at Elland Road, where he had become a folk hero for engineering the Yorkshire club's return to the Premier League following a 16-year absence.

Early newspaper reports suggested the Argentinian was 'warming' to the prospect of taking on the Everton project. For his part, Dyche who had been out of work for a similar period, was said to be enthusiastic about the opportunity, even if it was on a short-term basis, just to keep Everton in the top flight.

It was widely believed Bielsa was the first choice of majority shareholder, Farhad Moshiri, but the former Leeds manager was famous for preferring to take new jobs in the summer, so that he could get the benefit of a full pre-season to bed in his methods and playing style.

According to reports, he proposed to Everton that he and his eight-person support staff take charge of the Under-21s for the rest of the season and then he would become first-team head coach at the end of the season.

That plan was unworkable, leaving Moshiri and the Board of Directors to turn to Dyche as the alternative, a safe pair of hands hopefully to guide the team to safety over the remaining 18 games of the season.

With Bielsa turning down the opportunity to take the first team reins with immediate effect, Everton finally confirmed Dyche as Lampard's replacement on 27 January 2023.

The 51-year-old signed a two-and-a-half-year deal and brought former Everton youth player Ian Woan in as his Assistant Manager, ex-England international Steve Stone as First-Team Coach, and Mark Howard to provide additional sports science expertise.

Dyche had been out of work since leaving Turf Moor, after a decade in charge of the Clarets. During his time at Burnley, he led them to European qualification in 2017/18, but was dismissed in April 2022 by new owners with the club heading for the Championship.

Burnley, under Dyche's long-term replacement, Vincent Kompany, were the runaway leaders of the second tier and on course to return to the top flight, whereas Everton's new boss was charged with making sure the Blues didn't pass them on the way down.

Dyche took over with the Blues on a run of just one win in 14 games and sitting joint-bottom of the Premier League. He faced a baptism of fire with clashes against leaders Arsenal and local rivals, Liverpool, in his first two matches.

"It's an honour to become Everton manager. My staff and I are ready and eager to help get this great club back on track," Dyche said on joining the club.

"I know about Everton's passionate fanbase and how precious this club is to them. We're ready to work and ready to give them what they want. That starts with sweat on the shirt, effort and getting back to some of the basic principles of what Everton Football Club has stood for over a long time.

"We want to bring back a good feeling. We need the fans, we need unity and we need everyone aligned. That starts with us as staff and players.

"Our aim is to put out a team that works, that fights and wears the badge with pride. The connection with the fans can then grow very quickly because they're so passionate."

***

If Sean Dyche had been promised any reinforcements to the squad, come transfer deadline day on 31 January, he must have privately felt as aghast as the fans when the club finished the day empty-handed.

Many Everton fans had billed it as potentially the most important transfer window in the club's history, but the club finished January weaker than before. Despite selling Anthony Gordon, Everton failed to make a single signing, while the teams struggling with them in the lower reaches of the Premier League table all strengthened their squads.

Somewhat gallingly, fellow strugglers Southampton ended up beating Everton to Stade Rennais winger Kamaldeen Sulemana, with the player ultimately plumping for St Mary's over Goodison Park after both clubs had bids of around £22 million accepted.

Links of varying veracity for the like of Genk striker Paul Onuachu, who also went to Southampton, Udinese striker Beto, Fenerbahçe's Michy Batshuayi and Manchester United's Anthony Elanga all came to nothing, on what was a damp squib of a transfer deadline day.

When the transfer deadline passed, the Blues were the only club in the top flight not to sign at least one player since the turn of the year, a staggering failing that left new manager Sean Dyche desperately short of creativity in the wide areas and goal scoring threat up front.

Only Wolves had scored fewer goals than Everton to that point in the season, but Dyche would have to engineer them from places that his predecessor Frank Lampard could not, and he would have to do it without the club's joint-top scorer, Anthony Gordon, who, like Richarlison before him, was sold without being replaced.

***

4 February 2023: Everton v Arsenal

The winds of change blew through Goodison Park again — not in the Boardroom, of course; but on that score, protest was in the air. Yet, so too was defiance and a refusal by almost 40,000 Evertonians to let their club sink without a fight. Sean Dyche took his place in Everton's dugout (or, more accurately, the touchline where, in contrast to his more passive predecessor, he was a constantly animated and vocal presence) for the first time. There he oversaw one of those electrifying home wins over a superior foe, amid an atmosphere that vanquishes visiting teams regardless of their talent and standing.

Likely needing at least seven more wins to stay up, this was one of the most difficult of Everton's remaining assignments in 2022/23. Arsenal, unbeaten in the Premier League since September under Mikel Arteta, were an excellent side. Yet there were precious few moments during the 90 minutes where they could exhibit their quality. They had just three shots on target and only one of them, a powerful drive from substitute Leandro Trossard 12 minutes from time, really tested Jordan Pickford.

Another effort from Bukayo Saka in the first half, might well have gone in on another day, but this time, the positioning of Conor Coady, rejuvenated and inspired along with the rest of the Blues' team in a highly organised 4-5-1 formation, was exemplary and he cleared his England squad-mate's volley off the line.

Eddie Nketiah and Martin Ødegaard wasted the other couple of decent chances that fell Arsenal's way, but the best opportunities came at the other end and had Everton won by two or three goals, Arteta probably couldn't have had many complaints. They might have done had Abdoulaye Doucouré and Dominic Calvert-Lewin not spurned excellent headed chances in the latter stages of the first half, but James Tarkowski's first goal for the Toffees, fittingly enough scored under the coach who really made him as a player, was all that was needed.

This was a day reminiscent of the first game Duncan Ferguson oversaw in December 2019 against Chelsea — a high-octane, determined and feisty display that leveraged the power and tenacity in the squad together with that legendary 12th man in the stands. On a day which saw thousands of Blues march from the Royal Oak, up Spellow Lane and around the Grand Old Lady before kick-off-time, fears that the demonstrations against the club's hierarchy would detract from support for the team proved unfounded, as the fans raised the roof once more to roar home three points.

The decisive goal came right on the hour mark. Everton won a corner on their right,

McNeil swung it in and Tarkowski muscled his way past Martin Ødergaard to meet it and guide a header back across goal past Ramsdale before wheeling away in celebration of his first goal for the Toffees.

Arsenal had howls for a penalty waved away not long afterwards and Leandro Trossard stung Pickford's palms with that strong shot that was beaten away and cleared before the Belgian missed the target with a curling attempt a few minutes later.

The Gunners were increasingly desperate by the end and were finding their hosts hard to break down. They would have just one more chance to salvage a point in stoppage time, but Oleksandr Zinchenko blasted it over the bar. And then, mercifully, it was over after six minutes of injury time, the referee's whistle triggering relief and celebration in the stands.

This wasn't quintessential Dyche-ball, as his reputation had, perhaps unfairly, painted him at Burnley. Yes, the Blues went direct when they needed and the deciding goal came off a set-piece but the new boss had clearly set out to put legs in midfield and marry the technical ability and speed over the ground that existed in the team with its physicality and aerial ability.

When combined with a disciplined shape and an effective mid-block without the ball, it's a formula that would stand him in very good stead.

Dyche was right, however, when he stressed in his post-match comments that this result is just a start. Wolves's win over Liverpool and West Ham's strong performance at Newcastle illustrated how difficult the fight was going to be at the bottom over the rest of the season.

It was going to take eight more performances of high effort and concentration at Goodison and some vastly improved results away from home if survival was to be achieved, but this win over the worthy League leaders definitely pointed the way.

Final score: Everton 1-0 Arsenal

***

18 February 2023: Everton v Leeds United

After the disappointment of a 2-0 away defeat in the Merseyside derby in a Monday night game at Anfield on 13 February, Sean Dyche registered his second successive home win as Everton manager, and the Blues lifted themselves out of the bottom three thanks to Seamus Coleman's stunning second-half strike against Leeds at Goodison Park.

Everton were the better side on the day but frequently let themselves down in final third, although Illan Meslier had to be at his best to deny James Tarkowski a first-half opener from a corner, Max Wöber headed out from under his own bar from Conor Coady, Weston McKennie cleared a Neal Maupay header off the line, and Abdoulaye Doucouré made a mess of a gilt-edged chance to put the game to bed at the end.

Leeds failed to test Jordan Pickford in the Blues' goal despite being gifted several chances to put the hosts' back line under pressure in the latter stages of the game.

Everton, by contrast, made most of the early running, with Amadou Onana and Idrissa Gueye missing the target, Vitalii Mykolenko seeing appeals for a penalty waved away and James Tarkowski testing the keeper Meslier with a header from a corner.

Then, in the second half, Neal Maupay failed to work the goalkeeper with a shot on the turn eight and Mykolenko had another effort comfortably saved before Coleman broke the deadlock in stunning fashion.

Iwobi chipped the ball over the last defender down the right flank to find the skipper's run and with no blue shirts gambling in the centre, Coleman appeared to chance his luck by going for goal from an almost impossible position, the ball arrowing behind the keeper and inside the far post to light up what had been a nervy Goodison Park.

An increasingly desperate Leeds side pegged Everton back after that but the Yorkshiremen weren't able to muster a decent goal scoring chance while Everton really should have killed the game in the 88th minute.

Ellis Simms, on for Maupay, did superbly to loft the ball over the top for Abdoulaye Doucouré to gallop towards the Leeds box but rather than gamble with a left-foot shot, he tried to bring it back into his right and it ended up getting caught under his feet before it was hacked clear.

Though there were wins for all three teams that had begun the day in the bottom three of the Premier League for the first time in eight years, this win vaulted the Toffees out of the relegation zone and into 16th place.

Final score: Everton 1-0 Leeds

***

After the match, Seamus Coleman said he probably wouldn't be able to replicate too often the brilliant finish that had settled the game, but he acknowledged how important it was.

"I knew that there was no one in the box and I presumed the keeper would anticipate that maybe a cross would come in and he would maybe go half a yard and I just tried to hit the target.

"Listen, I could do that 20 more times, 30 more times and I wouldn't hit it as sweet, so, thankfully, for me and the team, it went in."

"[The game] was very high stakes," the Irishman admitted. "You try and play it down as best you can before the game and see it as just 90 minutes of trying to be better than the opposition but in the back of your mind you're aware of how big the game would've been if Leeds had've won; they pull away a little bit.

"You could feel that in the stadium, but the fans were right behind us in every tackle, every ball we had to chase into a corner — they were so loud so they played a massive part in this."

Asked how difficult it is to keep your nerve when there is so much riding on the outcome of the game, Coleman said:

"It's tough; there's no getting away from it but you have to do the right things. You know, we've been stung a few times here at Goodison, where it's been 0-0 and we're trying to push for the first goal and we get stung on the counter-attack.

"So we're starting to learn a little bit from that and the manager's done a lot of work with us on that as well. So to get the goal and hold out was important, but there's no getting away from it — there were plenty of nervy moments."

***

11 March 2023: Everton v Brentford

Sean Dyche could not work his magic in the next home game against Aston Villa, where the Blues suffered a disappointing 2-0 defeat which dumped them back in the relegation places. That was followed by a 4-0 thrashing away at Arsenal, and a 2-2 draw away at Nottingham Forest, results which still left Everton 18th in the league a third of the way into March.

Every game was becoming a 'must win' and the tension around Goodison before the match when Brentford came to town was palpable.

The Bees had not lost in 12 Premier League matches coming into the weekend and had their eyes on an unlikely European qualification place but, though they showed why they have been such difficult opposition in what became an increasingly panicked second half from the Toffees' perspective, Dyche's men held firm.

Everton had set themselves on their way to what was a vital victory when Dwight McNeil put them ahead with just 35 seconds on the clock and they could have been out of sight by half time had David Raya not made two smart saves and Video Assistant Referee, David Coote, not scandalously overturned a Demarai Gray goal that would have made it 2-0 at the break.

It was the perfect start for Dyche's men, however, as they broke up a Brentford attack from kick-off and launched the ball forward quickly, with Alex Iwobi slipping it inside to Abdoulaye Doucouré, who moved it on to McNeil, approaching the opposition box.

The winger, reborn under his former manager at Burnley, exhibited close control before firing a crisp shot across Raya and into the far corner. It was a lovely finish,

Michael Keane headed a fine a chance wide, Amadou Onana spurned a gilt-edged opportunity, side-footing disappointingly wide from Iwobi's fizzed cross from the byline and Demarai Gray aimed a shot inside Raya's near post, but the goalie did well to divert it wide with an out-stretched leg. From the ensuing corner, Iwobi must have thought he had scored from just a couple of yards out, but Raya was there again to save with his foot and Onana mis-kicked the rebound wide.

Meanwhile, Bryan Mbeumo forced a first save from Pickford in the 24th minute that the England keeper initially spilled, but then gathered at the second attempt; while Ivan Toney was inches away from equalising with a header from a cross from the Bees' right a minute later.

The second goal that the Blues were so keen to get looked to have arrived three minutes before half-time when Keane headed a free-kick it into the area. Ethan Pinnock hooked the ball off the line but only into Gray's chest and it ricocheted into the net. The referee, Simon Hooper, allowed the goal to stand, but after taking a long look at an inconclusive replay, Coote on VAR overruled Simon Hooper's decision on the field and ruled it out.

If Dyche had hoped his men could keep the initiative and try to pad their lead in the second half, he would be disappointed. Brentford, spurred on by the much-lauded Thomas Frank, seized control of the contest almost from the restart.

However, the Toffees kept them at bay, with Coleman making a vital block from point-blank range to deny Rico Henry, McNeil rescuing Pickford after he had made a mess of coming for a resulting corner by whacking the ball off his goal line, and Raya coming forward for a corner in stoppage time, only to plant a header well off target.

The win, combined with defeats for Nottingham Forest and Leicester and Leeds United's home draw with Brighton lifted Everton out of the bottom three and into 15th place for the time being, and offered hope once more that they had enough to win their battle to avoid relegation for a second season running.

Final score: Everton 1-0 Brentford

2023: The Cult of Bill

> "[Kenwright] owns only 1.3 per cent of the club these days. Everton is - theoretically at least - under the control of the British-Iranian businessman Farhad Moshiri whose company Blue Heaven Holdings owns 94.1 per cent. But Kenwright remains front and central, for better and for worse.
>
> - Ian Ladyman, Daily Mail

2023 The Cult of Bill

With Everton Football Club on its knees following one close call with relegation in 2021/22, with another one looming in 2022/23, and forced into extreme austerity as the largesse and mis-steps of the Moshiri years started to bite, supporters had started to demand both accountability and change – in the Boardroom at first, but increasingly at the ownership level as well.

In line with the feeling in general that the club needed an injection of fresh ideas and genuine corporate, commercial and footballing expertise, the clamour for long-serving Chairman Bill Kenwright to either stand down or be moved aside by Moshiri was growing beyond a disaffected and vocal few in the fanbase.

Writing in the *Daily Mail* at the end of January, with Kenwright and the rest of the Directors in self-imposed exile from home matches and in the period of uncertainty between the sacking of Frank Lampard and the appointment of Sean Dyche, Ian Ladyman pulled few punches in describing what one insider at another club labelled the 'Cult of Bill':

> "He owns only 1.3 per cent of the club these days. Everton is – theoretically at least – under the control of the British-Iranian businessman Farhad Moshiri whose company Blue Heaven Holdings owns 94.1 per cent. But Kenwright remains front and central, for better and for worse. Given the stress and the heartache, why is he still putting himself through it for the sake of what is essentially someone else's football club? 'I asked him this at a game not long ago,' one senior executive at another big club tells *Sportsmail*. 'Usually, he just laughs and ducks it. But this time I pressed him and he just said it was impossible for him not to still care.'

> "[S]even years after the sale and with the club once-again managerless following the sacking of Frank Lampard, Kenwright, according to those who

know him, continues to believe that Everton would simply sink on Moshiri's solo watch.' Bill has a belief perhaps bordering on arrogance that he can still save the club from itself', said one long-term ally. 'Farhad likes big gestures. He can be impetuous. Bill thinks he needs to be there to temper them and gets frustrated that fans can't see this. Some think Bill feels guilty, that he feels he sold to the wrong person. I haven't heard him say that. He does have an insane love for the club but also for the limelight, even when that focus is bad. He loves the glory of being in the middle of a grand old football club, even one as broken and divided as this one. It's like a drug to him but it's one he needs to kick for his own sake. '

"'It's very much the Cult of Bill,' one Premier League chief executive tells *Sportsmail*. 'And it's the same when they come to us to be fair. But in a nice way. At many Premier League clubs it's hard to recognise anyone in the boardroom but it's not like that at Everton. It's like the old days and there is something to be said for that.'"

The insight in Ladyman's article came from the quotes from figures within the game and those close to the Chairman himself, and they exposed the confusing internal structure that existed at Everton thanks to the competing forces of Kenwright's acolytes and Moshiri's faction, which routinely affected everything from player recruitment and transfer negotiations to selecting the club's next manager.

Ladyman's piece also revealed Moshiri's inability or reluctance to hire his own people in place to run the club, as well as Kenwright's fear that if he didn't remain actively involved, the whole thing would fall apart. As things turned out, they almost did, despite his best efforts.

***

Around the same time, in January 2023, another figure seen as controversial by some elements within the fanbase took the opportunity to publicly deny having an out-sized influence on Farhad Moshiri when it came to player recruitment and even managerial candidates.

Using the same platform deployed by the Everton owner to defend himself, infamous player agent and facilitator Kia Joorabchian said on a call with Simon Jordan and Jim White on *TalkSport*, that his relationship with the Blues formed only a small part of what he and his operation did.

Rumoured to have been behind the push to sign Alex Iwobi from Arsenal at the eleventh hour on transfer deadline day and other less successful moves like the loan of Anwar El Ghazi from Aston Villa in the winter transfer window of 2022, Joorabchian's name had become synonymous with the meddling in transfers and controversial managerial appointments at Everton because of his close relationship with fellow Iranian, Moshiri.

The unease among supporters surrounding his influence over Moshiri had peaked in January 2022 when he recommended his client

Vitor Pereira for the vacant head coach role following the sacking of Rafael Benitez, but under a more collegiate decision-making process, Frank Lampard was chosen.

Joorabchian confirmed to Jordan and White that he had put Pereira's name forward for the Everton job but suggested that CEO Denise Barrett-Baxendale had been influential in pushing for Lampard instead.

He admitted that Anwar El Ghazi had been his doing but also claimed to have suggested players like Bruno Guimaraes and Militao to the club before they were expensive targets and Everton passed on them.

Whatever the truth of the matter, Joorabchian largely melted out of the picture from that point on, and stood to have any influence reduced to almost nothing were Moshiri to be successful in selling Everton.

2023: Blues' accounts reveal 'Going Concern' bombshell

Everton's financial position vis-à-vis Profitability and Sustainability rules had been a concern of the Premier League's since the end of the 2020/21 season, a time when clubs in England's top flight were beginning to recover from the effects of COVID-19 and to assess the impact the pandemic had had on their operations and bottom line.

To that end, the Blues had been required to maintain ongoing dialogue with the League regarding the club's finances, and all of their transfer business was subject to oversight, starting with the summer

2021 transfer window. From then on, Everton had operated on an austere sell-to-buy basis while also working hard to structure incoming transfer deals with small up-front payments and the fees spread over the lifetime of the players' contracts wherever possible.

The enforced pivot away from what had been a period of significant outlay on player transfers and salaries in the first five years since Farhad Moshiri had arrived on the scene at Everton had the effect of significantly trimming Everton's losses in the annual accounts for the 2021/22 financial year which were finally released on 31 March, 2023.

The report showed revenue of £181 million and losses totalling £44.7 million, a £76 million improvement on the previous year, but the club's cumulative three-year losses were in excess of £305 million and net debt had increased to £141.7 million.

The biggest outlay had been on construction costs at the new Everton Stadium at Bramley-Moore Dock, which topped £200 million, and £10.5 million was attributed in the accounts to compensation to former manager Rafael Benitez and his staff following his dismissal in January 2022.

However, player acquisitions like those of Nathan Patterson from Rangers and Vitalii Mykolenko from Dynamo Kiev in January 2022 were offset by the sale of Lucas Digne to Aston Villa that month and Richarlison to Tottenham Hotspur in June, while high-earning players like Bernard and James Rodriguez were also moved on.

The club attributed £90 million in crystallised losses and further unspecified 'uncrystallised' losses (for example, unrealised revenue from player trading that was affected by the pandemic lockdown) to the COVID-19 pandemic, the latter of which had been a major point of contention from rival clubs.

The statements from the club in the accounts revealed, however, the extent to which Everton FC still relied on Moshiri's willingness to cover its losses and they contained the bombshell revelation that the club's very survival might be at risk in the event of relegation from the Premier League, should the owner not cover the shortfall.

"Despite the substantial financial impact of several unexpected and unprecedented factors in recent seasons, the club remains in a secure financial position thanks to the continued support and commitment of our majority shareholder," a statement in the accounts read.

It was clear the club had become entirely dependent on Farhad Moshiri's own finances. The key question was, with Alisher Usmanov now barred from sponsoring the club, for how much longer would Farhad Moshiri continue to pump cash into his failed project?

Such was the uncertainty, the auditors insisted the Everton Board include this alarming statement in their annual report and accounts:

> "**GOING CONCERN:** As outlined in detail in the notes to the financial statements, the Directors recognise that there is uncertainty attached to the timing and quantum of the anticipated revenue levels, cost savings and the future funding required by the Group over the forecast period in a relegation scenario. Efforts are currently underway to secure funding as referenced in the Directors' report. If the assumptions in the relegation scenario were not achieved, then the Group would have to seek further funding from its majority shareholder. They have provided a letter of support confirming ongoing financial support will

> be provided to the Group but this letter does not represent a legally binding commitment. Collectively, the above conditions indicate the existence of a material uncertainty that may cast significant doubt about the group's ability to continue as a going concern." - Everton Football Club Report and Accounts 2021/22

In other words, if Everton was going down into the Championship, it may also lead to the club being plunged into administration. As time would tell, Farhad Moshiri's written commitment to provide the club with ongoing financial support would prove to be worthless.

2023: Everton referred by Premier League to 'Independent Commission'

When Everton's annual accounts for 2020/21 were published in 2022, showing further losses of £120 million, it had prompted Leeds United and Burnley to write a joint letter to the Premier League requesting that an independent commission be established to investigate Everton's finances, and threatening legal action should the Blues be found to have breached Profitability and Sustainability Rules.

Everton had responded with a statement insisting they were in compliance with the PSR rules, a claim that was bolstered by the revelation that at two separate Premier League shareholders' meetings, first in March 2022 and then again that summer, it was stated that the club had no case to answer.

"We have worked so closely with the Premier League to make sure we are compliant. We are comfortable we have complied with the rules," the correspondence from the Royal Liver Building read. "External auditors have told us what we can and cannot claim against the pandemic. If they want to take legal action then they can do so by all means."

So, it was to Everton's shock in late March 2023 when it emerged that the Premier League had referred the club to an independent panel after all, charging them with breaching PSR rules during the 2021/22 season. Meanwhile, some executives at other top-flight clubs were uneasy at the apparent U-turn by the governing body which some felt might have been was politically motivated — Premier League CEO Richard Masters was set to go before a Parliamentary hearing on sports governance where the Government would push for an independent regulator to oversee English football — while others were asking why, if the Toffees had broken the rules, had the matter not been dealt with in the summer of 2022?

"The Everton charge is very surprising," one Premier League executive told *The Mail On Sunday* at the time. "We sat in front of the Premier League around March last year and they categorically told us there was no case to answer.

"Then, in the summer, we were told Everton could sign players as they were working together with the League to stay the right side of the line, and their COVID losses made them compliant.

"The Premier League made these points in open meetings and also held private meetings with individual clubs who had expressed concerns."

With the Premier League's charge having no precedent and the exact nature of the infraction undisclosed, the football world was left to speculate about all aspects of the commission. Initially, there were no details of when the hearing would take place — preliminary estimates ranged from six months to a year and a half — who would make up the panel, or how long they would take to reach a decision, while potential penalties ranged from a fine or more official transfer embargo to a points penalty or even expulsion. The fact that the League had charged Manchester City with no fewer than 115 counts relating to their own commercial dealings, and the reporting thereof, simply added another dimension to the potential ramifications of the commission's ruling.

As the season reached it's final month, external criticism of the Everton owner and board was piling in from all directions and pressure was mounting from those clubs embroiled with them in the battle to avoid relegation for the situation to be resolved before the end of the season.

Some contested newspaper reports claimed that Leeds United, Leicester City, Nottingham Forest, Southampton and Burnley all believed they were entitled to compensation from Everton should the club be found guilty, and that they were preparing to sue the club for damages if Everton stayed up.

At the very least, the clubs concerned asked that the Premier League ensure the work of the independent commission be completed before the end of the 2022/23 season so that any sanctions could apply to the ongoing relegation battle, particularly where a points deduction was concerned.

However, the League had to inform them that they were powerless to bring forward the verdict of the commission as they had no say in how swiftly the review process would be completed.

As it turned out, the panel wouldn't meet until October that year and Everton would go into the 2023/24 season with the threat of an unknown punishment still hanging over their heads.

2023: Chairman Bill's letter

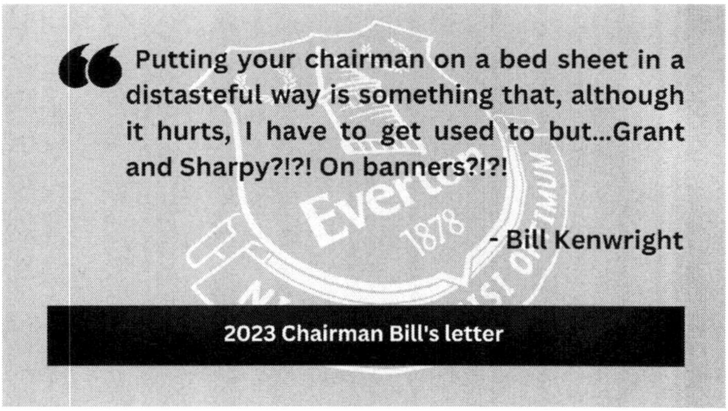

When Bill Kenwright's decade-long search for a billionaire benefactor to bankroll Everton's return to the elite of English football came to a seemingly successful conclusion with the arrival of Farhad Moshiri in February 2016, there was a school of thought that it might provide a watershed moment where the theatre impresario could begin to step aside after 12 years as chairman.

Though he had only been a major shareholder at the time, with a 49.9% stake, Moshiri's stated aim back in 2016 was to eventually increase his investment in the club. That would then provide him the opportunity to overhaul the club's leadership with fresh faces, new ideas and commercial acumen.

The British-Iranian businessman opted, instead, for continuity and a heavy emphasis on local influence, with Kenwright remaining in his post to offer his experience of running a Premier League club, even as his shareholding eventually dwindled to less than 2%. Moshiri, meanwhile, would resist taking a place in the boardroom himself until June 2023, almost two years after his representative on the Board, Sasha Ryazantsev had left the club.

Over time, however, as the progress promised by the new regime stalled, both on and off the pitch, confusion over just who was making the big decisions became a source of frustration for a growing contingent among the fanbase.

The agitation for change in the boardroom that had begun in earnest in December 2021, when it became clear that Rafael Benitez's tenure as manager was destined for failure, and it would build over the following 18 months as the Blues struggled to avoid relegation to the Championship. Fans began by imploring Moshiri to make personnel changes to the Board of Directors that could inject fresh blood and demonstrable expertise in business, commerce and top-level football into the club. By the turn of 2023, however, as Everton's situation in the Premier League became more perilous and a second successive fight for survival ensued under another failed head-coaching appointment in Frank Lampard, the clamour was now for a wholesale clear-out of the hierarchy.

That meant calls for removal of all the existing directors, including CEO Denise Barrett-Baxendale, Finance Director Grant Ingles, Non-Executive Director and playing legend Graeme Sharp, and

Chairman Kenwright himself, who had become a lightning rod for criticism from the most vocal opponents to the status quo at Everton.

Either a meddlesome and reactionary presence, a necessary check on Moshiri's more destructive impulses, or something in between, depending on which fans you asked, "Blue Bill" was seen by many as someone who would robustly defend his record without taking personal responsibility for the club's failings.

By January 2023. of course, Kenwright had been self-exiled from the Directors Box, with the members of the Board opting not attend home games, and he used the forum of the club's 2021/22 accounts to express his "pain" at not being able to attend Goodison Park.

In his Chairman's Statement at the front of the annual reports and accounts, he wrote:

"I may have been castigated by some fans for sharing my opinion, but I have enjoyed many [good?] times at Everton, and even though we have sadly been trophyless under my Chairmanship, it is with no fear of further criticism when I say two league games from last season's 38 will stay with me forever.

"Do I have to say more than that night against Crystal Palace? While the afternoon I stood alone in the stand at Leicester City after a monumental away, when listening to our outstanding travelling supporters, sing passionately and enthusiastically — for a full 20 minutes after the game had ended!! — was inspiring, humbling and genuinely moving.

"Memories of occasions like these have made the recent instruction given to myself and my fellow board members not to attend Goodison Park all the more painful that has hurt deeply.

"Looking forward, we know we have challenges to overcome. The absolute priority is, of course, to secure our Premier League status for a 70th consecutive season and we can all play a part in helping to secure that.

"As we proved in the run-in to last season, a unified football club is a stronger football club."

***

That unity would continue to prove elusive, however, and in April, the supporters movement going by the social media tag #AllTogetherNow, penned on open letter in which they reiterated their call and that of the 27 Campaign (now known as NSNOW) for the removal of the club's Board of Directors.

In their announcement, #AllTogetherNow said that the protests, staged before each home game since the turn of 2023, calling for wholesale change in the Boardroom, would cease if Moshiri confirmed that changes would occur in the running of the club.

Somewhat controversially, the movement's letter made mention of Kenwright's well-documented ill-health over the preceding few years as being a potential impediment to his running of the club, and this was addressed directly by the chairman in his own public response in which he defended the calibre of the Board's individual members.

In a highly personal letter, posted on the club's official website, Kenwright stressed that running the club in the competitive environment of the Premier League was difficult, as was securing the funding for Everton's new stadium at Bramley-Moore Dock.

He also dismissed the notion the club would be better off without the current board in place, when he wrote:

"Dear #Alltogethernow,

"I have read your letter to the Club. Firstly, can I thank you for your care and concern regarding my health. You may well know that in April 2015, I was advised I had a chronic illness that would probably be with me for the duration. This is, pretty inevitably, only the start of a journey where the issues usually increase. And they have. What you may also know is that most people find a spirit that will not give in and hopefully not be beaten. Sometimes it's not easy but there are many worse off than me.

"If I may, I will take this opportunity to address a couple of points from the rest of your letter. The Chairman does not run the football club. We have a Chief Executive Officer who does that, as is true with most clubs. In the eyes of most of the football world, Denise is amongst the best of the best. The truth is she has to be to deal with what every other Premier League club copes with in a hugely competitive environment in addition to the problems that the world has thrown at us over the last three years and, closer to home, in the last year or so. You may think it is not a massive challenge to relentlessly push forward the new stadium currently taking shape on the waterfront. I promise you it is! Financiers amongst your group will tell you why.

"You write that 'The rumours tell you from 'well placed and trustworthy sources' that investment is imminent.' Right now, that could be half right, a quarter right...etc. But that has been the situation for some time now. Again, those of you that know about raising hundreds of millions in investment will tell you it's a relentless journey where hopes are built and squashed in a heartbeat. But it's a quest that we undertake relentlessly and we will succeed. We are succeeding. Farhad and myself are on it hourly ... along with the Board and its advisors.

"For what you believe to be the best interests of the Club you are committed to the removal of this Board. As you've shown. For me, the horror of seeing Grant Ingles, our Chief Financial Officer, and Graeme Sharp being attacked is more than difficult to comprehend. Putting your chairman on a bed sheet in a distasteful way is something that, although it hurts, I have to get used to but...Grant and Sharpy?!?! On banners?!?! The short window you refer to will, you infer, be helped by the removal of your Board. Have you ever pondered whether your manager and players would agree with that? Whether Frank would have rubbed his hands with glee last year at the thought, rather than rushing to the Directors' Box to acknowledge where his biggest support had come from? And what about other clubs around us? Are they thinking 'the Everton Board has gone... it's going to be easier for us now!!!?' I'm confident of the answer to each of those questions. Finally, there is one indisputable fact. Your Board cares. It's not nice going through what we have gone through but it hasn't stopped the work rate, the desire to grow and improve and the loyalty to this Club and to Evertonians.

"I've often said that I would never deny the right of protest to any football fan, especially Evertonians. I know, inevitably, your day will of course come. Just as I knew that I would find you a billionaire when the loud and long protests claimed I wasn't even looking. In the meantime, I thank you again for worrying about my health problems. In truth, a week off would be great...but I can't see it happening...as it hasn't for many years. I wish you what I have wished every Evertonian since I joined the Blue Family nearly seven decades ago...a happy weekend...the season end we all hope for...and a return to better days thereafter."

Chairman Bill

***

It took just two days for the #AllTogetherNow Campaign to deliver a return salvo in what was becoming a public war of words with Kenwright, reiterating their calls for the Everton chairman to stand down.

Both the tone and the timing of the chairman's letter, coming as it did on the eve of an important match against Crystal Palace, were criticised by sections of the fanbase and in their follow-up, #AllTogetherNow cited Kenwright's response as further evidence of his unsuitability to the role he fulfilled at the club.

They pointed to Everton's desperate fight for survival in the Premier League as an indictment of the Board's failings and, describing his position as "untenable", they suggested he would never be able to restore the fans' faith in his ability to lead the club.

At that point, Everton sat in the bottom three of the Premier League with six games to go in the season, in danger of losing their top-flight status for the first time in 72 years. And, if that were to happen, the club's directors had confirmed just three weeks earlier that if the club was relegated, there was "material uncertainty about [its] ability to continue as a going concern."

Besides the Campaign's response to Kenwright, they took the decision to call off the scheduled protest before the potentially massive home game with Newcastle United on 27 April, and instead asked supporters to "stand shoulder to shoulder" to welcome the team outside Goodison Park.

#AllTogetherNow's second release followed statements issued on social media by both the Everton Fan Advisory Board and the Everton Fans' Forum expressing their disappointment with Kenwright's decision to release his letter at a time of distress and concern among supporters. It read:

Dear 'Chairman Bill',

"Every Evertonian is gobsmacked to read your reply to the All Together Now Movement. As Chairman of the Board, you are the apparent leader of OUR club. Under your control and leadership, our great club has endured its longest ever spell without a trophy and has been in more relegation battles than cup finals. You have thrown our CEO under the bus, something which will no doubt cause more upheaval in the boardroom of the worst-run club in the league.

"We now find ourselves in yet another relegation battle, our club's finances are shot, and we are under investigation by an Independent Panel of the Premier League. OUR club is in crisis. Yet, your first statement in months is to complain about bedsheets. We are afraid that all your letter has done is confirmed the size of the gulf between you, the board, and Everton's fans. The players alongside Evertonians kept our club up last season. You trying to claim credit for our survival last year is an insult to the Evertonians who greeted coaches and sung our hearts out. Frankly, your letter reads as delusional.

"Your letter adds weight to the fact that you cannot and will not ever win back the confidence of Everton fans, nor are you ever welcome back to Goodison Park. Your position is untenable, the timing of your self-centred response was scandalous. As a movement and Evertonians we care about the future of our club and are putting all of our effort into backing the team on Thursday as opposed to protesting, this is all despite your tone deaf media release on the eve of the huge Palace game.

"Out of respect for our club, go now and allow us to unite for the relegation fight your mismanagement has left us in."

#AllTogetherNow

***

Kenwright's controversial open letter to the #AllTogetherNow fan group elicited a further statement from the Everton Fan Advisory Board calling a vote of no confidence in the chairman.

The FAB – comprised of four elected representatives, including shareholder and then chair Jazz Bal, and fans drawn from supporters' groups, including the Everton Fans' Forum, Everton Supporters Club Committee and the Everton Heritage Society – was assembled to act as a liaison between Everton's ownership and Board on the one hand, and the fans on the other.

In the weeks preceding the war of words with Kenwright and supporters' groups, the Advisory Board had presented Everton's Board of Directors with several concerns raised by supporters at the running of the club, and the FAB itself had voiced their own reservations about a lack of timely or adequate communication from the hierarchy, particularly around player recruitment, the ongoing search for investment, the funding models for the new Everton Stadium, and owner Farhad

Moshiri's own medium- to long-term plans as they pertained to his position as majority shareholder.

In their statement, the FAB remarked on what was "a second successive relegation battle threatening our Premier League status", the alleged breach of financial rules, and their own calls for "proactive leadership, communication and engagement" from the club hierarchy, when the relationship between large parts of the fanbase and the Board had become fractured, and for some, irreparable.

***

Over the years as a journalist covering Everton for the *Liverpool Echo* and more recently the *Daily Mail*, Dominic King had defended the Everton hierarchy and Bill Kenwright from criticism, but as the club fought for its Premier League life, the evidence of "years of bad decisions" has finally opened King's eyes to what he saw as the biggest problems afflicting the club. He claimed, "The board have ripped the soul out of Everton and everything it stood for has gone."

In his article following Everton's demoralising second-half collapse against Newcastle in late April that left the club in 19th place in the Premier League, King blamed "a constant cycle of bad decisions from the board" that have been compounded by "a raft of performances that have been an affront – there is only so much misery people can take."

Even the *BBC* were commenting on the civil war between fans and board ripping Toffees apart. It was a rift symbolised by the fact that in March, the Everton Timeline panel dedicated to Kenwright's successful takeover of Everton in 1999 had been ripped off the wall of Goodison Park and thrown into a canal.

"To add to the toxicity and uncertainty around the Merseyside club, a civil war has erupted between the Everton board and disgruntled supporters, who feel chairman Bill Kenwright is not up to the job and owner Farhad Moshiri has squandered much of the £750 million he has invested," wrote Shamoon Hafez for *BBC Sport*.

There were few Evertonians who would have disagreed with that pithy summary.

2023: Dyche steers Blues to Premier League Survival

> I said to the players, 'We shouldn't be here. Enjoy this today and you've earned it, but at the end of the day it has got to change.' It's a horrible day for all concerned. There is no joy in it for me other than getting the job done.
>
> -Sean Dyche

2023 Dyche steers Blues to Premier League Survival

Everton's gritty win over Brentford on 1 March had been their third 1-0 home victory since Sean Dyche had taken charge and, like the slender triumphs over Arsenal and Leeds, seemed to have established a template by which the Toffees could save themselves from relegation to the Championship. They sat in 15th that day, albeit just one point above the bottom three, but they failed to win again for the next two months.

An impressive equaliser from Ellis Simms had salvaged a draw against Chelsea at Stamford Bridge; likewise a spectacular,

90th-minute Michael Keane goal against Tottenham at Goodison Park a fortnight after that, but those relative highs were followed by fairly dismal defeats to Manchester United at Old Trafford and to Fulham and Newcastle at home.

The 4-1 drubbing at the hands of Newcastle had been a particularly crushing blow. Everton had dropped back into the drop zone following a goalless draw at Crystal Palace five days earlier and, with home games running out, the visit of Eddie Howe's Champions League-chasing Magpies was seen as vital to Everton's survival hopes.

It was decided by the various activist groups that the pre-match protests against the owner and Board would be suspended for the week and another raucous, blue-hued coach welcome was planned to greet the players in the streets outside the ground. In short, Evertonians had planned to expend every ounce of effort in supporting the team with another of those famous "bear pit" atmospheres inside the Grand Old Lady, but what they got in return was a hefty loss.

It meant that Dyche's team had to eke enough points out of their final five matches of the season – four if they discounted the visit of Champions-elect Manchester City – to lift themselves back out of the bottom three before the end of the campaign.

***

1 May 2023: Leicester City v Everton

Clashes didn't come much more important than the one between Leicester and Everton on 1 May at the King Power Stadium, a veritable 'six pointer' between the teams sitting in 18th and 19th place respectively before kick-off. Victory for either club would have taken them a step towards guaranteed safety; as it was, each had to be content with just a point.

Everton left the East Midlands much the happier of the two having avoided another damaging defeat thanks to the heroics of Jordan Pickford and a redemptive second-half strike from Alex Iwobi.

With Dominic Calvert-Lewin making a third straight start to add a much-needed extra dimension to the Blues' attack, Everton were easily the more dangerous of the two teams for the first quarter of the contest.

And their early superiority was rewarded with a quarter of an hour gone when the ball was flighted towards Calvert-Lewin just inside the box, and he went down under a clear shove from Timothy Castagne that left referee Michael Oliver in no doubt about the award of a penalty.

Calvert-Lewin stepped up himself to take it and swept a perfectly struck effort high down the middle of Daniel Iversen's goal. There was a chance to make it 2-0 almost immediately when Iwobi played the striker in, but Calvert-Lewin's shot was blocked behind. Michael Keane could only nod the resulting corner wide at the back post.

The Toffees' lead lasted just seven minutes, though. Dwight McNeil gave away a cheap free-kick inside his own half and when James Maddison's set-piece wasn't dealt with, Wout Faes headed the ball back across goal. Keane failed to track Caglar Soyuncu and the Turkish defender swivelled it in off Pickford's hand to level the match at 1-1.

Iwobi, having received a let-off when dispossessed in midfield and Maddison's curling effort failed to test Pickford, was not so fortunate shortly afterwards. The Nigerian's ill-advised cross-field pass across the centre-circle was intercepted by Youri Tielemans, Maddison quickly threaded the ball through Everton's defence and the 36-year-old Jamie Vardy easily out-stripped Keane for pace, rounding the keeper and slamming it home to turn the match on its head.

To their credit, Everton responded, and when McNeil surged forward and cut the ball across to Calvert-Lewin almost on the goal-line, the striker somehow prodded the ball to the only part of the gaping goal where the keeper was, and Iversen kept it out.

Leicester counter-attacked immediately, when Vardy twisted Keane into knots before drawing Pickford and chipping a shot over him, but the ball bounced off the crossbar and over.

That wasn't to be the end of the first-half drama , though as Coleman, who had been having a very good game to that point, went down in a heap clutching in his knee after being pole-axed by Boubakary Soumare. He was eventually carried off – the skipper still geeing his teammates up from the stretcher – and replaced by Nathan Patterson.

Then, in the ensuing injury time, Iwobi lost the ball again in an advanced area, Leicester poured forward once more, and when Harvey Barnes's cross struck Keane's out-stretched arm, referee Oliver pointed to the spot again, this time in the home side's favour.

Pickford elected not to pick a corner, though, and stood tall in his goal to beat away Maddison's penalty as he tried to drive it down the middle, keeping it at 2-1 heading into the second half where the contest became more and more akin to a winner-takes-all cup tie.

Everton came out of the changing room the more purposeful of the two sides and almost got their reward again when Calvert-Lewin's effort was kept out by Iversen's out-stretched foot at the near post.

Two minutes later, however, it was 2-2. McNeil's cross came off the head of Faes and dropped invitingly to Iwobi arriving on the other side of the box and he steered a beautifully cushioned half-volley past the keeper.

That sparked a sustained period of Leicester pressure and James Tarkowski had to clear Vardy's goal bound header off his line. But as the game moved into the final quarter of an hour, it was Everton who looked the more likely to grab a winner and Doucouré went very close to stealing the points three minutes from the end. The Mali international found himself with time on the edge of the area to line up a left-footed shot that he despatched in search of the bottom corner, but Iversen had sight enough of the ball to dive to his right and palm the ball behind.

So, not the result that Everton needed with just four matches remaining – two of them against the daunting opposition of Brighton and Manchester City – and with the club still sitting in the bottom three of the Premier League.

Individual errors and amateur defending continued to be huge issues that Dyche seemed incapable of addressing but the manager was buoyed by the spirit shown by his team, the attacking threat they posed with Calvert-Lewin leading the line, and that they had scored twice away from home for the third time under his stewardship.

Salvation was still possible, but matters were out of the Blues' hands. They needed help in matches involving their relegation rivals until Everton could try to help themselves at the Amex Community Stadium the following Monday against Brighton and Hove Albion.

Final score: Leicester 2-2 Everton

***

After the match at the King Power Stadium, the club confirmed that Seamus Coleman had suffered a serious, season-ending injury.

"It's really unfortunate," manager Sean Dyche said. "We're waiting on news. "It could be serious, a knee injury. I thought he was terrific. The medics have had a look at it and it doesn't look great. We'll hope for the very best for him."

***

8 May 2023: Brighton v Everton

One of the surprise packages of the season, Brighton & Hove Albion had become somewhat of a feared opponent during the 2022/23 season. They had lost Graham Potter – the architect of their emergence as an established Premier League presence and their impressive possession-based style of play – to Chelsea earlier in the season but, far from lose their way in his absence, they had arguably become even better under his successor, Roberto de Zerbi.

By the time Everton travelled to the south coast in early May for a game billed on social media as the match between 'a well run club' vs 'a poorly run club,', the Seagulls were in eighth place, just four points shy of fifth. The general consensus was that the Toffees would do well to get anything from the game, particularly in view of what had happened in the reverse fixture at Goodison Park at the turn of the year.

Indeed, the bookies had given Brighton 7/19 for the win; Everton, with only two away wins in the last 34 games, were 8/1 for the victory. In the end, fans on both sides could hardly believe their eyes, as the visitors defied the odds.

By the final whistle, the jubilant hordes in the rammed away end easily outnumbered the rapidly diminishing home crowd, most of whom had seen enough by halftime to believe it would not be their day.

Everton had blown much-vaunted Brighton away on their own ground, registered their biggest win in 4½ years and lifted themselves out of the relegation zone with a counter-attacking masterclass at the Amex Stadium. In the context of their battle for survival, it was up there with the most important results of the season.

For Everton, the result was also a remarkable reverse of the match between the two teams at Goodison Park the preceding January when Brighton tore them apart on the way to a 4-1 win that drove another nail into the coffin of Frank Lampard's tenure as the Toffees' boss. It was also their best result on their travels since beating Sean Dyche's Burnley by the same scoreline under Marco Silva in December 2018.

With Dyche finally caving and dropping Michael Keane back to the bench, Yerry Mina returned to the team for a rare start at centre-half alongside James Tarkowski while Nathan Patterson came in at right-back for the injured Seamus Coleman and James Garner kept his place in central midfield.

And Everton got off to the perfect start with a goal after just 33 seconds. Patterson made an important block to intercept Kaoru Mitoma's attempt to knock it past him, Dominic Calvert-Lewin executed a perfect pirouette to take Alex Iwobi's pass around his marker and after driving into the box, the striker crossed perfectly for Doucouré to knock it in assuredly at the back post.

In the 26th minute it was 2-0. Dwight McNeil raced away down the left flank, spotted Doucouré free on the other side of the penalty area and found him with a perfect cross, which the Mali international volleyed home brilliantly.

Remarkably, it was 3-0 six minutes after that, and the goal came from another superbly executed breakaway. Iwobi's ball into the box was a little too far ahead of Doucouré, but he kept it alive and found McNeil, who took it to the byline and attempted to drive it across the face of goal. The cross caught Steele's out-stretched leg, though, and bounced in.

McNeil squandered yet another promising counter when he just failed to find Calvert-Lewin as the pair raced away in a two-on-two and Garner must have thought he had registered his first Premier League goal when he side-footed wide of the keeper from close range, but Lewis Dunk got in a crucial block that ensured Brighton's deficit was only three at the halfway stage.

Roberto de Zerbi responded by making four changes at the interval, throwing on exciting young striker Evan Ferguson and the tricky Julio Enciso and for the first 15 minutes of the second half it was one-way traffic towards Jordan Pickford's goal.

The England keeper stood tall, however, saving bravely at his near post inside the first minute of the restart, parrying Enciso's fierce drive up and behind to safety and then brilliantly turning a Ferguson header onto the post with a one-handed save at full stretch. Ferguson grazed the crossbar with a shot via Pickford's fingertips and, from the ensuing corner, then Alexis Mac Allister thumped a header off the face of the bar as Everton just about kept their clean sheet intact.

Dunk dropped a header wide of the far post shortly afterwards and Pickford made another top-drawer save to palm Mac Allister's header away before Everton defied all expectations by scoring a fourth.

Iwobi surged down the left flank this time and drew one defender to him that opened up the space for McNeil to steal into and. When the Nigerian found him with a perfectly-weighted pass, the former Burnley man faked to shoot, turned inside the last man and keeper and walked the ball into net before wheeling away in delight.

Brighton reduced their arrears to three again almost immediately when Mitoma slid in to meet a deep cross from the right. Although he could only steer the ball onto the post, it bounced off Mac Allister and then into the empty net to make it 4-1 with 11 minutes to go.

The Amex Stadium began to empty at 4-0, and those who remained did not get to witness a miraculous recovery. Indeed, it was Everton and McNeil who put the icing on the cake in stoppage time.

Once more it was a counter-attack, this time sparked by sub Amadou Onana's ball from inside his own half that released McNeil who used Iwobi in the middle as a decoy before leathering it inside the near post and into the top corner of Steele's goal.

A quite stunning result, against a very good side who could still have mathematically moved as high as fifth if they won their games in hand, lifted Everton out of the bottom three, taking full advantage of Leicester's 5-3 defeat at Fulham and Leeds United's loss at Manchester City that weekend.

Everton's next clash, with the new League leaders Manchester City at Goodison Park, promised to be a Herculean task of even bigger proportions but Dyche's men had given themselves a great chance of preserving the club's top-flight status providing they could reproduce this kind of form in their final three fixtures.

Final score: Brighton 1-5 Everton

***

20 May 2023: Wolverhampton Wanderers v Everton

Everton's comedown from that miraculous display in Brighton was swift and predictable as champions-elect Manchester City and Ilkay Gündogan, in particular, underlined the chasm in class between the two clubs with another world-class performance and a comprehensive 3-0 victory at Goodison Park.

Knowing that the Blues' final two games against Wolves and Bournemouth offered far greater opportunity for picking up valuable points, Sean Dyche, no doubt, was keeping the bigger picture in mind.

Watching from the sidelines as the match at Molineux ticked into the ninth minute of injury time with his side 1-0 down, the Everton boss must have felt his side had left far too much to chance for the final day clash with the Cherries. Indeed, were the Blues to lose to Wolves, a Leicester victory at Newcastle two days later would vault the Foxes into 17th place and wrest control of their destiny from Dyche and company's hands.

What followed, delivered by folk hero Yerry Mina as the clock reached 98:52, was another stunning moment in Everton's fourth great escape of the Premier League era.

With Calvert-Lewin passed fit despite feeling tightness in his groin during the defeat to City, Sean Dyche and his men were no doubt confident that, despite having to start Dwight McNeil at left back in place of the injured Vitalii Mykolenko, they could carry on from their magnificent performance at Brighton, and pick up three precious points against a Wolves side that had already secured their Premier League future.

And they started well, with Calvert-Lewin firing into the side-netting and then despatching Alex Iwobi's dangerous centre narrowly over the crossbar. However, the injury crisis at full back was about to get worse as Nathan Patterson was involved in a collision of legs that would force him off with an injury with less than half an hour gone.

Everton remained the dominant side and their best chance of the first period should have fallen to Calvert-Lewin, but Mina got in ahead of him to meet McNeil's corner and the defender couldn't keep his header down.

The visitors' momentum and good work to that point was undone shortly afterwards, when Doucouré's weak pass was intercepted deep in Wolves territory and the hosts broke away through Adama Traoré. Jordan Pickford saved his shot but could only palm it into the path of the untracked Hwang Hee-chan who turned the loose ball home.

As if the afternoon couldn't get much worse, Calvert-Lewin's afternoon also came to a premature end on the stroke of half-time when he went to ground grasping his thigh before putting his head in hands. It was yet another recurrence of his troublesome hamstring injury and it would be mid-September before he saw action again.

With Calvert-Lewin and Patterson missing and Demarai Gray and Michael Keane on in their place, Everton struggled for coherence and balance in the second half. There had a few bright moments but after Pablo Sarabia passed up a great chance to kill the contest when he curled his shot, the Blues' attempts to grab something from the contest became increasingly desperate and ineffective.

By this point, Keane had been pushed forward into an emergency striker's role after Dyche had introduced Mason Holgate in place of Amadou Onana, and the visitors then launched the ball forward hoping for something to break their way.

Wolves almost put the game to bed two minutes into the nine added on by referee David Coote for stoppages, when Matheus Nunes raced clear on the breakaway, but Pickford denied him with an out-stretched foot that diverted the Portuguese's shot wide.

Then, just when it looked as though Everton's huffing, puffing and ineffective long-ball football was to be in vain, Gray flighted a long ball to the back post. Tarkowski beat Bentley's gloves to the ball to head it downwards where Keane knocked it square and Mina converted from close range to send the distraught visiting fans into delirium on their side of the stadium.

In the battle to avoid relegation, the Toffees had really needed a victory but the draw salvaged with almost the last kick of the game would prove to be one more crucial result overseen by Dyche during those final few weeks of the campaign.

Final score: Wolves 1-1 Everton

***

28 May 2023: Everton v AFC Bournemouth

The point secured against Wolves ended up proving vital, as did the 88th-minute save by Newcastle United's Nick Pope on Monday 22 May that denied Timothy Castagne a dramatic winner for Leicester City at St James's Park. It meant that, going into the final day of the

2022/23, Everton needed to win to once again secure their Premier League status and preserve 69 years of unbroken top-flight football at Goodison Park. Anything else and the Toffees would be at the mercy of the results in the matches between Leeds and Tottenham at Elland Road and, more pertinently, Leicester and West Ham at the King Power Stadium.

The visitors to the Grand Old Lady were Bournemouth who had already twice beaten Everton in convincing fashion at the Vitality Stadium back in November, so there would be nothing routine about the fixture.

With Dominic Calvert-Lewin and Vitalii Mykolenko ruled out, Sean Dyche had to cobble together a team capable of beating the Cherries, who had already achieved safety but had not travelled to Merseyside to simply make up the numbers.

The manager turned to a starting back three for the first time since taking over from Frank Lampard, deploying Dwight McNeil and the excellent James Garner as wing-backs, with Demarai Gray charged with leading the line.

It was Everton who began the game on the front foot, but it took them a quarter of an hour to threaten the visitors' goal when Gray drilled a shot that faded away from the target. Idrissa Gueye was then played in superbly by Amadou Onana, but Mark Travers tipped his rising effort over the crossbar, and the goalkeeper had to be alert a few minutes later to push away another strong effort from the Senegalese international.

An error by Tarkowski almost condemned the Blues to a half-time deficit but Yerry Mina got back to get a crucial touch on Dominic Solanke's shot to divert it behind while, back down the other end,

Garner's curling effort was heading for the top corner, but Travers batted it behind.

At the halfway stage, Everton were heading out of the Premier League, with Leicester - who had a superior goal difference - beating West Ham, but the Blues had another 45 minutes to save themselves from relegation and potential financial Armageddon.

That breakthrough should have come just six minutes after the restart, but Gray failed with a gilt-edged chance from close range. The ball was nodded on to him in the six-yard box and he just had to get a decisive touch but, perhaps fearing contact from an approaching defender, he miscued his header and Travers pushed it off the line before it was prodded behind to safety.

Six minutes after that, though, Abdoulaye Doucouré imprinted his name indelibly on Goodison folklore with a stunning 20-yard strike. Gueye's floated ball was initially cleared by a Bournemouth defender and when it fell to Doucouré, he smashed it home with such velocity that Travers barely moved.

The Old Lady erupted as one in elation. There were incredible scenes of joy in the stadium before the hosts dug in to try to both defend the lead and extend it if they could.

Gary O'Neil's introduction of Kieffer Moore threatened to add unwanted drama to the occasion. The Welsh international's added height caused havoc. It was his knock-down that fell to Solanke in the box, but Pickford made a decisive intervention, apparently dislocating a finger in the process, while Mina finished the job by clearing his lines.

With Gray wasting one great opportunity when he slipped trying to test the keeper from the angle, the industrious Alex Iwobi seeing a shot deflect inches wide of the far post and Tarkowski heading over following a corner, a second goal to settle the nerves never came.

Instead, Goodison held its collective breath at the other end as substitute Matias Viña lined up a crisp volley that Pickford beat away to safety.

Anguished Evertonians bayed for the final whistle as a couple of late free kicks gave the visitors chances to heave the ball into the box, but Everton's back line held before referee Stuart Attwell finally blew for full-time. For that season at least, Everton were safe, and the relief was palpable.

Final score: Everton 1-0 Bournemouth

***

With his post-match comments, Dyche struck a purposeful and less restrained chord, saying that the necessary work to change things significantly at Everton was already underway.

The 51-year-old had completed his initial remit of keeping the Blues in the top flight by steering them to safety, despite the loss of key players and having an imbalanced squad. He quickly dispensed with his well-worn rhetoric around shifting the mentality in the dressing room to talk of making Everton think and operate like a big club again.

His message carried a tacit challenge to the hierarchy to assist in that transformation, but it was also grounded by what would be possible in the short term, with Dyche insisting there was a lot of work ahead and there would be no quick fixes.

Dyche told the media, "I said to the players, 'we shouldn't be here. Enjoy this today and you've earned it, but at the end of the day it has got to change.' It's a horrible day for all concerned. There is no joy in it for me other than getting the job done.

"There is no point in sitting on it and saying, 'Look how great we are,' because it is not like that. There is loads to change here and a lot of work to be done, but it was a big step to secure it.

"The work on next season started the day I got in here. Don't think I thought this was an easy fix, because it is not. Far from it. There is a massive amount of work to be done. The thing I've learnt about Everton is the fans have been amazing. They want the club to be in the top end of the market, but the club is not at the top end of the market.

"It's a big club, big history, but we are not performing like a big club. We have to find a way of changing that. This is two seasons now. There is a massive amount of change to build to a new dawn, a new future, a bigger future.

"I think the Evertonians, as remarkable as they have been, have to remember that. This is a bigger project than just, 'Oh well, it's all right now.' I don't have magic dust, I can only make things happen I think are believable. It is definitely a reason to be happy, but we have to demand more internally. The fans know the truth. They know this wasn't a walk in the park.

"You have to build a belief in a new culture. If you ask five die-hard Evertonians what the club stood for, they would probably give me five different answers. The club has to realign. There was a time when it was 'earthy, hard-working. Give a lot to the shirt. Pride'. I'm not sure they are as obvious now.

"That's the base I want to build but I want to play good, attractive, winning football but it has to start with something. There have been signs this team will work, fight and give everything. Don't think Pep's [Guardiola's Manchester City] side just play beautiful football. They work, they defend, play hard, as well as being ultra-top footballers.

"There's a chance [I'll have to sell players]. I'll find out about that. There's been peripheral talks based on ifs, buts and maybes. I'd be very surprised if they say there is going to be another war chest. There is a beautiful stadium down the road and someone has to pay for that.

"But that will come over the coming weeks when we find out the truth of what we have got. We had to get this sorted out. We've got it over the line."

2023: The Search Continues for New Investors

As Everton fought for their Premier League lives throughout the spring of 2023, confusion continued to surround the future ownership of the club. Press speculation over much of the season had suggested that Farhad Moshiri was prepared to listen to offers for his majority stake, but the Iranian-born businessman had been steadfast in insisting that the club was not for sale.

Media reports in March had put that down to Moshiri's concerns that selling Everton could cause his relationship with Alisher Usmanov – who was already sanctioned by the United Kingdom and

European Union following Russia's invasion of Ukraine in 2022 – to be scrutinised by the U.K. Government.

Indeed, Government sources had told the *The Daily Mail* that they were keeping a watchful eye on any sale of Everton. Perhaps there was still a suspicion – first aroused by the leak of the so-called Paradise Papers in 2017 - that Moshiri's original shareholding in Arsenal had been a gift from Usmanov. It was the proceeds from the sale of his Arsenal shares which Moshiri had used to buy into Everton in 2016.

Any involvement from Usmanov in the running of Everton was always denied strongly, both by the club and Moshiri's camp, but it remained a constant source of conjecture in the media, not least when it was claimed that as many as five prospective candidates for the Everton manager's had reported having held direct conversations with Usmanov during their interview processes.

Everton had cut their commercial ties with Usmanov's business entities in the spring of 2022 following Vladimir Putin's attack on Ukraine, which meant the loss of key sponsorships from USM Holdings and subsidiary Megafon, but there remained a possibility that Moshiri might yet be drawn into the sanctions equation. This concern grew when Usmanov and USM were reported to have been targeted with further sanctions by the U.K. government amid scrutiny of individuals and companies whom it accused of acting as "financial fixers" for Russian oligarchs like Usmanov and Roman Abramovich.

Britain's Foreign Office said in a statement, that they were aiming the new measures at those helping the two prominent businessmen (Usmanov and Abramovich) to avoid the full cost of financial sanctions which, by implication, could have included his long-time business partner – and the "M" in USM – Moshiri.

Indeed, *The Guardian*'s Simon Goodley reported that the Treasury's "sanctions police" were investigating Moshiri's finances, considering his long-time association with Usmanov which made him a "person of interest" to the Office of Financial Sanctions Implementation (OFSI).

That reportedly prompted the Everton owner to hire an expert sanctions lawyer at Peters & Peters, 'one of the U.K.'s largest law firms', but in an echo of the situation at Chelsea where Roman Abramovich had been forced to sell his club while receiving none of the proceeds, Goodley raised the possibility that an offer of investment or buy-out of Everton "would result in Moshiri losing control of the club without being paid a penny" if he, too, was subject to punitive measures by the Government. Or if it was proved conclusively that Usmanov's money directly funded his shares in the club.

USM Holdings bristled at the moves by Whitehall, saying in a statement:

"We consider the U.K. sanctions adopted against USM Holdings and its shareholders to be unjust and unfounded. Alisher Usmanov has not been engaged in business activity for a long period of time," the statement added.

Moshiri rejected the allegation in the same way he had strenuously denied claims it was Usmanov who effectively owned and controlled Everton, and that the oligarch had been in attendance during interviews for managerial candidates like Rafael Benitez and Frank Lampard.

***

In the meantime, Moshiri and the club continued negotiations with prospective investors in Everton from the United States. Talks with Florida-based private equity firm 777 Partners over a full takeover had reportedly stalled in March, and MSP Sports Capital took their place at the negotiating table with an offer of investment up to £150 million in return for a minority stake, perhaps in the form of preferential, convertible shares.

MSP, headed by former sport agent Jeff Moorad and businessman Jahm Najafi, secured exclusivity in their talks with Moshiri as a precursor to a proposed investment deal that was intended to provide Everton with much-needed funds, largely for the remaining construction costs on the stadium at Bramley-Moore Dock, and would also lead to change at boardroom level.

The New York-based investment firm, who already had stakes in Bundesliga side Augsburg, Spanish club AD Alcorcon, Estoril in Portugal and Belgian outfit Beveren, as well McClaren's Formula One team and the X Games, had been in discussions with Moshiri on and off for months and, by May 2023, all the indications were that an agreement was imminent.

However, a deal that would see MSP Sports Capital take an initial stake in Everton never materialised. Weeks passed and the 2023/24 season dawned without any sign of badly-needed funds to cover the next tranche due to stadium contractors, Laing O'Rourke. Then, on 23 August it was reported that MSP had withdrawn from talks with Moshiri.

No official reason was ever given but the claim was made by Matt Slater, Senior Football Reporter at *The Athletic*, that one of the stumbling blocks to the proposed deal had come in the form of opposition from Rights and Media Funding Limited, the offshore lender with whom the Blues had an estimated £200 million in outstanding loans and who had 'negative pledge clauses' which prevented Everton from pledging any assets if doing so would jeopardise R&MF's security.

According to Slater's report, that made MSP's proposal unworkable, with R&MF not convinced that the New York company would be injecting enough capital in return for its planned equity position of 25% unless they paid off tens of millions of pounds of what the club owed them first.

Nevertheless, MSP did agree to furnish the club with a £100 million loan for the Everton Stadium. In the meantime, the door was left open for 777 Partners who would soon reach a non-binding agreement with Moshiri regarding an outright takeover of his 94% stake in the Blues.

2023: Three step down from Everton Board

2023 Three step down from Everton Board

The winds of change in Everton's Boardroom finally arrived in June 2023 with the announcement that Chief Executive Denise Barrett-Baxendale, Finance Director Grant Ingles and Non-Executive Director Graeme Sharp had all stepped down from their respective roles with immediate effect.

The fate of chairman Bill Kenwright was expected to be announced shortly thereafter but it would take another 11 days before his position was clarified and, ultimately, it was Farhad Moshiri's preference that the 77-year-old theatre impresario remain in his post.

“We have all been fully committed during our time here and are disappointed to have made the decision to leave Everton,” a statement from Barrett-Baxendale, Sharp and Ingles said.

“We have worked tirelessly alongside our chairman in what has been a challenging period to deliver some of the most significant projects in Everton’s history – projects that will safeguard and sustain the commercial future of the club for generations to come.

“We are proud of the commercial growth projects progressed during our time on the board, including the construction of the club’s new waterfront stadium. This construction project — the largest currently on site in the U.K. — is progressing at pace.

“It has been an honour and a privilege to serve as directors. We would like to thank everyone who has supported us during our time here. We wish the club we have loved to serve every success in the future.”

***

On 15 June, Andy Hunter from *The Guardian* reported Everton fans had vowed to intensify protests against the club’s hierarchy unless they removed Bill Kenwright as chairman. He wrote:

"Given the clear need for improvements in a squad that has only just survived two relegation battles in succession, and this latest example of Everton’s dysfunction, the supporters group #AllTogetherNow has urged Moshiri to take decisive action.

"The group, which represents several Everton fan organisations, stated: 'We call for the immediate removal of the chairman of this football club – who has been the most unsuccessful chairman in our history. For the football club to move forward, and fans to unite, this without doubt has to happen. The protests will not cease and will only further intensify if you [Moshiri] allow ‘Chairman Bill’ to stumble on, continuing to fail in his position, despite clear evidence for a need for change. We ask you to respond without delay to this loyal fanbase, do not cause any further unnecessary hold up to a deadline that the football club’s leadership team set out.'

"Kenwright described the outgoing directors as 'a great board' when their departures were announced on Monday. While work is advancing on an impressive new stadium at Bramley Moore dock, Moshiri is yet to secure the funding needed to complete the project. Everton face other financial problems, including the threat of legal action from Leicester, Leeds, Southampton and Burnley should they be found to have breached Premier League financial rules. Their former manager Carlo Ancelotti is also suing the club in London’s high court. The #AllTogetherNow statement added: 'That ‘great board’ have left us in a perilous financial position with constant poor decision-making, leaving the club in a dire situation with an FFP court case hanging over our heads. They have brought us zero trophies and two back-to-back relegation battles. Not forgetting in recent times throwing the club’s biggest asset, its fans, under a bus with no remorse or apology.' "

2023: Moshiri joins Kenwright on Everton board

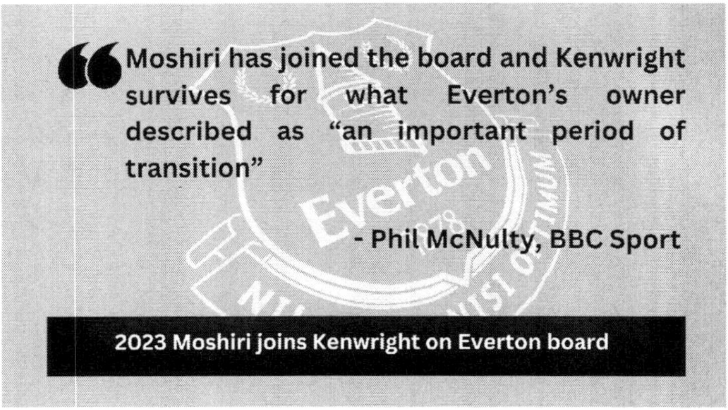

On 23 June, the position of Bill Kenwright and the make-up of Everton's interim Board of Directors were clarified when the club released of a statement in which it was announced that Colin Chong had been appointed as interim Chief Executive Officer and director.

Chong had served as the Chief Stadium Development Officer, focused on the delivery of Everton Stadium, as well as "the operational management of the club's business headquarters at the Royal Liver Building."

James Maryniak was promoted from Director of Finance to interim Chief Finance Officer, while two Non-Executive Directors were added to the Board in the form of the majority shareholder himself, Farhad Moshiri, and John Spellman, a Chartered Accountant, businessman and lifelong Blues fan.

Kenwright would remain as chairman, with Moshiri saying: "I wanted Bill to remain as our chairman during this important period of transition for the Club and I am delighted that he has accepted my request to do so. Bill's knowledge and vast experience will be crucial for us as we look to reset, deliver on external investment and position Everton for a successful future.

"In John, we have an experienced finance professional who has held Chief Executive and senior finance roles for international firms and I welcome him to the Club.

"In Colin and James, we have two experienced senior club professionals who have agreed to take on enhanced roles on an interim basis, and who we know can and will deliver immediately."

***

In an article for *BBC Sport*, Chief football writer Phil McNulty wrote of his scepticism that the news at boardroom level was unlikely to quell the mood of rebellion among fans:

"The early expectation after chief executive Denise Barrett-Baxendale, finance officer Grant Ingles and non-executive director and former player Graeme Sharp left the board was that long-serving Kenwright would follow.

"They formed a boardroom quartet whose relationship with the fanbase was so broken they have decided not to attend home games since January, citing safety reasons, amid growing protests among supporters, with Kenwright and owner Farhad Moshiri primary targets.

"Instead, Moshiri has joined the board and Kenwright survives for what Everton's owner described as 'an important period of transition' as incoming investment is expected from New York-based MSP Sports Capital to secure more funding for the club's new stadium at Bramley Moore Dock.

"It may well be that this is a boardroom holding operation until the MSP deal is finalised as it is expected they will understandably demand a strong boardroom presence in return for their investment, but the continued presence of Kenwright is in danger of overshadowing the wider context.

"Everton supporters' groups had already vowed to intensify protests if Kenwright stayed on and there is no doubt Moshiri has risked the further wrath of large numbers of fans by placing his faith in the 77-year-old, even if it may only be for a short period.

"Kenwright and Moshiri have taken heavy criticism for Everton's current parlous plight after two seasons of near relegation and being referred to an independent commission by the Premier League for alleged breaches of financial fair play rules.

"If Everton's statement was intended to calm the mood among discontented fans, early indications suggest it has had the opposite effect."

2023: Interim CEO updates fans on stadium progress

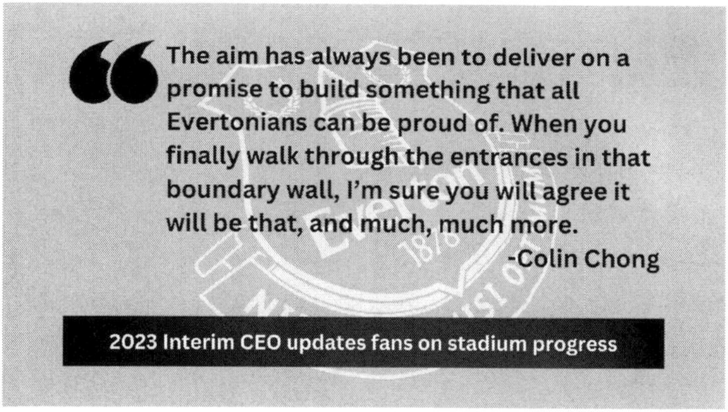

Colin Chong would serve in his dual role as Interim Chief Executive Officer and Chief Stadium Development Officer at Everton, and within days of his addition to the Board he would provide an update on progress made on Everton Stadium which had, by this stage, taken full shape at Bramley-Moore Dock.

He took the opportunity to address supporters in his capacity as acting CEO and address mischievous tabloid reports suggesting that the stadium was behind schedule:

"There was a time, not long ago, when peering over the boundary wall, or looking through the gates, was necessary to check on the progress of our future home on the banks of the River Mersey.

"Now, Everton Stadium towers into the north Liverpool skyline, and we've all enjoyed watching this magnificent super-structure emerge from the former dock.

"The scale of progress in the past 12 months has been staggering, and that is testament to the planning, commitment, professionalism and ingenuity of our trusted construction partners, Laing O'Rourke and their partnership with the hard-working staff here at Everton.

"A year ago, the site was receiving the delivery of steel work and we were seeing the skeleton of each of our stands come to life. Since then, we have seen milestones that have included the arrival and departure of tower cranes, terracing lifted into place, brick panels delivered and installed, a complex series of roof truss lifts completed and the ramping up of internal works, which has included making the building watertight and the start of the mechanical, engineering and plumbing fit-out.

"Within one year, the site is literally unrecognisable.

"Supporters have understandably shown a great interest in the project, from concept to consultation, and for that, I warmly thank you.

"It's also fair to say the one question I'm asked more than any other is 'when will the stadium be ready and finished'?

"Contrary to some ill-informed media reports, there is no delay, and the project remains firmly on track and on-schedule.

"A precise moving-in date for our new stadium has never been publicly set by the Club. We have repeatedly stated that the schedule of the development will see the keys for our new home handed to us from Laing O'Rourke during the 2024/25 season.

"This means we won't be starting the 2024 season at Everton Stadium – but, to reiterate, the Club has never publicly confirmed an intention to begin the 2024/25 season at our new home. If the project remains on schedule, it raises the question as to whether the Club moves in mid-season or alternatively, do we wait and give the Grand Old Lady a fitting send-off before commencing competitive league games for the senior men's team at the start of the 2025/26 season?

"Whatever decision is reached, it won't be based on sentiment; it will be reached in consultation with fans, while also considering the impacts it will have across our football club in terms of our football operation, our commercial partners and third-party contracts, our staff, seasonal workflows and the impact, of course, on supporters.

"Moving mid-season may offer some commercial benefits, but also presents a series of challenges and hurdles that could negatively impact other aspects of the Club – and other commercial considerations.

"What I can say categorically is that, today, the project is several weeks ahead of schedule, with another winter to come.

"The aim has always been to deliver on a promise to build something that all Evertonians can be proud of. When you finally walk through the entrances in that boundary wall, I'm sure you will agree it will be that, and much, much more."

***

While there was no indication how long Chong would remain as interim CEO – the assumption was that he would remain at the helm until there was clarity over investment into the club or an outright takeover was agreed – he assumed the role having overseen the one shining light of Farhad Moshiri's reign as majority shareholder.

Everton Stadium had been rising out of the north Liverpool docks precisely according to architect Dan Meis' vision and its successful completion promised to be one of the most important developments in the club's history. Financially, it offered stability, if not salvation – given the mountain of debt with which the Blues had been saddled – but that stability was also dependent on Everton's continuing membership of the Premier League, a status that would come under renewed threat during the 2023/24 season.

2023: Another Fine Mess You Got Me Into

> Bill has a belief perhaps bordering on arrogance that he can still save the club from itself', said one long-term ally. Farhad likes big gestures. He can be impetuous. Bill thinks he needs to be there to temper them and gets frustrated that fans can't see this. Some think Bill feels guilty, that he feels he sold to the wrong person.
>
> \- Ian Ladyman, Daily Mail

2023 Another fine mess you got me into

On 12 March 2016, Moshiri wrote in the matchday programme: "Most importantly, Everton is about great football and winning matches."

His intent was clear, but the results under his ownership have been far from impressive.

In the 276 league games played since Moshiri bought his stake in the club until the start of the 2023/24 season, the team achieved only a 34.4% win rate, with a goal difference of minus 101. It was a desperately poor return from such a significant outlay in transfer fees, players' wages and the cost of managers, directors and support staff.

Everton's Cup runs had been no better. After the League Cup Semi Final defeat against Manchester City and the FA Cup Semi Final defeat against Manchester United in Roberto Martinez' last season, the Blues had exited both the League Cup and FA Cup in the early rounds on five occasions. They had not progressed beyond the Quarter Final stage in either competition since 2016. The club's only foray into Europe ended with elimination at the group stage of the Europa League in 2017.

The absence of a footballing identity and strategy had been alarming since the early days of Moshiri's tenure, and it was somewhat ironic that the closer the Iranian-born businessman got to the exit door at Everton, the more coherent the overall vision on the playing side had looked – as forced as it has been by circumstance, austerity and a need to get back to basics.

A club that in seven years, had burned through eight managers and coaching teams, two interim managers, plus three Directors of Football, looked lost at sea. The result had been a plethora of coaching ideologies, haphazard recruitment of players and managers, multiple power-bases in and around the club – each using favoured agents, advisors and media to promote their vested interests.

In the years of Harry Catterick, Everton was known as 'The School of Science'; in the mid-eighties, Howard Kendall's side was acclaimed by Brian Clough as the "best young side in Europe," after winning the League Title and the European Cup Winners Cup in 1985. Joe Royle's 'Dogs of War' won the FA Cup in 1995. David Moyes' teams were tough, pragmatic and productive, enabling the club to hold the 'best of the rest' title for years. But what moniker could be applied to Everton during the Moshiri era? 'The Magnificent 7th' in 2016/17 was Moshiri's high-water mark.

Even the golden half-season under Carlo Ancelotti in 2021 - when the club was second in the league on Boxing Day – turned out to be a prelude to a slide into mid-table obscurity, in which Ancelotti seemed to lose interest and eventually left the club in the lurch at the end of that season. Hindsight is a wonderful thing, but Ancelotti leaving for a more prestigious club was always going to be on the cards, wasn't it?

In Moshiri's opening communiqué, he also wrote, "I have committed to providing additional funds for transfers and retaining our key players to ensure we have a strong core to build on in the future." Yet, his pledge to keep key players turned out to be hollow. Within his first two years, the club had sold John Stones, Romelu Lukaku and Gerard Deulofeu.

Yet he did offer an open chequebook to Ronald Koeman, as he explained on *TalkSport* in November 2016:

> "**We have no restrictions to spend**. The manager is totally committed and ruthless; if a player is not up to it he uses another player and eventually he buys one. There are no sentimental issues there. The manager will strengthen the team in the areas he feels necessary. Koeman is Koeman: he does what he wants and I support him. I think the job of an owner and chairman is simply to hire and fire the manager; the rest is down to him. He has the personality, aura and ability and

> we trust him. In Everton's culture the manager is the most important individual."

Moshiri's actions would once again prove to be at variance with his rhetoric. Indeed, he supported Koeman for a further twelve months, until he sacked him.

Furthermore, despite Moshiri's claim that: "the job of an owner and chairman is simply to hire and fire the manager, the rest is down to him." it became increasingly clear that was not how he and his chairman behaved.

The Dutchman was followed into the Everton manager's hot seat by as varied a group as you could wish to meet: each one hired and fired by Moshiri and Kenwright. The cost of early termination of Martinez and his six successors, plus their support teams exceeded £50 million.

Of course Everton was not the only club in the Premier League to hire and fire managers. Yet the lack of a clear footballing strategy and the absence of a consistent identity at the club, led to a chaotic merry-go-round that burned money whilst only yielding that 34.4% win rate.

In the results business of football it's impossible not to draw comparisons, and in the football-mad city of Liverpool the benchmark club sits just half-a-mile away, across Stanley Park.

Since signing for Liverpool on 5 October 2015 – just five months before Farhad Moshiri's arrival at Everton – Jürgen Klopp had faced Everton 17 times by the start of the 2023/24 season. He had won ten of those matches, drawn six and lost one. He had faced eight different Everton managers. The anticipation of who would come next presumably keeps him on his toes.

2023: Following the money

Back in March 2016, Farhad Moshiri also made a commitment to provide funding for the team, as well as for a new stadium. It was a hugely ambitious statement, but he was apparently a man with a plan and access to significant assets.

Remember, he graduated with a degree in accountancy from the University of London and worked at Ernst & Young and Pannell Kerr Forster before joining Deloitte & Touche. He then spent twenty years tracking the business plans and performance of Alisher Usmanov's companies.

Before he bought into Everton, Moshiri produced a business plan complete with spreadsheets and financial projections, all based on his key assumptions. His plan was verified by 18 months of due diligence and detailed discussions with Bill Kenwright. Even if Kenwright purported not to know what 'other operating costs' were, the qualified accountant who would become Everton's owner most certainly knew.

***

What Moshiri's spreadsheets did not tell him was by early 2023 he would have already pumped £750 million into the club through his own companies, he would still need to find another £350 million to complete the stadium, and even more to fund his loss-making club's working capital and squad-investment needs.

The cash requirements of the football club had spiralled far beyond the projections made in his business plan. The mismanagement of the club, by Moshiri and his board, had turned Everton from a tightly-run but undercapitalised unit in 2015, into an organisation that was still haemorrhaging cash in 2023.

In making his public assertion in January 2023 that the stadium project would top out at £760 million, Moshiri was confirming the cost was perhaps three times his original estimate. And, because of planning delays, COVID-19 and other factors, the projected cash-flow benefits of playing at Bramley Moore Dock in front of a crowd of over 52,000 had been pushed into 2025.

Once Moshiri's principal benefactor and intended naming rights sponsor for the new stadium, Alisher Usmanov, had been taken out of the game thanks to the events in Ukraine, Moshiri was financially standing all alone.

***

It was clear since the days when Moshiri and Usmanov owned 30% of Arsenal FC that the two men and their finances were closely linked. Moshiri sold his shares in Arsenal to his friend, Usmanov, in order to fund his initial stake in Everton. What's more, Usmanov's companies became Everton's principal sponsors between March 2016 and February 2022.

What is less clear, is how Moshiri funded his ongoing investment in the club after he arrived.

According to Simon Goodley, writing in *The Guardian* on 26 September 2023:

"The Everton Football Club owner, Farhad Moshiri, received more than £400 million from Alisher Usmanov companies in the run-up to the Russian billionaire being placed under sanctions, documents suggest, raising fresh questions about the financial ties between the two men.

"Records seen by *The Guardian* appear to show that Moshiri borrowed £145m from a company wholly owned by the Russian-Uzbek tycoon from about 2020. The papers also set out how, between 2018 and 2022, Moshiri sold about £270 million of shares in a company whose largest shareholder was Usmanov. Moshiri did not pay for those shares, public accounts imply, which accounting experts suggested could mean the share sales were a gift.

"After being presented with the information laid out in the internal documents, a spokesperson for Usmanov declined to discuss precise details of the funding but said: "Mr Moshiri and his companies are indeed indebted to Mr Usmanov and entities affiliated with him. We hope that the debt will be repaid after Mr Moshiri closes the sale of the Everton club, which is now being actively announced in the press."

Putin's decision to invade Ukraine shocked the world, even after months of Russian forces posturing on their neighbour's border. Then, in the aftermath of 24 February 2022, Usmanov, was sanctioned by the British and EU governments. Sponsorship funding from Everton's principal sponsor literally dried up overnight. What's more, Moshiri was suddenly and unexpectedly required to resign from the chairmanship of the $20 billion Metalloinvest Management Company Limited - the Moscow headquartered company owned 60% by Usmanov and 10% by Moshiri. With much of Moshiri's personal wealth tied up in the company, his Russian bank accounts were apparently frozen as part of the sanctions.

To his credit, Moshiri did not shirk his responsibilities to provide funds to the football club through his own companies – he said he would, and he did that at tremendous cost. That ongoing support throughout 2022 enabled the stadium build to continue, and the club to function semi-normally, albeit under a 'special measures' regime from the Premier League.

To date, he has paid out £300 million to Everton for new shares, and £490 million in shareholder loans. (Source: Everton FC Annual Report & Accounts; and TheEsk.org)

However, as Moshiri's funds dried up in 2023, the club was forced to extend its credit facilities with anyone who would lend it money. By September, the club's borrowings included:

- A £200 million rolling credit facility provided by Rights and Media Funding – funding provided by offshore entities at annual interest rates of around 12%. That facility being secured against all the assets of the football club, including future TV revenues, bank accounts and properties (excluding the new stadium).

- £140 million of debt provided by MSP Sports Capital (including Andy Bell and George Downing as limited partners) – secured against the shares of the Everton Stadium Development Holding Company.

- A COVID related loan of approximately £25 million with Santander.

Unsurprisingly, by the beginning of the 2023/24 season, with Moshiri's magic money tree looking sadly bare and every asset owned by the club currently mortgaged to the hilt, Everton's financial position was more precarious than ever.

***

In 1849, Charles Dickens wrote about the relationship between money and happiness: "Annual income twenty pounds, annual expenditure nineteen pounds, nineteen and sixpence, result happiness. Annual income twenty pounds, annual expenditure twenty pounds and sixpence, result misery."

If only Moshiri and the Everton board members he appointed had adhered to that principle from day-1 of his ownership, rather than follow a fatally-flawed 'money is no barrier to success' model.

A look back over Moshiri's years of ownership highlights a progressively worsening situation:

In Moshiri's first full year in charge (2016/17) the club achieved a turnover of £171 million[1], a massive £50 million increase on the previous year thanks largely to the bumper new TV broadcast deals. Operating costs also increased significantly to £184 million, resulting in an operating loss of (£12 million). Nevertheless, after the sale of John Stones and with a profit on player trading of £52 million, there was a **pre-tax profit of £31 million.**

The following year (2017/18), turnover increased to £189 million. Yet operating costs shot up to £287 million, bringing about an operating loss of (£98 million). It took the sale of Romelu Lukaku to push the profit on player trading to £88 million, ensuring **the pre-tax loss for the year was only (£13 million).**

2018/19 was the first year the club's finances spiralled out of control. Turnover dropped slightly to £188 million, while operating costs increased still further to £315 million. This resulted in an operating loss of (£127 million). With the club's previous top two playing assets already plying their trade at the other end of the

East Lancs Road, profit on player trading was only £20.5 million. **The pre-tax loss rose to (£112 million).**

A similar picture emerged in 2019/20. Once again, turnover fell slightly to £186 million, whereas operating costs were £361 million, and the operating loss a resulting massive (£175 million). Profit from player trading was £41 million, and **the pre-tax loss came in at (£140 million).**

In 2020/21, turnover rose slightly to £193 million, and operating costs fell slightly to £319 million, meaning there was another huge operating loss of (£126 million). After a modest £13.2 million profit on player trading, the **pre-tax loss for the year came in at (£121 million).**

The latest club results to be released are for the year 2021/22. Turnover fell back to £181 million. Operating costs were still high at £284 million, bringing about an operating loss of (£103 million). The sale of Richarlison to Spurs brought about a £67.7 million profit on player trading, and **resulted in a pre-tax loss of (£44.7 million)**.

It was at that point that the club directors were obliged by the auditors to issue a blunt notice about the club's continuation as a going concern, in the event of relegation. The auditors signed off the accounts only having received a (non-legally-binding) commitment from Farhad Moshiri to continue to fund the club.

***

In summary, in the first six years of Farhad Moshiri's reign, he and his Board oversaw a period where costs exceeded turnover by more than £640 million. The club's operating losses were reduced by making a £282 million profit on player trading in that period, meaning the pre-tax loss was 'only' £400 million.

Moshiri and the club would argue that the losses in 2017/18, 2018/19 and 2019/20 included around £50 million of exceptional stadium-related costs. All stadium costs incurred after planning permission was granted in 2021 have been capitalised and are included on the club's balance sheet.

The Board claimed significant COVID-19 related losses were also incurred. Besides obvious losses, such as gate receipts for all the games played behind closed doors, the club included losses relating to player trading during the depressed transfer market.

Moshiri may also point to delays in the Bramley-Moore Dock project – partly due to COVID and partly due to the need to submit a revised planning application; the consequences of which mean that the expected £50 million per annum of additional stadium-related revenue will only materialise several years later than his original assumptions.

Approximately £50 million of the club's operating costs resulted from compensation in the hiring and firing of managers and their coaching staff during the chaotic managerial merry-go-round that has characterised the Moshiri era.

Interest costs sapped a further £40 million from the club. And now, with external debt spiralling, at a time when interest rates for borrowers have quadrupled, the interest bill will only grow in the short-to-medium term.

Half of Moshiri's investment has gone to fund the operating losses in the football club.

***

In Farhad Moshiri's business plan, he expected revenue growth to play a major part in the turnaround of the club's fortunes. Billionaires are not averse to investing money to enable a promising project to get off the ground. The successful projects achieve good returns. The failed projects either get culled or sold on, hopefully before the losses become too serious. This is what billionaires do.

Farhad Moshiri and Alisher Usmanov had each owned a 15% stake in Arsenal since 2007. We don't know what turnover forecast Moshiri had pencilled in for Everton, but his experience at Arsenal must have been on his mind. The Gunners had moved to their new stadium in 2006 and attracted crowds of 60,000 who paid to watch Premier League football, Champions League matches, and plenty of domestic cup games. Their new stadium attracted Emirates Airlines as its naming-rights sponsor, and its extensive corporate hospitality facilities proved highly profitable.

With a turnover of £344 million in 2014/15, Arsenal could afford to spend £192 million on wages (well under the sustainable limit of 70%) and still make a profit of over £24 million. Was that the aspiration Farhad Moshiri had for Everton? If so, the Blues had a lot of ground to make up. In that same year of 2014/15, Everton's turnover was only £126 million. With wages of £78 million, the club was left with a loss before tax of £4 million. [2]

Billionaires, like Moshiri and Usmanov, are not typically known for their patience. After ten games in charge, Roberto Martinez became the first casualty of the new Moshiri era – although it cost £11.3 million to get rid of him.

Ronald Koeman replaced Martinez, and a new position of Director of Football had been filled by former Leicester City Head Scout, Steve Walsh. It was their job to ensure Everton upped their game and became more competitive, in order to give the Top 4 a run for their money in the race for Champions League places every season. In the meantime, Moshiri and his board nominee, Sasha Ryazantsev, moved ahead with the urgent task of building a new stadium, while simultaneously attempting to grow the club's revenue streams.

***

Revenue Streams:

Broadcasting Revenues: Everton's first growth spurt was expected to come from a hike in broadcasting revenues, which in 2015/16 - the season of Farhad Moshiri's takeover at Everton - stood at £81.7 million. In 2016/17, broadcasting revenue rose to £130.5 million on the back of the new TV deal.

Did Moshiri and the Everton board believe the TV rights would provide an ever-increasing income stream? Whatever their assumption, by 2021/22, Everton actually saw its broadcasting income fall back to £115 million. Failure on the pitch, including the lack of success in the domestic cups, meant the club relied solely on income from league matches. The profitable drama and income from hoped-for European football was replaced by the nail-biting reality of relegation battles. [3]

***

Gate Receipts: In 2014/15, with Farhad Moshiri eyeing up the acquisition of Everton FC, whilst still an Arsenal shareholder, he saw Everton's matchday income of £17.9 million totally eclipsed by Arsenal's £100.4 million. No wonder Moshiri prioritised the new stadium project in his first address to the Everton faithful.

Yet, it is still likely to be season 2025/26 before the Blues first run out to Z-Cars at Bramley Moore Dock. In the meantime, Goodison Park is full every week. With no European games, and few domestic cup matches, gate receipts have remained static at around £16 million. [4]

***

Sponsorship/Merchandising: Another area where Everton had previously lagged way behind the likes of Arsenal was in sponsorship and merchandising. Alisher Usmanov was unable to invest in equity at Everton while he remained an Arsenal shareholder, but providing sponsorship was another matter. By 2021/22 Everton's Sponsorship/Merchandising income had risen to £35 million, largely thanks to the club's deals with Usmanov's companies, USM and MegaFon.

But in February 2022, in the wake of Vladimir Putin's invasion of Ukraine, the club announced that Farhad Moshiri had immediately severed his links with Metalloinvest, the Russia-based conglomerate he helped found with Usmanov. That move came only days after the Blues announced they were suspending their sponsorship deals with USM Holdings and two Usmanov-owned telecoms subsidiaries, MegaFon and Yota. The club removed signage relating to MegaFon from Goodison Park overnight and Everton Women played their match against Aston Villa with blank jerseys after the same company's logo was dropped from their kit. The financial impact of these cancelled sponsorship deals (estimated at £20 million per annum) will become known when the club publishes its 2022/23 accounts. It remains to be seen whether Everton have been able to fill this significant gap by finding other major sponsorship and merchandising deals. An even bigger blow to the club, was the loss of the USM naming rights deal on the Bramley-Moore stadium, worth an estimated £200 million.

***

Operating Costs:

Without sight of Farhad Moshiri's business plan for the Everton FC acquisition, we will never know how quickly he expected his new club to achieve Arsenal-like annual revenue figures of circa £300-£350 million. However, he wasted little time in allowing the club's operating costs to emulate those of their illustrious North-London rivals. And when the turnover growth failed to materialise, he did little to cut costs; thereby creating a £642 million operating loss in the first 6 years of his ownership.

It's time to take a deeper dive into the main drivers behind the 'operating costs explosion' under Farhad Moshiri.

***

Wages:

The biggest cost to any football club is the wage bill for the players and staff.

Under the regimes of various managers and Directors of Football, Everton's Wages/Turnover ratio ramped up from 61% in 2016/17 to an unsustainable 95% in 2020/21. [5]

Not only were many players signed on high wages, but long-term contracts were handed out to average performers at the tail-end of their careers.

For many of the players recruited by Moshiri and his appointees, their deal with Everton marked the high-wage point of their career. If they failed to perform at Everton, no other club would pay them what they earned. It was virtually impossible to loan them out, unless Everton picked up most of their wage bill. Sales of these players proved virtually impossible, so most stayed on the Goodison Park payroll until their contract expired.

Consider the following roll-call:

Bolasie: £22.5 million fee. 5 year contract.£19.5 million wages
Schneiderlin: £20 million fee. 4 year contract. £20.8 million wages
Williams: £9 million fee. 3 year contract. £10.8 million wages
Sigurdsson: £44.5 million fee. 5year contract. £26 million wages
Rooney: No fee. 2 year contract. £16.8 million wages
Sandro: £5.2 million fee. 4 year contract. £13.5 million wages
Tosun: £21 million fee. 5 year contract. £15.6 million wages
Walcott: £20 million fee. 3.5 year contract. £18.2 million wages
Mina: £28.5 million fee. 5 year contract. £31.2 million wages
Bernard: No fee. 4 year contract. £25 million wages
Gomes: £28 million fee. 5 year contract. £29 million wages
Gbamin: £23 million fee. 5 year contract. £19.5 million wages
Delph: £8 million fee. 3 year contract. £12.6 million wages
Dele Alli: No fee. 3 year contract. £15.6 million wages
Maupay: £13 million fee. 3 year contract. £7.8 million wages

It's a sobering thought that over £500 million of Moshiri's cash went to pay the transfer fees and wages of these fifteen players, some of whom rarely played for the club, all of whom failed to justify their huge wages, and none of whom provided the club with a decent sell-on fee. (Source: Spotrac.com and ToffeeWeb.com)

***

Other wage costs:

Player costs are the main cost driver, but headcount was allowed to balloon across the entire organisation. Prior to Farhad Moshiri's arrival, the club employed 274 people. By June 2022, the number had swollen to 491, with all departments seeing a significant growth in headcount and costs.

Players, training, management: 98 (2014/15); 169 (2021/22)
Youth Academy: 38 (2014/15); 66 (2021/22)
Marketing & Media: 32 (2014/15); 78 (2021/22)
Management & Admin: 71 (2014/15); 116 (2021/22)
Security/pitch/safety: 35 (2014/15); 62 (2021/22)
Total: 274 (2014/15); 491 (2021/22)
Total wage costs : £77.5 million (2014/15); £162 million (2021/22)[6]

Except for Colin Chong and his team supervising the work of Laing O'Rourke at Bramley-Moore Dock, and the growth of the Women's Football team, it's hard to imagine why the club which finished 16th in the league in 2021/22 should require a significantly more complex and costly organisation than the one which had finished 11th in the league six years earlier.

***

Financing the Stadium:

When Farhad Moshiri announced in March 2016 that he would look into the best options for the stadium and how to finance it, there was no mention of how much he had budgeted for this in his business plan. However, he knew it had cost Arsenal £390 million to build their 60,000 capacity stadium on an industrial and waste disposal site in Ashburton Grove in 2004. Emirates Airline bought the naming rights for the stadium, in a 15-year deal estimated at £100 million that also included a 7-year shirt sponsorship, starting in the 2006/07 season. Emirates and Arsenal agreed a new deal worth £150 million in November 2012, and shirt-sponsorship was extended by five years while they extended naming rights to 2028.

Another reference point could have been the City of Manchester Stadium, which was built at a cost of £110 million as the home for the 2002 Commonwealth Games. It had a capacity of 35,000, part of which was temporary seating. Soon after the event, the athletics track and pitch were removed, and the ground lowered to create space for additional tiers of seating in a football-specific configuration. The temporary stand behind one goal was dismantled and replaced by another permanent construction, identical to the one at the other end. This all cost an extra £30 million and enabled Manchester City to move there from their historical ground – Maine Road – after signing a 250-year lease. In 2011, the club was given a naming rights deal with Etihad Airlines for £150 million. It was a record deal for British football. Further investment will take the capacity of the Etihad Stadium to 60,000.

Everton had their own reference point in Kirkby, where they proposed to build a 50,000-seat stadium. It was estimated to cost £150 million and be the centrepiece of a huge retail development in a scheme driven by supermarket giant, Tesco. The Destination Kirkby project had a divisive effect as soon as it was announced and when Bill Kenwright opened the decision to a vote of 36,662 Everton fans. The outcome in August 2007 was 15,230 in favour, with 10,468 against and a further 10,901 abstaining. As Andy Hunter wrote in *The Guardian* on 25 November 2009: "The vote followed claims from Everton's then chief executive, Keith Wyness, that Kirkby represented 'the deal of the century' for a club that currently cannot afford a new stadium without an enabling project. It was also voted on before details of the new stadium were revealed and which, when published, prompted the leader of Liverpool City Council, Warren Bradley, to describe it as 'A glorified cow shed built in a small town outside Liverpool.' The project was finally ditched, when government Communities Secretary, John Denham, rejected the club's proposals."

Three Premier League clubs, three stadium projects, in a cost range from £150-£390 million, two of which had attracted sizeable naming rights deals to help them defray the capital costs. Was that the ballpark that Farhad Moshiri was thinking of when he prepared his business plan?

If so, the decision to develop the new Everton stadium on the banks of the Mersey as part of the Peel Holdings' Liverpool Waters scheme, then a World Heritage Organisation site, quickly blew those ideas out of the water. In committing to Bramley-Moore dock, the club had to pay around £30 million to Peel Holdings for the site, paid tens of millions to drain and infill the dock, and committed to spend "more than £55 million to preserve, restore and celebrate the heritage assets at Bramley-Moore Dock.

In selecting that city-centre, waterfront location and the magnificent design from Dan Meis, Moshiri aimed high. No glorified cow shed for him; instead, he committed to build Everton their Nil Satis Nisi Optimum stadium, one that would come to be nicknamed Liverpool's "fourth grace" and be selected as a host venue for the 2028 European Championships.

Club officials had long suggested the project would cost £505 million and Denise Barrett-Baxendale, then chief executive, was credited with negotiating a fixed price with contractors, Laing O'Rourke. But in an interview on TalkSport with Jim White in January 2023 and a meeting with the Everton Fan Advisory Board, Farhad Moshiri revealed that the completed stadium development project would cost around £760 million.

Though external funding had always been part of the original plans for paying for the Everton Stadium, none was secured until the summer of 2023 – and even then it was in the form of loans rather than investment. Up to that point, Farhad Moshiri had found himself in the painful predicament of everything coming out of his bank account. **Current estimates are that Moshiri has already paid out £400 million, for everything from the site cost, design and planning to the renovation of the heritage assets and construction costs to date.**

That left around £360 million to find over the final 18 months of the construction timeline.

Combined with funding the loss-making club to the tune of around £500 million since 2016, it's easy to see where over £800 million of Moshiri's money had gone.

No wonder he was desperately searching for additional funding.

His plan, ever since signing an exclusivity deal with MSP Sports Capital in May 2023, seemed to be based on the acceptance of their offer to inject over £100 million into the stadium funding pot and £50 million into the club, in return for granting MSP two places on the Everton board.

He hoped the MSP funding could not only trigger construction finance from major investment banks, but would also enable him to restructure the Everton board and bring in fresh ideas on how to take the club forward.

As had proved to be the case all too often, events did not work out the way Farhad Moshiri expected them to.

As the Toffees began their 121st season in the top-flight, on and off the field, the situation was about to become even more precarious.

---

1. Everton FC Annual Report & Accounts -2016/17
2. Arsenal Report & Accounts 2014/15; Everton Report & Accounts 2014/15
3. Everton Report & Accounts
4. Everton Report & Accounts
5. Everton FC Annual Report & Accounts

6. Everton FC Annual Report & Accounts

2023: Moshiri's Everton walking the tightrope

While Sean Dyche had successfully steered Everton to Premier League safety by almost the slimmest of margins thanks to that final-day win over Bournemouth in May, the club had remained under a cloud of uncertainty heading into the 2023/24 season.

The situation was summarised in gloomy fashion by Phil McNulty in his pre-season Premier League prediction column for *BBC Sport*:

"Where to start with a club who have narrowly escaped relegation for the last two seasons, and have yet to show any evidence they have learned the lessons? Everton have lacked quality back up for injury-plagued striker Dominic Calvert-Lewin for 12 months and they have yet to bring in anyone who looks ready to fill that role, with Leicester City's Patson Daka the latest to be linked.

"The scale of Everton's financial mismanagement over recent years means they are scraping around in the bargain basement. The squad is currently smaller than the one that escaped the drop on the final day of last term, although the addition of 38-year-old Ashley Young on a free transfer may be a very smart move.

"Everton's expected reset at board level has yet to materialise, along with the long-touted investment from American group MSP Sports Capital. Three boardroom members left in June but deeply divisive chairman Bill Kenwright remains in post, which continues to be a source of discontent among fans. The 77-year-old has not even felt able to attend a game at Goodison Park since January, citing security concerns.

"Manager Sean Dyche's organisational skills may just keep Everton up, although there is also the concern about a hearing in October after the club was referred to an independent commission for an alleged breach of the Premier League's Financial Fair Play rules. Everton strongly deny any wrongdoing but the prospect of a points deduction lingers if they are found guilty, which will obviously impact this particular prediction. Prediction: Everton to finish in 16th place."

Three games into the new season, Everton had managed to underperform McNulty's predictions. With a record of 3 games played, 3 losses, no goals scored, 6 goals conceded, zero points, the club sat bottom of the Premier League – the worst start in its history.

The bad news was not confined to the football results. On 23 August, Matt Slater of *The Athletic* reported:

"Everton's hopes of improving their financial situation have received a huge hit after MSP Sports Capital withdrew from talks about taking a minority stake in the club. The New York-based investment group signed an exclusivity deal with the Premier League side in May and the plan was to invest up to £150 million ($190 million) in convertible debt that would become a stake of approximately 25 per cent in the 145-year-old club.

"In a complicated deal, £100 million of that investment was meant for Everton Stadium Development Company, the subsidiary club owner Farhad Moshiri set up in 2017 to oversee the construction of Everton's new ground at Bramley-Moore Dock, with the rest going to the club. But that exclusivity period is now over and the deal is dead, with the stumbling block being opposition from one of Everton's existing offshore lenders, Rights and Media Funding Limited."

For many Evertonians, the news that a relatively unknown lender, Rights and Media Funding could block the new investment deal came as a shock. It raised many questions, including who was behind Rights and Media?

It was a question that had been partly answered at Everton's AGM in November 2015, just three months before Farhad Moshiri took over at Everton. In an article written by Ed Aarons in *The Guardian* in December 2016, he recalled how:

"The CEO, Robert Elstone castigated shareholders who asked questions about [Philip] Green's potential involvement before revealing that the club's net debt had increased from £28.1 million in 2013/14 to £31.3 million in 2014/15, despite announcing record turnover and a bumper TV deal. 'We have three sources of lending,' he said. 'We have a long-term loan with the Prudential that expires in 2026, an overdraft with Barclays that is not enough to manage the day-to-day cash flow of the football club and, to address that, we borrow from JG Funding (a private company) against the TV money. It is all fully disclosed in our accounts, is approved by the Premier League and paid back at the end of the year.' "

Less than six months after the latest loan with JG Funding was taken out, Moshiri paid his £87.5m for a 49.9% share in Everton, valuing the club at £175 million. The publication of Everton's 2015/16 accounts revealed the Iranian businessman had also provided an interest-free loan of £80 million 'with no agreed repayment date.' That funding was used post year-end to reduce the club's long-term debt by repaying the entire other loans balance of £54.8 million at 31 May 2016.

Despite that, Everton's accounts showed that another loan was taken out on 26 August 2016. This time, it was registered to a company called Rights and Media Funding Limited, which had changed its name from JG Funding at the end of 2015.

This practice of 'payday' lending, whereby clubs borrow at higher-than-market interest rates from offshore entities, was not a new practice, nor was it unique to Everton. The security offered against the loan was typically the club's TV rights money. The loan is normally repaid annually and renewed as necessary. As Aarons explained in the same article in *The Guardian*:

"By the start of the 2011/12 season, Everton had debts of more than £40 million and faced the prospect of having to sell some of their better players to balance the books. With banks unwilling to lend in the wake of the financial crash, Kenwright turned to Vibrac [Corporation] to arrange a deal worth £14 million a year, although they were to take out loans worth more than £80 million in loans over the next four years. Fulham also borrowed £16 million, while Reading took out an £11.7 million loan for which they were later fined £30,000 for contravening Football League rules."

A recent search on the Companies House website revealed that Rights and Media Holdings is a U.K. company based in Altrincham. It has no employees and two directors, David McKnight and Jonathan McMorrow. In its accounts, for the year to 30 June 2021, it had assets of £190,934,023. The lenders of these assets were named in the charge documents as:

- M H Finance Limited, a company incorporated and registered in Bermuda.

- Galloway (Cyprus) Ltd, a company incorporated and registered in Cyprus.

- Carroch (Bahamas) Ltd, a company incorporated and registered in Nassau.

But who is behind these companies?

In *Football's Secret Trade,* published by Bloomberg in 2017, Alex Duff and Tariq Panja revealed that the British tax exile and racehorse owner, Michael Tabor – who made his fortune selling the 114-shop

Arthur Price betting chain to Coral in 1995, and subsequently split his time between homes in Monte Carlo and Barbados – "Employed David McKnight, a soft-spoken Mancunian in his late 50s... Tabor also called in Graham Shear, a partner at law firm Berwin Leighton Paisner, who could put together a contract in as little as 24 hours."

According to Duff and Panja, Tabor used McKnight and Shear to organise loans to Athletico Madrid, Deportivo La Coruña and Getafe. Tabor also "took over some of the business of Investec in English football, advancing money due to Everton, Southampton, Fulham and Reading before the start of each season, in return for promissory notes from the Premier League....The arrangements in the UK were through another company domiciled in the British Virgin Islands, called Vibrac Corporation."

Michael Tabor's name is nowhere to be seen on the loan agreements between Everton Football Club Company Limited and Rights and Media Funding Limited, but the agreements are signed for Rights and Media by David McKnight. The documents are copied to Bryan Cave Leighton Paisner LLP, for the attention of Graham Shear.

Seven years after Farhad Moshiri took over at Everton, the club is more indebted to Rights and Media Funding than ever. According to Everton's 2021/22 accounts the club's borrowings, aside from shareholder loans, amounted to £174.1 million. Included in that figure was a £150 million, 5-year facility with Rights and Media Funding, which appeared to be fully utilised. The club is likely to be paying 10-12% interest on that loan.

In the charge document signed by Everton directors, for the loan taken out from Rights and Media Funding on 22 August 2016, there is a negative pledge attached to the loan. That means the terms of the loan agreement prohibit or restrict the company (Everton) from creating a further security that will rank equally with or ahead of the charge.

In layman's terms, you can't mortgage your house twice, at least not without the consent of your first lender.

This is standard practice in such matters, and MSP Sports Capital must have known about the club's loans from Rights and Media Funding. Why it took so long for this to become the deal-breaker (if indeed it was), remains an open question.

So at the start of the 2023/24 season, Everton remained in financial limbo. Farhad Moshiri continued the search for his own messiah investor –someone who would help him keep the club afloat, and enable him to fulfil the dream of a new stadium for the Blues to play in. In the meantime, the owner, the club and its fans continued their tortuous tightrope walk; knowing that a slip into the Championship could prove fatal.

2023: From Moshiri's frying pan into the 777 fire?

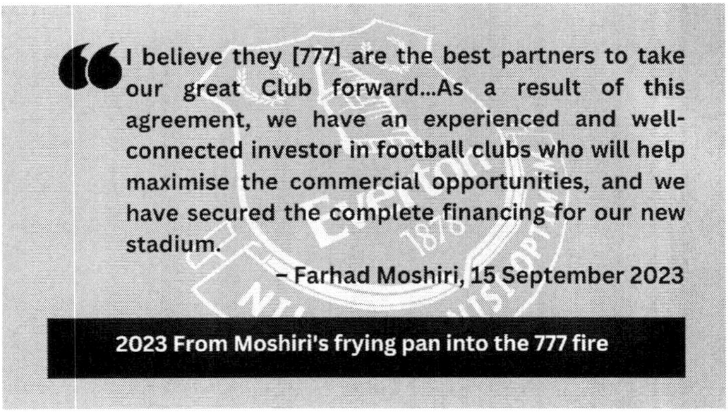

By the turn of 2023, Farhad Moshiri's search for external investors in Everton had become reminiscent of Bill Kenwright's increasingly desperate efforts to find his own billionaire more than a decade before, but Moshiri's discussions with USA-based investment firms MSP Sports Capital and 777 Partners hinted at progress on that front as the year wore on.

The narrative had initially been around Moshiri trying to find a co-funder for the stadium. Yet the fallout of Russia's war against Ukraine, the resulting sanctions against Alisher Usmanov, and Everton's worsening predicament on the pitch, moved Moshiri's discussions towards the outright sale of the football club and its half-finished stadium.

Less than six months after providing a (non-legally-binding) letter to the auditors confirming his ongoing financial support for Everton Football Club, news broke on 15 September, that Moshiri had signed an agreement with 777 Partners to acquire his full 94.1% stake in the club. The precise nature of the deal remained opaque, with the exact terms of the agreement undisclosed, but *The Telegraph* reported that it could eventually total £500 million with the Miami-based private equity firm agreeing to making staged payments over a period of years that would depend very much on whether the club remained in the Premier League.

In an open letter to Evertonians, Moshiri said:

> "The nature of ownership and financing of top football clubs has changed immeasurably since I first invested in Everton over seven years ago. The days of an owner/benefactor are seemingly out of reach for most, and the biggest clubs are now typically owned by well-resourced PE [Private Equity] firms, specialist sports investors or state-backed companies and funds. I have been open about the need to bring in new investment and complete the financing for our iconic new stadium at Bramley-Moore Dock, on the banks of the Mersey, which I have predominantly financed to date.

> "I have spoken to a number of parties and considered some strong potential opportunities. However, **it is through my lengthy discussions with 777 that I believe they are the best partners to take our great Club forward, with all the benefits of their multi-club investment model. As a result of this agreement, we have an experienced and well-connected investor in football clubs who will help maximise the commercial opportunities, and we have secured the complete financing for our new stadium, which will be the critical element in the future success of Everton."**

Completion of the transaction was expected to occur by the end of the year but the 777 bid was subject to regulatory approval, including from the Premier League, the Football Association, and the Financial Conduct Authority (FCA). As a slew of newspaper and investigative pieces published over the ensuing weeks illustrated, this promised to be no mere formality.

Despite Moshiri's claims that 777 were "the best partners to take our great Club forward," serious doubts were being expressed over the American firm's ability to follow through on their purchase of the club in the first place, with numerous observers questioning whether they had the funds necessary to complete the deal, even on a phased basis.

Beyond that, reports of missed or delayed payments in parts of their existing sporting portfolio – one that includes Sevilla, Standard

Liege, Genoa, Hertha Berlin and Vasco da Gama in football and the British Basketball League – placed a question mark over 777's ability to complete Everton Stadium, cover any debt that must be repaid in the event of a successful takeover, fund day-to-day operations, and invest in the playing squad.

As if all of that weren't enough, concerns were being raised as high up as the UK Government over 777 Partners' suitability for buying into the Premier League based on their ongoing involvement in several court cases in the United States. 777 and sister company Sutton Park had been accused of fraud, offering illegal loans and failing to pay bills totalling hundreds of thousands of dollars, all potentially disqualifying events under the Premier League's beefed up owners' and directors' test.

That was the "postage stamp" version. The seedier and unsavoury accounts of how co-founders Josh Wander and Steve Pasko had built 777 Partners in the first place could form the outline for a Hollywood film. Originally under the banner of Sutton Park, the pair had found their niche in the lucrative business of "structured settlements" – the practice of offering highly discounted cash settlements, often to victims of accidents who have been awarded annuities in compensation for their injuries – and they had grown the firm into arguably the biggest player in its sphere in the US.

Starting with Wander's arrest for drug trafficking and possession as a student at the University of Florida (for which he was later sentenced to 15 years' probation for possession of drug paraphernalia after pleading no contest to the charges), through the lawsuits filed by two American women accusing 777 subsidiaries of predatory lending practices and allegations of racketeering activities, including 'kidnapping, bribery, extortion and dealing in a controlled substance,' all the way to claims of fraud and breach of contract in relation to their budget airline business, legal problems have never been too far away from Everton's prospective buyers.

Where the experience, the financial resources and the management skills to take forward a club the size of Everton were concerned, there was little evidence that 777 would have the wherewithal to pull it off.

At the time of their takeover bid, the firm had barely two years of experience in owning and controlling football clubs and their success rate in that time had been decidedly mixed. As Paul Brown and Philippe Auclair wrote in the first of a number of exposés of 777 for *Josimar*, a Norwegian investigative publication, in July 2023, "Multiple club-owner 777 ... has a patchy record in honouring its financial commitments.

"[I]n less than two years, 777, a private company which insists it does not invest other people's money but only the wealth of its owners, has become a multiple club owner only surpassed by a handful of operators such as Abu Dhabi's controlling entity City Football Group in terms of the depth and breadth of their investments in club football.

"777 now owns in full or in part seven football clubs in seven different countries on three continents, for an outlay which Josimar estimates could run up to 900 million dollars in total, debt burden not included, a colossal sum for a company which is nowhere near as cash-rich as other US equity funds which have recently set their eyes on, in particular, European clubs."

Though 777 Partners' moral and ethical compass appeared to be at odds with a great British footballing institution that prides itself on its standing and work in the community, it was their ability to successfully fund and run Everton FC that was of greatest concern to its supporters. In that respect, the sight of fans of Standard Liege and Hertha Berlin displaying banners of protest aimed at their club's Floridian owners, reports from Brazil that FIFA had threatened Vasco da Gama with a transfer ban for non-payment of transfer fees (777 came up with the payments at the eleventh hour) and further delayed tranches related to their investment in British basketball all cast doubt over a company that claims to have the funding necessary to acquire and develop a major Premier League club.

No one could say for sure, as the end of 2023 approached and the club awaited the conclusion of the vetting by the Premier League and FCA of the bid from Florida, whether a takeover by 777 Partners would be a good thing or a bad thing for Everton FC. Though 777 had a chequered history of meeting their obligations in a timely manner, they had a habit of finding the money in the end and there were signs in 2023 that their stewardship of Genoa, in particular, had brought stability and firmer fiscal foundations than had previously existed.

Indeed, 777 at least appear to be going about things in the right way in terms of structuring a portfolio of clubs across three continents in fairly short order. Don Dransfield, formerly the Chief Strategy Officer at City Football Group, was appointed Chief Executive Officer of a dedicated 777 Football Group division in May 2022. He met with Everton supporter representatives as well as finance expert Paul The Esk and joined Wander and Pasko in the Directors Box at Goodison Park for the home game against Luton Town in September 2023.

Additionally — and equally as encouraging from the point of view of structure and intent — Johannes Spors, previously director of football at Vitesse Arnhem, now General Manager at Genoa, and someone who was seriously considered for a senior role by Tottenham, was appointed Sporting Director for the 777 Football Group, reporting to Dransfield.

777's intent, as Wander told French newspaper *L'Equipe*, is to invest in a club's long-term success rather than to try and turn a quick profit.

"What is important in our eyes is not to build a club which generates profit just for the sake of profit," he said. "We want clubs that are capable of living and developing over a number of decades."

Those goals were echoed by Spors in an interview with *The Telegraph* in December 2023 in which he described Everton in terms of being "the missing link" in the firm's stable of clubs.

"We want the clubs to be the best versions of themselves," the German explained. "We have the challenge that every club that joined the group was having, in recent history, a development going in the wrong direction. We have to turn around all the clubs' development and all of them are now in a better situation.

"So we made the teams younger, we made every team cheaper in terms of the wage bill, but we increased the value of the squad."

Everton's financial hole is considerably deeper than any of the teams 777 Partners have acquired to date; nevertheless, against the backdrop of a drumbeat of negative headlines around the company – at the time this book went to print, reports emerged that the US Department of Justice had launched an investigation in 777's financial dealings – Messers Wander and Pasko were making good on their intent to invest in Everton. By the end of 2023 they had furnished the club with loans in excess of £100 million, to cover working capital and the ongoing cost of building the new stadium at Bramley-Moore Dock.

Would that form the starting point for a takeover that would end the Moshiri Era or would the mysterious money-men from Miami become the latest in a lengthening line of Everton's creditors?

2023: The End of an Era

> "There can be no mistaking that Bill loved Everton Football Club. He admired the hard work, dedication and effort of every member of staff across the club and Everton in the Community but most of all he recognised and empathised with the passion, loyalty and support all the Everton teams have had from Evertonians be that at home, away or abroad.
>
> \- Farhad Moshiri

2023 The end of an era as Bill Kenwright dies

Ever since he and his True Blue Holdings Consortium had launched their successful bid to buy the club from Peter Johnson in 1999, the figure of Bill Kenwright had loomed large over Everton. It would be another five years before he assumed the mantle of chairman but, in everything from the firing of Walter Smith and the appointment of his successor David Moyes in 2002, to the formulation of the Blues' first proposed waterfront stadium at the Kings Dock two years later, there was no question who was shaping the club's future.

Even after Farhad Moshiri came on board in 2016 and eventually increased his holdings to 94.1%, reducing Kenwright's stake to a 1.3% in the process, the renowned theatre impresario remained entwined in many key aspects of running the club, especially when the Board of Directors – and he in particular – had become a lightning rod for criticism and frustration from supporters.

This was true even as he battled ill-health in his 70s but, in the summer of 2023, Kenwright was admitted to intensive care for a period of weeks due to complications following surgery to remove a cancerous tumour from his liver. He returned home to begin his recovery but apparently suffered a heart attack shortly thereafter. He passed away on 23 October at the age of 78 surrounded by his loved ones, bringing to a close a defined era in the club's history.

"The club has lost a chairman, a leader, a friend, and an inspiration," a statement from Everton read.

The club's majority shareholder, Farhad Moshiri, sent his own message via evertonfc.com in which he expressed his sadness at the passing of his "great friend".

"There can be no mistaking that Bill loved Everton Football Club," Moshiri wrote. "He spoke with an infectious enthusiasm about every aspect of Everton, from the legends of yesteryear to his unconditional support for everyone that wears the Blue shirt and represents the club. He admired the hard work, dedication and effort of every member of staff across the club and Everton in the Community but most of all he recognised and empathised with the passion, loyalty and support all the Everton teams have had from Evertonians be that at home, away or abroad. He was a special soul, a man successful in so many different walks of life. We will miss him but never forget him."

A life-long Everton fan and one-time small-part actor on *Coronation Street*, Kenwright built his career as a nationally renowned producer of plays. He was first elected to the Everton Board of Directors on 23 October 1989, and, after leading the successful takeover a decade later, he decided to take the title Vice-Chairman and installed former supremo, Sir Philip Carter, as Chairman before eventually taking the helm himself in 2004 when Carter became Life President until his passing in 2015.

Though the first decade of Kenwright's tenure as chairman would see much-needed stability on the pitch under David Moyes, the club's financial footing was gradually eroded as the Board battled to keep the team competitive on the increasingly un-level playing field of the Premier League.

He had always maintained that he was the ordinary fan from the Boys Pen who had 'done good' and realised the dream of owning his beloved Blues; merely the custodian waiting for someone with deeper pockets and much bigger resources to eventually step in and buy him out. It took him longer than he initially envisaged but he eventually found someone fitting that bill in the form of Farhad Moshiri.

Likely even by his own admission, the next seven years didn't pan out the way Kenwright had envisaged. His dream of a new home for the Toffees on the banks of the Mersey was well on the way to being realised but his death came at a time of deep uncertainty at Everton, both on and off the pitch, with the club struggling financially and facing the prospect of a third successive battle to avoid relegation.

His role in the decline in Everton's fortunes during the Moshiri Era may have been debatable, but in the minds of many supporters he had, unfortunately, come to be seen as complicit in the majority shareholder's failings. Though he had been retained as chairman while the rest of the board stepped down in the summer of 2023, it was expected that in the event of any takeover, Kenwright's time as chairman would have come to an end anyway.

He would not get to see that next chapter in the history of his beloved Blues, nor take a seat at Bramley-Moore Dock but Bill Kenwright had left an indelible mark on the club. A memorial service was held for him on 18 December at the Anglican Cathedral in Liverpool.

2023: Everton stunned by Independent Commission's verdict

The decision in March 2023 by the Premier League to refer Everton to an independent commission after charging the club with breaching its Profitability and Sustainability Rules (PSR) during the 2021/22 season had hung in the background while the Blues first battled to avoid relegation for a second successive season and then set about trying to improve their playing squad. All the while, they were still operating under strict austerity measures that had, by that point, been in place for two years.

The club's attempts to not only remain compliant with the League's spending rules, but also take demonstrable strides towards improving their standing vis-à-vis PSR, required Director of Football Kevin Thelwell to work the loan market and structure deals for incoming players in such a way that required the bare minimum in up-front payments.

38-year-old Ashley Young was drafted in on a free transfer following his departure from Aston Villa. While Arnaut Danjuma, the player who had infamously snubbed a move to Goodison Park at the 11th hour in the January transfer window, was secured on loan at the second attempt. Another season-long loan arrangement was concluded for Leeds United winger Jack Harrison, and Youssef Chermiti, a promising teenage striker was signed from Sporting Clube de Portugal in a deal that could eventually total £12 million.

The initial outlay for the youngster was thought to be a quarter of that, and when another January target in the form of another Portuguese striker Beto was secured shortly before the summer deadline for £26 million, Thelwell and the club were able to structure the deal in such a way that no payments were due until the next financial year.

Meanwhile, the outgoings continued. Yerry Mina's £6 million-plus annual salary was jettisoned from the wage bill when his contract expired, and almost £50 million was raised with the sale of seven players from the first and Under-21 teams, with Alex Iwobi the most prominent when he left for Fulham in a £22 million deal. When added to the departures of the likes of Anthony Gordon and Moise Kean earlier in 2023 it meant that Everton had realised close to £120 million in outgoing transfers for the calendar year while spending almost nothing by comparison on the five new faces they were able to welcome to the club.

It may have been an imperative given the parlous state of the club's finances, a situation that would require further loans from external lenders to prop up day-to-day operations as the year wore on, but it also represented significant risk. Sean Dyche had been left with a more balanced playing squad that finally had striking alternatives to Dominic Calvert-Lewin, whose 2021/22 and 2022/23 campaigns had been wrecked by injury, but there was precious little depth. Any significant injury crisis could have seriously undermined what was expected to be another long fight for top-flight survival.

All of those moves to slash the losses racked up in the preceding years came too late for the purposes of the Commission that finally heard the Premier League's case against Everton and their PSR breach in October. A three-person panel made up of David Phillips KC, Alan Greenwood and Nick Igoe was appointed by the Premier League to hear the case. With no precedent or established framework for sanctions in place, the Commission's powers of censure were essentially limitless.

While outright expulsion from the Premier League was deemed unlikely in the extreme, speculation among observers varied from Everton being handed a fine or temporary transfer embargo on the less punitive end of the scale to a points deduction on the other. In what was a hugely controversial development, however, newspaper reports surfaced on 25 October that the League were pushing for a points deduction of as much as 12 points and it would later emerge that they had advanced a formula by which the Commission might calculate an appropriate sanction: 6 points for the initial breach and then 1 point for every £5 million Everton had gone over the £105 million threshold.

So it was that on 17 November, it was announced, to the astonishment of Everton FC, its fans and much of the domestic football that the Commission had recommended the club be deducted 10 points with immediate effect, plunging the Blues back into the relegation zone. Worse, it was also revealed that in a decision reached by Mr Phillips in May earlier in the year, the door was opened for the likes of Burnley, Leeds United and Leicester City to launch their reported £300 million joint lawsuit against Everton for lost revenue due to relegation in the two preceding seasons which, they would argue, would not have occurred had Everton not broken spending rules.

In the Commission's report, it was detailed that Everton had admitted to breaching PSR but only by £9.7 million, an assertion the Premier League countered with their own calculation that the club had gone over the limit by £19.5 million. Mitigating factors put forward by the club's counsel relating to the outbreak of the war in Ukraine that led to the suspension of key sponsorship deals with USM Holdings; the club's firing of Player X following his arrest in December 2021; interest paid on costs related to the construction of Everton Stadium; further losses and complications caused by the COVID-19 pandemic, including the inability to raise funds with the sale of Player Y; and the Premier League's 4% Transfer Levy on transfer fees were all dismissed as considerations.

Instead, the League put forward a number of Aggravating Factors that they felt were appropriate in determining the extent of Everton's culpability, including "overspend despite repeated warnings", "misleading the Premier League about stadium interest" and "misleading the Premier League about the intention to sell Player Y". The Commission decided to eliminate the last factor from consideration and agreed with Everton's assertion that an improving trend towards PSR compliance went "some limited way to diminish [the club's] culpability", but they ultimately sided with the League on the other factors, agreed that Everton had, to an extent, acted in bad faith. The Commission ruled that only a sporting sanction not a financial penalty would be appropriate for 'a serious breach', given owner Farhad Moshiri's personal wealth.

On the day the 10-point penalty was announced, Everton issued a statement saying they were "shocked and disappointed by the ruling of the Premier League's Commission. The Club believes that the Commission has imposed a wholly disproportionate and unjust sporting sanction." An appeal of the decision was lodged 14 days later, with a new independent panel to be appointed to assess its validity in the coming months.

In the meantime, an Everton team that, under Dyche, had started putting a run of form together and was climbing the Premier League table was thrust into another battle for survival. The struggle on the part of the three newly-promoted clubs – Burnley, Sheffield United and Luton Town – offered hope that the Blues could overcome the significant handicap of losing 10 points and stay up. Even if they managed it, however, the club's parlous financial state and the uncertainty over 777 Partners' takeover bid continued to pose further existential threats to one of Britain's oldest and most venerated institutions.

2023: We Shall Not Be Moved

With Farhad Moshiri's signature on an exclusive agreement with 777 Partners to acquire his full stake in the club, the Iranian-British businessman's active ownership of Everton effectively came to an end on 15 September, 2023 – but the deal could only be completed if the Florida-based investment firm passed the Premier League's owners and directors test. Originally expected to take around 12 weeks and be wrapped up Christmas, that vetting and approval process would bleed well into 2024, with the prospect that the sale might not come to fruition at all growing ever stronger.

With the Blues already indebted to 777 to the tune of a reported £142 million – that on top of the other liabilities that had piled up under the Monaco-based billionaire's reign – it wasn't clear what would happen should the takeover collapse, and where that would leave the club.

In the meantime, the peril in which Everton had been placed by the Moshiri years deepened with the announcement by the Premier League on the 15 January 2024 that the Blues had been referred to *another* independent commission for a *second* alleged breach of Profitability and Sustainability Rules for the three-year period ending 30 June 2023.

Under new guidelines from the League aimed at expediting any penalties for contravening spending rules, member clubs had been required to submit their preliminary accounts and PSR calculations by the end of December 2023. Still in the process of preparing for their appeal against the first charge and sanction, Everton had been forced to submit accounts in line with the decision from the first independent accounts and declare themselves in breach of PSR.

If found guilty, of course, that carried the threat of a further points deduction, to be imposed before the end of the 2023/24 season, and the very real prospect that Everton could be relegated from the top flight – with all the existential crises that would trigger.

Everton responded to the second charge with a pointed statement highlighting the fact that 75% of the financial period in question overlapped seasons for which the club had already been penalised, a sanction for which they were currently appealing:

"The Premier League does not have guidelines which prevent a club being sanctioned for alleged breaches in financial periods which have already been subject to punishment, unlike other governing bodies, including the EFL. As a result – and because of the Premier League's new commitment to deal with such matters "in-season" – the club is in a position where it has had no option but to submit a PSR calculation which remains subject to change, pending the outcome of the appeal.

"The club must now defend another Premier League complaint which includes the very same financial periods for which it has already been sanctioned, before that appeal has even been heard. The Club takes the view that this results from a clear deficiency in the Premier League's rules."

The situation meant that outcome of that appeal, expected to heard in February 2024, was of critical importance to the club's future and to Moshiri's legacy as Everton's owner.

Moshiri's track record in accountancy and consulting, together with his skills and experience in mergers and acquisitions, had once taken him to the chairmanship of Metalloinvest, Alisher Usmanov's $16 billion conglomerate, and the reward from the oligarch of a 10% shareholding in the company.

Yet Everton's appalling performance on and off the field over his almost eight years at the helm, the club's referral to two independent commissions, coupled with the deep concerns around Moshiri's choice of buyer in 777 Partners all raise serious questions about his governance and judgement.

As we've seen repeatedly in The Unofficial Everton Timeline, since taking control in 2016, Moshiri's miscalculations had caused considerable damage to the football club and to his own reputation.

After nine years as an Arsenal shareholder, he must have felt as though he knew what it took to run a successful football club. Arsenal may have been an entirely different kettle of fish to Everton –on the field, Arsène Wenger provided the leadership and regular Champions League football, and the Gunners had completed construction of the Emirates Stadium before Moshiri and Usmanov showed up – but, as the intervening years have shown, the Boardroom leadership of Arsenal has been far more suited to steering an elite Premier League football club.

Given his other responsibilities as chairman of Metalloinvest, Moshiri surely never intended to be involved in the day-to-day running of Everton. Nor should he have been. His job was to appoint serious, heavyweight, experienced professionals to the Everton Board. Instead, he allowed Bill Kenwright to convince him that some continuation of the old regime was the answer. When it came time to appoint a new chief executive, a new finance director and a non-executive director, he allowed Bill Kenwright to fill those posts with his devotees rather than bring in industry-leading expertise to establish a forward-looking, innovative Boardroom. And when it came to the big decisions on the playing side, Moshiri never seemed able to resist the temptation to meddle, or to take the advice of self-interested 'advisors' from outside the club.

Indeed, while Sheikh Mansour hired top professionals to run Manchester City, leaving them to recruit Pep Guardiola, provide him with the funds to recruit the players he needed, and lay the foundations for City to win 14 major trophies since 2017, Moshiri, in that same period, interfered in areas he had no expertise in and has experienced nothing but failure. He personally hand-picked a succession of managers and coaches, most of them with little in common in terms of their approach and style, while Directors of Football also proved ineffective within Moshiri's structure, where he and Kenwright remained in charge of player recruitment.

Moshiri clearly had good intentions when he arrived at Everton and he did have an aggressive plan for the first few years following his takeover aimed at vaulting the Toffees into the promised land of the Premier League's top four and the Champions League.

He once told an AGM of shareholders that while he was at the club, money would never be in short supply, no doubt because he had mistakenly banked on the continuing financial support from his friend and business partner, Alisher Usmanov, and his companies. And Moshiri described to the independent commission in October 2023 his strategy of significant outlay on upgrading the playing squad in his first three or four seasons as major shareholder.

As Evertonian and finance expert, Paul the Esk, commented in November 2021:

"The casual abandon with which cash was spent in the early days of the Moshiri reign, combined with extremely poor recruitment decisions on and off the pitch, have created a significant cost and liability that Moshiri could not have foreseen when he arrived in February 2016."

It shouldn't be overlooked that Moshiri's efforts at building a successful team were hampered by some terrible luck, in terms of serious injuries to the likes of Yannick Bolasie, Jean-Philippe Gbamin, Andre Gomes and Yerry Mina. Such setbacks robbed the Toffees of their services for long periods and prevented them from ever having a significant impact on the team's fortunes. But while his ambitions were grandiose, Moshiri's plans lacked any contingency for the eventuality that either European football's gravy train proved elusive, the supply of funds from USM Holdings was cut off – or both! Putin's invasion of Ukraine was never in the plan, and the consequences of the UK government's immediate sanctions on Usmanov deprived the club of its main sponsors overnight. It also dashed any hopes Moshiri had of completing a £200 million naming rights deal for the new ground at Bramley-Moore Dock.

Beyond the shorter term speculation on a 'Hollywood' manager and big-money signings, with the goal of Champions League qualification within three or four years and all the riches that would entail to fund future growth, Everton Stadium was seen as the main solution to the club's problems.

The planning, design and execution of the new stadium stood in stark contrast to the shambles that Moshiri's reign became on the pitch and if the good ship Everton is able to ride out the stormy waters currently threatening to pull her under, the reclusive and somewhat enigmatic British-Iranian will have solved one problem that had vexed successive owners for generations.

Yet as the stadium continues to rise out of Liverpool's north docks, the existential threat that Moshiri referred to in his videoed meeting with Jazz Bal of the Fan Advisory Board in January 2023 hangs heavier than ever over the club.

With the club's interim directors in the process of appealing against the ten-point deduction imposed by the Premier League's Independent Commission, the threat of further sanction posed by a second panel, and with Captain Moshiri about to abandon ship, off the field the club's future remains far from certain.

***

On the field, however, things were looking up as 2023 drew to a close. Even though the Premier League had handed Everton the largest sporting sanction in English top-flight history, plunging it into another battle against relegation, it had taken the Blues just two weeks to win the same amount of points back and haul themselves out of the bottom three, as Sean Dyche and his side shrugged off the setback against Manchester United on 26 November by winning four straight matches.

Indeed, it was fitting that Chelsea – the free-spending Londoners – were the opponents at Goodison Park on 10 December. Fitting because the respective experience of the two clubs over the majority of the Premier League era, and their standing in the game with regard to treatment by the media and the powers-that-be, had been so very different.

In hoarding players and farming them out on loan to places like sibling club Vitesse Arnhem, and in spending close to £1 billion on incoming transfers in just a couple of years, and by signing those players on seven and eight-year contracts, Chelsea had bent the rules to breaking point.

They may yet have their day in front of an independent commission for their own PSR breaches, but few could miss the irony – not to mention the mockery of the notion of financial fair play –in Mauricio Pochettino's response to his team's latest defeat at Goodison Park, being a call to spend yet more money on transfers in the upcoming January transfer window.

Everton, by contrast, will almost certainly have to sell one of their crown jewels in the next few months to cover costs and spiralling debt, especially if the regulatory scrutiny of 777 Partners' proposed takeover of the club drags further into 2024, or if their buy-out falters altogether. But under Dyche, Everton have in spades what money can seldom purchase: and that is spirit, mentality and belief.

It may have been tempting for neutral observers to put those four Everton wins prior to Christmas 2023 down to the galvanising effect of the Premier League's potentially devastating sanction, but Dyche's team were already on the march before the unfair and disproportionate loss of those ten points.

Indeed, their win at Burnley in mid-December had been their tenth win in their previous 14 matches in all competitions, seven of them in the League. Extrapolated over a full season, that top-four calibre return of 25 points from 36 would be enough to propel them into contention for a place in Europe.

"If you get a group of players who give everything to win, it's a powerful thing," Dyche had said in the aftermath of the win over Chelsea. The team's winning streak, unfortunately, came to an end with a painful exit from the Carabao Cup in a penalty shootout and three successive League defeats that left the club hovering above the bottom three to close out the year.

The appeal against the points deduction might yet ease the threat of relegation with the return of some of those lost points back. In the meantime, however, the manager and his players would be challenged by injuries and suspensions while, of course, a second independent commission loomed. Yet there was no doubt that Everton would push on, displaying the kind of character, defiance and fight for the badge that Dyche had so admirably harnessed in his first year in charge at Goodison. That baseline of determination and togetherness, on the pitch and in the stands, would continue to be a vital ingredient in a season that could yet finish far more positively than it might have done.

Or, to put it in fewer but all-encompassing words: We shall not be moved.

THE CONTINUING STORY...

That's the end of this edition of *The Unofficial Everton Timeline.*

Thank you for following the long and complex story of what has been one of the most fascinating and traumatic decades in the history of Everton Football Club.

Why is this edition so long? It's simple. There's a lot to tell, and rarely a day goes by when the club is out of the news. The second half of this season could be even more tumultuous than the first half. Imagine that!

We'll be back with more *Unofficial Everton Timeline* insights: telling the story, on and off the pitch, and giving perspectives that will never be shown on the club website, nor mounted on the walls of Goodison Park or Bramley-Moore Dock.

Until then, Up The Toffees!

Steve and Lyndon

ACKNOWLEDGEMENTS

Huge thanks go to Lord Grantchester, Keith Wyness, Tony Tighe, David France plus his wife Elizabeth, and the other wonderful people associated with The Everton Collection, who developed The Everton Timeline which adorns Goodison Park.

Owned by The Everton Collection Charitable Trust, the collection is housed at the Liverpool Record Office where it is conserved in purpose-built facilities meeting the highest standards for long-term preservation and under the care of professional archivists. With support from the Heritage Lottery Fund, the Trust acquired The David France Collection – treasures lauded by experts at Christies and Sotheby's as the world's greatest club collection of football memorabilia – in late 2007 for a fraction of its market value. In addition, Dr France and his wife donated the priceless 29 official minute books, which document all board meetings between 1886 – 1964, to the Trust and detail the decisions made at 5,000 meetings recorded in over 10,000 handwritten pages signed by the likes of John Houlding, George Mahon, Will Cuff and John Moores.

The archive also contains over 6,000 football programmes, around 90% of all programmes involving Everton in league games, cup competitions, friendlies and reserve-team fixtures since 1885, including all home editions from the inaugural League season. Other highlights include season tickets from the club's days at Stanley Park, Priory Road and Anfield, gold medals for every major competition won by Everton including an example of the first-ever League Championship medal in 1890, the earliest team photograph taken shortly after the club changed its name from St. Domingo in 1881, players' contracts dating back to 1890, the tender documents for construction of the grandstand at Anfield in 1884 and much more.

The club's own modest archive was added to The David France Collection to form The Everton Collection. In total, it contains 20,000-plus items which chronicle the week-by-week story of life as well as football on Merseyside.

Further information can be found at www.evertoncollection.org.uk

In addition, the authors would like to express their appreciation to David France (Life President, Everton FC Shareholders' Association) for his contribution to the book. In turn, he would like to extol the unyielding dedication and tireless hard work of Colin Chong (interim CEO), Richard Kenyon (Chief Commercial and Communications Officer) and their staffs at the Royal Liver Building, Finch Farm and Goodison Park following the departures of the club's chief executive, chief finance and strategy officer and non-executive director in June 2023, and the death of chairman Bill Kenwright in October 2023.

It would be impossible for the authors to write a book about Everton and its amazing supporters without also acknowledging the tireless and essential work of all those involved in the 'Everton In The Community' charity https://www.evertoninthecommunity.org/, as well as Speedo Mick and all the incredible fundraising work he does for mental health charities through the speedomickfoundation.org

On a personal note, Steve would like to thank his family and close friends for helping him deal with his Everton addiction.

Lyndon would like to thank his wife, Natalie, and two daughters, Elyssa and Anna, for putting up with his passion for Everton FC, the many hours of devotion that goes into covering the club for almost three decades and all the wild emotional highs and lows that go with it!

About the Authors

Steve Dickinson

Steve was born in Liverpool, England in 1957. At the age of three, his grandad 'introduced him to the Blues.' The rest, as they say for a lifelong Evertonian, is history. His first memories of watching the Blues on TV was their 3-2 win against Sheffield Wednesday in the 1966 FA Cup Final. His first live match at Goodison Park was a 2-0 win against West Ham, during the league-winning season of 1969/70. Life for the Toffees was sweet back then.

Between then and now, he graduated with an engineering degree from the University of Liverpool and spent a forty-year career in the world of construction and manufacturing: running projects and businesses, restructuring companies in the UK and overseas, and travelling the globe.

He is now an author, publisher and Everton season ticket holder.

Steve can be found at SteveDickinsonBooks.com and on Twitter/X @TopBalconyMan

***

Lyndon Lloyd

Born in Johannesburg, South Africa, Lyndon was chosen to be an Evertonian comparatively late in life when he moved to England at the age of 12. Though he graduated from the University of Wales, Swansea with a Masters in History, he pursued a career in graphic and web design that took him to California during the Dotcom boom at the turn of the Century.

In parallel, he built Evertonia.com, an independent website covering the Toffees, that was merged with ToffeeWeb in 2001. The resulting behemoth is the biggest and longest-running website devoted to Everton, and one of the oldest football sites still in existence.

Lyndon can be found at ToffeeWeb.com, on Twitter/X @EFCLyndon, and on the weekly ToffeeWeb Podcast.

Did you enjoy this book?

Thank you for reading *The Unofficial Everton Timeline: 2014-2023 The Moshiri Years*

Your feedback helps us provide the best quality books and helps readers like you discover great books. It would mean the world to us if you took two minutes to share your thoughts about this book as a review. You can leave a review online, wherever you obtained the book, and/or send us an email with your honest feedback.

Best wishes and Up The Toffees!

Steve@SteveDickinsonBooks.com

Lyndon@ToffeeWeb.com

Printed in Great Britain
by Amazon

38312836R00391